THE POLITICS OF REFLEXIVITY

The Politics
of Reflexivity

Narrative and the Constitutive Poetics of Culture

ROBERT SIEGLE

The Johns Hopkins University Press

BALTIMORE AND LONDON

This book has been brought to publication with the generous assistance of the Andrew W. Mellon Foundation.

The Johns Hopkins University Press,
701 West 40th Street,
Baltimore, Maryland 21211
The Johns Hopkins Press Ltd., London

The paper used in this publication meets the minimum requirements of American National Standard for Information Sciences—Permanence of Paper for Printed Library Materials, ANSI Z39.48–1984.

Library of Congress Cataloging in Publication Data

Siegle, Robert.
   The politics of reflexivity.

   Bibliography: p.
   Includes index.
   1. English fiction—History and criticism. 2. Point of view (Literature)
   3. Narration (Rhetoric) I. Title.
PR830.P57S54   1986   823'.009'23   86-2700
ISBN 0-8018-3334-5 (alk. paper)

For My Parents

Contents

Contents

Preface and
Acknowledgments

Hugh Holman used to tell the story of his seventh-grade book report on
Vanity Fair. Rolling along with great enthusiasm, he was stopped cold—
very likely for the only time in his life—by his teacher's question, "And
what does the subtitle [*A Novel without a Hero*] mean?" Stung that he
had not already asked himself this killer query, he vowed not to be
caught again. I believe he modeled both his scholarship and his teaching
on just this kind of question that arrests the rush to easy closure and
leads to the real heart of an issue. Though far from having perfected that
difficult art, I have nonetheless taken seriously Professor Holman's suggestion to "look into these dramatized narrators and see what you find."
I have even wondered at times whether his sending me off to read
Robert Scholes's *Introduction to Structuralism* wasn't another artful
stroke of a master teacher, an indication that he knew that there in the
Gallic upheavals I would find ways to ask my questions about the all
too easy closure of traditional narrative poetics. In any case, it is one of
my keenest regrets that Professor Holman did not live long enough to
rock back in his desk chair, cock his eyebrow, and fire a shot straight
into the heart of whatever hasty conclusions remain in this book.

As for the critical underpinnings of the study, I have for the most
part assumed rather than belabored them. We are, I believe, in the midst
of what some would call a "paradigm shift" from one methodological
environment to another, and this study does not explicate basic post-
structuralist notions—a number of primers have appeared that are better
introductions. Instead, I have focused on tracing the implications of
poststructuralist insights for how we manage the traditional critical
vocabulary concerning narrative point of view.

My debts are many, of course—to undergraduate teachers like Lamarr
Smith and Robert Denham, who started me thinking about literature,
and certainly to Hugh Holman, who in graduate school taught me to do
so in a far more disciplined way. More recently I have accrued an enormous debt to J. Hillis Miller, who has gone infinitely beyond his duties

to read and encourage my work in the years since a remarkably stimulating National Endowment for the Humanities summer seminar. It is difficult to imagine working at all without the possibilities his books and essays have created for rethinking critical issues.

To Eric Halpern of the Johns Hopkins University Press I owe a special debt for his belief in the value of the project. To Alice Bennett we all owe very much indeed for her meticulous care in editing the manuscript. I am grateful, too, for the efforts of the design and production staff at Hopkins, one that certainly deserves its reputation for fine craftsmanship.

Summer grants from NEH and from the Center for Programs in the Humanities at Virginia Polytechnic Institute aided greatly in countering to some extent the battlefield conditions under which this manuscript has been written—heavy teaching loads, including much freshman composition, have considerably slowed the progress of the work, and without such timely funding the book would have been even longer in the making.

Finally, to my (lamentably) former colleague Cheryl Herr I owe perhaps the greatest debt of all. In the middle of an always overcrowded schedule she found time to read much of this study in the kind of early version we all prefer to forget ever existed, making many useful suggestions and enduring theoretical enthusiasms tangential to her own work in Joyce.

I am grateful to the following journals and presses for permission to include copyrighted material in this study:

From *Herzog* by Saul Bellow. Copyright © 1961, 1963, 1964 by Saul Bellow. All rights reserved. Reprinted by permission of Viking Penguin, Inc.

From *98.6* by Ronald Sukenick. Copyright © 1975 by Ronald Sukenick. Reprinted by permission of the Fiction Collective.

From *Moving Parts* by Steve Katz. Copyright © 1977 by Steve Katz. Reprinted by permission of the Fiction Collective.

From *Fireworks* by Angela Carter. Copyright © 1974 by Angela Carter. Reprinted by permission of Harper & Row, Publishers, Inc.

From *Chance* by Joseph Conrad. Copyright © 1913, 1921 by Doubleday & Company, Inc. Reprinted by permission of Doubleday & Company, Inc.

From the author's essays in *The Kentucky Review* 5, 2 (Winter 1984), *College Literature* 10, 2 (Spring 1983), *Conradiana* 16, 2 (1984), *Essays in Literature* 8, 2 (Fall 1981). Material from these essays used with permission of the editors of the journals.

THE POLITICS OF REFLEXIVITY

ONE

Narrative Reflexivity
and Constitutive Poetics

This book explores the ideological implications of our basic forms of narrative thought and reconsiders that set of critical terms whose map of the territory has often been fully naturalized as its actual topography. It assumes that the ideological resonance of themes, conceptions, and the conventions through which they are conveyed provides a subtle history of military, economic, and institutional politics. Accustomed as we may have become recently to literature "as a socially symbolic act," we have yet to redefine our narrative poetics. Our terms and our teaching are still loaded with preconceptions that hinder our task of seeing all that narratives accomplish. In the final analysis reflexivity is a way of understanding the semiotic, philosophical, and ideological processes taking place in any narrative alongside those issues our existing poetics equips us to find. Hence in this first chapter I wish to suggest the complexity of "reflexivity" as a fundamental trait of narrative, look at how that complexity seems to be limited in our discussions of the phenomenon, and note the kinds of issues a "constitutive poetics" might require us to address.

The Concept of Reflexivity

Partly, then, this book is about what has happened to the shepherd's crook since the era before the Greek pastoral meant a literary idyll. Having admired the staff's sinuous curve back upon itself, the Romans took the Greek word for "crook" and used it to mean to bend, bow, curve, and turn or turn around (offshoots meant a curved blade or pruning hook, pliant or flexible, and other derivatives closer to bending or curving). That marks a loss of meaning, one must say, since all the herding functions of "crook" (by this date *flectō*) are lost, as well as the sense of its curving back on itself. Producing the word "reflex" from this Latin root thus requires that the prefix *re-* be added to *flectō* to

1

restore the sense of "back upon itself." One senses redundancy, since we have a bending shape twice directed back on itself (once in the original stem, once in the prefix), thereby making the word an effective illustration of how we cover over the figurative origins of language. But this more literal sense of "reflex" is essential in a number of ways to the use I wish to make of the term. I want to talk about something that turns back upon itself in the very process of its getting out again to where it was pointing before it started—the figure, in other words, that flexes back upon itself and then *re*peats the movement, like this:

Figure 1. The Reflexive Circuit

That circling looks almost like an eye or an eyelet through which one would look to frame a view—and appropriately so, since we are used to talking about a text as a framed view of the world.

But obviously there must be more important results of this different sense of "reflex." Covered over in its everyday usage is the double bend, the double turn, that in fact has the narrative line going literally in every direction at once. That is, a circle can theoretically be cut into an infinite number of straight lines pointing in every possible direction. Usually when we hear of reflexive, self-reflexive, or self-conscious narrative, we think of novels like *Tristram Shandy* that explicitly talk about themselves and hence turn back upon themselves. But we know that *Tristram Shandy* also has a great deal to say about what is not itself, about almost everything in fact—hence this new figure of "reflexive" seems more appropriate. It describes in fact a line that, *in order to* finish out its trip from one end to another, must turn back on itself and then turn back on its turning; its marking feature is this rotation, this looking all around itself.

Several of the points I have to make about reflexivity in narrative require this change in our sense of the figure within the term. The more simple reflex motion—a single turn back on itself—suggests that reflexive narrative has to do only with itself, that it turns away from what is represented and loses itself in self-contemplation. A reflexive narrative would thus be about "only" art and would tell us little else. It would not affect our view of reality, our essential values and philosophical assumptions—would be, in other words, a safe but frivolous project. For example, to confine reflexivity to the term "metafiction," a fiction that is *about* fiction rather than, presumably, about other things besides, risks circumscribing reflexivity to relatively overt examples and its significance to mainly aesthetic issues.[1] Moreover, the notion of "turned back" (as if a reversal) suggests that reflexive narrative turns its back on its destiny, betrays its essential direction, and is preoccupied with a single aspect of its nature, perhaps the least important one at that. Finally, this simple figure of reflex would thus impose an either/or choice for narrative between the referential and the reflexive.

My use of "reflexive," however, suggests that reflexivity uncovers a great deal about the whole narrative circuit—the codes by which we organize reality, the means by which we organize words about it into narrative, the implications of the linguistic medium we use to do so, the means by which readers are drawn into narrative, and the nature of our relation to "actual" states of reality. Hence reflexivity is not a single-minded focus upon art for art's sake, and hardly a betrayal of the larger issues challenging the narrative artist, but rather is the most comprehensive fulfillment of those challenges that considers not only what it will say but the philosophical grounds and means for saying it. Moreover, far from being a single focus chosen from one of two options (reality or itself), reflexivity focuses on all possible topics and their potentially simultaneous achievement (its completed course points everywhere at once).

Thus my discussion of etymology is a means of stepping out of a theoretical tradition laden with unnecessary critical, epistemological, and metaphysical assumptions. If one considers current meanings of the term's metaphor, one can see several of the false starts we have made toward understanding its implications in narrative theory. For example, the use of "self-reflective" (or "-reflexive") is akin to "self-conscious" and clearly depends upon metaphors of selfhood and consciousness that seem confusing and misleading when we are talking about a text rather than a person.[2] In a medium perfectly capable of contesting the entire apparatus of Western metaphysics from which such metaphors derive, it is well to have a critical approach that, as much as possible, has not already preformulated its conclusions, that can let the text prescribe its own terms, insofar as that is possible, rather than imposing them upon it. Moreover, a myth of literature struggling toward a mature self-awareness is implicit in "conscious" or "reflective" and thus obscures the fact that reflexivity is a basic capability of narrative exercised in every period, historical schematizations notwithstanding. Reflexivity has always been with us and is not just a function of the modern novel's reflection of the breakdown of cultural consensus. As has been argued in a number of recent debates, a critical theory that already presupposes a fictional history is unlikely to yield reliable results for a history of fiction. Finally, the notion of "self-conscious" for "reflexive" suggests merely an occasional text, or even a moment in *a* text, given over to self-contemplation before getting on with the main business at hand. Giving up these misleading terms or definitions of reflexivity frees us to accept what we find when we carefully sift discussions of reflexivity and reflexive narratives themselves—that it is everywhere in narrative, in all periods and forms, sometimes explicit and sometimes implicit, always revealing the conceptual puddle over which fiction gallantly casts its narrative cloak so we can cross untroubled by the fluidity of our footing.

The idea of "reflex" in the sense of an involuntary, irrational response—to the doctor's tap on the knee—can also mislead one about this element of narrative. Perhaps this is how those who object to the breaking of fictional illusion think of reflexivity—those comments by the narrator about his problems are spastic twitches of the authorial dendrons, unintentional slips a bit ridiculous to see and as distracting as a nervous tic and hence destructive of what a speaker might wish to say. Reflex in the sense of reflecting light, images, or heat also indicates a mimetic bias that understands narrative solely in terms of mirroring reality as it is in itself, with any curious working on the mirror's surface a distraction from art's moral function to reflect what the world truly is. This definition is a restrictive rather than a liberating way to understand reflexivity in narrative.

These paragraphs, then, are meant to suggest that the metaphorical applications of "reflex" during its linguistic career have limited and misled the way we organize our thinking about the activity in narrative to which we apply the term. We need a change in figure for the term to allow us to work out a fuller and more exact description of that activity.

Reflexivity and Mimetic Poetics

The effect of the essentially mimetic poetics of Anglo-American narrative theory has been to straighten out the shepherd's crook, to make it less an instrument to pull in all the stray significations of the narrative herd than a prod to push selected members toward a narrowed conception of what narrative is about: it is "only" a picture of the world. I do not really wish to disparage previous thinking about reflexivity, for it has produced some powerful readings of individual narratives, but I think a look at a few examples shows how a mimetic focus blurs all but one arc along the narrative orbit sketched out by reflexivity.

4

One thinks, for example, of one of the earlier explicit treatments of "reflexive attitudes" in fiction. Albert Cook notes that art interests itself not only in the appearance "to be found in the 'sheen' of things" but also in "its own appearance, the artifice it constitutes of paint or sound or words organized."[3] He notes that the novelist's problem "of inventing a coherent artifice, an appearance, is bewildering just because of the mass of detail or experience he must contemplate." Reality seems too complex and multitudinous to fit into the "coherent artifice" he might structure, and hence the reflexive novelist refers to his work as "the artifice which it must perforce be as selected and, hence, in one sense distant from reality." This kind of reference is in the "initial conception" of novels by Sterne, Gogol, Gide, and Cervantes, "and it is implicit in the formalism of most well-made novels since Flaubert."

Here we seem to have a very suggestive formulation of reflexivity in narrative. What, then, happens when fiction looks at itself as "words organized"? It seems in Cook's account to discover an unclosable distance between the artificiality of its coherence and the "mass of detail or experience" we term "reality." Artifice is "distant from reality," and the practitioner steeped in his genre cannot help but be at least implicitly aware of this. Here we are on the brink of a Derridean sense of the novel's self-deconstruction, the text's revelation that its organization and presumably its thematic coherence are artifical rather than centered in some freestanding reality. The brink, however, is not the abyss, and Cook quickly retreats from the radical implications of his initial formulation. He argues that reflexive artifices "must in some way designate the reality *from which they spring*. When a novel uses reflexivity it must *discover* a reality" (italics mine). Now, instead of being a writer's invention, the work's structures "spring" like a beast directly from reality into the novel. The "coherent artifice" is now suddenly the presence of reality's essence, its center, its being. Now we realize that when Cook describes the artifice as "selected," he means its structure and meaning, not just its details; he continues this model of mediation with the metaphor of exploring and discovering reality, as well as the notion of definition ("must . . . designate") of a presumably preexisting entity. Cook does not really respect the distance from reality he marks in relation to artifice, and he insists that "reflexivity, like any literary device . . . does not or should not operate in a void." Like most mimetic theorists, he manages to argue that while narrative is distant from and not the same as reality, it also springs into the text from reality. That contradiction, I think, is an important indicator of what it attempts to hide. Having clearly formulated the way fiction that reflects upon its devices looks across a gap or void to reality, recognizing itself as artifice,

5

Cook then cancels the void or, to use his own metaphor, "springs" across it.[4]

For Cook, the meaning of "reflexive" is that of a mirror: we *do* look at a surface of artifice, but what we see there has sprung into view as a reflection of reality. In the most extended treatment of this subject, Robert Alter pursues reflexivity as an involuntary turn back upon the self, using "reflect" in the sense of bouncing back from mental walls.[5] Hence he defines what he calls the "self-concious novel" as one "that systematically flaunts its own condition of artifice and that by so doing probes into the problematic relationship between real-seeming artifice and reality," in which "there is a consistent effort to convey to us a sense of the fictional world as an authorial construct set up against a background of literary tradition and convention."[6] In discussing the secular skepticism of Cervantes, Alter shows that "art is obviously questionable because it is understood to be ultimately arbitrary, while nature is still more problematic because it is so entrammeled with art, so universally mediated by art, shaped by art's peculiar habits of vision, that it becomes difficult to know what, if anything, nature in and of itself may be" (28–29). This statement clearly stakes out the epistemological skepticism we have seen in Cook's essay. That skepticism shows up in Sterne as well, when Alter notes that "a central insight of his novel is that any literary convention means a schematization—and thus a misrepresentation—of reality" (33). The self-conscious novelist, then, is one who feels thrown back upon the workings of his own mind as his subject matter.

Alter takes this hypothesis even a step further by observing that Sterne's work also illustrates "that a new 'authentic' literature liberated from conventions is a sheer impossibility"; as a result, the writer "makes us continually conscious of the conventions, exploring their limits, their implicit falsity, their paradoxical power to transmit fractional truths of experience" (33). This formulation seems to take the exposure of authorial rhetoric to the final stop on the line: it is all false, misleading. But what are "fractional truths"? If authorial structuring and investing of meaning is misrepresentation, where does the truth come from? And if it is fractional, where is the whole integer of truth centered? Somehow the reflexive novel "reflects a greater fidelity to reality than other kinds of fiction" (70). How, if we invalidate authorial rhetoric about the world, is this so? How, that is, can the author's reflection of his own mind, or even of the conventions, be any less "entrammeled" or "mediated" by art than nature is? Or even more puzzling, how do we measure relative "fidelity"?

The answer, for Alter at least, is implicit in his key term. "Self-conscious" implies a present awareness of the self, and this self turns out to be the savior of truth for Alter. *Tristram Shandy,* for example, turns out to be "existential realism" (43), a shift of mimesis from the outer to the inner world.[7] Sterne's novel is presented as a realistic portrait of the "restless dynamic of the mind interacting with itself as the indisputable reality we inhabit, and thus his extreme consciousness of artifice and reader-response becomes an instrument of realism" (50–51). There is obviously much of value here, since Sterne does indeed present his narrator playing over the materials. But Alter himself points to what unsettles his formulation when he speaks of the mental processes involved in portrayal as "themselves conditioned by culture." Such conditioning suggests that both the picture of consciousness and consciousness itself are as problematic as Alter has already shown the picture of nature to be. It seems that Alter drives an arbitrary stake into the Derridean slope down which he is sliding.

A self that is coherent, stable, and knowable provides a center of fixed truth, a fact clear not only from Alter's terms, as I have noted, but also from his dependence upon a sense of "the actuality of personal and historical time" as the criterion for successful experimental fiction (232). But there is yet another stake in that Derridean slope. Alter's whole project in *Partial Magic* is to confine self-consciousness to a subgenre of the novel. He excludes *Lord Jim* and *Vanity Fair* from his genre of self-conscious fiction on the grounds that in these novels "the conspicuous elaboration of narrative artifice is performed in the service of moral and psychological realism, operating even in its occasional improbabilities as a technique of verisimilitude, not as a testing of the ontological status of the fiction" (xiii). That is, Conrad and Thackeray are cycled out of the sweeping cultural critique of the self-conscious novel, while Cervantes, Sterne, and the like become a curious sideshoot off the novel's family tree—the mad hatters of the narrative wonderland.

Alter's attempt to absorb *Tristram Shandy* into psychological realism points to the absence of a secure wall between mimesis and reflexivity; rather, between them is a permeable membrane, a two-way corridor, different walls of the same room, arcs on the same circular line describing the orbit of narrative itself. Self-consciousness, or more properly reflexivity, then, is not subdivided off into some curious aberrant subgenre but is at the heart of narrative itself. Alter sometimes seems to confine reflexivity to explicit comments about artifice, but the "elaboration of narrative artifice" he brackets off in Conrad is merely the implicit reflexivity never entirely absent from any narrative. This omnipresence means not only that obviously reflexive narratives like *Vanity Fair* must be granted their reflexivity, but that any myth that reflexivity

7

is a distinctly historical fad is misleading at best.[8] The worst form of this myth is one that views eighteenth-century fiction as emerging from satire and apologue through reflexivity toward nineteenth-century realism, when the novel reached its zenith as the revelation of moral truth and order; in the twentieth century, sadly enough, the novel lost confidence in itself and has gradually degenerated into such symptoms of decadence as unreliable narration, hopelessly reflexive disparagement of its own truth claims, fabulation, and the like. We will not find many to endorse this expression of the myth, for its bald statement points up its absurdity, but the elegiac longing for the Victorian novelist's authority tinges a great deal of theorizing about the nature and history of narrative. By overcoming this historical myth and the mimetic blinders to narrative theory derived from it, one can achieve a much fuller understanding of the Victorian novelist's sense of his own limitations and the modern novelist's sense of achievement in the face of those same limitations.

Two recent studies are cause for optimism that we are moving in the right direction. Linda Hutcheon, for example, focuses upon the reader's role in *Narcissistic Narrative,* and if one regrets that her phenomenological orientation preserves familiar notions of self (as in her title), her formalism those of organic unity ("Literature remains a self-sufficient aesthetic system of internal relations among parts that aim at an Aristotelian harmony" [90]), and her conservative semiotics those of mimeticism (reflexivity is a representation of the *process* of making fiction), one can still admire the vigor with which she disparages our tendency to make nineteenth-century realism the definition of all narrative and the acuteness with which she analyzes the modes and means of "narcissistic" narrative.[9] Perhaps even more encouraging is Patricia Waugh's *Metafiction: The Theory and Practice of Self-Conscious Fiction.* Such terms as "metafiction" and "self-conscious" may risk the kinds of misconceptions already noted, and Waugh seems interested mainly in those moments when metafiction "sets up an opposition . . . to the language of the realistic novel,"[10] as if "the realistic novel" did not itself have more than its share of reflexive moments. But overschematic notions of literary history aside, Waugh's study pursues a number of the more radical formal and philosophical implications of overt reflexivity in current fiction, and her command of this century's explicitly reflexive works is extraordinary. The real project remaining, then, is to extend the reflexive frame of reference to all narrative and to make the corresponding revisions in narrative poetics that such an extension would enable. The various curbs on reflexivity we have seen have served, whatever their motivations, as strategies of containment limiting the effects reflexivity has on our poetics, our sense of the philosophical underpinnings of that poetics, and our recognition of the ideological ramifications both of narrative itself and of our reading habits.

Toward a Constitutive Poetics

The mimetic theorist most likely sees reflexivity as a merely "comic" or addlepated shimmying of the reflective mirror of narrative. If it is held still and authoritatively, we have a reliable presentation; otherwise one plunges into the abyss of unreliability.[11] One can, however, conceive of passing beyond the brittle surface of mirror theories to a constitutive rather than a mimetic poetics. In some ways one would think "constitutive" poetics the more commonsensical, since we know that fiction inevitably composes a world different from the one it seems to represent; whether it is Cervantes setting out to lambaste falsification by romances, or Hawthorne celebrating the mingling of the actual and the imaginary, or James seeking to exploit to the fullest the organizing powers of narrative, commentators have pointed to this difference as crucial to the nature of fiction. Within that difference one finds the way that fiction interprets, composes, structures, or posits a world—constitutes it out of the innumerable code elements collected by means of the allusive powers of language.

Perhaps one of the most influential statements of recent critical theory, Paul de Man's *Blindness and Insight,* might provide a useful reference point here:

> The self-reflecting mirror-effect by means of which a work of fiction asserts, by its very existence, its separation from empirical reality, its divergence, as a sign, from meaning that depends for its existence on the constitutive activity of this sign, characterizes the work of literature in its essence. It is always against the explicit assertion of the writer that readers degrade the fiction by confusing it with a reality from which it has forever taken leave.[12]

One notes here the double divergence from "reality": first that of the sign from meaning as presence (i.e., the thing itself), and second that of meaning itself from such immediacy, since it "depends for its existence" *not* upon reality, but upon "the constitutive activity of this sign." Texts both defer (by pointing rather than making present) and diverge or differ (by constituting through codes of one kind or another rather than by replicating)—hence the Derridean polemics of *"différance."*[13] Reflexivity may be said to emerge in the space between these divergences.

As the semiotics of Umberto Eco teaches us, any code system divides up an expression continuum (from sounds and marks to phonemes and graphemes) by an arbitrary act that parallels the equally arbitrary way culture segments the content continuum (of things and experiences) and elaborates rules for the combination of these units (grammar and syntax for language, clothing and mores for behavior, politics and economics for group behavior, genres and conventions for art, concepts and theoretical systems for philosophy or theology or poetics).

By (reflexively) forcing awareness of these codes on readers, texts "train semiosis," as Eco puts it, by compelling them to reconsider the various codes and discover new possibilities in them. This training quickly erodes our sense that these codes are "natural" or permanent. Eco spells out this erosion in the following key passage:

> While doing this [training semiosis], the aesthetic experience challenges the accepted organization of the content and suggests that the semantic system could be differently ordered, had the existing organization been sufficiently frequently and persuasively challenged by some aspect of the text.
> But to change semantic systems means *to change the way in which culture "sees" the world.* Thus a text of the aesthetic type which was so frequently supposed to be absolutely extraneous to any truth conditions (and to exist at a level on which disbelief is totally "suspended") arouses the suspicion that the correspondence between the present organization of the content and "actual" states of the world is neither the best nor the ultimate. The world could be defined and organized (and therefore perceived and known) through other semantic (that is: conceptual) models. [14]

But since there are only models and no unmediated vision of " 'actual' states of the world," "correspondence" is not exactly the point. Thomas Kuhn argues that we "have to relinquish the notion, explicit or implicit, that changes of paradigm ['paradigms' being similar to Eco's 'models'] carry scientists and those who learn from them closer and closer to the truth" (170), arguing for the probabilistic Darwinian model of change rather than for the teleological plot it replaced. Hence there is "no neutral algorithm for theory-choice" (200), and the alternative to one paradigm-shaped way of seeing "is not some hypothetical 'fixed' vision, but vision through another paradigm." [15]

The "truth" of a statement is thus measured by its satisfaction of a reigning paradigm, and even the competition between paradigms is governed not by what Kuhn dismisses as "the methodological stereotype of falsification by direct comparison with nature" (77) but by a process of paradigm competition decided ultimately by the needs of the community at that point. Kuhn thus all but cycles us back to Nietzsche's contention that "Truth is the kind of error without which a certain species of life could not live" [16] and is measured by our needs rather than by nature as it is in itself. As Nietzsche comments, "we have projected the conditions of *our* preservation as predicates of being in general" (276). Nietzsche, of course, is much more radical than Kuhn, holding that all of the "categories of reason" actually "represent nothing more than the expediency of a certain race and species—their utility alone is their 'truth'" (278). Narrative of one kind or another may well be the central medium by which culture "naturalizes" these categories, while its reflexive dimension works equally hard to show how such naturalization takes place.

We are talking, then, in terms of a basically semiotic model of "knowledge" as codes that compete for prevalence in a given community. But this process is clearly also *ideological,* since the "way culture 'sees' the world" has enormous material consequences, and since the means by which one cluster of codes gains dominance over another through paradigm competition is inescapably political in every sense of the term. One need not necessarily depend upon the likes of Althusser or Adorno to see that reflexivity is highly charged ideologically precisely because it denaturalizes far more than merely literary codes and pertains to more than the aesthetic "heterocosm" to which some theorists might wish to restrict it.[17] To "train semiosis" is to train revolution, as consciousness-raising groups and Maoist cells demonstrate. World coding, once understood as constituted rather than copied or reflected, is up for grabs, and we come to that point at which a thoroughgoing semiotics borders on ideological critique.

The border is also shared, however, by a philosophical version of reflexivity's activity. Richard Rorty traces the difficulty of redefining philosophy to "a notion shared by Platonists, Kantians, and positivists: that man has an essence—namely, to discover essences. The notion that our chief task is to mirror accurately, in our own Glassy Essence, the universe around us is the complement of the notion, common to Democritus and Descartes, that the universe is made up of very simple, clearly and distinctly knowable things, knowledge of whose essences provides the master-vocabulary which permits commensuration of all discourses."[18] To picture narrative as a glassy essence mirroring a "true order" of events is to plunge into the threadbare problematics Rorty explores at length, taking his cue from the work of Dewey, the late Wittgenstein, and the late Heidegger, who "hammer away at the holistic point that words take their meanings from other words rather than by virtue of their representative character, and the corollary that vocabularies acquire their privileges from the men who use them rather than from their transparency to the real" (368). De Man, Eco, Kuhn, Nietzsche, Rorty, and a host of ideologically oriented theorists all seem to be recommending that

11

we be content with comparing discourse to discourse rather than sup-posing that we are correlating discourse with the nondiscursive. Ulti-mately their reasoning leads to the imperative that we perceive the crucial interrelations among themes and models made available in the inter-disciplinary theory emerging in semiotic, ideological, and philosophical critique.[19]

Constitutive poetics is thus a specialized application of a larger study of how a culture—whether in literature, cultural coding in general, science, or philosophy—composes its identity and that of its individuals and constitutes the "world" within which it takes place.[20] This special-ized application might thus yield many insights that are not included in a representational poetics but are a necessary part of the field that poetics assumes it masters; it is a supplement to it in the Derridean sense of be-ing an integral part that is at the same time an addition to our custom-ary mimetic attitudes toward fiction. Were I a traditional structuralist, I might offer a diagram to illustrate:

Modes	Referential Focus	Reflexive Focus
Representational	"Realism"—making pic-tures of the "world"	Mechanics and assumptions of knowing and showing
Constitutive	"Irrealism"—various types of "fabulation"	Mechanics and assumptions of composing, interpreting, structuring, positing

Traditional poetics feels comfortable only in the zone where the refer-ential focus intersects with representational poetics; Alter branches out into that square where the reflexive and representational intersect, since he is attracted to some of the epistemological issues reflexivity raises. Someone like Robert Scholes in his more flamboyant moments finds himself thinking out the implications of the intersection of the referential and the constitutive, particularly in contemporary American fiction. The greatest resistance among established theorists, however, seems to come when constitutive poetics and reflexive narrative ele-ments set up the "self-reflecting mirror-effect" de Man describes, for it is here that theory menaces all the stable reference points of meta-physics, point of view theory, and other equivalent contenders for a "center" from which one can stabilize, fix, and survey the field of narrative.

Since I am not a traditional structuralist, however, I suggest that the bottom right cell of this diagram is one that exceeds the boundary lines .

by which it is constituted, thereby not only affecting the other "three" divisions and making clear the illusory nature of their supposed independence from the reflexive and constitutive, but also affecting all those cultural divisions of activity adjacent to narrative (whether in parallel, as in poetry or drama or film, or in serial, as in other types of discourse, and beyond discourse in many possible arrays of coded cultural behaviors). Hence the importance of a close attention to the implications of narrative reflexivity and constitutive poetics: we find here a blueprint of the basic cultural act that is in the final analysis less that of knowing than of making coherent narrative explanations out of whatever data happen to be registered from the "content continuum" of the nondiscursive.

At bottom, of course, we are talking about the process by which energies are formed into subjects—"subjects" as both the subject matter of representation and as what occupies the place of the grammatical subject of representation. It is difficult not to think of this latter subject with the metaphor of computers; that is, of a subject as the *user* of a narrative program. The word "program" suggests a political platform, of course, and not inappropriately so, since the formation of subjects is the primal political process. But its meaning within the computer community also stresses the interplay between its enabling or generative power and its more or less covert limiting and channeling of that generative power within the juridical configuration of the program. A user becomes that mix of actions and inclinations encouraged or enabled by the program and grows away from those discouraged or not permitted. Popular narrative forms like Victorian fiction and contemporary film participate in a larger process of legislating what we may call, if you will, the culture's aesthetics of forming subjects.

As for narrative theory, its traditional forms have been largely "logocentric," as Derrida would call it—wholly within the metaphysical tradition of Western thought.[21] The key elements of point of view theory, for example, have always been discussed as almost ahistorical metaphysical beings—the narrator, the characters, the author, the reader. In the following chapters I will look at these key theoretical elements to see how their reflexive functioning in several narratives reshapes our theories along nonmetaphysical lines. As they circle their own functioning, they clearly mark their orbits within a semiotic rather than a metaphysical sphere, and to the extent that it is possible to conceive of it, we will try to imagine what a "grammatological" rather than a "logocentric" poetics would look like. A fully "grammatological" poetics is, I think, impossible, since there is little hope of escaping the tendencies of language to import all manner of ontological assumptions. And yet it should be possible to begin the work of conceiving of the key centers

13

of point of view theory in terms that reflect their position *in* texts rather than working as if the texts were reflections *of* them. We may find ourselves pondering whether authors exist without texts, whether readers can be without texts. If it is *in* texts that they enact these functions or roles, then they are semiotic rather than metaphysical beings. We will also find ourselves confronting the larger social and economic interests involved in both the metaphysics of narrative and the long tradition of regarding mimetic poetics as natural, transparent, and sufficient. Considering that Anglo-American narrative theory has been almost exclusively preoccupied with point of view and has thus existed in that mainly ontological frame, it has seemed to me essential to approach my task by looking squarely at the key terms of that frame and to invert each into its reflexive and constitutive counterpart.

Following this introduction, then, I examine four periods in the history of narrative, each in terms of an element of modern poetics subjected to radical redefinition within the fiction itself. My purpose in addressing these four periods is not to rewrite literary history *my* way, but to indicate why I have little sympathy for discussions that seem to confine reflexivity to recent avant-garde works, as if the novel had "evolved" into metafictional cleverness sometime during the 1960s or were more an American than an English phenomenon. Reflexivity seems so "current" mainly because poststructuralist theory allows us to understand it fully at the same time that current fictional practice has forced an at times almost reactionary critical establishment either to ignore it or to devise rather elaborate strategies for its containment. Each section emphasizes one work in detail to answer the perennial call for extended demonstration while referring to sufficient contemporary works to forestall the charge of special pleading. Hence within the confines of the Thackeray chapter one will find summaries of the chapters I might have written on Trollope, Hawthorne, Dickens, Melville, and Eliot, with backward glances at Cervantes and Fielding. These lateral references also allow a greater range along the continuum between explicit and implicit reflexivity, but since the distinction between *diegesis* and *mimesis* is itself a function of a certain limiting theory classifying discourses for its own purposes, perhaps my heavy scrutiny of commentary is less of a danger than one might at first suppose. Even the dialogue "selected" by a narrator for "transcription," that is, should be seen more as commentary than as objective or neutral "fact." Each of the major works, moreover, differs greatly in time, place, degree of "canonicity," and formal design so that, with the briefer readings, they may together support my contention that few narratives indeed can take place without addressing the kinds of points I explore.

Each of the texts chosen for extended analysis may thus be viewed as novels that, one way or another, sum up or epitomize a large network of fiction with which it is roughly contemporaneous. Hence *Vanity Fair* seems preeminently Victorian, a compendium of points of view, stylistic qualities, and conventional devices and structures. Conrad's *Chance,* on the other hand, shows a key figure in early modernism reflecting upon the shift away from Victorian assumptions engineered by writers such as James, Conrad, and Ford and continued in the next decade or two by the American high modernists. Warren's *World Enough and Time* catches us midcentury and feels something like a "late modernist" reconsideration of the modernist ambivalence toward romanticism, its frame historian combining a nostalgia for the convictions powering the heroic with considerable scruples about the historical and philosophical monstrosities spawned by such force of will. *The French Lieutenant's Woman,* finally, positions itself on that most contemporary of thresholds between the existentialist rescue of individuality and the poststructural demystification that has succeeded it as a prevailing paradigm.

But each of these principal works also leads to a specific issue for narrative poetics. My attention to *Vanity Fair* is directed toward that novel's deanthropomorphizing of "narrative voice"—a venerable term in Anglo-American criticism that too exclusively connotes subjectivity as its ground—and its denaturalizing of narrative stance. My interest in *Chance* bears on its exploration, at the expense of simplistic notions about representation and nature, of the narrator's relation to cultural reality. *World Enough and Time* permits an approach to subjectivity as the object of narrative, illustrating ways identity and culture are constituted out of available materials in the culture's interpretive systems. *The French Lieutenant's Woman* enables an analysis of our traditional concept of the "author" that should alarm those readers of the novel for whom the existentialism of the 1940s seems an adequate interpretation of its materials. Voice, narrator, "reality," character, author: the constitutive dimension of these elements of narrative theory reorients our thinking not only about narrative but necessarily about criticism as well, an issue the final chapter addresses.

TWO

Thackeray and Nineteenth-Century Fiction: Narrators and Readers

In *Vanity Fair*, his first well-funded opportunity to blend *Punch* with novelistic expanse, Thackeray made good use of the chance to work through the premises on which his contemporaries were inventing the modern middle-class consciousness. The effect was to play them off against each other reflexively, thereby illuminating the constitutive poetics by which this genre shaped for a century the reality within which the Western imagination dwelt. At its simplest, this anatomy of the "voice" of the emerging mass culture becomes very blunt: " 'I' is here introduced to personify the world in general—the Mrs. Grundy of each respected reader's private circle."[1] Mrs. Grundy is, of course, the distillate of the same middle- to upper-middle-class popular wisdom the novel genre embodies. Hence it is no exaggeration to say that *Vanity Fair* draws our attention most compellingly—and explicitly in such a remark—in terms of its reflexive attention to the social and philosophical dimensions of narrative voice, perhaps one of the vaguer terms in the critical vocabulary. "Voice," the rubric under which we analyze the "speaker" of a text, carries with it a range of obvious anthropomorphic connotations that *Vanity Fair* undermines through its play with the two primary constituents of voice. As for style, the novel exhibits a persistent and omnivorous irony that has perplexed and confounded critics from the first. Lacing the celebrated fluidity of Thackeray's prose, irony links each line of the novel to the larger social and literary conventions of which it is a function, making any stylistic "fix" upon "his" view problematic. Similarly, "narrative stance," the other primary constituent of voice, is anything but a simple choice—it becomes an anthology of options ranging from the author-god of the mainstream Victorian novel through the historian, the personal observer, the participant, and even the puppeteer staging his Punch and Judy show at the fair.

Hence as he weaves together the elements that constitute his narrative voice, and as he reaches for the conventional stances from which that voice presents the events of the novel, Thackeray cannot seem to help marking the disparate sources of those elements and the variations in philosophical assumptions and readers' roles predicated by those stances. Each brings its attendant connotations deriving from its own discursive sources in theology (omniscient narrators), history (the investigator), autobiography (the participant-observer), and drama (the puppeteer). What emerges from such blending, marking, and dispersing is a complex structure of interplay in which, reflexively, the constitutive properties of these narrative elements gradually move into the foreground of the novel's field of activity. And no single element, perhaps, makes such activity more lively than the irony that suffuses the voice carrying these stances.

The Ironic Voice

We are accustomed to ordering the language of narrative voice into the contours of an individual identity that we project behind it; we assume there is a person talking to us, as if on a printing telephone held before our eyes instead of the standard receiver. In fact, however, the lesson of *Vanity Fair* is that there is not one "human" voice behind a narrative, but *the* one human voice of culture. With its varied history of texts, its repertoire of many patternings, devices, stances, and other unspoken contracts between authors and readers about reality, that culture *is* the narrative voice. It is thus far less univocal (and hence less consistent, "reliable," and "coherent") than we may be accustomed to thinking. Thackeray depends heavily upon irony to deflate the pomposity of dominant conventions, usually by emphasizing the sources from which they derive. This tactic reminds us of the fictive status of those conventions, a status normally effaced as the conventions become naturalized— as they pass, that is, from fictions or innovations into conventions and thus "common sense," as we charitably call it.

Many writers attempt to arrest this evolution once these conceptual fictions become canonized as "natural" or "commonsensical" but before they are subject to the corrosives of irony. Blunt dogmatism is one strategy, of course, but a more sophisticated tactic is to argue limits to the effects of irony. Wayne Booth, for example, approaches irony as simply another technique of persuasion, a contractual if sophisticated arrangement by which the reader "reconstructs" an ironic passage as a means of reaching the author's intended message.[2] Since this involves rejecting the literal because of some significant incongruity, then exploring alternative interpretations and correlating them with the author's beliefs, irony places considerable demands upon the linguistic and literary competency of the reader and creates many possible pitfalls for the unwary and unable. Nonetheless, the possibility of what amounts to "decoding" irony persists, for the clear implication of the metaphor of "reconstruction" is that one rebuilds mentally along the same lines by which the author originated the structure before us. Hence Booth suggests that irony may be stable or unstable depending upon readers' certainty that they have accurately represented the authorial reasoning, a distinction clearly dependent upon an essentially representational poetics and the epistemological metaphor of the mirror upon which it rests. Moreoever, irony may be overt or covert depending on whether the ironic disparity is explicit or disguised, a distinction that assumes the absolute and definitive control only a powerful and univocal being could impose upon a text. Finally, Booth argues, irony may be local or infinite, depending on whether its import is somehow limited or whether it affects the universe itself or the very possibility of discourse. This last distinction is a crucial implicit assertion that irony can *ever* be limited or localized, and that the nonironic language against which it works is "normally" reliable and accurate as a representation of the nonverbal realm it purports to convey.

The more one pursues reflexivity, the more untenable these kinds of assumptions become. Indeed, to compare Wayne Booth's discussion of irony with Paul de Man's earlier treatment of it is to recognize the difference it makes whether one touches base with the Continental tradition of thinking about irony important in de Man but largely absent in Booth. In irony, according to de Man, "the sign points to something that differs from its literal meaning and has for its function the thematization of this difference."[3] This is close to Booth's notion of "incongruity," but to thematize difference is not necessarily to inaugurate a reconstruction of an authorial edifice—it is to point to a gap, an oscillation between two contending centers, neither of which suffices in itself as the meaning. To return to our initial comparison of Wayne Booth and Paul de Man, then, is to recognize that reflexive irony undoes the search for a center by bending that search back around its starting assumptions. The oscillation between convention and subject, or between either of these and culture, disperses any originary prime mover or first cause and makes *the oscillation itself* the crucial constitutive energy of the cultural, narrative, or individual act.

Indeed, the disparity in the two critics' contexts is indicated in de Man's next sentence: "But this important structural aspect may well be a description of figural language in general" (192). "Rhetoric" for de Man is not simply the stable Boothian context of speaker persuading listener, but also the slippery realm of figurative rhetoric in which language betrays its distance from any referent. Such distance signals one source of the inauthenticity inevitable in any process of understanding, whether of self or of world, and the result takes us far from the possibility of stable, overt, and local irony. As de Man puts it, "a far from harmless process gets underway. It may start as a casual bit of play with a stray loose end of the fabric, but before long the entire texture of the self is unraveled and comes apart. The whole process happens at an unsettling speed. Irony possesses an inherent tendency to gain momentum and not to stop until it has run its full course; from the small and apparently innocuous exposure of a small self-deception it soon reaches the dimensions of the absolute" (197). It is de Man's rather than Booth's sense of irony that one finds if one looks reflexively at *Vanity Fair,* and it prods us into recognizing how much more than Amelia's sentimentality or Becky's rapaciousness is undermined; the entire narrative medium we use to understand these characters and the world within which we place them is also subject to the irony begun with these stray loose ends of the cultural fabric.

Such irony does begin, nonetheless, with stray ends that compose the first stage of the novel's reflexive concerns—the extent to which the novel depends upon irony to make the reader feel he or she imposes upon the material the norms by which it is to be judged. The nod of assent or smile of perception is the first step beyond passive acceptance of dominant narrative or social coding in a text, for even as an ironic passage depends upon those conventions, it highlights them as such. Especially given the historical context in which Thackeray courts a serial audience looking for more intellectual stimulation than it had typically found in the medium, Thackeray frequently resorts to such irony in order to take his audience beyond the naive complicity of merely popular fiction.

Thackeray's chapter titles are the most elementary examples of fostering this reflexive awareness in the reader. Chapter 11, for example, is called "Arcadian Simplicity," hence invoking classical and Renaissance ideals of virtue and tranquillity hardly applicable to Mrs. Bute's plot to make a match between Becky and Rawdon or to Miss Crawley's imperious rule at Queen's Crawley. Neither the conventional ideal nor the social reality fares well as the reader correlates an obviously literary frame with what appears to be actual experience. Later we may come to rethink the status of that "actual experience," but at first dip into the novel we find the reader motivated toward a wittily ironic perspective upon discrepancies between formalizations of experience and experience itself. Such a discrepancy is, of course, recognized as the hallmark of Thackeray's irony, and examples of it are numerous.

Chapter 31, "In Which Jos Sedley Takes Care of His Sister," shows Jos completing his elaborate toilette and ordering his meals with great care instead of looking after his hysterical sister; the ideal of brotherly love and solicitude within which he conceives himself is no more convincing than his equally conventionalized sense of himself as a military buck complete with epaulets and mustachios. And chapter 41, "In Which Becky Revisits the Halls of Her Ancestors," delights the reader with its obvious sarcasm at the expense of the novel of high fashion in which Becky now feels herself a protagonist.

One need only skim the table of contents of *Vanity Fair* to multiply the number of examples in which the irony plays specifically off the literary or conventional frames within which a character is constituted. Thackeray also uses character tags this way. Dubbing Betsy Horrocks "the Ribbons" throughout the narrative keeps before us the role she attempts to play out of the pages of the Victorian equivalent of *Cosmopolitan*. Calling the senior Osborne "the old aristocrat" indicates the stereotype he tries with only partial success to work himself into. When Miss Pinkerton is tagged "the Semiramis of Hammersmith" or "Minerva," or when Lady Southdown is said to rise up "as magnificent as Mrs. Siddons in Lady Macbeth," a reader becomes familiar with the inability of characters to separate any sense of themselves or their behavior from roles as stylized as the florid conventions of the melodramatic Victorian theater. It is perhaps only a step away from readers' applying such an insight to their own roles in living and in reading.

To look very closely at all at the modifiers Thackeray uses for characters and events is to realize how pervasively he denaturalizes human behavior. Shortly after arriving for her visit to the Sedleys, for example, Becky comes down the stairs "the picture of youth, unprotected innocence, and humble virgin simplicity" (1:27; 3). Though readers have not yet seen Becky display the full range of her talents, they already know enough at this point in the novel to react against such extravagant posturing. If this is an accurate description of Becky on the stairs, it is accurate only because it is as carefully posed as a period portrait. Innocence, humility, and simplicity are the markers of the role she plays, and she is "unprotected" only in the sense that she lacks a mother to extract a proposal from Jos and "virginal" only in that her full involvement with the Reverend Mr. Crisp remains unknown.[4]

A more complex passage pertains to Dobbin later in the novel. When he is considering George's dilemma as a penniless married man, he imagines George selling out his commission and roughing it with Amelia in Canada. In other words, he imagines their lives in terms of an Arcadian fantasy compounded of *Daphnis and Chloe* and *Sergeant Preston of the*

Yukon. The narrator calls attention to this conventionalized frame both by commenting directly upon it and by juxtaposing another frame of reference to it: "With such a partner Dobbin thought he would not mind Siberia—and, strange to say, this absurd and utterly imprudent young fellow never for a moment considered that the want of means to keep a nice carriage and horses, and of an income which should enable its possessors to entertain their friends genteelly, ought to operate as bars to the union of George and Miss Sedley" (1:235–36; 20). There is indeed something "strange to say" about this comment, but it is not a simple matter to unravel. Dobbin is "absurd," we know by now, because of the extent to which he allows his fantasies to be programmed by popular fiction. As in the case of a number of characters we have glanced at, his inner life turns out to be blueprinted by the external media of popular culture. But to call him "utterly imprudent" necessarily invokes, however ironically, a materialist frame of reference elaborated in the final lines of the passage and itself compounded of the shrewdness of middle-class self-improvement literature and the pretentious emulation provoked by fiction of the high and the fashionable— still two best-selling types of popular literature. This passage, then, not only undoes the character by accenting its scripting by convention, but also unravels the narrator's stance from which that convention is exposed as such. Moreover, to the extent that "imprudent" is ironic and Dobbin is in some way affirmed, the reader faces the impossibility of mediating in a nebulous zone between frames. In addition to the omnipresence of scripting conventions, the point here is that this passage typifies a tactic in the novel by which no standard of judgment escapes the dubious status of stylized convention and by which the reader is left with no absolute point at which to arrest the escalation of irony.

One could approach a number of other passages with similar effects, including the famous passage refusing to settle the question of Becky's "guilt" with Lord Steyne. The narrator interrupts the scene to ask, "Who could tell what was truth which came from those lips; or if that corrupt heart was in this case pure?" All that she has accomplished, we are told, has "come to this bankruptcy" (2:229; 53). G. Armour Craig has argued the point of this indeterminacy as the assertion that "market values and moral values are discontinuous and separate" in Vanity Fair.[5] The point may well be, of course, that market and moral values are all too continuous and interrelated, as the passage implies by tumbling together the moral language of "corrupt" or "pure" with the accounting metaphors adding up to bankruptcy. The moral dimension we assume to be grounded on absolute or transcendental underpinnings is again inextricably bound up with all but antithetical materialism. Both, of course, are finally rooted in the linguistic medium, for the crucial evidence is always semiotic, whether it comes from "those lips" or from the signs of wealth being totted up as jewels on the floor and bank notes folded away in a cashbox. The effect of such a passage is to raise the issues of market versus moral values, to cause the reader to consider the complications of the case more thoroughly,[6] and to bring out other such referential themes; but by undermining the stability from which narrator and reader more typically assess the characters they share, the passage encourages the reader to reflect upon the whole process by which fiction establishes and reinforces the lines along which we evaluate matters. It means its crucial question literally rather than rhetorically— "Who could tell what was truth?"—for the telling would require a stance outside the cultural framework.

Another striking passage that caused even more controversy among contemporary reviewers,[7] and that features Becky speculating in terms we might now call situation ethics, also nurtures a reflexive awareness in readers.

> "It isn't difficult to be a country gentleman's wife," Rebecca thought. "I think I could be a good woman if I had five thousand a year. I could dawdle about in the nursery, and count the apricots on the wall. . . . I could pay everybody, if I had but the money. This is what the conjurers here pride themselves upon doing. They look down with pity upon us miserable sinners who have none. They think themselves generous if they give our children a five-pound note, and us contemptible if we are without one." And who knows but Rebecca was right in her speculations—and that it was only a question of money and fortune which made the difference between her and an honest woman? If you take temptations into account, who is to say that he is better than his neighbour? A comfortable career of prosperity, if it does not make people honest, at least keeps them so. An alderman coming from a turtle feast will not step out of his carriage to steal a leg of mutton; but put him to starve and see if he will not purloin a loaf. Becky consoled herself by so balancing the chances and equalizing the distribution of good and evil in the world. (2:80–81; 41)

Within the quotation marks, Becky unfolds clearly worldly ethics condemning the snobbery of those among whom she seeks to live. Hypocrisy is the rule when both virtue and social standing are economically determined. With the rhetorical question in the middle of the passage, the narrator takes over and appears to extend Becky's reasoning and complicate any judgment of her because her career is environmentally induced. We should exhibit sympathy for Becky as a victim rather than pride ourselves upon a repudiation of her shabby ethics. It is this section of the passage—especially when the alderman comes into the picture— that riled Lewes and led other reviewers to conclude that Thackeray was immoral and a threat to the public welfare. There have been a sprinkling of readers since then who have repeated this moral condemnation of Thackeray, just as there have been isolated apologists for Becky defending the apparent line of reasoning here.

But the final sentence of the paragraph inverts this reading: we discover that we have been tricked into a reading error by the narrator's ambiguity. That is, the sly "so balancing . . . equalizing" in that last sentence suddenly shows us that the long passage about the alderman purloining a loaf, a strictly economic view of crime, derives from Becky's assessment of the case rather than from the narrator's. We discover that what follows the dash is not the narrator's voice reporting his own thoughts, but rather his voice summarizing the rest of Becky's internal monologue. We have in our hands a text that allows us to misread precisely at the point at which the moral and the mercenary interpenetrate. Ideologically, the culture holds them to be separate realms; practically speaking, they are both more words from "those lips" of cultural coding. Both in the economic determinacy toyed with in the reasoning and in the accounting metaphors of "balancing" and "equalizing," the passage introduces one frame into another and throws the reader back upon the task of reflecting upon the relations between them not normally pursued in the popular literature of Thackeray's day. Whether we approach the question in terms of the relations between an economic substructure and Victorian morality or more generally in terms of the texture of overlapping semiotic matrixes, we have moved beyond an uncritical scripting by such conventions to a critical reordering *of* them, precisely one of reflexivity's key effects.

In these cases we have seen the text throwing the reader back upon his own philosophical resources to question not only the material itself, but the grounds of that material and the act of understanding it. The text presses hardest against a reader, perhaps, when it disperses conceptual grounds into the mere conventions of culture, especially when it is the popular culture of all members of the society rather than the classical learning of the elite. Hence more popular forms and genres to which we have seen brief allusions can also be found providing more extensive dimensions of irony as well. The parodist of *Punch's Prize Novelists,* adept at using stylistic play in anatomizing the prevailing conventions of Victorian popular fiction, comes alive with a vengeance in the "Vauxhall" chapter (6) of *Vanity Fair.* As he recounts Becky's campaign for Jos, the narrator breaks off for a bit to generate alternative treatments of his subject matter. He notes that "we might have treated this subject in the genteel, or in the romantic, or in the facetious manner. Suppose we had laid the scene in Grosvenor Square, with the very same adventures—

would not some people have listened? Suppose we had shown how Lord Joseph Sedley fell in love, and the Marquis of Osborne became attached to Lady Amelia, with the full consent of the duke, her noble father" (1:59; 6). And so on, through the kitchen narrative and the Newgate novel, even though the long "Night Attack" was deleted after serial publication. "Some people" might have listened with their preconceptions about high society, their expectations of a roman à clef exposing the privacies of the wellborn, their hunger for a glittering world where wit and polish are the primary values pulling to themselves implicitly the moral force of ancillary values (virtue, wealth, success, beauty) in a thrilling but comfortably regulated system.

Some people, however, might have opted for the "downstairs" version of battling cooks and coachmen in which the unruly passions and eccentricities of the lower orders justify their inferior place in society. The adventurous excitement of the Newgate version, on the other hand, appeals to the wish for some relief from the dull pace of ordinary living, some flirtation with the night world of lawlessness that would be sanctioned by the tidy final dispensing of justice that underscores the comforting notion of providentially set limits to terror. The full sequence of four or five such options sets up different expectations for the conduct of the narrative, and the reader crawls into the niche precarved for him by literary convention. But too, as I have sketched, there are wider implications whose strings are attached to the literary and stylistic systems here. The irony deflates the pretentiousness of these highly stylized stances and indeed employs the interplay among them to make the reader aware of how thoroughly these conceptual schemes frame both the presentation and the interpretation of fiction.

Something happens in a page or two, however, that carries these concerns a step further. The narrator tells us: "This mystery served to keep Amelia's gentle bosom in a perpetual flutter of excitement. If she did not speak with Rebecca on the tender subject, she compensated herself with long and intimate conversations with Mrs. Blenkinsop" (1:61; 6). If readers were to miss altogether the stylized elements here, they would undoubtedly find themselves yearning for the match that hurries the plot of much sentimental fiction. For most readers, certainly for most of Thackeray's contemporaries, this reaction is probably never wholly absent; the response is too firmly coded into the structuring of human experience as the mythos of love, matchmaking, and perpetual happiness. But an ironic awareness of all this is induced partly by the fact that Amelia's heart is fluttering over the match between an obese narcissist and a ruthless scavenger and partly by the lesson in stylization the narrator has taught in the preceding pages.

What is normally a conventional assumption about the mythos of youth and the conduct of narrative is here turned against not only the elements of the assumption but also those readers who have not sufficiently examined that assumption and are thus no more perceptive than the characters. The stakes are clearly higher than literary satire—the sociopolitical ramifications of this mythos are not hard to find. Persuading the populace through mass culture that romance is its central concern and primary means of self-validation ties up its energies in sexuality rather than in challenges to the existing political and industrial conditions. In psychological terms, the mythos underwrites the individual's sense of incompleteness and thus his never-ending search for something outside himself to complete his desire for plenitude. In metaphysical terms, the mythos is homologous with the aspiration to some form of union with an ideal or divine realm. In literary terms, the mythos is an allegory of the desire to unite the linguistic realm of human knowledge with the nonverbal other of external reality—the epistemological foundation of realism.

When at the beginning of the chapter these stylized worldviews are clearly announced and parodied, a reader's easy recognition of them may well limit their implications in the immediate context to literary parody—and indeed the usual reading of such a passage stresses Thackeray's care in distinguishing his realism from the unrealistic forms of popular fiction. But in this later passage the text shows the seemingly inevitable seepage into what appears to be realistic and therefore truthful narrative of the same kinds of stylistic cues to whole structures of assumptions. Hence even if one strives just to reflect reality, that reality is always assimilated to some form of verbal and conceptual stylization. Indeed, its "realistic" force may well depend upon just how subtly it uses reigning stylizations to make its material consistent with the larger context of assumptions to which they are related. The sense of "reality," in other words, derives from a narrative's conformity to a set of reigning assumptions rather than directly to any nonverbal "reality."

At the same time, to apply fully this lesson on stylization to the text is to produce further perplexity. As readers of Thackeray's earlier works are aware, such passages as these themselves operate according to a conventional pattern in which a stylization is stylized—such double or triple stylizing places the narrator's ironic frame *within* the process it unmasks. Pardoxically, that is, the passage operates by undoing both the procedure targeted and its own. Competition among conventions, then, is one insight such a process achieves, but another is the competition *within* conventions by all the code elements assimilated inevitably from "rival" conventions or paradigms—as is never more obvious than in irony, dependent for its very operation upon the structures it critiques. Is not irony thus the "normal" rather than an aberrant function of language?

Such a possibility opens yet another side to the effect of this passage. If it is impossible to pretend that the passage is not ironic, that Thackeray is outrageously sentimental, it is equally impossible to decide to what extent he is otherwise—clearheaded, hard-nosed, practical. The legendary confusion of critics over whether Thackeray is sentimental or cynical, over whether Amelia is an abused heroine or a rapaciously egoistic emotional leech, derives from the extent to which this kind of irony undoes any basis for passing reliable judgments. If one cannot see, let alone narrate, without the optics of stylizing sets of assumptions, then one cannot discriminate between "genuine" emotion and emotion that is a function of the stimulus and response mechanism of highly conventionalized cues. Not only is unmediated insight unavailable, but the very integrity of narrative "voice," let alone ironic voice, is problematic. It is a debatable but undecidable mix of frames and paradigms of assumptions that are themselves mixtures of further mixtures. Such inevitably regressive reflexive analysis is a valuable insight into the complications involved in the accretion of a "voice." Rather than the presence of an individual viewpoint, voice signifies the endlessly intertextual and mutually constitutive conventions interacting to form a "voice." It is a *personal* voice only if we revise the metaphysics of that adjective to accommodate the semiotic medium of its being. What we gain in rigor, however, we lose in certainty: the absolutist or transcendental epistemology of Boothian irony has shown its constitution to be by means of de Man's Schlegellian snowball. The discourse originates, then, not in authorial stratagem but in an eminently semiotic cave of Echo, and it exists not as an authoritative insight but as a composite willed into a shape that nonetheless reveals its multifariousness and, by traditional lights, its compromised integrity. This irony is not simply, then, the narrator or Thackeray exposing *himself* in a "self-reflexive" irony but is the very "voice" of the conventions marking voice as such.

This "philosophical" conclusion has its less abstract consequences as well, however. If the "I" behind *Vanity Fair* is to be the collective "Mrs. Grundy" of the middle class, to experience the voice of that "I" as a dispersion of individuality and its grounds is to threaten the ethos of that class. The critical history of *Vanity Fair*, with its preoccupation with degrees of guilt or the psychology of individual characters, might suggest that many readers still understand the genre according to the degree to which Defoe's journalistic fiction played off the middle-class desire to master facts or Richardson's epistolary narrative grew out of primers for would-be letter writers. The novel, that is, is the middle-class blueprint for its forms of being. *Vanity Fair,* of course, is more complicated than that, as is the fiction of both Defoe and Richardson. But in its effort to deal with the sweep of middle-class existence in midcentury England, the novel does through irony mark the anxiety over the grounds and thus the security of middle-class being. Subjectivity, the province of the class, is imperiled by those philosophical problems inherent in its collective "voice" that are suggested by the play of irony in this novel. To look at the rather different practice of irony by such contemporaries of Thackeray as Trollope and Hawthorne is to see how pervasive this topic of concern can be.

In considering Trollope's *The Warden,* it is certainly difficult not to take the protagonist, Mr. Harding, as a type of the narrator. Even within the novel, other characters are forced to "wait" until he answers the primordial narrative question—What next? It is no easy matter, of course, since the primary institutions of his culture bear down upon him seeking to impose an ending. Through his daughter the family, along with its mythos of romantic love, tugs in one direction. The press, embodied in John Bold, seeks to harness local social services under the yoke of technocratic efficiency (and predictably enough conflicts with the family as an older social form claiming the same turf). The church, of course, works through Archdeacon Grantly contending for the same ground of action in the world, arguing that its material forms (its sinecures, charities, and emoluments) are immune to the criteria espoused in the sensationalized journalism of the press. And Parliament, not to be undervalued in this clearly ideological struggle, threatens to step in and legislate—to legitimate one disposition or another of the social resources, to mandate the lines and forms of legitimacy, and to readjust through its considerable power the social space in which Mr. Harding finds himself.

To carry out the middle-class function of nineteenth-century narrative—that of evoking the individual's struggle to achieve a secure point in the field of larger forces at work in history—Mr. Harding must negotiate a difficult multidimensional tissue of alliances among these contending institutions. He is made the key of the narrative action, that point at which action must take place despite the odds. Trollope's superb device for suggesting the impossibility of being the individual called for by the nineteenth-century ethos is Harding's musical turn. That is, those who use language are those who operate as the vehicles of the power of larger institutions. Least verbal of all is his daughter, muted as the force within the embattled institution of the family, muted as a woman in a man's world. Louder in the world of discourse, however, are the flashy editorialist, the overbearing archdeacon, the drafters of the threatening parliamentary legislation, the magistrates ready to write a judicial disposition of the case.

Mr. Harding, however, insofar as he fails to merge himself with the enabling power of institutional force, instead plays music—a nonverbal art. Even worse, however, are the versions of removal of even this often potent form of "moving" people. That is, his lifework appears to be transforming the music that once moved congregations into a beautiful art object, a photogravure sarcophagus of vellum. Still more drastic is his nervous habit, whenever the stress of his unenviable situation becomes unbearable, of sawing soundless music out of an imaginary instrument. Three or four times removed from an answer comprehensible within the discursive rules of his culture, his "music" is a fitting image for the necessary displacement in Victorian fiction of the answers to its central questions about the individual in society. The novel dramatizes the highly discursive realm in which institutions contend for the allegiance of speakers, but it also dramatizes the impossibility either of speaking as an individual or of acting (or not acting) outside the options generated by the interplay of those institutions.

Thackeray traverses this ground by suffusing voice with a manic irony that shows no actions or judgments not already co-opted by stylized forms in which we must necessarily lose confidence. But Trollope just as persuasively indicates the impasse reached by individualism in a culture increasingly dominated by institutions and the forms of discourse they distribute. Neither feels comfortable with a stance from which the individual may contend within the discursive province of culture.

For a third version of this class fable, one might well turn to Hawthorne's "The Gray Champion," an odd little sketch that by these lights becomes the dream narrative of collectivity in all its shockingly violent and confrontational quality. This mysterious figure of authority, according to the interpretively useful if aesthetically cumbersome exposition, appears to function as (literally) the people's voice only at those rare moments when the collective will is galvanized sufficiently to face explicitly the ideological stresses of the communal life rather than allowing them to remain latent within the "normal" institutional practice sensationalized in *The Warden* or in the social fiction of Dickens. The governor depends upon several tributaries of social form to sustain his position at the pinnacle of colonial society, among them the legal word of the royal charter, the sacred word of God's minister, the ritual language of the royal procession, and the raw military power of the soldiers deployed under his command. The dream, of course, is that the will of the people is sufficient to dispense with the configurations of institutional power when they become concentrated and arbitrarily exercised.

It is, of course, the middle class that dreams this myth of the legitimate, of the rights of man limiting those of the state, and of the naturalness of these limits that both enables and validates them. Like *Vanity Fair* and *The Warden,* in other words, this story suggests the extent to which classic Anglo-American fiction narratizes historical conflicts, most obviously that of the individual subject and the social forms through which he or she is expressed. The gradual shift that takes place in "The Gray Champion" from realistic narrative to two-dimensional allegory emphasizes the increasingly remote historical probability, as the nineteenth century proceeds, of a single voice explicitly articulating a stance outside such social institutions as appear in the tale. That is, the historical possibility that appears to sustain the early part of the tale thins out to the purely verbal realm of the heavily expository ending. As those institutions increasingly assimilate individuals to the impersonal forms of modern society, the sacramental power vaguely invoked by an older, theologically legitimated voice becomes inaccessible. Its language of truth fades from political confrontations that must, by the Gray Champion's Bunker Hill "appearance," be fought materially rather than rhetorically. The vision that has powered the middle class and its narrative forms is hence marked as a dream, a displacement of history necessary in order to contain the terror of losing that middle ground between the aristocracy and the rabble—the same ground on which, not coincidentally, the Gray Champion makes his last tangible stand.

The Issue of Narrative Stance

The history of criticism of Thackeray's *Vanity Fair* shows recurrent attempts to treat the novel as if it functioned like the "prototypical Victorian novel," itself a mythical construct reflecting the cultural need to believe in coherence and harmony among individual, social, and metaphysical orders. Thackeray, who had himself experienced unexpected flux in all three orders, had spent what we call his "apprenticeship" ridiculing the disjunctions between the tidying effects of literary form and reality, a ridicule we have seen put to increasingly intense purposes in *Vanity Fair.* It is important, then, to recognize the novel's parodic relationship to stylistic conventions and fictional modes,[8] its satiric relationship to society,[9] its growth and development during the writing

29

and publishing process,[10] and even what moral grounds it offers for thematic consistency and rhetorical coherence.[11] But insofar as such approaches still treat *Vanity Fair* as a univocal rhetorical construct, they obscure basic facts about the novel—the narrator, for example, is not a single unified identity but a complex of discordant intertextual strains signaled by conflicting claims about his grounds of narration, conflicting facts about his "personal identity," and conflicting stylistic strains and, value judgments. Univocal readings of *Vanity Fair* also belie a persistent unease among readers that has led in the modern era to efforts to explain away the source of that unease in psychological terms ranging from the simplistic (in, say, the work of J. Y. T. Greig) to the relatively sophisticated (in Bernard Paris's work).[12] Perhaps, however, the most insightful statements of this unease come from Thackeray's contemporary critics.

G. H. Lewes, for example, noted in his review that "Thackeray laughs all around; his impartiality has something terrible in it; so complete is the irony that he turns it even upon himself."[13] This "something terrible" distressed a number of contemporary ciritics. Samuel Phillips noted in the *Times* that "a series of novels, based upon the principle which Mr. Thackeray delights to illustrate, would utterly destroy this knowledge [of the efficacy of the good] and render us a race of unbelievers"; Thackeray is "our clever but too skeptical companion" with whom "it [is] impossible to feel happy or at ease."[14] Often we seem to work hard at straightening out and justifying what causes such philosophical unease in readers—Geoffrey Tillotson's landmark study is an excellent example[15]—but it is equally important to search for the nature of the "something terrible" lurking in this novel and to accept its reflexive implications, however uneasy they may leave us.

What do we make, for example, of the apparent contradictions in the self-characterization of the narrator? We are told he is a lonely bachelor at Vauxhall (1:65; 6), a rapt observer of weddings (1:189–90; 16) who nonetheless knows the emotions involved only at second hand (1:259; 22). The same Dobbinesque wistfulness haunts his sense of children, whom he observes with some care from coachtops (1:273; 23), noting his childlessness with a mix in undecidable proportions of irony and poignancy (2:3; 36). Thus he has the outsider's mix of detached judgment and unquenchable desire to participate, whether he talks of family matters or is invited "to fill a vacant place" at dinners (2:2; 36) or finds himself "from the outside gazing over the policemen's shoulders at the bewildering beauties as they pass into Court or ball" (2:194; 51).

The trick, of course, is that his privilege exceeds the boundaries these details might suggest. Though, as he tells us, he has seen only the "vast wall in front" of Steyne's palace (2:138–39; 47), he either contrives informants or simply enters anyway to describe interiors and events within those walls. It is the epitome of how the narrator, though his circumstances should rule him outside given zones of experience, often crosses over into those zones, displaying a solid sense of their interiors. Such crossing of the boundaries not only mocks the convention by which fiction sets up reflectors, *ficelles,* and first-person narrators, but also whatever popular notions valorize lived experiences over imagined ones. Each seems equally real within the body of experience that makes up the "selfhood" of our imaginary narrator. The blurring of this line becomes literal when our usually single narrator speaks of himself and his dear wife Julia as role playing with their children for the sake of an inheritance (1:104; 9). The outsider is also insider, a positing of incompatible alternatives that undermines the whole logic based upon the superiority of the realistic, the experienced, and the known over the fantastic, the imagined, and the merely posited. What is fantasized to fill in the gaps left from interviews, letters, and direct observation is as "real" as what is more "reliably" documented; what is imagined is as solid as what is experienced; what seems known establishes no privilege over what is clearly posited; whatever is so conventional that it has often passed unnoticed is as real as what purports to *be* the real and the true.

Thackeray presses this multiplicity of selves within the narrator far beyond the playfulness of a single novel by indexing within "him" all the major narrative perspectives of Victorian fiction. After all, one finds a puppeteer, an almost swaggering omniscient novelist, a melancholy commentator, a historian sifting documents, an acquaintance of the characters themselves, a fellow worldling of the reader—all dissolved into what seems to be the same voice (as far as we would mark it by general tone and characteristic devices, at least), but exercising different privileges and predicating different roles for the reader in his own act of interpretation. We can imagine some of the roles combined (novelist and commentator, for example, or fellow worldling and historian), but not others (puppeteer and historian? novelist and acquaintance of the characters?). At some point the orchestrated dissonance of these incompatible points of view must come to our attention and force us to understand not just the arbitrary literary nature of these conventions but the epistemological and metaphysical consequences of that arbitrary quality.

What do we make, for example, of the puppeteer? Juliet McMaster's fine study of *Vanity Fair* examines the prologue in which the frame with the puppeteer is erected, discussing it in the context of its reinforcement of the realism of Thackeray's treatment of Victorian society, of the narrator's own humility, and of the importance of the reader's learning from the novel.[16] How does one begin to consider the reflexive dimension of this passage?

Such a show takes place within a tightly structured set of conventions shared by its manager and audience, conventions that "accept" oversimplifications of human nature in characterization, unrealistic elements in personal relations, and extraordinarily heightened dramatic scenes—a blow-by-blow account in a puppet show is hardly documentary realism; it is fantasy in which normal undercurrents of hostility or antagonism, or simply of difference, surface as clubbings and abuse. But to valorize what he calls "a reflective turn of mind" in the same two-page preface that presents this comparison is to change the terms of the agreement by which we unreflectingly accept such conventions. The popular genres Thackeray had been lampooning for years before writing *Vanity Fair* are not essentially different from a puppet show in positing such thoroughly structured conventions; nor, one might observe, is the "realistic" fiction dominating the narrative high road. The characters in Thackeray's novel, "real" enough to embody third-force psychological constructs for Bernard Paris, are still oversimplifications, even if perhaps to a lesser degree than Punch and Judy. The plot effaces huge stretches of boring commonplace affairs and much excitement that might prove distracting, all in order to conform to quite assumption-laden expectations about what kinds of events "qualify" for treatment in a Victorian novel and about how exaggerated relationships must be before they rise to fictional notice. It may be that we are to take these puppet shows in Smithfield more seriously, questioning the moral and psychological assumptions they embody, but we should also understand the nature of narrative—even realistic narrative—as shaped by unquestionably arbitrary conventions that impose their grid of assumptions upon the reality they pretend simply to represent.

Puppets "carved and dressed with the greatest care by the artist" and "on which no expense has been spared" are obviously products of a proud artificer unashamed to have given them their shape, dress, traits, and fates. Whether this godlike mastery enhances the manager or diminishes God is quite another matter. The divine paradigm of mastery in knowledge and action, itself analogous to the metaphysics of realism, is further scathed by the irreverent reference to the fantasy that "Old Nick will fetch away" the wicked nobleman after the performance. In fact, it is not divine justice but the aging, disease, and death of a thoroughly demystified human temporality that, in the course of the novel, claim Steyne. Though this seems to be the soul of realism itself, the very provision of the details of his death is not demanded by an objective account of Becky's and Amelia's affairs (happening as it does in 1830, long after things are settled with the main characters). And the details themselves—Steyne dies amid fits and the theft of his valuables by mistresses and valets—suggest the discredited principle of poetic justice.[17] The narrator responds to an unrealistic need for a patterned narrative (and what is the End of Steyne?) in a novel where, as we have seen, patterns are stylizations full of fictive assumptions about exterior reality. In the strictly temporal environment of this "Novel without a Hero," with its corresponding absence of absolutes or ideals, no formal pattern can be imposed without introducing the distortions implicit in retrospective ordering and interpreting. These lines, then, make evident how much metaphysical overreading occurs when, even in apparently realistic narrative, the author as puppeteer imposes pattern upon experience.

Certainly the dramatic source of the preface speaks to this issue as well. "Punch and Judy," after all, is an episodic narrative in which Punch murders a series of victims, violating successively "higher" institutional authority as he goes. According to a roughly contemporary version,[18] he kills his neighbor, his child, his wife (after which he wins Pretty Polly from *The Beggar's Opera,* a nice intertextual touch), the doctor, a servant, a blind man, and Jack Ketch. Having thus embodied a diabolical lack of any restraint, Punch takes on paradoxically the role of divine avenger and kills the devil himself, removing the embodiment of evil and thereby apparently restoring what was perhaps a dubious moral order to begin with. This model of lawless drama ending with moral order may well fit the novel's final compromise with conventional patterning (we indeed end with the curtain coming down on a marriage), but it also draws upon the religious roots of such a pattern, particularly since Punch and Judy are themselves descendants of Pontius Pilate and Judas Iscariot via popular religious dramatic traditions of several centuries' standing. Though the puppet show of the preface may well contrast, then, with the realistic narrative within the main body of the novel, it also clearly marks the common closure of each within the transcendental teleology of Western culture's central fiction.

At the end of the novel, the puppet master tells us, "Come, Children, let us shut up the box and the puppets, for our play is played out." Apparently it is not possible to move from the reader as child to the reader as adult, for the readers are children in the novel's final sentence, and the sentencing is to "*Vanitas, Vanitatum!* Which of us is happy in this world? Which of us has his desire? or having it, is satisfied?" The line has pessimistic implications for realistic narrative's aims, to say the least. The desire of Dobbin for his Amelia, the desire of readers for their comforting illusions, the desire of the novelist for mastery over his material, the desire of the critic for the perfect interpretation and for the perfect theoretical model—these desires for happy plenitude are aligned as shadows of each other cast by the textual candles, and they must include that desire of realism for the perfect copy of reality. For in the fulfillment of a desire, we discover only its imperfect approximation of the dimensions of human longing. In the fulfillment of a realistic narrative, we find only its imperfect approximation of the dimensions of that nonverbal reality beyond the self. It may be that the structure of values and assumptions in the preunderstanding is what permits us to see as much as we do, but what we see is necessarily a projection from that structure rather than simply a reading of an illusory "whole." It may be that the stance as puppeteer sets up a contrast that heightens the impact of the "realistic narrative" within the frame, but the very act of framing underscores the *posit* at the heart of composition.

Stances within the Frame

As we move into the body of the novel, narrative stance becomes predictably more complicated as variously incompatible stances compete. Curiously, these variations are either scorned for inconsistency[19] or rationalized,[20] and both these perspectives anticipate and valorize a univocal speaker. What we have seen thus far, of course, suggests that this is a misleading and rather transcendental expectation and that narrators are actually hybrids of a number of semiotic strands—the issue is thus a false one, and we need not make the choice among the stances or interpretations that is mandated by traditional expectations of *a* speaker behind the voice. In any case, the shifts do not make a great deal of sense until the novel is read reflexively, an approach for which Thackeray's earlier sketches and fiction should be more than adequate preparation. What we discover is that the primary stances Thackeray explores in *Vanity Fair* become vehicles for elucidating precisely what each requires its readers to assume, uncritically, in fiction that lives primarily within the letter of the conventional laws. The three stances this section considers together—the narrator as character, as historian, and as omniscient novelist—probe respectively the appeals for authority to immediate perception, to rational inquiry and research, and to perfect mastery of absolute truth or knowledge. As one might expect in reflexive fiction, *Vanity Fair* undoes the easy assurance by which narrators and readers normally conspire to perpetuate these modes of cognition, and the implications of this play extend far beyond the confines of this novel.

The narrator as character is a stance that depends upon two corollary assumptions, both of which center on the special privilege obtained by presence—on the one hand the mutual presence of narrator and reader meeting in a conversational relationship, and on the other hand the presence of the narrator on the scene at certain key moments, most memorably at Pumpernickel. The first supposes the full communication of an intimate chat and will be more thoroughly addressed later on, since it occupies so major a place in the rhetoric of *Vanity Fair*. The second, however, involves the first of three major cultural illusions targeted by the reflexive play among these stances.

An excellent example of how both referential and reflexive interests are served by the same device is the multiplication of conflicting identities for the character the narrator portrays himself to be. In the Vauxhall chapter, for example, we begin to feel sorry for Dobbin, left out of the party by the two couples, but we also find this response itself a bit sentimental; at this point the narrator tells us, "It wasn't very good fun for Dobbin—and, indeed, to be alone at Vauxhall, I have found, from my own experience, to be one of the most dismal sports ever entered into by a bachelor" (1:65; 6). This carefully adjusted emotional response—we thereby sympathize without sniffling—illustrates the disciplining power of this narrative stance in regulating the reader's reactions, hence serving well the referential dimension of the narrative.

At the same time, however, it conflicts with another passage in which the narrator produces a wife. After suggesting the family's competition for Miss Crawley's favor, then turning the matter to the reader's own courtship of his or her Aunt McWhirter's fortune, the narrator then includes himself: "Ah, gracious powers! I wish you would send me an old aunt—a maiden aunt—an aunt with a lozenge on her carriage, and a front of light coffee-coloured hair—how my children should work workbags for her, and my Julia and I would make her comfortable! Sweet—sweet vision! Foolish—foolish dream!" (1:104; 9). The narrator's comment certainly foreshadows the futility of the most avid suitors among the Crawleys, reminds the reader not to take too smug a view of such a mercenary family, and universalizes by including himself as a perpetrator. But it also does violence to the bachelor at Vauxhall or to the character who wistfully begins "were I blessed with child" (2:3; 36). As such contradictions multiply in the course of the novel, we are driven to recognize that the normal referential strategy to build a single coherent, consistent, unified entity from whom the narration may logically flow is being undercut by a reflexive marking of our need to constitute an authoritative being out of relatively few strokes of the pen.

To take seriously such a revised sense of the personal stance would be to find inconsistencies or conflicts, variations or shifts, no longer the same kind of critical crux they have been in traditional narrative criticism. Rather than resolving differences into the logical frame of the supposed divided identity of author or character or into the organic frame of the development of author or character, we might instead find dissonance of one kind or another a "natural" or even inevitable mark of voice. Such dissonance would then become an opportunity to identify the mix of semiotic frames and the implications of the particular game plan by which the narrative plays them out together. Reflexivity typically directs our attention to the resonances among surface conventions, the underlying codes that identify and relate the specific elements that feed into these conventions, and the founding assumptions upon which conventions and codes rest. In terms of the stance of the narrator as character, reflexivity suggests we consider the extent to which this stance draws upon the degree of conviction that intersubjective relationships normally inspire, even though its observations come from a moving, shifting, elusive "center" whose discursiveness we prefer to modulate into metaphysical terms.

The reliability of precisely those metaphysical terms is the ultimate target of the reflexive play in this stance. The novel pursues this question most fully when the narrator appears as an impetuous, vigorous youth at Pumpernickel longing for another glimpse of "that nice-looking woman" (2:349; 62). With remarkably clear memory, the narrator recalls the grand manner and appetite of both Jos and Georgy, Amelia's amusements at Georgy's feats, and Dobbin's sly teasing of the boy. Then we get some close observation at a performance of *Fidelio:*

> From our places in the stalls we could see our four friends of the table d'hôte, in the loge which Schwendler of the Erbprinz kept for his best guests: and I could not help remarking the effect which the magnificent actress and music produced upon Mrs. Osborne, for so we heard the stout gentleman in the moustachios call her. During the astonishing Chorus of the Prisoners, over which the delightful voice of the actress rose and soared in the most ravishing harmony, the English lady's face wore such an expression of wonder and delight that it struck even little Fipps, the *blasé* attaché. . . . And in the Prison Scene where Fidelio, rushing to her husband, cries "Nichts, nichts, mein Florestan," she fairly lost herself and covered her face with her handkerchief. (2:345; 62)

There are marvelous satirical implications here; certainly it is no accident that the opera Amelia watches is *Fidelio,* for the ironic contrasts between its plot and hers are abundant. The prison scene, for example, in which Leonore is still disguised as a man, sets Amelia off, perhaps because she could hardly begin to carry off a pretense of "masculinity"—

she does not have Leonore's capacity to step outside the stereotypical role prescribed for her by social conventions and to act directly and decisively.

More important than the ironies one could play out, however, is the doubly reflexive framework we are given here. That is, we watch a character who is herself a fully stylized sentimental heroine call attention to that stylization by her utterly conventional responses. Second, we see that she constructs her sense of herself not upon the lines of sentimental fiction by which we see her, but of heroic opera—much the way George styles himself upon the adventure hero, Rawdon upon the rake, Jos upon the romantic cavalier, and Dobbin upon the courtly lover. Such passages, in other words, undo the idea of characters along lines similar to what we found in our study of irony: the "selfhood" of each is a construct scripted by the conventions of popular narrative. They can see neither themselves nor each other except in these discursive terms. "Vanity Fair," in the final analysis, may well boil down to the networks of cultural conventions that, rather than the intersubjective authenticity current idealizations propose, control how we see and relate to each other and to ourselves.

That these prefabricated forms enter into and complicate the truth claims of the narrator's approach is made clear in the aftermath of this passage. Just after the part quoted, the narrator notes without any obvious marks of irony that "every woman in the house was snivelling at the time: but I suppose it was because it was predestined that I was to write this particular lady's memoirs that I remarked her" (2:345-46; 62). The judgmental note of "snivelling" seems to clash with the youthful exuberance with which this experiencing narrator responds to Amelia. One has, after all, the absurdly fervent patriotism satirized in the account of *Die Schlacht bei Vittoria* the next evening, the ecstatic response to Amelia's "curtsy, for which everybody might be thankful," and the fervent hope that she "would be induced to stay some time in the town" (2:348, 349; 62). Like Dobbin, this experiencing narrator loses all proper distance from his material and sees her as an unqualified exemplar of the heroine in the prototypical sentimental romance. Moreover, he monumentalizes her as a unique and especially significant figure, as indeed a narrator must for a protagonist, at the same time that his text "inadvertently" confesses she is no different from "every woman in the house." There is, then, no special trait of Amelia to single her out except that she exemplifies the current fashion of stylized behavior. If perception depends upon correspondence to stylized patterns, then this woman who is remarkable but no different from other women is noteworthy only because the narrator can follow Dobbin's lead in mentally editing her to "fit" the fashionable image.

Part of that mental editing is signaled by the narrator's curious claim that he "was predestined to write this particular lady's memoirs." How do we make sense of such predestination? Memory, it seems, is edited once he launches the narrative project, so that "to write" causes him in fact to have "remarked her" indeed, but in the sense of marking again according to the image called for by his present narrative.[21] The key epistemological presence, then, is not intersubjective but semiotic. Whether it be in the initial perception, in which cultural fashion pre-selects and preforms the perceived, or in the retrospective act in which narrative convention edits memory, the meaning of "presence" is a semiotic matrix that necessarily distances the referent even while pre-tending, as representationalist poetics seems to do, that the immediacy of a narrator on the scene enhances either the authority or the reliability of the presentation. As Thackeray demonstrated repeatedly in such "trap" narratives as *Barry Lyndon* and *Major Gahagan,* convention takes us in on this point, and it is only when, especially in the latter case, the narrative explodes in our face or, more subtly, when it marks reflexively its epistemological gambit, as in this passage, that we easily recognize just what is entailed philosophically in the stance of the narrator as character.

Such passages, indeed, point toward the impressionist fiction James and his followers found in realism, in which the subject half of the Cartesian dichotomy expands to fill the domain of the fiction. If we cannot really be objective, then what we *must* be is omnivorously sub-jective, making all features of "reality" over into our own impressions. At the same time, though, *Vanity Fair* also suggests that once we look at the structures of subjective impressions, we find neither the phe-nomenology of mind nor the radical individuality of being, but the sem-iotic matrix of which both subject and object, both "self" and "world," are functions. The stance as character thus progressively empties itself of the grounds for its authority as it more rigorously applies itself to the material it masters. In *Vanity Fair* the phenomenon is made ines-capable through the extreme conventionality as we see in these passages, but as we could not with any confidence draw a boundary between such conventions and an unmediated and thus "authentic" engagement with experience, we are persuaded of the phenomenon's general rele-vance to a poetics detailing the constitutive magic of discourse.

If we consider this stance in other narratives, we discover how consis-tently the reflexive energies of narrative are expended in exploring the curious implications of narrators who are themselves characters in the action of the novel. Tristram Shandy is, of course, virtually archetypal here in his frustration at the literal impossibility of making a record of the life one witnesses. His frustrations reflect eighteenth-century epistemological debates, just as Emily Brontë's Lockwood, Nelly, and company index a rather different set of empirical limits—the inadequacy of convention, so admirably epitomized by Lockwood in the literary sense and Nelly in the social context, to experience what by some means or another at least appears to dwell beyond the ken of culture in the odd realm of pure ontology Brontë projects in that turbulent masterpiece. Even if the intense drama in which Heathcliff and Catherine feel themselves taking part is only a function of desire and imaginative fantasy, "their" world is one that narrative conventions are able to portray only by means of something akin to a drawing class experimenting with negative space. That is, through Nelly and Lockwood, Brontë blocks out all those narrative possibilities that fall short of the magnitude of the two main protagonists, which in fact contain only the level of experience attained by the novel's second(ary) generation and its narrators. Lockwood, that is, may be described as Brontë's summary of the male sentimental domestic narrative tradition with its reduction of life to leisured love relationships and of women to objects of male fantasy. Nelly, on the other hand, represents the middle-class Brontë's notion of what working-class wisdom might be. The "Brontë" we infer looking over their shoulders is yet another convention, however rarer, affected by the positioning of class, sex, and other conditions and shaped by the desire to resolve contradictions that run deeper in the culture than her narrative quite comprehends. Characters who become, like Heathcliff and Catherine, something like pure subjectivity simply elude the capacity of conventions to specify what happens for them. The mystified would argue that this is precisely because conventions inevitably diminish the mystical power of authentic selfhood, pure being. But the same material also supports the reasoning that conventions of presentation or of content (to preserve for a moment the fiction of such a distinction) are all there is, and the "pure subjectivity" Brontë desires eludes narrative form because it eludes the primal desire of all humanity for a pure ground of being that is safely, securely, permanently, and consistently *there* as a court of final appeal. Such characters are a collective wish fulfillment in nineteenth-century culture, finally ossifying among the types in Gothic romance as another dead end of cultural dreamwork. Adding this conceptual limit to the empirical limits Sterne celebrates, one has a clear grasp of the consensus about narrating characters drawn upon by a novel like *Vanity Fair*.

After all, if one looks laterally from *Vanity Fair* at the quintessential contemporary exemplar of this narrative stance, one finds the energetic example of Dickens's works. David Copperfield, Pip, Esther Summerson, and of course, as always the case in Dickens, more—all show us a similar process. All, that is, set out to write autobiographies so as to explain their essential or phenomenological being. Each makes discoveries similar to those we have found in *Vanity Fair:* individual existence is less a process of growth and individuation than of the internalization and enactment of "external"models. When David, for example, models himself upon the dashing figure of Steerforth and marries the boss's impossible fashion-book doll of a daughter, he sets himself up for a process in which he gradually finds these signs emptying themselves of any essential content. Steerforth is indeed as much a rhetorical figure as his name implies; Dora is herself a figure of Victorian male desire and stylization; as their inactivity in the novel suggests, neither is really there except as a blank space in the semiotic network signifying in relation to all the other signs they differ from. Significantly, of course, both these semiotic characters die, washed up on the narrative beach, their rhetorical power washed out for a protagonist who sees them finally as signifiers in his own psychodrama. The only fate thinkable for one who has discovered the semiotic rather than ontological status of signs ("characters" rather than "beings") is to empty *himself*—to turn from deeds in the world to writing of the world, to practice mingling those code elements he has come to see as constituting his own or anyone else's being.

Great Expectations presents a more complexly wrought case of expectations constituted by socially arbitrated values coded into dress, manners, and professions. Pip acquires the code elements of a gentleman and finds that his ambition, emotions, and tastes are similarly constituted in him through the same process of socialization. His distaste for Magwitch is as automatic as his late abortive proposal to Biddy is perfunctory and nostalgic. The latter is, in fact, part of a larger nostalgia for the simplistic childhood coding in which good and evil function as distinct binary opposites, a nostalgia Pip shares with many critics of the novel who speak of his coming to a state of wisdom and maturity in which he eschews the false social conventions that misled him for so long. In fact, every experience he has suggests that each binary value is alloyed with the other and that the coding of cop or criminal, grouch or goodhearted, friend or foe is a question of the specific positioning of preeminently semiotic terms and the relations pertaining at a given moment.

In *Great Expectations,* we might have expected to see individual subjectivity predominate according to traditional expectations of both "Dickens" (as the sign for a certain unified practice of assumptions and narrative technique) and "the Victorian novel" (as a similarly constituted sign). In fact, however, individuals in this novel are themselves like empty Saussurian signs, and we watch them change their coding as they come into different relations. The frightening criminal becomes comforting father; the protective police become destructive and arbitrary authority; the belligerent Herbert becomes a passive helper; Pip as aggressive social climber gives way to Pip as melancholy loner and dependent. And so on. These changes depend less upon any internal, permanent substrate of "essence" than they do upon characters' circulation in a semiotic economy in which characters as signs bear the traces of all from which they differ, including themselves, and thus "mean" and function in narrative sentences more according to context than essence. Pip expects an *organic* relation between a self and a system each authenticated by its ground, respectively, in transcendent spirituality and in principles of truth. What he finds instead is that self and system are coconstitutive in terms of the semiotic matrix within which both take place. He had expected to act out the romantic drama of imperial selfhood, the inner reality triumphant in the field of self-actualization; he ends, having encountered the narrative constitution of self and the fictive quality of the discourse of culture, as a quiet functionary in the quintessential symbol of the semiotic economy of culture—the Continental branch of a multinational corporation. It is no accident that the formal narrative of these events emerges in Pip's later years when, like David Copperfield, he no longer sees the semiotic as transparent.

Nor is *Bleak House* a more promising field for the immediacy of subjective vision, for it records the progressive contraction of the possibility for individual action. Only the institution acts, and those whose wealth (like Jarndyce's) or position (like Jaggers's) makes them an outlet or pressure point for institutions. "Individuals" retreat into protective microcosms of the whole, whether moated castles or custom-built downsized country estates, and ultimately choose exile into a Canadian wilderness where, presumably, institutions have not so thoroughly permeated the daily round. *Bleak House* thus suggests that even if one leaves intact some ground for selfhood—a premise as questionable elsewhere in Dickens as it is in *Vanity Fair*—the *exercise* of that selfhood is a more than dubious task. Esther is not a powerful ego waging its will against the inert backdrop of nature and experience, but a curiously annoying line of chatter amid the cocktail party of an institutionally governed culture. She is an empty anachronism against the broad and specifically institutional range of her counternarrator, that omniscient voice who takes the narrative into the larger world of the press, the courts, and the class system that both shapes and limits the semiotic being that Esther

41

and her circle inhabit. The novel, in other words, devastates the subjective ground of personal narration in a different way than *Great Expectations* or *David Copperfield.* In those novels being seems redefined from within as semiotic rather than ontological; in *Bleak House,* whatever space there is in the scheme of things for the possibility of ontological being is crowded out by the larger institutional constructs that dominate the landscape as surely as the dinosaur of the famous opening. At best, from a traditional point of view, we can argue that the institutional simply crushes the individual; at worst, from that same view, the individual was never really there in the first place except as a node in larger matrixes that we may call institutional, thus emphasizing the sociopolitical, or the semiotic—thus emphasizing the means of their functioning.

* * * * *

As the narrating character brings us into the issue and means of retrospection, he stitches his seam with another narrative stance, that of the historian. The narrator as historian must necessarily confront the constitutive quality of our various concepts of time in a number of those passages where he draws upon his interviews with key characters, ostensibly to lend credibility to his "realistic" account. Hence "Captain Dobbin has since informed" him of the dress Amelia wore at her wedding to George (1:259; 22). Similarly, Becky "never told until long afterwards how painful" nursing Miss Crawley became (1:160; 14). "Becky, who penetrated into the very centre of fashion, and saw the great George IV face to face, has owned since that there too was Vanity" (2:188; 51). Each of these examples shows the conventional gesture by which historians underwrite their own versions of events with the testimony of the principals. Each, that is, bids to secure reliability on the basis of the direct observation of those involved—the experiental or empirical standard, if you will. But the questionableness of that standard is heightened by the temporal gap here between the time each event was witnessed and the time, many years later, when a dress style, an emotion, or a judgment was rendered.

In each case, then, narrative, which treats time as a succession of events, is based upon memory, which treats time as a collection of eternal presents—a temporal version of the spatial presence undone in the preceding stance—accessible to the consciousness. The narrative mode assigns significance and order in terms of a moment's place in a sequence. Memory is more like an imaginative environment in which one shapes and stages events around one's own needs. Normally we oscillate back and forth between these two conceptions of time without pondering their incompatibility, indeed regarding a fixation in either of them as the aberration of the irresponsible (who live in a succession of presents with no regard for past or future) and of the obsessive-compulsive (who are driven by excruciating anxiety to master the sequential flow of time). This split characterizes any narrative act, since the chronology of succession is imaginatively present in the writer or narrator as he works. It is also characteristic of the reading process, however, since one must read line by line, but also within a gestalt of the "whole" as one thinks of it at any given time. It is in the oscillation between these two conflicting models of time that narrative *constitutes* the texture of its realm, and the frequency with which the narrator as historian points this out testifies to the novel's sense of this as a fundamental trait of the form's poetics.

The stance we have just considered manages temporal dynamics through the apparent authenticity of direct observation and the coherence of the narrator's personal identity. The reader trusts the unmediated vision (or trusts that he or she can calculate the essential angle of diffraction) and the coherence of the personal vision (so that even an "unreliable" narrator is predictably, consistently, and hence reliably so). As one turns to the narrator as historian, one still has the personal force of the voice, but also the stature brought by the rigors of rational inquiry and meticulous research. If the narrator as character taps the romantic valorization of the spontaneous and thus authentic self, the narrator as historian taps the rationalist valorization of the methodically reflective self. The cohabitation of the two elements is, of course, nothing new; one need only recall Fielding's mixture of "history" in his title and his coach-riding intimacy with readers. One should not underestimate the force of convention behind this mixture—the eighteenth century was content to mix a wide range of discursive options within the essay tradition to which Thackeray was so well attuned. But Thackeray nonetheless pursues a relatively specific analysis of the historian's stance in ways that keep inescapable the cultural fiction it sustains.

One comic version of this analysis occurs when the narrator adduces an anecdote from his club to gloss an event in the narrative (Becky's hurling the "Dixonary" out the coach window):

Miss Sedley was almost as flurried at the act of defiance as Miss Jemima had been; for, consider, it was but one minute that she had left school, and the impressions of six years are not got over in that space of time. Nay, with some persons those awes and terrors of youth last for ever and ever. I know, for instance, an old gentleman of sixty-eight, who said to me one morning at breakfast, with a very agitated countenance, "I dreamed last night that I was flogged by Dr.

43

Raine." Fancy had carried him back five-and-fifty years in the course of that evening. Dr. Raine and his rod were just as awful to him in his heart, then, at sixty-eight, as they had been at thirteen. If the Doctor, with a large birch, had appeared bodily to him, even at the age of three score and eight, and had said in awful voice, "Boy, take down your pant * *"? Well, well, Miss Sedley was exceedingly alarmed at this act of insubordination. (1:10; 2)

Juliet McMaster has read this passage as a universalizing "appeal to our common experience of childhood subjection," so that "Becky's act of rebellion stands out as a gesture of myth-making stature."[22] Her reading, in other words, heeds the convention by which the narrator who experiences reinforces the one who narrates. The intimacy produced by personal revelations, most acute in confessional narratives, fosters a closeness of judgment by which understanding of human nature is shared, reinforced, enlarged—even universalized, as she argues in this case.

But does this reading suffice? I think not, because the passage is far too deflating to be called "myth making," and it is not merely the characters who are deflated. Certainly the passage begins as if the narrator merely intends to justify Amelia's alarm, "for consider" that some impressions remain quite vivid; that this should be, however, after the passage of a single minute indicates a less serious form of moralizing than we might have supposed. The elaborateness of the justification, the contrast of fifty-five years (and the passage mentions the old man's age three times) to one minute, and the analogy between a startled schoolgirl and an old man trembling with his pants down can end only in the "well, well" by which the narrator reduces the whole process to proper absurdity. The narrator's "personal" experience explodes rather than reinforces the responses one sees—whether in characters like Amelia or Becky or in the frame occupied by the narrator's acquaintance. The narrator works conventionally in precisely the way McMaster argues, but in this case he is using that very convention to arrest the reader's uncritical passivity to the teller and to call attention to the device by which monumentalized or exaggerated episodes carry such rhetorical force as McMaster finds.

Hence the passage works reflexively to undermine the passive role assigned the listener or the reader of historical narrative. But it also begins a deeper theme questioning the nature of historical reasoning. The doubling of Amelia (as perceiver) with the old man (as retrospective and thus historian), and of narrative scene with remembered dream (itself of a memory), doubly foregrounds the formalized quality of the historian's sources. The old man's experience of Dr. Raine, that is, appears as a dream so stylized the narrator can flesh it out further before allowing it to blow away. It has been subjected first to perception, then to memory, then to dreamwork, then to at least two retellings, and each formal remove subjects the experience to another layer of the stylization we have seen at work throughout the narrative. By doubling himself in Amelia (as character) and the old man (as historical source), the narrator (as historian) undermines the differences in status often felt to separate these three sources of information in narrative. Each has monumentalized some experience that subsequently disciplines (with the rod, if necessary) the narrative of which it becomes the effective organizational center.[23]

In addition to showing this fix upon a "center" that then functions to shape the material, the historian also demonstrates how liable he too is to the stylization dominating his sources. A case that carries several of these themes is the narrator's interview with Dobbin, an aside that serves almost as a parable of historical endeavors and the problem of mimetic art they share with fiction generally. The narrator tells us at one point that "very likely Amelia was not like the portrait the major had formed of her," an important observation, since at least part of the portrait the narrator gives us is supposedly based upon interviews with Dobbin. The narrator goes on to support this opinion by mentioning a page from a fashion book Dobbin has pasted in his writing desk. Dobbin, of course, fancies that it resembles Amelia, "whereas I have seen it, and can vouch that it is but the picture of a high-waisted gown with an impossible doll's face simpering over it—and, perhaps, Mr. Dobbin's sentimental Amelia was no more like the real one than this absurd little print which he cherished" (2:97; 43). That this portrait persists in the writing desk through all the changes in what Dobbin thinks and feels about Amelia is remarkable. Somehow, that is, this early notion of Amelia persists long enough for the historian to have seen it himself, though he is considerably younger than Dobbin and comes to the major's acquaintance only after the novel's main events.

What is most curious, however, is the rhetoric of the narrator in this passage. Most of what he seems to offer he also takes away. We seem, that is, to get a series of negative equations: the print is not Amelia, Dobbin's mental portrait is not Amelia, and the print is not Dobbin's mental portrait except in its inaccuracies, its failure to correspond to Amelia. What we actually have is by no means clear. The print is a gown, not a person, an equation neatly expressing the narrator's sense of the unreality of the print, and perhaps another indication of how thoroughly the "real" Amelia fades into the fashion that makes men notice her in the first place. Above the gown, moreover, is "an impossible doll's face," a further emphasis upon unrealistic artifice that accords with the usual interpretation of the passage.

But the passage does *not* say that Amelia herself does not have this doll's face, just that the print does. Does the unrealistic nature of the print stem from the fact that Amelia has anything but a doll's face, or that the print shows only the doll's face that she has and not the less benign wrinkles of her character? Does "impossible" refer to more than a difference of taste in beauty between two men, appropriate since they are of different generations? Does it mean that the benign face is an impossibly sentimental interpretation of a human being, or that the narrator cannot stand personally to be around a person so sweet? When we see the phrase "Dobbin's sentimental Amelia," does it mean the genuinely sentimental Amelia who is Dobbin's, or his sentimentalizing of whatever the "real" Amelia is? At some point, perhaps, this becomes syntactic haggling, but the one conclusion that does seem clear from such a passage is that Amelia as she really is and Amelia as she melts into stylized perceptions (by Dobbin, by the narrator) become so indistinguishable that the historical effort to achieve a portrait never can escape the epistemological limitations implicit in "portrait" (i.e., selection of details, distorting emphases, thematic investiture, and so forth). What is achieved is, perhaps, never more than *not* what it is supposed to be, the distinctive negative equations here suggesting the inevitable divergence of discourse from its purported destination into its fictive byways.

Indeed, it seems that every effort the historian makes to interview someone who will tell it like it is finds only another character who foregrounds the "like" more than the "is." In reporting Amelia's high-spirited refusal of old Osborne's first offer for Georgy, the historian goes to someone we might expect to have an ideally objective perspective on the scene—Mr. Poe, the lawyer. Foreshortening the scene to quote just her outburst, the narrator ends the passage neatly with " '—and she bowed me out of the room like a tragedy Queen,' said the lawyer who told the story" (2:133; 46). It is a handy storytelling technique, for it is a plausible abbreviation of the story for dinner conversation. The emphasis upon the stylized behavior points out the grand emotional excesses to which we must become accustomed in Amelia's behavior, the element of genuine tragedy in a mother whose son is about to be taken from her, but also the difficulty of acting in such a situation—or even of conceiving oneself in it—without the patternings of social and literary conventions dictating one's lines and gestures. Nor, of course, can one witness even a stranger's behavior outside such conventions. The passage both undermines and enhances Amelia on the referential side, and on the reflexive side it dissolves her individuality into the collective formalization of culture. What we know when we nod in recognition at this comparison has to do not so much with Amelia as with necessarily reductive types in the popular imagination.

A more comic example of the effects of stylization upon the historical record is Thackeray's witty send-up of the American correspondent. The dinner at Gaunt House is supposedly above the social world of our narrator, but Mr. John Paul Jefferson Jones of the New York *Demagogue* has gotten an invitation through his connections with the American embassy. This marvelously gauche, obtuse, and materialistic American journalist estimates the cost of everything and complains of losing "my Helen," "a very pleasing and witty fashionable, the brilliant and exclusive Mrs. Rawdon Crawley" (2:168; 49). The inflated style effectively diminishes Becky (hardly as worthy as Helen, hardly pleasing, hardly fashionable or exclusive except in the most uncomplimentary sense of the terms). More to the point, both narrators are outsiders trying first to perceive and then to record the inside, and we as readers find ourselves calculating ironic trajectories from a novel presenting a historian faced with the pages of a tabloid. At every point along this chain from first to last we find figures interpreting interpretations, and with both the successive removes from immediate experience and the stylizations that silt up in the course of its flow, we have never the same river twice, and in fact never *the* river but only the multiple channels it cuts through the distinctly semiotic cultural delta.

The historian's sources, of course, can be much less innocent than a Mr. Poe or the Dr. Pestler who attends Amelia during her hysterical grief over weaning Georgy (to his wife's undying jealousy). For example, we hear in the middle of Dobbin's enlightenment about Becky's past history that "it was at that very table years ago that the present writer had the pleasure of hearing the tale. Tufto, Steyne, the Crawleys, and their history" (2:404; 66). All of the affair at Curzon Street he heard at dinner from Tapeworm, secretary of the legation to Pumpernickel, he who "knew everything and a great deal besides, about all the world." Is the pivotal event of Becky's career, and of this novel, part of what Tapeworm knew about all the world, or about a great deal besides? How much has the narrator added or suppressed in his memory of that conversation "years ago"?

The same difficulties attend the case of Tom Eaves, the historian's favorite informant for the high society so far above his own head. Eaves, we discover, is a dubious source, for he is a tale monger, name dropper, and social climber—"for every shilling of which, and a great deal more, little Tom Eaves . . . is ready to account" (2:139; 47) is the same verbal formula used for Tapeworm. It is customary to point out that these admissions playfully subvert novelistic conventions and require readers to test events against their own sense of the characters involved. But in light of the issues we have found thus far, we would have to give a greater role to these passages than simply passing potshots at the rhetoric of fiction. In one sense we are untroubled by the passage, since we know that *every* source of information in the novel is ultimately referable to the imagination of Thackeray. But this comforting deflection of the question rests upon a correlative deflection of such questions away from the models of history, biography, and knowledge in general we hold normally sacred and reliable. We proceed as a matter of course as if we "knew everything" and as if we did *not* also know "a great deal besides," as if we did not always add "a great deal more" to any accounting we make of the experiences we interpret. The real reason we should be relatively untroubled about the implications of a Tapeworm or an Eaves is that we must always proceed under these conditions anyway. Hearsay, elaboration, self-interest, and warping cultural matrixes— whether metaphysical or social climbing—constitute inevitable conditions of our "knowing," and liking or disliking this fact is merely another feature of our conceptual optics. More than a question of juxtaposing a right, true, or reliable realist mode against these defective models of narrative, the historian's troubles with his craft query the line we customarily draw between the two.

Indeed, one encounters a number of passages in which the historian breaks off his project to share his quandary with the reader. Customarily read as making the reader cocreative in judging by moral criteria, this device more literally requires readers to make decisions that cannot be made. The narrator's perplexity after one of the most crucial scenes in the novel, Rawdon's attack on Steyne, has frequently been noticed: "What *had* happened? Was she guilty or not? She said not; but who could tell what was truth which came from those lips; or if that corrupt heart was in this case pure?" (2:229; 53). The richness of critical speculation on this point illustrates the effectiveness of such a strategy in framing a moral evaluation of a character's behavior.

Perhaps the passage *does* refer us to the level of morality rather than of event, and perhaps its reticence has much to do with propriety. But, literally, it asks "Who could tell what was truth which came from those lips?" thus—depending upon whether one has the relative clause modify "truth" or "what"—querying what is truth if it emerges from those lips, what from those lips could be called truth, and who could be in a position to "tell" us? Not, it appears, the historian. The first possibility makes "truth" a function of a speaker's status, that is, a situational matter; the second assumes a more absolute and transcendent model of truth; the third gives up the possibility of choosing within or between these models. Equally of note is the confusion over "corrupt" and "pure," normally categories that are both absolute and mutually exclusive. Here, however, they are (un)decidable case by case and hence quite situational, but at the same time paradoxically essential (a "corrupt heart" being, it seems, constitutional rather than variable). The question matters because it is the moral historian's business to sort out individual events and to reveal their moral bearings. If that historian's moral framework oscillates between the essential and the existential, and if the very possibility of any stance from which one "could tell" is questionable, then such passages are more than urbane disclaimers— they are moments of profound nostalgia for the illusory certitude promised by the historian's stance itself.

The narrator also wonders whether George was more attentive to Amelia the night his father forbade the marriage because of his concern at her disappointment or because of his valuing the prize he might lose— Does one impose a generous or a selfish motivation upon George's behavior? Posing the question requires the reader to decide what is undecidable, to choose a frame that causes the passage to comply with the implicit assumptions of that frame and thus to become an effect cited as the cause. Similar occasions ask us to make moral readings where "making" is literally the case—did frustrated pride or paternal affection most pain Osborne at his son's death? Was it shame or dislike for his neighbors that confined old Sir Pitt in his last years? The historian's concern for the problems of interpretation forces these issues upon us.

The narrator as historian becomes the model for the problems in interpretation, the mediating agents that have always already acted in the interpretive process. The reflexivity initiated by these passages is neither local nor finite, to borrow terms from Booth's discussion of irony, for their point is not merely to shift us from inauthentic to some authentic interpretation. Rather, they clarify the now common point in historiography that no matter how necessary it is to make the record, that record falls within the stylized conventions that determine its content as well as its form. Interpretation is willed, not found, and the rationality and objectivity of the historian's stance are achieved by a nonrational leap into anything but an objective, "open-minded" perspective.

If the narrator as character leaves us seeing narrative coherence as an oscillation among culture, convention, and the subject, as historian he makes narrative arise out of the oscillation among an inaccessible actuality, the stylized interpretations in his various sources, and the discursive pressures of his own practice—between, in other words, the sequence of moments that have gone by and the innumerable interpretations present

49

for him to mix in his record. The reflexive dimension of each stance thus works against the credence conventionally given it.

Thackeray's analysis of history is neither unique nor unprecedented, of course, and we must see this phase of *Vanity Fair* as a summation of a persistent strain in narrative rather than as a quirk of the era's wittiest author. Scholes and Kellogg some time ago proposed the empirical and the fictional as the basic vectors of narrative energy,[24] and though their schema might lead us to expect these to function as exclusive categories, we know of course that in practice they describe the arc of oscillation along which narrative constitutes its worlds, and that they have long been the subject of debate.

This is one issue surfacing, for example, when Cervantes pauses in his sequel to respond to the theoretical principles invoked against *Don Quixote*. The issue is superficially one of narrative propriety, but more profoundly that of the relation between interpretive principle and "historical" fact, and I open with Sampson Carrasco's citation of the critics:

> "some who have read your history say that they would have been glad if the authors had left out a few of the countless beatings which Don Quixote received in various encounters."
> "That's where the truth of the story comes in," said Sancho.
> "Yet they might in fairness have kept quiet about them," said Don Quixote, "for there is no reason to record those actions which do not change or affect the truth of the story, if they redound to the discredit of the hero. Aeneas was not as pious as Virgil paints him, I promise you, nor Ulysses as prudent as Homer describes him."
> "That is true," replied Sampson; "but it is one thing to write as a poet, and another as a historian. The poet can relate and sing things, not as they were but as they should have been, without in any way affecting the truth of the matter."[25]

It is a slightly confused tripartite confrontation. Sampson argues for generic decorum, a neat separation of poetry (in its primal rather than its formal sense) and history; Thackeray's mixture of these discursive types presages related attacks by Conrad, Warren, and Fowles, as we shall see. But Cervantes has already led an implicit probing of the possibilities of this generic law first by enclosing Sampson within a fiction through which he argues the primacy of reason and facts; as the logic of history spins out of a character in a fiction who takes that fiction as exemplifying history, we find it increasingly difficult to take that logic seriously as the whole truth. Second, by using him as a key force opposing the don's imaginative vision, Cervantes embroils Sampson in the sort of local ideological issue that makes history polemical, as we see when Sampson begins "staging" the narrative events intended to debunk the don's ongoing narrative vision and to replace it with his own rationalist narratology. Without getting into the classic debates on this question, we can see clearly that Cervantes makes an issue here of whether it is possible to decide this critical crux in Cervantes criticism (Whose side are we supposed to be on?), however inevitable a question in our own response it may be. One would have to know the line between history and fiction to answer the question definitively and thus not to feel the sense of loss that pervades the atmosphere in the wake of the don. Certainly this question has remained one on which virtually every narrative critic has had to take a position.

But Sampson's generic terms are only part of the question raised by the passage. Sancho and the don think in terms not of literary convention but of truth. Sancho's label is "story," a significant imprecision fusing the critical categories of Sampson or of Scholes and Kellogg. It is of minor importance to me that this seems part of the larger debate between realism and idealism—it seems actually closer to one between satiric slapstick and heroic romance. What *is* significant, however, is that for both characters the "truth of the story" inheres in the selection of details and their foregrounding through the formal techniques of the narrative, decisions determined by specific preexisting interpretive outlooks. Both, that is, see the materials of the story as vehicles for rigid interpretations that *should,* at least, exclude contrary possibilities. Since for them this story is not only history but *their* history, we cannot pretend that the novel does not begin by exploring its own generic assumptions. That is, history for Sancho and the don does not appear in its proper form as neutral facts or objective chronology; its essence is interpretation (i.e., fictive constructions about history). Just as the worlds of Sancho and the don mutually critique each other, so do their interpretive frames stand comparably rigid, flawed, and simplistic precisely in their assumption of the possibility of "valid" interpretation.

This debate, then, quickly transcends its local relevance as an episode in *Don Quixote* and bridges to *Vanity Fair*'s efforts to outline the implicit assumptions of this narrative stance. Cervantes's best English disciple carries the issue into a different national literature but in very similar terms. In *Tom Jones,* for example, Fielding argues as follows: "But so matters fell out, and so I must relate them; and if any reader is shocked at their appearing unnatural, I cannot help it. I must remind such persons that I am not writing a system, but a history, and I am not obliged to reconcile every matter to the received notions concerning truth and nature."[26] It is a beautifully ironic manifesto proclaiming the freedom of historical narrative from "system" and from "received notions." We are in trouble immediately, however we construe the passage. If we take the theory seriously—history's "every matter" follows

51

independent of interpretive principles—we are soon overwhelmed (indeed, by this point in the novel we already have been) by Fielding's practice. Surely few narratives make so extended a use of these complexly contrived appearances, exits, and hidden coincidences from the Restoration stage. Fielding's quarrel with Richardson was not, of course, over the issue of exemplary plots and characters, but over which class's ethos they should exemplify. That is, Fielding uses the ideologically innocent "system" of morality to condemn the one path to upward mobility Richardson's lower-class heroine can follow, just as Richardson uses it to dramatize the aristocratic expectation of privilege. Such apparently neutral oppositions as morality and sexuality, "system" and history, truth and nature, become the interpretive headings under which each "history" wages a bit of ideologically charged class struggle. Practice confounds theory to demonstrate how thoroughly the selection, arrangement, and presentation of details suits interpretive vision despite whatever aspiration might exist for the state of pure objectivity.

Whether we reach this point after some resistance or begin with an ironic interpretation of the passage, we come to see that acts appear "unnatural" here only insofar as they diverge from the interpretive "system" brought to bear upon them. The presumed contrast of system and history is a polemic maneuver for advancing "received notions concerning truth and nature" at variance with other received notions. History, it seems, is precisely the vehicle for insinuating interpretation under the guise of facts that *Vanity Fair* demonstrates it to be, just as history in its nondiscursive sense is the field upon which different ideological systems contend for rhetorical dominance of the cultural imagination. The stance of historian, far from liberating narrative from the quicksand of unreliable narration and setting it on the firm ground of facts, instead brings with it all the problematic and ideological conflicts afflicting historiography. Perhaps in the process it also marks the fictional strategies of historical rhetoric.

If Fielding is the quintessential realist of the eighteenth century, certainly George Eliot plays that role among the major nineteenth-century writers, and her own questions about the historical model are lucidly explained in J. Hillis Miller's crucial essay on narrative and history in *Middlemarch.* Among the guiding traits Miller isolates are

the notions of origin and end ("archaeology" and "teleology"); of unity and totality or "totalization"; of underlying "reason" or "ground"; of selfhood, consciousness, or "human nature"; of the homogeneity, linearity, and continuity of time; of necessary progress; of "fate," "destiny," or "Providence"; of causality; of gradually emerging "meaning"; of representation and truth. [27]

Miller's list reads like an index of this study, and the extent to which Eliot's novel works out this same agenda of issues testifies to the pervasiveness of reflexivity in Victorian narrative. More specifically, Miller cycles through the various analogues of history as a system (religion, love, science, art, superstition), showing how for each of these the narrator "demystifies the illusion" that details make wholes governed by a single center and that history is "progressive, teleological" (Miller, 464–66). What remains in the wake of this dispersal of the metaphysical ground of history, and thus that of *Middlemarch* as well, is "the free and contradictory struggle of individual human energies, each seen as a center of interpretation, which means misinterpretation, of the whole" (467). History, fiction, and interpretation thus fall together as versions of the same paradigm of discourse, despite their rhetorical positioning in relation to each other. We might wish to qualify Miller's emphasis upon how "free" such a struggle is, in light of the force of semiotic conventions always already internalized and the pressure of various institutional practices reinforcing this or that cluster of conventions. Subservience to a masculine career like Will Ladislaw's parliamentary involvement (itself an immersion in institutionally prescribed roles) is, after all, the ladies' law even for so radiant a being as Dorothea, forced as she is to take Will's prophetic name, and repeatedly in *Middlemarch* characters' perceptions of their own possibilities are circumscribed by the particular set of conventions within which they narrate their ongoing histories. But the central message persists in this novel, in which the point of view is something of a hybrid between the omniscient narrator and the narrator as historian: for all its rhetorical and ideological potency, the historical model is every bit as immersed in constitutive poetics as the fiction it seems intended to reinforce.

The pursuit of this primal relation between history and narrative continues in a later chapter, but the point here is the consistency with which discussions of this relation have all but destroyed the boundary in the very effort to mark it. Fiction absorbs history, and the fictional narrator whose stance is that of a historian seems inevitably to raise the question that drops open the trapdoor in the platform he stands on.

* * * * *

In many ways the narrator as omniscient novelist sums up everything we would say about style and stance in voice. The omniscient narrator, that is, subsumes all imaginable functions and privileges for point of view. Hence we should expect to see the omniscient narrator used to expose stylizing conventions as such, to critique teleological interpretations of experience, to define discourse as a willed power over material and readers alike, and to mark the inevitable closure of narrative rhetoric within the limitations and logical legerdemain to which all these traits contribute. I suggested in reference to *Bleak House* that its omniscient narrator voiced the power of fiction as a cultural institution treating other cultural institutions on the Victorian scene, a level of analytical awareness beyond Esther's narrative, and a sphere of activity precluding any agent so peripheral as a private individual. The implication is less to strengthen the hand of the omniscient narrator than to show the limits to power and knowledge that both his and the various institutional rhetorics seek to obscure. *Vanity Fair* marks the operation of the omniscient narrator in ways that enable a demystification of its status even as it continues its power over our imagination. There is, one surmises, no escape from the fictive force of discourse even for those who become aware of its modus operandi.

Much of the playfulness of this stance is at the expense of conventions so naturalized by the late 1840s that they coded reality for many readers. Just after Amelia's wedding, for example, the narrator calls attention to the difference between his story and the conventional romance: "As his hero and heroine pass the matrimonial barrier, the novelist generally drops the curtain, as if the drama were over then: the doubts and struggles of life ended: as if, once landed in the marriage country, all were green and pleasant there: and wife and husband had nothing but to link each other's arms together, and wander gently downwards towards old age and perfect fruition" (1:316–17; 26). The passage asks us to consider the extent to which both our expectations and those of the characters are conditioned by the conventional fictions of the day and prompts us to recall a number of equally conditioned acts in the novel—Dobbin's uncritical adoration of Amelia based upon his culture's celebration of the tender, clinging parasite, everyone's adoration of George based upon his culture's admiration of the heroic and athletic type, the near universal admiration of Georgy as a pretty and rich male child, and so forth. Hence this passage works well to show how dependent omniscient narrators are upon the reigning conventions by which they contain characters, events, and readers. Moreover, the irony at the expense of how such drama typically "ended" pushes beyond stylization into the logical structure of narrative—marital teleology, we might call it. As I suggested earlier, structures like sentimental romance underwrite all the institutions and structures of knowledge by which a culture maintains its stability, even in so reflexive a novel raising such arbitrary patternings from the unconscious. This novel, for example, also ends with the long awaited marriage of central characters and hence does not go so far as to imagine what a culture not preoccupied with romance might be like were its energies redirected from fantasy to reality. But it does work to denaturalize these preformulated visions of reality by foregrounding the conventions and structures by which they normalize experience.

The omniscient narrator is also used to foreground how easily these conventions shape readers' expectations and responses. Much earlier in the novel, for example, we have this passage when the narrator is dallying with Jos and Becky: "There is no need of giving a special report of the conversation which now took place between Mr. Sedley and the young lady; for the conversation, as may be judged from the foregoing specimen, was not especially witty or eloquent; it seldom is in private societies, or anywhere except in very high-flown and ingenious novels" (1:38; 4). Thackeray gets out of a tedious scene, to be sure, but he also marks the degree to which Jos's sense of his own awkwardness and Becky's sense of her strategic options are conditioned by their role models, the exemplars of courtship in popular romances. Moreover, in the face of our seemingly instinctive wish for the union, we must realize our own vulnerability as readers to the expectations prescribed in the romantic conventions despite the fact that the lovers' scene is here being played by an obese nabob and a penniless scavenger—a far cry from Lord Orville and Evelina. The power of the omniscient narrator is to a great extent a function of his ability to impose such naturalized interpretations of reality and to appear as the originator of their "fresh insights" into the intricacies of human behavior. As Thackeray's horseplay suggests, a narrator's omniscience is mainly the repetition with fresh particulars of prevailing norms (i.e., fictions) about that behavior.

That this repetition has a sinister side is at least implied in Thackeray's treatment of censorship. Note, for example: "We must pass over a part of Mrs. Rebecca Crawley's biography with the lightness and delicacy which the world demands. . . . There are things we do and know perfectly well in Vanity Fair, though we never speak of them . . . and it has been the wish of the present writer, all through this story, deferentially to submit to the fashion at present prevailing, and only to hint at the existence of wickedness in a light, easy, and agreeable manner, so that nobody's fine feelings may be offended" (2:364; 64). In pragmatic terms, this is a way of telling us Becky became something of a whore without using quite those words or painting the scenes necessary to show it.

Aside from narrative convenience, the passage also displays Thackeray's restiveness within the conventions that exclude this sector of reality. The aggregate effect of such phrases as "the world demands," "though we never speak them," "light, easy, and agreeable manner," and "nobody's fine feelings" is to undermine with irony both the naturalization and the stature of censorship standards. He certainly underscores their arbitrary nature and the groundlessness of their rationale by describing them as "the fashion at present prevailing." "Fashion" reduces them to the status of spats or Easter bonnets, one that is predictably class related, while "present" underscores their transitory and even capricious quality and "prevailing" their status as mere consensus rather than natural or absolute truth. At the same time, of course, Thackeray complies even while marking the expanse of reality they exclude. In effect, asking us to compare the conventions of sentimental romance and moralistic censorship undermines the stature of each code's implicit assumptions. We might easily take censorship as the norm of cultural discourse—it achieves order by excluding from its body of permissible "sememes" whatever would disturb the social status quo that both function to maintain.[28] This passage, for example, sides however ironically with a social class that conducts its degradation under cover of wealth and privilege, just as the earlier passage about Jos and Becky suggests that sentimental romance depends more upon a man's ability to buy a beauty than upon the virtues celebrated on the surface of the genre. Generic logic and conventions are most fully exposed by the omniscient narrator because he most fully subsumes within himself the institutional voice of culture that sustains genre.

The omniscient narrator makes most explicit his implausible claims to knowledge, truth, and mastery by advertising his privilege. When he goes into Jos's mind for the first time, for example, he does so explaining that "novelists have the privilege of knowing everything" (1:29; 3), a phrase that certainly has the effect of setting Becky's campaign for the nabob into the diminishing frame of narrative comedy. "The novelist, who knows everything," can expose Becky's scheming by revealing that the trophies Rawdon sent his aunt were purchased by Becky from the relic dealers, again dwarfing the comedy with Olympian condescension (1:408; 33). "The novelist, it has been said before, knows everything," hence he can expose the lying and cheating by which the Crawleys live on nothing a year (2:2; 36). In these instances we are raised to a superior position with the narrator, who determines for us the relevant facts and final opinions while forestalling any possibility of empathy with the characters. The narrator is above us in the sense of imposing his judgments upon us but holds us above the characters he belittles. That in his other stances he assumes a position equivalent to that of his characters or, as historian, to that of his readers is just the most obvious way these competing stances jostle the workings of conventions against each other.

More penetrating questions turn up when the narrator insists we compare points at which he exercises his omniscient privilege in different ways. In one he asks, "What think you were the private feelings of Miss, no (begging her pardon) of Mrs. Rebecca? If, a few pages back, the present writer claimed the privilege of peeping into Miss Amelia Sedley's bed-room, and understanding with the omniscience of the novelist all the gentle pains and passions which were tossing upon that innocent pillow, why should he not declare himself to be Rebecca's confidante too, master of her secrets, and seal-keeper of that young woman's conscience?" (1:183; 15). In this passage about Becky, the omniscience is stressed overtly; what follows are ironic taunts about Becky's miscalculations: "Well, then, in the first place, Rebecca gave way to some very sincere and touching regrets that a piece of marvellous good fortune should have been so near her, and she actually obliged to decline it." The passage continues full of ironic modifiers for Becky as "a hardworking, ingenious, meritorious girl." The narrator has clearly gone out of his way to raise us to a seat of judgment over Becky.

The passage the narrator refers to as being "a few pages back" operates quite differently. It is a view of Amelia "looking at the moon . . . and thinking to herself how her hero was employed" (1:143; 13). She is thinking of the grave responsibilities she imagines occupying her George, but the narrator reveals in a virtual pique that the unheroic George is instead drinking punch and singing bawdy songs. He further strengthens the condemnation of George by deifying Amelia with "her kind thoughts" that "sped away as if they were angels and had wings." Here, though he is clearly being an omniscient narrator by reporting her thoughts, the effect is to pull us close to Amelia so that we will despise the greater target, George. The potential for ironic damage to Amelia in "her hero" and in the angelic comparison is not exploited by a narrator who at other points is at pains to demonstrate the liabilities of a sentimental egoist.

The narrator, it seems, is indulging in precisely the same process of deification lampooned in Amelia's elevation of George and her son, and at other points in Dobbin's glorification of Amelia. He cannot himself manipulate material without aligning it with the conventions, despite his ironic deflation of those same conventions elsewhere in the novel. The omniscient narrator reminds us that there is no escape from the cultural voice. Here the "lapse" (a logically inappropriate term, since there is no alternative) is obvious, almost comic. But in the world of narrative it is not always so clear. The text requires us to realize that, as we found in de Man's comments on irony, its deflation and denaturalization do not necessarily lead to authenticity. Since "narrative voice" is cultural rather than individual, it cannot be expected to elude the limitation of the cultural assumptions of which it is a function.

As for the effect upon the reader, the comparison also makes clear how readily readers abase themselves before any godlike dispenser of truth. The rhetorical punch of an omniscient narrator's praise is so potent that even being aware of it does not completely vitiate its effect upon our judgments of the novel's characters—hence Thackeray's ability to use such a passage to prune our responses at this particular moment in the narrative and also to jolt our awareness of the way fiction making controls our sense of experience. We know we are being suckered as we give in, for in the passage about Becky the overtness of omniscient privilege is used to diminish her, while here its covertness pulls us just as decisively toward the character.

The reasons for such power have much to do with the great hunger of the middle class for an authoritative guide whose expertise and judgment are definitive, one who can provide them with a secure platform above the less able, less astute, less well equipped—above those who, in other words, are like the helpless characters in a novel at the beck and call of the master novelist. Political messiah, technical expert, intellectual sage, artistic genius—all are versions of the figure of power that thrives upon the need of middle-class readers for whatever particular etiquette they themselves seek to master. As we have already seen, that figure manages its position through its skill in deploying the appropriate modules of convention, naturalized sufficiently that they have the "ring of truth" for the audience.

This comparison thus requires readers to become conscious of the power of the omniscient novelist and its broader cultural implications. It should therefore also prompt them to question the stance's claim to knowledge and truth, especially in "realistic narrative" attempting to represent not the subjectivity of a narrator or the repertoire of conventions on his shelf, but the world "out there," for the relation of "truth" and absolute mastery is inescapable. Such mastery is presumption, of course, an illusion willed by one who functions as if he or she accepted the assumption that reality is an open book one can read and then know. The reflexive play with stance we have been examining easily accepts the metaphor of reality as a book, except that no nonmetaphoric alternative is envisioned, and the metaphor's full implications are continually stressed. What crosses the line between the world and the text is not truth, experience, or facts but a certain version of the codes by which all three are regulated.

The cultural analysis emerging from this examination of omniscient narrators is anything but unique to Thackeray. One can, for example, usefully refer to Herman Melville's fiction as showing a similarly mixed relation to the culture and its fictional forms. When it depends upon characters as narrators, the result is an interesting blend of perplexity and pieces of the cultural sky that are falling around Melville. In "The Piazza," for example, the leisure-class gentleman feels "the vastness and the lonesomeness are so oceanic, and the silence and the sameness, too,"[29] that he begins to fantasize some relief from his sterile life in the social scheme. This relief is partly sexual, as with the fairies, fantasy creatures whose lithe dances, mischief, and diminutiveness reflect the conflation of male desire, bafflement by the feminine, and will to master the "weaker," smaller sex. But our now familiar issues of class and convention soon enter with his typically aristocratic idyll of a beautiful and innocent peasant girl languishing in a distant cabin that becomes for him the site of a modern pastoral idyll. Nor, of course, is this the only thoroughly conventional frame he invokes for his experience. He sees his natural surroundings as Sunday artists' landscapes, their features as mythological and literary allusions, and his responses as poetic clichés ("the season's new-dropped lamb, its earliest fleece"; "for then, once more, with frosted beard, I pace the sleety deck"). Saturated with cultural frames, he is scarcely able to deal with what he finds when he makes his pilgrimage to Arcadia: "she" is there, but not as Marie Antoinette in a milkmaid's outfit. Rather, she works dawn to dark sewing piecework and cooking for her brother (who works a similar schedule at hard labor). They are barely able to subsist, and Marianna shares with the narrator both the need to escape into fantasy and the cultural programming that defines the objects and forms of her displaced desires. His bourgeois house seems a marble palace to her, he a Prince Charming; her "companions" are shadows she personifies and addresses, though her work does not leave her the time actually to look at them. They are doubly removed from her reality, then, for she sits in an economic cave unable to see even the shadows of her cultural ideals.

Reflexivity enters, as it so often does with narrating characters, as we become aware of the process of the telling. This narrator is amazed that "to you shadows are as things, though you speak of them as of phantoms . . . [and] that to you these lifeless shadows are as living friends" (100–101). He does not see how fully his comment applies to his own Charlemagne, Canute, Hecate, or Shakespeare. Both use narrative topoi to resolve imaginatively the oppressive historical conditions under which they live, and both their narratives work by masking those conditions from the dreamer of shadows; they reveal themselves only to the analyst, and he sees *as* shadows only those narratives projected by another. His own remain the "things" and "living friends" by which he masters the unruly elements of his own experience. In his last line he begins, perhaps, the sort of play we have found in *Vanity Fair*, for he describes himself as "haunted by Marianna's face, and many as real a story" (102). Her face, that is, is no more real than a story, no doubt because it is already assimilated to his repertoire of conventional frames. Or alternatively, her face *is* very real to him, and he associates it with his changed response to many a similar (real) story of economic oppression. The passage oscillates between the two readings because it identifies the crucial point at which culture and history contend: even as narrative seeks to reveal historical crises, it has always already begun to regulate, assimilate, and domesticate them from the unthinkable displacement of order by disorder to an aberration from the prevailing norm we can safely reestablish. Whether that norm is overtly ideological or is masked as morality or logic, it functions as a "nature" from which cultural history lapses. More generally, one sees writing as a process of mastery through forms and conventions, casting their shadows rather than presenting the living faces of things.

Melville's tales thus intersect with Thackeray's analysis of the interplay of class and convention, the narrator of "The Piazza" being as appropriate a version of the generic voice as Mrs. Grundy herself. In *Billy Budd* the historian-narrator juxtaposes a whole series of narratives about Billy in a tale pulled apart by the failure to decide whether theodicy or the relation between the individual and cultural institutions is to be the central focus. Within the latter context, each narrative becomes the voice of a single faction in the social microcosm of the ship, and each reveals part of Melville's broader social analysis. Billy, the worker in this economic drama, literally has no voice: he can submit, or he can strike out in futile and self-destructive blind rage. Vere's narrative reflects his allegiance to the social hierarchy of which he is a functionary; it shows both the executive's freedom to be aware of the personal side of his relations with inferiors and also the requirement that he act inflexibly as the voice of the institution. Claggart's narrative embodies the irrational, arbitrary, but very real malevolence of institutional power as it comes down upon the individual with all its "brute force," showing thereby the full impersonality of the procedure. The doctor, voice of science, tries to explain events in his depersonalized way, just as the purser resorts to something akin to superstition to narratize Billy. The chaplain, more than once emphasized as in the pay of the navy—the church as economically subservient institution—conducts religious rites over Billy and holds morning services after the execution, both narrative minidramas serving to close off a course of events that could lead to revolution if it is not contained (as long as Billy is dead and forgiven, and as long as obedience is reestablished with the formal integration wrought by religious ritual, then there is little space or reason for the sailors to imagine change). The official record, quoted near the end of the narrative, rewrites events in a way that is baldly self-serving for the institution. The sailors' song at the very end—the last word in many published versions of the tale—manages in ways familiar from "The Piazza" to narratize Billy into a comfortable frame (death is not really murder, it is much needed "sleep") and yet also to slip in a utopian political ideal, the nonhierarchical model of cameraderie ("Donald he has promised to stand by the plank") that would eliminate such examples of the arbitrary exercise of power. As something close to pure anomaly—the innocent victim—Billy provokes the full energies of all involved in this microcosm; they all must assimilate him into a narrative that "makes sense" without allowing the threat he poses to received notions. Narrative, in other words, may well be a means of coming to understand events, but it is inevitably ideological, a basic fact that *Billy Budd* makes inescapable by lining up so many versions, each of which owes one clearly displayed debt to the place of its voice in the social hierarchy of the ship and another (really a version of the first) to the discursive convention governing that place.

"The Bell-Tower" features an omniscient narrator telling the archetypal tale of Western culture: the technological project to build a monument to the ego, one that would regulate the daily lives of the citizens (by marking time), one that represents man as a mechanical servant of his master, and finally, one that is a narrative of sorts—its appeal is the scene that climaxes every hour for all to read. Interpretations abound—townspeople read through superstition, the "milder magistrate" through the depictions in contemporary art of such sinister figures as Sisera and Deborah, others through civic pride, Bannadonna himself through near-satanic ego. The simplest by far of these tales by Melville, it would be of no interest here were its recasting of the tower of Babel not so clearly an allegory of mimetic narrative's attempt to represent the daily round of the individual, just as Bannadonna's narrative represents the man striking his hours productively and punctually. To reduce man to a representation is to murder being, confining it to the linear tracks along which Bannadonna's domino must move. This allegory overlaps, of course, with that of the technocrat who murders as he mechanizes, the economically privileged who depersonalizes as he employs, the egoist who abuses all as he self-aggrandizes. For a stance whose voice *is* that of the culture at large, it is not surprising to have

61

these nested bells all ringing at once. Perhaps, then, it is appropriate to leave Melville and his omniscient narrator resonating within these levels of significance behind narrative form, for in the intersection of these interpretations we find an expression of the symmetry among all the discursive types that reflexive narrative keeps drawing into its self-analysis, a symmetry growing out of the troubled relation between will, order, and the unknown.

The Reader as a Narrative Stance

Indeed, one could argue that the reader is the real focus of all this reflexive play with stance, and especially with the stance of the commentator—one that could function out of any of the three major points of view we have examined and whose consistency accounts for the prevailing tendency to speak of just one narrator in *Vanity Fair*. The reader in the final analysis is the definitive point of view for a novel. Representationalist poetics, of course, cannot afford to emphasize this because such a view would admit the resultant indeterminacy as a trait of narrative rather than classifying it as a "problem" for critical theory. Such an admission naturally weakens the concept of culture as an effort to know the nature of reality rather than as our imaginative domicile— hence our tradition's emphasis upon validity, control, and presentation. Even in this novel, the energies of much of the narrative rhetoric are directed at structuring the reader's stance as tightly as possible. As it turns out, however, the commentator is a perceptive observer of both the vulnerability and the power of readers, their struggle as almost passive victims of narrative rhetoric and their arrogance in acting as masters of the text, its critics and judges.

I suggest five propositions about the use of the reader as a point of view, all of which take place within a by now familiar combination— the authority is both exercised, as power usually is, and exposed in the process:

1. Deferring to the reader's opinion in fact controls readers by forcing them not only to interpret, but to do so within what is usually a limited range of options. For example, Maria Osborne becomes fearful at one point that Amelia will steal her own Bullock, and so she engages him in a precious conversation informing him that Amelia is engaged to an excellent shot and that they are all, of course, "so fond" of her. When the narrator then asks, "Who can calculate the depth of affection expressed in that enthusiastic *so?*" the reader has been primed with the answer: the depth is incalculable because it is nonexistent (1:131; 12).

2. Such deference characteristically compels readers to see an incident in conventional moral terms. A case in point concerns the Osborne sisters when they are drifting apart after Maria has married young Bullock and begun her social climb: "the intercourse between the two grew fainter continually. 'Jane and I do not move in the same sphere of life,' Mrs. Bullock said. 'I regard her as a sister, of course'—which means— what does it mean when a lady says that she regards Jane as a sister?" (2:89; 42). Such a comment still does not leave the reader a great deal of freedom, and it requires that he or she come out of any passive role and supply the conventional norms absent in young Mrs. Bullock.

3. The more reflexive the exercise of this device, the more it reveals the interpenetration of spheres normally thought separate. "Which, I wonder, brother reader, is the better lot, to die prosperous and famous, or poor and disappointed? To have, and to be forced to yield; or to sink out of life, having played and lost the game?" (2:323; 61). This moral judgment is taxing because there is no direct indication that the alternatives are deceptive (both are extremes and purely economic patterns that thus exclude any number of alternatives framed by different values). In another such case he supposes at one point that no pair battle as fiercely as former friends over money problems—in this case Osborne and Sedley—and asks, "Who has not remarked the readiness with which the closest of friends and honestest of men suspect and accuse each other of cheating when they fall out over money matters?" (1:212; 18). The same nexus of cash and class is behind old Osborne's rankling over his son's gentlemanly airs. The narrator, at least, asks if the reader has not also discovered that "there is no character which a low-minded man so much mistrusts, as that of a gentleman" (1:254; 21).

4. The more the reflexive device focuses upon questions of constitutive poetics, the more it reveals various indexes of provinciality in the norm it brings into play. The following comment on Amelia's dullness in polite society has implications that go beyond her own case: "Thus, my dear and civilized reader, if you and I were to find ourselves this evening in a society of greengrocers, let us say, it is probable that our conversation would not be brilliant; if, on the other hand, a greengrocer should find himself at your refined and polite tea-table, where everybody was saying witty things, and everybody of fashion and repute tearing her friends to pieces in the most delightful manner, it is possible that the stranger would not be very talkative, and by no means interesting or interested" (2:343; 62). The ostensible point is that since Amelia has "been domineered over hitherto by vulgar intellects" (which "is the lot of many a woman"), she has not had the chance to develop her own conversational skills. Moreover, the values implicit in those skills, as the

sarcasm in this passage makes clear enough, are nothing to be proud about. Nor, I suppose, would those of the greengrocers' conversation were we to have equal opportunity to eavesdrop in that society. That is, more than simply a moral putdown of a judgmental reader, the passage assumes a class analysis of prevailing norms of dullness and wit, tying those norms not so much to a permanent moral or intellectual standard as to the prevailing consensus of a specific subset of the culture. The economic determinants we saw implicit in earlier passages here become part of the differentiae in defining various semiotic pockets of the larger culture. Since the narrator specifically includes himself in this particular pocket, there is no reason to suppose that other semiotic habits he shares with his like-minded readers are any less subject to parochial limitations. At the broadest level, of course, the passage marks once again the class of which the novel is the "voice."

5. Ultimately this stance reveals readers' responses as a will to power "trumped" by the way culture codes or programs both the objects and the instruments of desire. At one point, for example, the narrator summarizes all of George's triumphs in athletics, noting that "wherever he went, women and men had admired and envied him." The narrator then breaks off to exclaim: "What qualities are there for which a man gets so speedy a return of applause, as those of bodily superiority, activity, and valour? Time out of mind strength and courage have been the theme of bards and romances; and from the story of Troy down to to-day, poetry has always chosen a soldier for a hero. I wonder is it because men are cowards in heart that they admire bravery so much, and place military valour so far beyond every other quality for reward and worship?" (1:369; 30). In other words, all the fashions *Vanity Fair* has worked to foreground reflexively prevail in the culture not because they correspond to the reality they pretend to embody or, more modestly, to represent, but precisely because they *do not*. They are compensatory illusions by which a culture pretends to master circumstances and ideals quite beyond the grasp of its members. If heroic romance derives from inner cowardice, does sentimental romance derive from the frustration of sexual desire? Does realism derive from the uncontrollability of history? Does critical theory derive from the elusiveness of the "primary" text? The ultimate effect of a narrative's stance is thus that of a bellows, a narrative play upon mass ideals that both fills readers with a false sense of expansiveness and deflates them of such conceptual biliousness. It exacerbates the individual's sense of lack by dwarfing him with the ideal, and it assuages the resulting sense of inadequacy by indulging wish fulfillment and by allowing the reader the illusion of superiority (as one who knows more than the protagonist

at any one time and as one who can hold "the whole story" in his head). A reflexive narrative like *Vanity Fair* necessarily plays this game, but it also opens the rule book to remind readers the narrative unfolds not according to the laws of the nature of things or of instincts, but according to a cultural dynamics founded upon the need to will the illusion of power. It is precisely toward that will and the expedients of narrative it employs that reflexivity repeatedly turns us.

What narrative shifts in *Vanity Fair* show more than anything else, then, is the makeup of the monolithic cultural voice that articulates the discourse of being. When a narrative voice begins individuating itself, becoming historian, observer, even participant, then that discourse is being led back around upon itself, and the "I" that purports to be the individual identity of a concretely embodied metaphysical essence unmasks itself as a symptom of the collective "neurosis" that generates the discourse of culture. Thackeray, who spent the first ten years of his writing career assimilating along parodic lines the fictional and expository forms of his era, spent the finest two years penning sketches of the convergence of these forms of cultural discourse in the "I" we all take to be the most absolute truth, the most verifiable fact of *cogito*. That "I" is the multivoiced constellation of discursive elements we choose to call the individual, and the very ease with which Thackeray juggles incompatible I's within the same fictional utterance alters our often unexamined concept of "voice" from anthropomorphic to semiotic terms, with all that shift implies about both identity and narrative as its mode of production. For the critic, then, "voice" becomes not the autocratic determinant of "meaning" but a nexus of discursive conventions that, if carefully traced in all their full and quite likely discordant difference, can teach us much about how a culture at a given point distills "identity" or "subjectivity" out of the cultural ether.

Class ideology, stylization in forms of mass entertainment *and* in more elite forms of art, conceptual frames within which we compose an order that enables a sense of mastery and control—all of these factors are marked for our consideration by this reflexive dimension of narrative. What we need to accomplish now is a closer look at the narrative relation, a subject upon which no narrative is more reflexive than the Marlow narratives of Joseph Conrad.

THREE

❧

Conrad, Early Modernism, and the Narrator's Relation to His Material

Although it seems to lack some of the fire of earlier Marlow narratives, Joseph Conrad's *Chance* was, surprisingly to many modern readers, a very heartening popular success for its author. Indeed, in his often-quoted "Author's Note" Conrad pauses over this success: "What makes this book memorable to me apart from the natural sentiment one has for one's creation is the response it provoked. The general public responded largely, more largely perhaps than to any other book of mine, in the only way the general public can respond, that is by buying a certain number of copies. This gave me a considerable amount of pleasure, because what I always feared most was drifting unconsciously into the position of a writer for a limited coterie" (x).[1] One must add that, given his always precarious financial state, Conrad could not have minded the purely material aspect of the response, but his concern about becoming "a writer for a limited coterie" was also quite real for him. This fear of becoming too limited in appeal stems, I suspect, from the extent to which his fiction embodied his own keen interest in the formal and philosophical issues his mentors were exploring.[2] He had, after all, experienced close literary and personal relationships with both Henry James and Ford Madox Ford, relationships that had to raise his awareness of the intricate technical issues that both those writers often discussed, even if Conrad himself says relatively little about such issues explicitly. *Chance,* the most reflexive of all the Marlow narratives, provided a means for conducting his critical speculations implicitly in his fiction. That reflexive nature was accented by the original subtitle of the novel, *An Episodic Tale, with Comments,* a promise carried out even more extensively in the serial version that began 21 January 1912 in the magazine section of the *New York Herald.*[3] His anxiety about being a coterie writer no doubt accounts for his cutting a number of rather interesting passages from that serial form, many of them useful in defining Conrad's reflexive interests in *Chance.*

Normally, of course, the narrator's relation to his material is conceived as a rhetorical issue of strategic distances—that is, the moral, psychological, and presentational attitudes that shape the way the narrator sees the events and characters of the story. Under the pressure of this study's emphasis upon the reflexive, however, this vital element of point of view theory turns round to the more fundamental issues upon which the entire narrative act rests. Issues of presentation can reside within an entirely representational poetics. *Chance* makes it clear that these technical issues have much larger implications than those of interest mainly to a coterie of craftsmen, and that they lead us to the heart of a constitutive poetics for cultural form.[4]

Marlow and the Margins of Culture

In the most general terms, *Chance* pursues a radical examination of the position of the narrator in relation to his material. In *Vanity Fair* this problem took the form of investigating the implications of the point of view for the relations between narrator and reader. Here the problem takes an even more elemental form by returning repeatedly, perhaps even compulsively, to narrative as the fundamental point of conceptual contact between the individual and the experiences that become his world. In part this motif raises the perennial Marlovian issues about how much of experience can be conveyed by narrative and what happens to that experience when it passes through cultural conventions into narrative, but *Chance* also demands attention to why that passage seems so necessary to both Marlow and his listeners, and ultimately to the significance of the narrative mode of consciousness within the culture prescribing it. One of the richer passages deleted from the serial version of the novel illustrates just how such issues surface in the narrative. At one point Marlow stages a "chance" meeting with Flora de Barral outside Captain Anthony's hotel, partially to prevent her running into Fyne as he remonstrates with the captain, but perhaps even more just to nose into her feelings and memories. In both versions of the tale, he reveals that the source of his interest in the "lovers" is precisely that they seem to be outside the conventions of the normal plot that culture provides its young: "those two were outside all conventions. They would be as untrammelled in a sense as the first man and the first woman" (210). In the serial edition, at least, this apparent freedom calls for punctuation with an exclamation point.

But just before and after this passage, the serial edition provides some very interesting additional comments. For example, Marlow observes:

> For most people the pages of life are ruled like the pages of a copybook headed with some sound moral maxim at the top. They can turn them over with the certitude that the very catastrophes shall keep to the traced lines. And it is comforting, in a way, to one's friends and even to one's self to think that one's very misfortunes, if any, will be of the foreseen type. (7 April)

The metaphors of the passage provide some useful insights into *why* Marlow would care about the differences between the Anthonys and "most people." If life is a copybook that people in a culture maintain for themselves, then their sense of their identity is a function of those texts that have been copied—that is, of the narratives providing the conceptual models by which a life line is formed. Hence the emphasis in *Chance* is upon ruling the pages, with its pun conflating a will to mastery and the artificiality of drawing boundaries and guidelines. Consciousness for "most people" seems thus to consist of an intertextual plot that imposes a sense of self upon the blank pages of personal history. That the pages are "headed with some sound moral maxim" adds to this awareness of the fictional quality of personal and cultural texts a distrust of the conventional morality of the culture, a morality portrayed here as the ideological headings that orient the course of the ordinary consciousness. It may be that the animosity in Marlow's ironic tone here derives from his own anxious rather than "comforting" feelings, his perplexity rather than "certitude," and his disappointment that such solaces of the culture are illusory. A novel entitled *Chance*, if it is about anything, would seem to be about what intervenes from outside the cultural margins to upset the "foreseen type," a phrase that suggests the culture's will to master time into predictable narrative conventions and to master variation into distinct abstract categories. This key passage, then, collects several issues pervasive in the novel:

1. the derivative, intertextual nature of copybook lives,
2. the suspect standing of abstract systems ("maxims") of morality, psychology, and the like,
3. the role of those systems in a wider will to mastery over time (so that the future is "foreseen") and circumstance (so that "the very catastrophes shall keep to the traced lines"),
4. the role of these themes as features of the process by which the consciousness fills and binds its pages into a narrative grasp of personal and cultural existence, and
5. a set of necessarily elusive forces grouped under the general heading of "chance" that threaten this cultural ordering of experience.

It is no wonder, then, that Marlow should be struck by Flora because she is "an exceptional case." Marlow is fully aware that "conventions make both joy and suffering easier to bear in a becoming manner," but his tone makes it equally clear that to be "becoming" is no great accomplishment. As he goes on (in the serial version), Marlow observes that "conventions exist only as embodied in the people who, so to speak, stand around to watch the game. And they [Flora and Anthony] would have no one to watch them." The metaphor of a game emphasizes the cultural rather than the "natural" quality of human lives, and equating conventions (from social patterns to "moral maxims" to the attempt to dominate natural catastrophes) with game rules opens a distance between those conventions and any ultimate or natural origins for them.[5] That they exist only as embodied in a spectator citizenry further emphasizes their artificiality (that is, they have no final ontological standing apart from cultural consensus) and alludes as well to the coercive element in the culture's will to mastery. Conrad touches upon this element frequently in his animus against, among others, policemen; the serial edition, for example, contains a long diatribe Marlow shares with Powell denouncing the bobby who conducts young Powell aboard ship in the opening chapter of the book version, and *Lord Jim* and *Heart of Darkness* contain similar though briefer passages.

It is precisely the outcome of escaping from these culturally prescribed margins that fascinates Marlow; he wants to see where the narrative can go if it scrawls itself off the conventional page. With "no one to watch them," he notes, "they would have nobody outside their two selves to refer to any consequences" of the relationship.[6] At this point in the serial, Marlow pauses to make this focus unmistakable: "Do you see now why I was interested in the whole thing, with its touch of romance and its possibility of being an idyl. Why not an idyl? Must an idyl necessarily have rustic surroundings—the green fields, the murmuring stream, the leafy shade of sheltered nooks? Or is the freshness of unsophisticated hearts enough to create an idyllic atmosphere about two lives exposed to the rough salt winds of the open sea?" (7 April). By means of some nostalgia for the nineteenth-century attempt to locate authenticity in innocence, Marlow hopes to ride this story beyond the cultural margins to the essentials, the "realities" of the human situation beyond all the games and spectators. But his own search seems doomed. He follows this comment by defending his hopes with the example of "sundry story tellers" whose idylls have been set in both slums and drawing rooms. It is a self-destructive argument, for it means either that storytelling conventions quite routinely break through to the supposed authenticity of the idyll, hence devaluing his project, or that the idyll form is so hollow in its conventionality that it can be imposed upon any stretch of experience. In the first case, one can gain the pure ground beyond cultural complications by locating "unsophisticated hearts" in any setting—a doubtful project in the first place (Is any heart free of the complications of cultural conditioning?) and in any case one that would be of little use to the sophisticated searcher. *Chance* gradually moves us toward the second case, in which such illusory authenticity is no more than convention "as embodied in people who, so to speak, stand around to watch the game" and discover what their preconceptions school them to find. Marlow, the quintessential watcher, must work hard during the novel to hold this romantic line against materials that constantly threaten to overrun it.

He is, then, one of those maintaining a copybook of sorts, and his task is to arrange the pages of his materials so that the culture's narrative line is coherent. His problem, as he makes clear when the book version rejoins the serial, is "that I could not imagine anything about Flora de Barral and the brother of Mrs. Fyne. Or if you like, I could imagine *anything* which comes practically to the same thing. Darkness and chaos are first cousins. I should have liked to ask the girl for a word which would give my imagination its line" (210–11). Since these two *seem* to be "outside the pale"—yet another metaphor for a stake marking a boundary or margin—Marlow has no conventional script by which to foresee their "joy and suffering." At the same time, therefore, he can also generate any number of plots and project them onto their futures. His cosmological metaphors of "darkness and chaos" for these two possibilities underscore the primal nature of narrative as a setting of margins and boundaries through the darkness of ignorance and the chaos of unlimited possibilities. Marlow wants to know that shadowy region beyond the lights of the cultural conventions, but he also wants the primal narrative word, the "line" by which his imagination can survey the topography of the wilderness.

It is a contradictory movement, then, between Marlow's wish to distance himself from the easy moral maxims of the Fynes and his wish to achieve narrative coherence out of the materials of the Anthonys and de Barrals. He is both fascinated by what lies beyond the margins and reliant upon the most conventionalized form of those margins. In pursuing the transactions between the two, his narrative becomes a demonstration of the linear or narrative—that is, the logocentric—means by which we attempt to master experience. Having indexed among his concerns the cosmological, philosophical, psychological, social, and literary, Marlow has brought into a narrative about Flora de Barral all the primal building blocks of culture itself. But rather than using them as some sort of inert backdrop external to the novel against which the internal plot takes place, *Chance* in effect makes them internal functions of narrative. That is, narrative becomes the type or even the center of all cultural activity. The novel's reflexive focus returns persistently to the role of narrative in establishing entities and identities of all kinds and at all levels of endeavor. It was one among a number of skilled strokes that Ian Watt, in his recent study of Conrad, should have seized upon "consuetudinal" as a term for one role of time in the narrative technique.[7] The word, of course, means "habitual" and therefore constitutive of an entity or characteristic of its identity, and it derives ultimately from the Indo-European root for "-self," the reflexive pronoun. At the risk of overworking my title, it seems that to pursue Marlow's reflexive narration is to follow that circuit by which cultures, individuals, and "sundry story tellers"—among them Marlow—habituate time according to a culturally derived but, at this point in our history, naturalized narratology of closure, causation, identity, and so forth on through the litany of logocentric premises. Hence Watt's term reverberates cannily back through the etymological history to the philosophical premises of narration itself.

Marlow's near obsessive hovering about these primal issues results in the curious movement by which the novel seems almost to neglect the forward progress of the narrative. Contemporary critics complained enough about this to prompt Conrad into one of his more sarcastic ripostes: "No doubt that by selecting a certain method and taking great pains the whole story might have been written out on a cigarette paper. For that matter, the whole history of mankind could be written thus if only approached with sufficient detachment" (x). One could argue that the lengthy expansion of what could otherwise be a brief tale is precisely an attempt to portray "the whole history of mankind" as a function of the nature of narrative. *Chance* might thus serve as in this sense the prototypical reflexive narrative extending the imperial realm of the narrative paradigm to the furthest reaches of our knowledge, that point at which what we can see dissolves in uncertainties as hopelessly impenetrable as the mists upon the Congo or the fogs of the Pacific.

The Narrative Stance

One of the more curious aspects of the novel, and one that contributes to the sense of delay or avoidance of narrative, is that there is almost no story. A lonely sea captain shelters a homeless girl and the ex-convict who is her father, and the feelings gradually developing in each of them come into the open after a nosy second mate disrupts the father's jealous attempt to poison his son-in-law. The father poisons himself instead, the marriage is finally consummated, and the second mate years later weds the captain's widow. Virtually nothing else occurs except that any number of characters, including the principals, struggle against the unusual and the mysteries of chance to compose a narrative that will satisfy their desire to make sense of things. It is this struggle, more than anything else, that draws Marlow's interest, and in fact no one attracts Marlow's interest who is *not* engaged in it. Each figure in the narrative is less important as an actor in a drama than as one of many narrative centers seeking to draw others into a recognizable plot, usually arranged around itself, that displays a meaningfully interrelated cast progressing through a coherent series of events toward an appropriate state of rest at the end of it all. Even characters like young Powell, who seems by nature quite uninterested in the narrative enterprise, are drawn into its workings and socialized by their seniors into the world-making activity of culture.

Among these narrators there are even an absurd number of namesakes. Young Powell gets a job because a captain thinks he is a relation of old Powell, the shipping master. Young Powell's first name is Charles, as is Marlow's, as is that of the "cousin" of the governess whose buoyancy and good looks weave a romance plot in Flora's young imagination. But the doublets in name are nothing compared with the doublets in function. Old Powell, for example, superintends a scene in which the innocence of young Powell and the distraction of Captain Anthony allow him to fabricate a validating origin for the future second mate: Anthony thinks the youth "looks very respectable," to which the shipping master replies, "Certainly. His name is Powell," a reply that causes Anthony to acquiesce in signing the youth. Old Powell doesn't correct Anthony when the latter calls the youth "your young friend," that is, relative, and squints at the youth's certificate in order to be able to blend in his first name quite familiarly. He appears, to young Powell at least, to have given the boy "the real start in life" by means of this mythic origin, and Marlow's comparison of him to Socrates (7–8) neatly links the scene weaver with the father (at least according to Plato's fiction) of our logocentric philosophy. Like a highly cooperative deconstructive text, however, the shipping master is quick to displace any such sense of his primary position in this scheme of things—"'Oh, no, no,' says he. 'I guess it's that shipment of explosives waiting down the river which has done most for you. Forty tons of dynamite have been your best friend to-day, young man'" (22). The chance accident to Anthony's second mate, Powell's chance meeting with a friend who sent him to the shipping master, the coincidence of names, and other such "chances" that explode upon the scene all complicate the linear thread of coherence being spun at this point. Old Powell, who seems the shaping narrator of the living scene, is no more master of its margins than others for whom life has overrun the copybook's pages. Old Powell, however, is a bit unlike many of the mininarrators in that he knows how limited his steps toward coherent control must be and leaves quite open the narrative he seems to have begun: "Don't be in a hurry to thank me," he says to the youth. "The voyage isn't finished yet."

To this model of an open narrator, most of the other examples stand in contrast. They double not the part of Marlow that seeks out the exceptional, the atypical, the unformed—the nonlogocentric?—but the margin-ruling activity in Marlow's approach to his task. The moneylender at whose establishment Marlow catches his one glimpse of de Barral is one case, however minor. Here is a figure one always seems to find "busy at that marvellous writing table," deciding whether to expend himself for the characters who pass before his desk, a decision certainly akin to that made by the novelist who must also decide where to invest his imaginative wealth for the best return. He is attracted to de Barral because of the narrative mystery about him: "That's a deep fellow, if you like. We all know where he started from and where he got to; but nobody knows what he means to do." He has plotted out the beginning and volume one of de Barral's narrative, but does not know how to achieve the sense of an ending that would confer coherence and meaning upon it all. He becomes "thoughtful for a moment" and adds "as if speaking to himself" a final query, "I wonder what his game is" (78). Half of Marlow's interest in de Barral is precisely that "there was no game, no game of any sort, or shape, or kind" in de Barral's career and that he was thus seemingly as far beyond the margins of the copybooks as Flora and Captain Anthony. De Barral is thus a frustrating case for the moneylender's efforts to draw him within the normal narrative margins he has learned to draw at this desk. Perhaps his enthusiasm for this conceptual mechanism matches that for his *garniture de cheminée,* for curiously enough Conrad makes him a collector of these contrivances that are a suitable figure for Marlow's own means of channeling experience up the flues of the cultural furnace.

In any case, old Powell and the moneylender give us brief exemplars of the open and closed poles of narration between which the rest of the cast arranges itself. The novel makes it clear, for example, that Marlow is drawn to the Fynes not because of their personalities or intellects (see his slights of them on pp. 57, 61, 137, 143) but because they become narrators. He tells us that "My liking for her [Mrs. Fyne] began while she was trying to tell me of the night she spent by the girl's bed-side" (138). And he is fascinated that Fyne "had set himself the mental task of discovering the self-interest" of de Barral's cousin in taking care of Flora. Marlow muses, "And so, Mr. Fyne listened, observed and medi-tated. . . . That's an excellent way of coming to a conclusion" (173). Fyne's hypothesis (the cousin hoped de Barral had hidden enough money to reward him later on) is, of course, pure conjecture, and even Marlow had not "thought him [Fyne] capable of so much cynicism" but approves and incorporates Fyne's guesswork along with the rest of the more factual material he derives from their conversations together. [8]

Other minor narrators in this anthology of a novel include Franklin, with his effort to explain de Barral through a plot of diabolic possession — an extreme form of the recourse to the metaphysical to make narrative sense of things. The framing narrator is himself a novelist who thinks de Barral an apt subject for a tale by Poe (18 February), takes both teasing (25 February) and deference (17 March) from Marlow because of his craft, and comments on his appetite for "digging under the emotions of trivial existences, wherein the rich significance of things is often found — as a mine of diamonds may be discovered in commonplace surroundings" (28 January). It is, after all, *his* "certain amount of scribbling, the results of which are now before your eyes" (28 April). And de Barral's cousin, who in the serial is a commercial book "manufacturer" (3 March), draws Marlow's admiration as a "really remarkable individual in his way" (169) for his capacity to stage a scene maximizing the "consternation" of the Fynes, a discomfort "the fellow was aware of, and enjoyed quietly" (167).

Powell is a more reluctant participant in these authorial pursuits. In the opening chapter he is a dazed and innocent youth who, once he reaches the *Ferndale,* must meet at first only the "unusual of an obvious kind" and benefit from Franklin's tutelage in constituting narrative, or he "would have been perfectly useless for my purpose," as Marlow puts it (272). For "signs can be seen only by a sharp and practised eye," and Powell becomes interesting and useful to Marlow only as he begins to master that eminently cultural semiotic art. We soon begin to see him projecting "some mysterious grievance" as a history for de Barral, a conjecture "young Powell could not help thinking" (278). Once de Barral actually speaks to him, he becomes as obsessed as Marlow does with the case: "it was distinctly at that moment that he became aware of something unusual not only in this encounter but generally around him, about everybody, in the atmosphere" (292). He perceives anomaly and begins the attempt to rule it back within the margins. At the very sug-gestion of the unexplainable, one becomes the center of a suddenly vulnerable narrative. We are told that young Powell "felt it. He felt it in the sudden sense of his isolation; the trustworthy, powerful ship of his first acquaintance reduced to a speck, to something almost undistinguishable, the mere support for the soles of his two feet before that unexpected old man becoming so suddenly articulate in a darkening universe" (292–93). Instead of the ship's being the trustworthy microcosm of the Western cultural tradition, it is an indistinguishable speck in an ocean of unruled possibility, support for the soles of feet rather than for the souls of man "in a darkening universe."

From this point on Powell is increasingly occupied by his Marlovian function, though when the story takes place he is ill equipped to fulfill it. For example, we find that "he tried to 'get hold of that thing' by some side which would fit in with his simple notions of psychology" (308), a simpler but not categorically distinct version of Marlow's own penchant for psychologizing about individuals, professions, sexes, and types. Like Lord Jim (and, of course, Marlow), he has a capacity to fill out imaginatively the scenic possibilities ("he did not know how scared he had been, not generally but of that very thing his imagination had conjured, till it was all over" [320]). Key signs like the single word overheard from de Barral cause him to curse "'Damn!' quite heartily . . . ; that hostile word 'jailor' had given the situation an air of reality" (407), and he passes sufficiently beyond the simplistic framework of conventional thinking to realize "that there was something mysterious in such beings as the absurd Franklin, and even in such beings as himself. . . . He was foolish in a way totally unforeseen by himself. Pushing this self-analysis further, he reflected that the springs of his conduct were just as obscure" (410). The "air of reality" alters the comforting context with its margins of consciousness to a puzzling text in which sea, self, psyche, and others all become mysterious threats to order, clarity, and coherence.

The Powell on the scene, as Marlow points out several times, is not of course the Powell who narrates to and through Marlow; he is "a Mr. Powell, much slenderer than our robust friend is now, with the bloom of innocence not quite rubbed off his smooth cheeks" (282). As Marlow explains, "there of course all he could do was to look at the surface. The inwardness of what was passing before his eyes was hidden from him, who had looked on, more impenetrably than from me who at a distance of years was listening to his words" (426). The "inwardness," the rationale of causality of motives and character that makes sense of events, is accessible only from a distance that is temporal, spatial, and psychic, like Marlow's here, although the passage also reminds us of the description of the frame narrator's novelistic skills. One needs room to create, to draw the connecting lines that reconstitute a system of margins to the course of events. Marlow, in fact, is moved by the spectacle of Powell's struggle for understanding to give us one of his more notable meditations on experience and narrative: "The surprise, it is easy to understand, would arise from the inability to interpret aright the signs which experience (a thing mysterious in itself) makes to our understanding and emotions. For it is never more than that. Our experience never gets into our blood and bones. It always remains outside of us" (282). Marlow is fascinated by Powell's surprise at his experiences, precisely because as something like a "nonverbal other" they cannot fit the semiotic systems the young man has intact at this point in his life. In fact, what Marlow points to here is the archetypal moment when the narrative artist rearranges within the margins of his own typescript the signs he derives from the nonverbal. Significantly, the experiences themselves are ruled out—we take in only the signs, for "our experience never gets into our blood and bones."

Powell, of course, lacks Marlow's sophisticated grasp of these delicate issues and so, as we have seen, finds himself "at sea" in a very different sense from what he expected when he joined the crew of the *Ferndale*. Marlow's own insecurities about the relation between the semiotic and the nonverbal show in his recurrent fascination with characters who are fitting things together, drawing signs from their experiences and assimilating those signs into larger frames of reference. It is as if he must constantly retrace the lines along which the narrative deed is done in order to feel some support beneath him. Certainly much of his interest in Flora de Barral is of this kind. One must suspect, of course, that part of his interest is unacknowledged sexual attraction. More than once he says something of the order that "there are in life moments when one positively regrets not being married" (136) and of Flora that "she was an appealing and—yes—she was a desirable little figure" (201). And as we have already seen, he is interested in how her apparent unconventionality might reveal some more "authentic" or "natural" possibilities.

But he is also drawn to the way in which, like Powell, she is first isolated, then forced into generating narrative coherence for the events and characters surrounding her. In her talks with Mrs. Fyne, Flora recalls the venomous outburst of her governess as the beginning of her efforts to build some sort of order; in response to the governess's calling her a fool, she tells Mrs. Fyne: "I do assure you I had never yet thought at all; never of anything in the world, till then. I just went on living. And one can't be a fool without one has at least tried to think. But what had I ever to think about?" (119). An unthinking creature living unconsciously within the margins of a very comfortable gentility in Brighton, she has simply accepted the givens provided by her father. This is the state of innocence akin to what Powell initially prefers—being "too busy to think of the lady 'that mustn't be disturbed,' or of his captain—or of anything else unconnected with his immediate duties" (276). The collapse of de Barral's financial empire, however, shears away the economic support to her childlike condition, and the governess's venom poisons the emotional and psychological tranquillity of her unreflective adolescence. Marlow, of course, is keenly interested in this transition and breaks into the narrative—or rather resumes his extended commentary—to define this shift:

> "And no doubt," commented Marlow, "her life had been a mere life of sensations—the response to which can neither be foolish nor wise. It can only be temperamental; and I believe that she was of a generally happy disposition, a child of the average kind. . . . When she was viciously assured that she was in heart, mind, manner and appearance an utterly common and insipid creature, she listened without indignation, without anger. She stood, a frail and passive vessel into which the other went on pouring all the accumulated dislike for her pupils, her scorn of all her employers. (119)

The image of a "frail and passive vessel" is allied to Powell's sense of how his "powerful ship" becomes "a speck," and it suggests the same pattern of the isolated and vulnerable ego suddenly aware of the incoherent swirl of unsuspected cross- and countercurrents moving everywhere beneath the surface of conventional life.

Perhaps more effectively than Powell, Flora begins reabsorbing these shocking experiences into an acceptable order. The tension between experience and order is always distressing to her. Later in the novel we read that "she said to herself that it was good not to be bothered with what all these things meant in the scheme of creation (if indeed anything had a meaning), or were just piled-up matter without any sense" (337). The contrast between the orderly "scheme of creation" and the fear that things are "just piled-up matter without any sense" is primary in the novel, and Flora, like others we have looked at, strives for some way of interpreting things and thereby restoring comfortable margins to a frightening world. This passage, in fact, provides some insight into this way of approaching matters as it continues: "She felt how she had always been unrelated to this world. She was hanging on to it merely by that one arm grasped firmly just above the elbow. It was a captivity. So be it" (337). "Relation," a word that combines the causality of procreation, the dynamics of intersubjectivity, and the narrative act, is a particularly apt choice for the passage. The motherless child who becomes a de facto orphan, the victim of deceptive relations with the governess and Charley, the "woman for whom there is no clear place in the world" (281) and hence no plot—Flora must make her own. Hence Captain Anthony's arm becomes a connection, and *his* plot for her the "captivity" in which she finds some margins within which to dwell.

As for the past, she begins early on to reconstruct that. This passage, for example, is a textbook case for retrospective narrative at its freest as Flora equivocates for Charley and seeks something akin to young Powell's "simple notions" to give her a hold on the governess: "For Charley she found excuses. He at any rate had not said anything while he had looked very gloomy and miserable. He couldn't have taken part against his aunt—could he? But after all he did, when she called upon him, take 'that cruel woman away.' He had dragged her out by the arm. She had seen that plainly. She remembered it. That was it! The woman was mad. 'Oh! Mrs. Fyne, don't tell me she wasn't mad. If you had only seen her face' " (139). She seizes upon madness as a way to rule out the behavior of the governess and protect her own innocence from the implications of such fury, duplicity, and self-interest. If the governess is outside the normal, then nothing she says, does, or represents can or should affect that norm and those living within it. While excluding the governess, she reformulates Charley in language that effectively highlights the editing required for the narrative. The equivocation of "at any rate," the tentativeness of "could he?" and the willful insistence in "had seen that plainly" doubled in "she remembered it" all show the will to narrative mastery clearly at work.[9]

It is not an easy art to keep up, for events often fail to conform to their place in narrative continuity. As soon as she picks up her father, for example, she becomes distressed that "everything was so different from what she imagined it would be" (361), and she finds that her father was only "her companion. He was hardly anything more by this time. Except for her childhood's impressions he was just—a man. Almost a stranger. How was one to deal with him?" (366). Instead of filling out the character assigned him by her "childhood's impressions," he is a stranger—which basically means he has his own egoistic, possessive ends—his own plot—to which he wants her to conform. She finds that "she couldn't fathom his thoughts" (380), and she is troubled at the deceptiveness of those childhood impressions of what she now sees as a "well-remembered glance in which she had never read anything as a child, except the consciousness of her existence" (358). That mere consciousness had been "enough for a child who had never known demonstrative affection," enough to allow him to become in her private mythology "the only human being that really cared for her, absolutely, evidently, completely—to the end" (380). But it is not enough when he forces her to choose between himself and Anthony by trying to poison her husband.

Nor is Anthony any easier to keep in narrative line. The progress of their relationship from her initial comparison of it with the "peace and rest in the grave" (221) to the "kindness and safety" she finally feels once, in his love, "all the world, all life were transformed for me" (444), is no easy matter. As we have already seen, she feels herself "the captive of Anthony's masterful generosity" (423), scarcely comprehending its nature and motivation. The celibacy of the marriage confuses and distresses her from the first: "She felt bound in honour to accept the situation for ever and ever unless . . . Ah, unless . . . She dissembled all her sentiments, but it was not duplicity on her part. All she wanted was to get at the truth; to see what would come of it" (341). She is not really able to find in herself her own attraction to the captain, or her own frustration at his willingness to forbear. Her identification of "truth" with "what would come of it" is a significant link of narrative with meaning, a link we have seen repeated in the thinking of all Marlow's characters. The puzzle arises only because of the discontinuity in the narratives each is composing; his willingness not to take advantage of her, required by the injunctions of gentility and honor Fyne puts to him, strikes her as something quite different: "she went stiff all over, her hand resting on the edge of the table, her face set like a carving of white marble. It was all over. It was as that abominable governess had said. She was insignificant, contemptible. Nobody could love her. Humiliation clung to her like a cold shroud—never to be shaken off" (335). The plot her governess writes for her keeps surfacing to conflict with the one she seeks and with that offered by Anthony.

He is also suffering, however, as "the chafing captive of his generosity" (395) in his "life of solitude and silence—and desire" (328). The communication between the two is blocked by this sort of narrative dissonance; he supposes that because he has "dragged the poor defenceless thing by the hair of her head, as it were, on board that ship," that "she must fatally detest and fear him" (396–97). When she tells him she is not "keeping anything back from you," she is sending a sexual signal that he reads as referring only to "her deplorable history" (343–44), and "quite unable to understand the extent of Anthony's delicacy, she said to herself that 'he didn't care'" (396). Both resent the other's failure to fall into their own narrative lines; "somehow he resented this very attitude" of generosity he had to maintain (397), and she "discovered in herself a resentment" (342), "was beginning to be irritated with this man a little" (374), "felt angry" (389) with Anthony's blindness to her uneasiness, and so forth. It is not until a vial of poison brings together three or more individual plots that the narrative lines are broken enough to be reformed more closely in parallel.

Flora thus both suffers and succeeds through her essentially narrative grasp of her world, even though as an intensely egoistic world making it is subject to the dangers of conflict and misunderstanding as it comes in contact with other egoistic narrative worlds. Like other characters in the novel, she draws upon the dubious devices of revisionist memory, causal fictions, and what we might call "characterization"—turning others into types for her own psychodrama—in order to connect past and future along a narrative line that promises some coherence, some margin of safety, and some protection for the essentially isolated and vulnerable state of the individual in a vast and indifferent cosmos.

It would not be difficult to argue that all of Conrad's characters, particularly those in Marlow's narratives, are seen in similar terms: Lord Jim, who seeks constantly to lay out and fulfill a narrative in keeping with his romantic plot lines; Kurtz, who seeks to carry out the quintessential teleological plot of Western culture and to take the Congo with him; the multitude of ancillary narrators who watch and reconstruct, if they can, these principals in accordance with their own views of things. In *Chance* the many examples would be tedious to exhaust, but one ought to remember that each principal character in the novel is someone who interests Marlow because his or her established world, more or less drifted into, is then swept away.[10] It is their efforts to narrate new worlds for themselves that excite Marlow's curiosity.

One might suppose from this fixation upon the narrative stance that the narrative pacing would not have been so turgid as to have drawn so much early criticism of the novel. But as we have seen, it is not the actual conduct of narrative that fascinates Marlow, but the conceptual conditions invoked to make it possible. It is not Fyne as a person but Fyne as he tries to find a position from which to assemble the pieces that interests Marlow. As he puts it, "Little Fyne had never interested me so much since the beginning of the de Barral–Anthony affair when I first perceived possibilities in him. The possibilities of dull men are exciting because when they happen they suggest legendary cases of 'possession' not exactly by the devil, but, anyhow, by a strange spirit" (251). At this point we can hypothesize that the "strange spirit" is that of the narrator exercising godlike arrogance (what Marlow calls "Satanic conceit" when Anthony exerts it [351]), positing a new testament of cosmic coherence. And as we have also seen by focusing upon the principal characters, such creative acts are extraordinarily difficult to manage. The value of *Chance* is that its multiple versions of the narrative act clarify some of the forces, conceptual and otherwise, that take "possession" of us as we narrate. It is in the nuances of a series of oppositions among these forces that Conrad achieves so much, and hence any real sense of them must be earned through close readings. But we can begin with the suggestion that these often metaphoric oppositions serve as the narrative margins that waver as Marlow attempts to follow them, and that among the more important of them are

1. linear clarity and labyrinthine confusion,
2. shore life and seacraft,
3. formal abstraction and its deconstruction, and
4. the larger conflict between the ideas of order and of chance.

Linear Clarity and Labyrinthine Confusion

An indulgence in metaphor, a deferral of the "story," and an effort at verbal overture, the opening chapter of *Chance* is "about" young Powell's passing his exam and getting his berth aboard the *Ferndale*. In strictest terms, it is minimally relevant to the rest of the novel. One could certainly establish him as a naive youth far more economically, especially than in the serial version with its long passages cut from the book's first chapter. But among the themes this overture sounds are several that provide basic motifs to follow. For example, one of these themes emerges in Powell's opening blast at the "establishment." I quote, adding in brackets material from the serial version: "Since he had retired from the sea he had been astonished to discover that the educated people were not much better than the others. No one seemed to take any proper pride in his work: from plumbers who were simply thieves to, say, newspaper men (he seemed to think them a specially intellectual class) who never by any chance gave a correct version of the simplest affair. [And growing almost disloyal to the glorious institutions of his country, he did not fear to say that he supposed the Queen's Ministers were not any better in that respect]" (4). Perhaps the instant rapport between Marlow and Powell derives from Marlow's interest in his new friend's antipathy to conventional narratives (from either the journalistic or the political establishment) and his apparent willingness to be disloyal to any institution that seems to block his access to the "correct version" of even "the simplest affair." Such an affair would certainly have linear clarity of the kind to which we have seen Powell trying futilely to reduce events. In general terms, however, the passage suggests that the mature Powell is no less likely than the younger Powell to be "astonished" by the labyrinthine complications of the many versions we have of the reality.

Indeed, the first sustained action of the novel features an almost allegorical descent by Powell into the bowels of St. Katherine's Dock House. Conrad wisely deletes from the serial a prolonged description of Powell taking his examination (the captain besieges him with one catastrophe after another trying, unsuccessfully, to break his command of his line of thought). This change lets the emphasis fall upon Powell's depression over not being able to parlay a certificate into a berth (Conrad also deletes a description of equivocating captains unwilling to tell him outright he lacks the experience necessary for hiring). In any case, Powell professes himself ready to go "boldly up to the devil" to get a job, a desperation reminiscent of Flora's suicidal moments or Anthony's blustery and nearly violent manner in proposing to her. He envies cabbies, bootblacks, bobbies, and sentries for having "their places in the scheme of the world's labour," reminding us of the isolation Flora and Anthony feel, and he also envies the bums "because they were too far gone to feel their degradation," reminding us of Flora's equally low self-esteem.

Hence Powell's expectation that the examination was his real test is disappointed, and he must cope with a far less straightforward route to his first professional post. Having earlier half-expected to be greeted "with songs and incense," he now enters the Dock House "in a slinking fashion" and "afraid of being stopped" by the doorkeeper, who in fact does begin to pursue him. He is not comforted by what he finds; as the text puts it, "The basement of St. Katherine's Dock House is vast in extent and confusing in its plan. Pale shafts of light slant from above into the gloom of its chilly passages. Powell wandered up and down there like an early Christian refugee in the catacombs; but what little faith he had in the success of his enterprise was oozing out at his fingertips. At a dark turn under a gas bracket whose flame was half turned down his self-confidence abandoned him altogether" (9–10). Feeling more like a "baffled thief" than a Christian, Powell finds not the catacombs of the faithful but the labyrinth stalked by a doorkeeper-minotaur threatening to cut off his last chance to find the thread into his future. He is, as the passage makes overly clear, in the dark, and he loses all faith and self-confidence. Opening a door in desperation, he finds not "the big shadowy cellar-like extent of the Shipping Office," but a "cupboard," a "little hold," a "gas-lighted grave" in which a "drab" and "dusty" bald little man who "looked as though he had been imprisoned for years" tells him in a "contemptuous squeaky voice" that "you've lost your way" (11–12). Powell scurries from this encounter pursued by "an amazed and scandalized voice" roaring, "Don't you know there's no admittance that way?"

One could easily go overboard in allegorical reconstruction with such an incident, but its dark shadows certainly flicker across Powell's shining visions of functionaries saluting him, whisking him down bright official hallways, and establishing him in a position of power, authority, and honor. Such positions, we are to understand, come only by the circuitous and confusing ways of hard work and chance. Once he gets to the older Powell, however, he still thinks things will now work out more or less neatly. We have already seen him watch stunned while the shipping master commits a penal offense, dupes Anthony into considering the boy his relative, and disavows any real responsibility for launching a career. Young Powell gapes as his senior explains the potential for byzantine maneuvers in the office politics—informants who could make it "look very black" in order to imprison him and usurp his position. "It's human nature," the master explains. The youth can only say that "I had never looked at mankind in that light before. When one's young human nature shocks one" (15). In other words, this second action in the novel repeats the first: the expectation of simple, straightforward linear progression becomes complicated in labyrinthine ambiguities, moral equivocations, and the eminent danger of ceasing altogether—as when the doorkeeper bursts in upon the two Powells and must be lied to in order to save the protagonist.

The third action features Powell gathering his things and finding his way to the ship; a seemingly innocent pastime, this too becomes a repetition. For one thing, he has innumerable errands to perform in only six hours in order to get ready for a two-year voyage. He feels he would like to "sit down on the kerb and hold my head in my hands," and he feels as if "an engine had been started going under my skull" that gathers "more way every minute" as he "rolled up and down the streets" to shops and aunts and lodgings—a very roundabout course until he is set down "suddenly at the entrance to the Dock before large iron gates in a dead wall." If he had been expecting a welcome, he finds only a dead wall and no little difficulty getting through. It is a "dark, narrow thoroughfare" with a "mean row of houses" without "the smallest gleam of light," the street itself "pitch black" beyond the glare of a distant gin palace (25). We have, in other words, a replica of the dark passageways of St. Katherine's—only, if possible, more sinister: "Some human shapes appearing mysteriously, as if they had sprung up from the dark ground, shunned the edge of the faint light thrown down by the gateway lamps. These figures were wary in their movements and perfectly silent of foot, like beasts of prey slinking about a camp fire"

(25). If young Powell stands as the campfire of hopefulness, seeking the pathway lit by his beacon of professional competence and earnest commitment, these figures become reminders of the diabolic realm of disorder hunting him to make him their own. The policeman who eventually takes him in hand tells him that one figure lacks the nerve, the other the ability, to commit any crime—each lacks one of Powell's two key assets, however embryonic they may be.

The nightmare scene climaxes when the policeman lets him in, "and slammed the gate violently with a loud clang. I was startled to discover how many night prowlers had collected in the darkness of the street in such a short time and without my being aware of it. Directly we were through they came surging against the bars, silent, like a mob of ugly spectres" (27). Specters beyond the margins of his awareness crowd into the momentary page of vision, only to be closed out by the policeman manning the cultural barrier against them. The reader's temptation to allegorize is intense, particularly since this is the third and most vivid version of the same scene. Powell continues his own plot line, but only by excluding much that he had not expected to discover and much more that he cannot know—like the awful row that "started as if Bedlam had broken loose" off down the street. The explosion of madness beyond the edge of his scene is emblematic of the chaos left in the labyrinthine darkness of reality as one composes. Indeed, the serial version gives the scene yet another twist by having Marlow defend the two "bandits" as at least "honest" to their limitations (hence only helping instead of trying to steal Powell's bags) and attack the policeman because he "imagined himself master of his fate" though no more than a slave to "momentary instincts," to "transcendental reveries of free will and duty and conscience," and most of all to the "vain pomp and privilege of authority" given him by his office (28 January). Both his mastery, then, and his "rightness" are illusions of his will to power. Marlow goes further by arguing that honesty too is entirely relative, but the point is that even Powell's chastened retrospective version of how the evening upset his expectations can be "surprised" yet again by a different perspective, another version of what is anything but "the simplest affair."

In any case, one would suppose we had had enough of the scene in which a naive belief in order is surprised by that which exceeds its control. There is, however, yet a fourth version of the same event—when Powell comes aboard ship. As Powell comes up to the ship, he has this reaction: "At once the head-gear in the gas light inspired me with interest and respect; the spars were big, the chains and ropes stout, and the whole thing looked powerful and trustworthy" (29). But, almost comically, he tells us that "I hit my shins cruelly against the end of the gangway," so we are not too far from finding that linear path more difficult and painful than anticipated. The ship is not so trustworthy that "an irregular round knob, of wood, perhaps," cannot turn out to be "the head of the shipkeeper." And it is not so healthy that the shipkeeper cannot turn out to be "the feeblest creature that ever breathed," gasping "in a fit of weak, pitiful coughing" (30). Nor is the environment so reassuring to Powell that he fails to recognize that "I was nothing but a second officer of a ship just like any other second officer to that constable" (29). And he is troubled to discover that the captain's wife is on board—an aberration whose exact explanation "nobody I ever heard on the subject could tell for certain" (31). By this point, at least, Powell has begun the attempt at more complex, speculative, open-ended narrative explanations of behavior. But as we have seen from the rest of the narrative, this is a lesson whose full content is as yet beyond him. Though a chapter that contributes very little to the "story" of the novel, this opener nonetheless, through its four versions of the onslaught of confusion upon our expectations of clarity and control, establishes the fundamental status of a narrator confronting the materials of a situation. The narrative thread leads him into dimly lit labyrinthine regions below the surface clarities and conventions, and what seemed like a clear progression turns out to be a confusing and at times arbitrary set of associations whose linearity is hard won and likely to be illusory.

Shore Life and Seacraft

Perhaps the most important sections in chapter 1 are those passages establishing the opposition of seacraft and shore life; appealed to often throughout the novel as the very type of moral experience and reliable communication, the metaphor of life at sea is extended in the serial version until it breaks under the metaphysical burden it is asked to carry. Numerous passages in both versions of the novel develop the sailor's outrage at the immorality and confusion of shore life, and the serial in particular creates an elaborate analogy between this contrast and fundamental attitudes toward the human condition. One of these fundamental attitudes is partly temperamental, for "sea-life fashions a man outwardly and stamps his soul with the mark of a certain prosaic fitness" to cope with daily realities (47). A sailor ashore feels something like Anthony's reaction: "The night of the town with its strings of lights, rigid, and crossed like a net of flames thrown over the sombre immensity of walls, closed round him, with its artificial brilliance overhung by an emphatic blackness, its unnatural animation of a restless, overdriven humanity" (346). As in the passages when, say, Flora urges her father to seek the sea as "the uncontaminated and spacious refuge for wounded souls," Anthony's sense of the sea/shore contrast has much to do with the "net of flames" that closes over the spirit and leaves it "overdriven" ashore, "what with the fads and proprieties and the ceremonies and affectations" that are "a perfect terror to a simple man" (221).

The moral component, however, is much more intense elsewhere. Typical of this attitude is Anthony's sudden lecture to Franklin: "It ought to teach you not to make rash surmises. You should leave that to the shore people. They are great hands at spying out something wrong. I dare say they know what they have made of the world. A dam' poor job they make of it, and that's plain. The world is a confoundedly ugly place, Mr. Franklin. You don't know anything of it? Well—no, we sailors don't. Only now and then one of us runs against something cruel or underhand, enough to make your hair stand on end. And when you do see a piece of their wickedness you find that to set it right is not so easy as it looks" (270-71). Anthony is already consigning the unrest Franklin feels to the "piece of their wickedness" he is trying to set right, a sort of "cruel or underhand" culture that has corrupted the world. The framing narrator, the audience for Powell and Marlow, notes that "the service of the sea and the service of the temple are both detached from the vanities and errors of a world which follows no severe rule" (32–33), an analogy that clearly allies the sea with a stable and moral worldview.

The serial version of the novel develops this contrast at even greater length in passages later cut from chapter 1 before book publication. The life at sea is "unchangeable" and "incorruptible"; moreover, "You cannot intrude passion into the exercise of seacraft, and as its perfect mastery brings no material recompense in its train it has nothing to fear from the wiles of enviousness, nor can it be made crooked by extraneous considerations tending to personal advantage" (28 January). "Theirs," he continues, "was a moral life" because "the welfare of your little world . . . depends on the faithful discharge of their trust by all the ship's company." Because "its exactions are simple and cannot be evaded or argued away," Marlow argues that "there is no room for that diversity of judgment which is the sign of insincerity and errors affecting the pursuit of the arts and trades and productions of this earth" (28 January).[11]

Seacraft thus provides escape from the crowds and the lights. It is an exacting discipline in which survival itself depends upon close communal effort and, above all, upon "the moral excellence of sea training, where [the] guiding principle is doing, not getting," and where "there are only two ways of going to work, the right way and the wrong way" (28 January). Such moral certitude and absolute truth are obviously attractive alternatives to life ashore. But this apparently stable contrast does not hold even in the serial version, where it receives its greatest elaboration. We have already seen troubled passions like Franklin's jealousy over losing his hold on the captain or Powell's attraction to Flora and his distaste for the old company's dislike of the de Barrals—life at sea becomes less than ideal in the novel. Anthony, after all, loses both his ship and his life, even though he follows "the book" to the letter. The trustworthiness and power of the ship and the absolute rule of seamanship are both compromised by events that take place or are summarized later in the novel.

Within the serial version, moreover, Powell and Marlow develop an extended analogy in which they think of transforming the world into something like the ship. Marlow laments, "It's a pity the earth is not more like a ship sent out on a voyage; it's a pity that it won't be steered or handled and navigated and kept fit to meet the dangers of space" (28 January). He muses that "it would make better men of her population if the earth were more like a ship that has got to be brought into a port of final discharge safely some day. But she isn't. She merely drifts." Marlow would like the teleology of tight cosmic plotting, firm narrative control over the unfolding of episodes, and the sense of direction and significance that comes from transcendent purpose. Unfortunately, he continues (still in the 28 January issue), "If the metaphor is to be carried on, I should say that our globe resembles rather a rudderless and unrigged hull launched haphazard upon the deep. Naturally the mob on board—you couldn't call them a ship's company, having no collective trust to keep and answer for, and nothing to do that really matters—go on fighting among themselves for the stores and the accommodation and clambering over each other for precedence." "Rudderless and unrigged," the human species is subject to the haphazard, not the well plotted. Marlow leaves the ideal of the sea far less accessible and reassuring than it seems at first.

For one thing, the "diversity of judgment" to which Marlow attributed the "insincerity and errors" of shore life is only artificially excluded at sea: "this tranquilizing view of our conduct can be distinguished with some clearness only in a world whose destiny, however humble, is practically, visibly, and sensibly dependent upon our action." Hence in both versions of the novel Marlow notes that "it's certainly unwise to admit any sort of responsibility for our actions, whose consequences we are never able to foresee" (23), a moral relativism that shows elsewhere as well, as in his disparagement of the policeman's conventional morality.

Marlow argues that "the incapacity to achieve anything distinctly good or evil is inherent in our earthly condition." The sea, rather than being a natural opposite to corrupt human culture, is instead a fragile fiction that can be preserved only under the atypical conditions of life at sea.

The novel thus defeats any attempt, by readers or by its own characters, to look to the sea for natural or transcendent values with which to draw the margins for their existential copybooks. Marlow's distinction is that, in the final metaphor of chapter 1, he is a seabird who deliberately perches on a shoreline tree: he both loves sea life and recognizes its fictional status. He sees even more, as in this passage: "The solitude of the sea intensifies the thoughts and the facts of one's experience which seems to lie at the very centre of the world, as the ship which carries one always remains the centre figure of the round horizon" (300). The sea intensifies, that is, the natural egoism of the individual in arranging "the world" around the central self. The plot of selfhood, indeed the very narrative discipline of seacraft, are functions of egoistic self-preservation (and self-creation, for that matter). Both involve positing a linear course eventuating in "a port of final discharge," a fulfillment of individual destiny justifying the journey. But at the same time that seacraft seems analogous to narrative crafting of the self, the sea also serves as a stubbornly undomesticated backdrop that dwarfs the self's pretensions.

For example, to look at Marlow's references to both sea and sky is to be disabused of any lingering romantic link between human selfhood and some sort of transcendental or teleological selfhood: "At sea, you know, there is no gallery. You hear no tormenting echoes of your own littleness there, where either a great elemental voice roars defiantly under the sky or else an elemental silence seems to be part of the infinite stillness of the universe" (326). In fact, it leads to the same sense of littleness. But the point here is that the eminently cultural distinction between "silence" and "voice" resolves into the "elemental" in a passage that is one of a long string of references to the indifference of nature.[12]

Rather than a contrast between authenticity and corruption, sea and shore become instead another version of the frustrated attempt to draw copybook margins that safely divide culture and chaos, or of the foiled efforts of narrators to set their plot line aright, or of young Powell's fall from linear innocence to labyrinthine complexity. Hence Marlow remains perched in a tree along the cultural shoreline, fascinated by the spectacle of human beings generating their fictions of order, civilization, and selfhood but struggling in the face of all that exceeds the logocentric mechanisms of the cultural process, "an object of incredulous commiseration like a bird, which, secretly, should have lost its faith in the high virtue of flying" (34).

Narrative and the Forms of Culture

Seacraft is only one of several cultural forms Marlow observes during the course of the narrative, marking both the arbitrary and the necessary aspects of these organizational fictions. That is, whether he is talking about conceptual systems, customs, or literary conventions, Marlow seems to feel that these forms of culture may be narrative fictions, but that they are also necessary for the individual to understand the experience around him. Moreover, despite their apparent differences, they are more like the multiple subplots of a novel than like categorically distinct and independent forms of discourse.

For example, a reader may discover several passages in which an almost anti-intellectual sentiment undermines the authority of any conceptual plot for order. For example, Marlow contrasts rationality and temperament: "Differences in politics, in ethics, and even in aesthetics need not arouse angry antagonism. . . . One's very conception of virtue is at the mercy of some felicitous temptation which may be sprung on one any day. All these things are perpetually on the swing. But a temperamental difference, temperament being immutable, is the parent of hate" (54). Though provoked by nothing more substantial than a difference in walking gaits between himself and Fyne, the passage nonetheless is one of those moments when Marlow hinges on the trivial an observation important to our understanding of his basic assumptions. Opinions, tastes, and morality are part of a constantly changing cultural construct that never manages to exert absolute mastery over the more basic (and noncultural?) temperament. It is as if the conceptual or thematic point of origin for narrative were instead a secondary disposition established over time by temperamental responses to whatever "felicitous temptation" happened to arise. A circumstantial narrative of responses becomes ossified as political, moral, or aesthetic philosophy and thus cut off from its nature as fiction.

Abstractions are subject to more than temperament, however; as Marlow observes, "our mental conclusions depend so much on momentary physical sensations" (56) that their supposed origin in a logical or rational realm seems a more than usually pretentious fiction (in this case it is Marlow's conclusion about character that is determined by lighting on the "stage" of the scene). In fact, he argues a bit later, "all these revolts and indignations, all these protests, revulsions of feeling, pangs of suffering and of rage, expressed but the uneasiness of sensual beings trying for their share in the joys of form, colour, sensations—the only riches of our world of senses" (62). At moments like this one,

Marlow is ready to resolve intellectual protests, personal relations, and social upheavals all into the struggle of animals in the "world of senses." The economic metaphors of "share" and "riches" allude to a Nietzschean will to power that makes a science of politics, ethics, aesthetics, or psychology more a function of that will than a means of primary insight into the nature of things themselves. Taken together, these passages suggest the degree to which rational fictions are shaped by such alogical forces as temperament, chance events, and human physiology. Determinism is much less the point here than Marlow's refusal to privilege rationality over narrative. Removing the line between the two, moreover, highlights the rationality of narrative and the narratological basis of rationality, thereby qualifying the epistemological claims of any rationally based discourse.

In any case, this distrust of reason's claims finds many echoes throughout the text. "Intelligence leads people astray" (37), presumably because they forget that this line between rationality and fiction is itself a fiction, and as Marlow observes, a "well-stocked intelligence weakens the impulse to action; an overstocked one leads gently to idiocy" (62). One would suppose that education gradually increases the number of competing potential plot lines until the individual sees no clear path before him. Marlow is willing at some points to suggest that "most sciences are farcical except those which teach us how to put things together" (152), a suggestion that seems a part of his nostalgia for the illusory certainties of practical systems like seamanship. He is also able to impress upon the framing narrator his sense of "the unreasonable complications the idealism of mankind puts into the simple but poignant problem of conduct on this earth" (325). He becomes positively gruff in contemplating "the troubles of transcendental good intentions, which, though ethically valuable, I have no doubt cause often more unhappiness than the plots of the most evil tendency" (376). Idealism and transcendentalism, and the rational systems that claim their origins in these logically insulated havens, have benefits (and are hence "valuable") for the social economy, but when they claim absolute rather than fictional status, they distort their clear lines into "unreasonable complications" as dangerous as the "most evil" forces.

This is not to say that recognizably arbitrary principles would necessarily escape unreasonableness or evil consequences, but it does coordinate with other efforts in the novel to qualify the power of philosophical abstraction as a source of narrative structure, closure, and authority. We have looked already at the passage that sees the order of signs as an unbreachable screen between the mind and experience (282–83), thereby precluding anything but semiotic fictions about that experience.

Marlow goes further in canvassing the treacheries of the theoretical, explaining at one point, for example—in a paragraph that leaves him "smiling to himself"—that "nothing is more disturbing than the upsetting of a preconceived idea. Each of us arranges the world according to his own notion of the fitness of things" (289).

Conceptual fiction may be inevitable, but it is also highly vulnerable. Indeed, this is how Marlow explains Flora's instability after her father's crash, and no doubt it accounts for much of his interest in her case: "Even a small child lives, plays and suffers in terms of its conception of its own existence. Imagine, if you can, a fact coming in suddenly with a force capable of shattering that very conception itself. . . . Luckily, people, whether mature or not mature (and who really is ever mature?), are for the most part quite incapable of understanding what is happening to them: a merciful provision of nature to preserve an average amount of sanity for working purposes in this world" (117). The egoistic conception of existence supplies the very "terms" of one's role in living. The fundamental error of confusing one's conceptual fiction with truth is nonlethal, the passage suggests, only because understanding never escapes one fiction or another long enough to see "what is happening" on the cruel and unconscious plane of natural fact. Maturity—presumably the escape from such childish fantasy—is itself an impossible fiction. One must suppose that the conceptual is an inevitably deluding but necessary strategem to achieve enough sanity "for working purposes."

Marlow elsewhere illustrates the operation and implications of this process of conceptual fictions. He distinguishes, for example, between information ("something one goes out to seek and puts away when found as you might do a piece of lead: ponderous, useful, unvibrating, dull") and knowledge (which "comes to one . . . a chance acquisition preserving in its repose a fine resonant quality") (88). The resonance of knowledge, of course, derives from the fragile tile the mind molds, paints, and fires in the imagination, a "conception of its own existence" that when sounded rings with all the harmonic qualities of a culturally attuned artifact. But as we have seen, it is vulnerable to additional chance information that may as easily shatter it as set it resonating.

Such knowledge is of course never absolute, but is only relative; one is always in the state of Marlow who, in speaking of Anthony, says that "I didn't know him so completely that by contrast I seemed to have known Miss de Barral—whom I had seen twice (altogether about sixty minutes) and with whom I had exchanged about sixty words—from the cradle so to speak" (144). Positive knowledge, in other words, is something of an illusory conception and is measured primarily not against the thing itself (an obvious impossibility) but against other subjects whose narrative coherence we have not yet constituted. Conviction comes not from the inert collection of "unvibrating" information, but from the dynamic "resonant quality" of narrative conception—knowledge.

Indeed, Marlow at times seems to chart no more than a choice between kinds of delusive fictions, one version of which comes in his (sexist) typing of male and female consciousness. Men depend upon the logocentric assumptions we have seen the novel undermine, the "well-known, well-established, I'll almost say hackneyed, illusions, without which the average male creature cannot get on" (94). Men must believe in the Western cult of egoistic mastery, whether in the form of the dutiful worker, the macho egotist, or the master of philosophical systems. By contrast, "The women's rougher, simpler, more upright judgment, embraces the whole truth, which their tact, their mistrust of masculine idealism, ever prevents them from speaking in its entirety. And their tact is unerring. We could not stand women speaking the truth. We could not bear it. It would cause infinite misery and bring about most awful disturbances in this rather mediocre, but still idealistic fool's paradise in which each of us lives his own little life" (144). This identification between idealism and the theme of egoistic fictions is the most negative moment of Marlow's distrust of the interpretive power of abstractions. But women, presumably because they have escaped the philosophical conditioning of workplace and university, perceive what idealism excludes, and therefore maintain a "secret scorn . . . for the capacity to consider judiciously and to express profoundly a meditated conclusion. . . . They have no use for these lofty exercises which they look upon as a sort of purely masculine game—game meaning a respectable occupation devised to kill time in this man-arranged life which must be got through somehow" (145).

It is, however, a game with the high stakes of sanity itself, of order, of meaning and purpose, and we have seen it played by more than men. But for Marlow, women follow a different cultural drummer: "What women's acuteness really respects are the inept 'ideas' and the sheeplike impulses by which our actions and opinions are determined in matters of real importance [i.e., matters of love, marriage, property, and so forth]" (145).[13] Women, in other words, draw more upon a cultural matrix of habits, and particularly customs and mores, than upon philosophical abstractions, and thus we find Marlow dealing with a second class of cultural form. Marlow, of course, benefits from a "composite temperament" that has in it a "small portion of 'femininity,' that drop of superior essence" that enables him to see logocentric abstraction and cultural mores as the composite workings of culture itself. That both these forms have a basic and necessary interrelationship with fiction is readily apparent, for we have already seen both at work in the self-narrating activities of the characters.

The effects of what amount to a cultural matrix of conventions are as unmistakable as one might have anticipated. For good or ill, the word of public judgment is "a sound, a mere disturbance of the air, [that] sinks into our very soul sometimes" and shapes us (264). Hence Marlow thinks Flora's suicidal impulses far more justified than she does and considers her guilt "very likely some obscure influence of common forms of speech, some traditional or inherited feeling—a vague notion that suicide is a legal crime; words of old moralists and preachers which remain in the air and help to form all the authorized moral conventions" (214). In this formulation one sees coming together philosophical or idealistic abstraction ("old moralists and preachers") and custom ("common forms of speech") to "authorize" a conventional narrative of the good life. Marlow seems for the moment to be a semiotician tracing the fictive origins of behavioral norms.

Another case in which Marlow observes idealism and custom joining to authorize behavior is the "dithyrambic phraseology for the expression of love. A man in love will accept any convention exalting the object of his passion and in this indirect way his passion itself" (234). Here the verbal patterning of the discourse of courtship is explicitly stressed, creating a narrative plot into which Flora falls, enhancing her sense of herself as the object of Anthony's passion, and into which Anthony falls as well, giving him a sense of purpose previously missing from his life. In demystifying love as primarily a form of culture Marlow goes so far as to say at one point that even "affections are, in a sense to be learned" (244).

As in the case of reason, Marlow is not arguing against custom but marking reflexively a relationship among reason, custom, and narrative so reciprocal that they seem versions of one another rather than fully distinct categories. Moreover, these cultural forms are not just options available for the consciousness to elect, but a necessary medium without which "consciousness" would not take place. Marlow, indeed, is at pains to make clear the role that literary fictions play both in the self-conceptions of his characters and in his own construction of a narrative. In one key passage explaining Powell as an observer-narrator, Marlow supposes "that to him life, perhaps not so much his own as that of others, was something still in the nature of a fairy-tale with a 'they lived happy ever after' termination. We are the creatures of our light literature much more than is generally suspected in a world which prides itself on being scientific and practical, and in possession of incontrovertible theories" (288). Hence the captain is a "prince of a fairy-tale" accountable only to "powers practically invisible and so distant, that they might well be looked upon as supernatural" like the Platonic forms or deities of the culture at large.

Powell is not the only character we find understanding himself or others in terms of light literature. Even Marlow, who after all speaks in the shadow of bookshelves (325, 350), thinks of Powell's narrative as "the sea-chapter, with such new personages as the sentimental and apoplectic chief-mate and the morose steward" (309) and Flora's life as a "tragi-comical adventure" (310). The frame narrator thinks that "this is like one of those Redskin stories where the noble savages carry off a girl and the honest backwoodsman with his incomparable knowledge follows the track and reads the signs of her fate in a footprint here, a broken twig there, a trinket dropped by the way. I have always liked such stories. Go on" (311). No doubt he has always liked them because they simulate so attractively the basic status of all the characters in the novel, himself included, trying to interpret signs into some coherent "fate" or plot. And if Powell thinks Flora "looked like a forsaken elf" and that Captain Anthony had "something African, something Moorish" like the swarthy sexual totems of a swashbuckling romance, then we have indeed further examples of characters and events perceived, conceived, and thus assimilated in terms of the "light literature" through which culture conveys its abstract beliefs and its customs.

Like light literature, popular drama also shapes the perceptions of characters in the novel, as when Marlow characterizes Flora's glance as "horrible even on the stage" (171). This is a significant example, since Marlow, not a witness, is seeking some stylized form to which he can relate Mrs. Fyne's nebulous description. Fyne, watching the departure of the governess, tells Marlow "that he was excited as if watching some action on the stage" (114), suggesting that for him, at this point, the narrative of Flora conformed to melodramatic conventions he found entertaining. Marlow thinks of Flora as in some sense a "comedian," savors the "dramatic fascination" of a scene between Flora and Mrs. Fyne, and in a confession that suggests the extent to which he all but identifies literary and real-life narrative, tells us that "as is my habit, or my weakness, or my gift, I don't know which, I visualized the story for myself. I really can't help it" (177). As we have come to see, he "can't help it" because imagining experience in scenic terms characterizes his consciousness. His three labels for this mode of perception derive from the three basic charges that a rational or logocentric mind makes against fiction: that it is an aberrant "habit" (as opposed to a purposeful—i.e., rational—pursuit); that it suffers from the "weakness" of fictionalizing rather than providing the "incontrovertible theories" of rationalism;

and that it is a rare "gift" for entertainment rather than the fundamental way of knowing.

Perhaps both the nature and the deception of literary frames is
summed up in the poet Carleon Anthony's description of his aim "to
glorify the result of six thousand years' evolution towards the refinement of thought, manners, and feelings" (38). Even Marlow cannot refrain from pointing out the arbitrariness of the time span and the failure
of the fiction of refinement to keep the poet from being a "savage sen-
timentalist," "implacable," "a terror," a man of "unforgiving selfish-
ness" (38–39). In any case, the claim that the entire history of culture
is epitomized in its aesthetic forms is a powerful polemic for bearing
down upon the exceptions, anomalies, and more obvious contradictions
of its theological, philosophical model of experience. It is no accident
that six thousand years is the literalists' biblical span for the Judeo-
Christian creation.

One also finds obvious literary shaping in Marlow's efforts to tell what
happened. Sometimes he is explicit—"we can imagine"—other times
self-assured—"we may be certain"; sometimes he simply hypothesizes
"something of that sort" and looks to see if his listener is "struck by
the absolute verisimilitude of this suggestion" (102), a notably literary
and philosophically problematic criterion. Marlow "imagines" that
Flora's watercolorist neither read nor understood the morning papers
(111), a fact obviously beyond his knowing, and when he is really rolling, he sputters that "this is no supposition. It is a fact" (159) when he
shapes an entirely hypothetical scene of courtship between Anthony
and Flora. He projects "an air of calculated discretion" onto Flora's
eyelashes (204) and depicts with conjecture entire scenes ("probably,"
"would be," "must have," together with narrated events drawn back
from outright fantasy only by question marks [206–7]). He resorts to
circumlocutions like "I thought to myself" (216), "That is it," and "I
am inclined to think that" (222), "I could imagine them" (230), "I
have the practical certitude that" (262), "and you may be sure that"
(263), and the "perhaps" and "possibly" and "may have been" of alternative versions (350). This rhetoric of fictional reconstruction, pervasive
despite the relatively strong sources Marlow has to draw upon, suggests
the inevitabiliy of fiction in any account, just as the role of light literature in the self-conceptions of his characters displaces even his sources
from any pure origin into the cultural realm of intertextuality.

To understand is thus to assimilate to preexisting narrative under-
standings. Thus Flora is celebrated as "not so much unreadable as
blank," and hence to be filled in as the narrator's needs, tastes, opinion,
temperament, and culture dictate. He can, for example, psychologize

95

freely to fill in her "blank" unconscious (as on 263f) or, less sweepingly, indulge in the "fantastic hallucination" of de Barral limping away. "Why limping? I don't know. That's how I see it. One has a notion of a maiming, crippling process; of the individual coming back [from prison] damaged in some subtle way" (352). In other words, Marlow fabricates gestures according to his narrative's need for metaphoric and thematic coherence. The element of "fantastic hallucination" in his narrative is thus an admission of the extent to which narrative constitutes the "real" it presents.

Lest we miss the conclusive role the narrator plays in shaping narrative, Marlow carries it into the "real" events—he is willing to stage scenes to produce the effects he wants. For example, Marlow is "indulging my chaffing humour," even becoming "vindictive" in order to provoke the Fynes into revealing more than they might have otherwise. He almost overplays it, in fact, producing Mrs. Fyne's exclamation "Mr. Marlow!" before he backs off and savors almost indecently the way "she had delivered herself into my hands" (149–50). He does the same thing later on by offering to go with Fyne to Captain Anthony's (191), for no other purpose, one assumes, than to witness the scene and help it along should it threaten to sag. He repeats the strategy by waiting around while Fyne goes in, then waylaying Flora and provoking *her* revelations through "murmuring by way of warning" that Mrs. Fyne has herself staged the confrontation between brother and husband. These seamen are great readers, for Marlow is no doubt like Powell, who admits that "I have a great liking for books. To this day I can't come near a book but I must know what it is about" (413). Marlow knows from reading novels what sorts of meetings make rich and revealing scenes, and he ensures that they arise.

Hence there is the potential—as we have seen between Flora and Anthony—for a good deal of mischief, or at least confusion, when a whole cast of egoistic plotters cross narrative paths, each seeking to order—mentally or otherwise—events according to conceptual prescriptions, customary courses, or literary forms. Indeed, when Marlow comments that "things are not what they seem" (201), he is not so much noting the traditional caution about the conflict between appearance and reality as backing off from the dissonance among three or more "plots" explaining Flora's hesitation to kill herself. That dissonance in itself should serve as an adequate commentary on the limitations of fiction and its cultural cousins, but we also have comments like Marlow's curious assertion that "everything may be said—indeed ought to be said—providing we know how to say it" (61). Given the theme of saying as fictionalizing, we perhaps need to see this principle not as a positivist assurance or an epistemological optimism, but as the archetypal narrator's belief that *some* technical strategem, some confluence of conventions, and some squiggle on the conceptual schematic exists that will offer hope of pulling phenomena within the narratable—if also problematic—margins of cultural comprehension.

It appears, then, that the kinds of preconceived plots provided by rational conceptions and whole systems of thought, by the customs and mores of a culture, and by the synthesis of such ideology and custom in literature all provide only the illusion of access to some stable and universal "true" order to which individuals and events may be meaningfully assimilated. Part of the poignancy of *Chance* is the fervor with which Marlow and his characters long for some sort of unmediated hold on truth or, for that matter, on each other. For example, Flora's idealization of the Victorian father nurtures her hope that if not Anthony, than at least her father loves her "for *her,* for her very own self" (380). Anthony's love is hopelessly mediated and displaced by his romantic notions of rescue and his idealistic celibacy, and hence his feelings come to her only through labyrinthine channels. But Marlow also leads us to see that "a residue of egoism remains in every affection—even paternal" (371), and that de Barral is ruthless in trying to force his daughter to cross over from her story line into his own. Early on, young Powell resists the fundamental cultural temptation to form "theories about facts" (261), hoping for some direct and thus authentic relation to experience, but we see that this temptation too cannot be resisted without sinking into idiocy and ineffectualness, and that he is helpless to resist the codified role of the knight when it presents itself to him. And when Marlow, at the end of the novel, belies all he has said about "light literature" and the follies of mere sentiment to stage manage an appropriate finale to his narrative view of things—the engagement of Powell and the widowed Flora—we have perhaps the ultimate demonstration of the individual's striving to manipulate chance and culture into narrative closure.[14] One may, it seems, long for and need such closure, may indeed be unable to think and act without it, and at the same time mark reflexively its groundlessness except as a useful and, if one is fortunate, satisfying fiction.

Order and Chance

There is a danger, however, in thinking of the relation between "reality" or "experience" and the logocentric order of narrative in purely adversarial terms; such a conception seems to repeat the culture's classic stress

97

upon mastery, upon the struggle between binary opposites, and upon understanding as somehow reconciling an abstract order with phenomena. Certainly, as we have seen, the novel displays its characters engaged, actually or conceptually, in such adversarial struggles, and it leads its readers to repeat such roles in the larger cultural drama. But there are moments, as one might expect in a reflexive narrative circling relentlessly its grounds and structures, when this simpler, heroic version of the character-narrator assimilating chaos into creation is set next to something different.

That something different involves the relation between narrative coherence and what the novel alludes to as chance, incertitude, the unknown, or the infinite; and attempting its expression implicates one in the most persistent of dilemmas. On the one hand, narrative or cultural order is a linear clarity imposed arbitrarily on nonlinear experience. Hence narrative, or any other version of cultural discourse, cannot bring the noncultural within the cultural margins: they are too straight and narrow. At the same time, however, the very drawing of those margins imposes a cultural order or at least a positioning upon what is only apparently beyond those margins—just designating it "beyond" gives it a place within a cultural frame of reference, gives it a word ("chance") by which we designate it. One would think, however, that the "other" of culture, whatever it might be, would be beyond even the capacity to designate it "beyond." Or to put the question teasingly, since this "other" is required in order to mark the margin of culture, just as two properties must be present to mark a boundary line, either we can draw that margin, in which case the "other" would be present and knowable and hence not really "other," or we cannot draw such a margin, in which case notions of boundaries or categories, of culture and "other," are all part of a fundamental cultural mythology. Since the first of these options is clearly nonsensical, the second must hold, in which case the task is to become aware of that deceptive maneuver by which culture exiles into an imaginary "other" those elements of its own experience it chooses to deny, and then effaces the decree of exile, naturalizing such a proscription into the "nature" of things.

Chance is remarkable in that it records Conrad's effort to make Marlow his means of pushing into this dilemma for traditional logic. Ultimately, so reflexive a question takes us to the very heart of the cultural process, and Conrad seems to have reached this extreme point of reference via three themes that have become increasingly familiar to contemporary theorists:

1. demystifying the remnant of transcendental metaphysics inherent in the opposition of void and presence,
2. exploring the implications of metaphor's omnipresence in discourse, and
3. recognizing the ultimate place of narrative as the constitutive paradigm of culture itself.

Taken together, these three themes begin to propose an understanding of "the narrator's relation to his material" fundamentally different from that which has shaped the largely rhetorical perspective of our narrative theory. *Chance,* that is, seems to call out for a complete redefinition of what this critical question really asks.

We can begin our approach to these difficult questions by noting how casually Marlow can, on occasion, collapse the binary logic characteristic of Western thought. In a passage not found in the book version (though, interestingly enough, left in the Yale manuscript that was meant to be the American edition), Marlow speculates upon the primal hope he perceives at the base of Anthony's "generous" proposal to Flora:

> How much hope there was in it besides—it is hard to say? No man can live without it any more than a fish can live out of the water. It pervades like subtly vivifying fluid the nooks and crannies of all our sentiments. The rashest counsels of despair contain something of it, for no man is certain that there is rest to be found anywhere in or out of the world. (25 May)

Hope for these forms of "rest" or completion, whether that rest is physical, psychological, philosophical, or narrative, is the very element of our being, the "vivifying fluid" of our emotions, the inspirational adulterant of our most despairing mix of attitudes. But the syntax of the final phrases is curious in its effect upon the meaning of the statement. One would almost expect another negative with the final verb (i.e., no man is certain there is *no* rest), "for" if one is not sure nihilism is true, then one need not despair utterly. But "if no man is certain that there *is* rest," then hope, like despair, thrives upon suspended rather than positive knowledge. Both, that is, are the same feeling of uncertainty that there is any positive meaning ("rest") in our lives.

Marlow seems to be beyond any expectation that one could "rest" intellectually upon the sort of positive knowledge that faith and nihilism both require. But the passage suggests more than a modest skepticism about the limits of our knowledge. If, that is, hope and despair are coequal functions of cultural mythology, then we have only an illusory difference between dwelling hopefully within the cultural margins of order and plunging despairingly into a "void" imagined to exist beyond those margins. Each, rather, is a variation upon the same fiction posited where Marlow would have remained suspended about such questions, preferring instead to lay out more limited fictions about individuals. Hence we do not have a line safely dividing metaphysical territory into binary simplicity; rather, we have a "chance" insight into the alogical complexity by which presence and void, order and chance, center and disintegration are the means by which logocentric law includes within itself the outlawed it appears to exclude. Like hope and despair, each of these oppositions emerges out of the absoluteness of its antonymical relations within the cultural myth and imposes a fictional line upon the nonverbal continuum. The separate realms on which each seems based— the presence (within which are truth, order, logic, fulfillment) and the void—are, as J. Hillis Miller had argued, features of the same figure, the walls and spaces of our logocentric labyrinth.[15]

Hence both the copybook margins are culturally defined. Marlow's efforts illustrate not the process of bringing the noncultural into the cultural record, but that of tracing and retracing the narrative linearity by which both the comfortably plotted (and thus foreseen) and the discomfiting events of chance and the nonrational are defined within that cultural structure so aptly figured by the labyrinth. Marlow often feels as if he were on the verge between the cultural and the void—that he operates, in the famous image from *Heart of Darkness,* in the haze of insight surrounding the hollow kernel of truth. But both that haze and the hollowness, indeed the "void" for which they are figures, may be like the typographical convenience of margins on the page and blank spaces between words and lines. It is, after all, "between the lines" that the critic works, just as it is the "blank" of Flora's mind that attracts Marlow's interest.[16]

Marlow's repetition of the narrative act by which new lines trace outward in reflecting precedent and assumption is not entirely dissimilar to the "recession of centers" Perry Meisel traces in *Heart of Darkness,* a pattern of apparently "grounded reality" turning into mere "representation of itself."[17] For Meisel it is more specifically language than narrative that omnivorously consumes grounds and realities, though the linguistic medium of narrative and the linearity of syntax supply a good case for absorbing them both into the analogical paradigms we have found. And J. Hillis Miller's influential study of *Lord Jim,* focusing upon metaphors of darkness and light, reaches a kindred conclusion:

No one of them is the original ground, the basis on which the others may be interpreted. *Lord Jim* is like a dictionary in which the entry under one word refers the reader to another word which refers him to another and then back to the first word again, in an endless circling; and Marlow sitting in his hotel room ceaselessly writing letters by the light of a single candle while Jim struggles with his conscience and the thunderstorm prepares in the darkness outside may be taken as an emblem of literature in its paradoxical relation to a nonverbal "reality" it seeks both to uncover and to evade in the creation of its own exclusively verbal realm.[18]

The metaphor one expects to find piercing to and partaking of the full essence of truth is instead in the "endless circling" of an orbit within the semiotic, depending ballistically upon the balance between the force of its own verbal trajectory and the gravitational pull of an imagined center it never reaches.

The work of both Meisel and Miller cues us to the second means by which we can approach Conrad's most challenging line of thought. Metaphor is an unavoidable topic at this point because of its central trait of disrupting any effort to achieve denotative, referential, or literal purity.[19] Metaphor makes unavoidable in thought a degree of figurative language, and therefore of fiction, and a degree of diacriticity since it disperses meaning beyond the "referent" to the matrixes of cultural associations within which both metaphor and referent take on whatever meaning they can have. Hence equally inevitable is a degree of that impurity of the alogical by which, through the figurative and the diacritical, the meaning of something becomes bound up in and a part of its apparent contrary, even if that contrary is supposed to be the "other" of culture itself, as in a highly crafted novel about chance.

To watch metaphor in *Chance* is to observe how its operation is congruent with narrative, a fact not surprising since metaphor essentially is a mininarrative projected behind a surface to explain how such an appearance came to be. Metaphor, that is, means not by embodying a consubstantial essence of its referent but by "narratizing" it. To describe the morning when Flora must return to de Barral's cousin as most resembling "the morning of an execution" (171), or to describe her as his "passive victim, quivering in every nerve, as if she were flayed" (164), is to constitute narrative explanations, not simply to name static traits. Metaphor shares more with narrative (and cultural discourse in general) than making meaning through a subject's place along a causal plot line. It also is very obviously fictional, arbitrary, and inadequate in its comprehension of that subject. These points are familiar enough not to detain us here, but in the examples above it is not exactly "true" that

Flora was flayed, except in one sense chosen arbitrarily from a number of possible codings, none of which are comprehensive in imaging her relationship to the de Barral cousins.

In any case, all these "disruptive" aspects of metaphor wreak the sort of havoc with the discourse of law and order now made familiar by deconstruction. The novel points reflexively to this phenomenon through the proliferation of violent metaphors like those associated with Flora. Predictably enough, metaphor emulates the plot of the larger narrative, as when Anthony's enthusiasm for his self-sacrifice in the marriage is described as "a special sort of exaltation which seemed to take him by the throat like an enemy" (339), a metaphor that becomes all but fact as de Barral attempts, like an enemy, to get a deadly poison down the captain's throat.[20] More important, however, these violent metaphors introduce the epitome of disorder into the heart of Marlow's effort to achieve a rational order based upon the familiar logics of identity and causality. Violence far beyond cultural prescriptions is a tool for organizing a linear order for events, just as events like Powell's voyeurism, de Barral's murder attempt and suicide, and Anthony's drowning become conventional and necessary steps in the causal chain whose end point is the upcoming marriage of Powell and Flora. This degree of suffusion into order by its contrary may well imply that the exiled elements were never really gone in the first place. As one attempts however subtly to glimpse beyond the cultural page, what one sees are the other leaves of the Western text. Indeed, order in any conventional discourse perhaps depends upon some appropriate violence to provide slope and velocity to its narrative line, a violence correlative with the act of constituting any form of order.

Hence one finds many marks of the alleged "other" within this novel about chance and understanding. Certainly its characters frequently falter in the struggle to define fully the causal coherence that seems the essential narrative logic. Indeed, the number of times the plot "hits" or "misses" purely because of chance makes very difficult the effort at that kind of definition, a difficulty that is often shown by characters' amazement that the illusion of coherence persists even when all effort at explanation fails. Powell, for one, is still struck by the way chance seems to create this illusion, for near the end of his tale to Marlow "he proceeded to call my [Marlow's] attention to the wonderful linking up of small facts with something of awe left yet, after all those years, at the precise workmanship of chance, fate, providence, call it what you will!" (411). The grammatical equation of Christianity (providence), pagan determinism (fate), and strict secularism (chance) is a good gauge to Marlow's sophistication in comparison with Powell's wonder; Marlow recognizes all three as permutations of the causality and often the teleology that logocentrism imposes, for even "chance" becomes a description of a mechanical causative network that accommodates the never quite entirely raw material of experience to Western frameworks. [21]

Indeed, the equation of chance with providence all but implies the principle of void or disorder as the most fully defined "center" of our cultural history—God himself. Chance is both the puzzle to coherence and the heart of its order. On the one hand it arouses our skepticism, since chance seems an alogical category that cannot fit our causal lines of explanation. But when chance *is* the explanation, institutionalized as the operative principle, it is a first cause, a prime mover, and inverts the classic oppositions of reliable/unreliable, truth/fiction, rational discourse/imaginative narrative, order/chaos. If the second term is the empty center of the logocentric hull, then the cultural craft's buoyancy depends upon the very cluster of normally "pejorative" terms in this list. [22]

What emerges in this discussion of a reflexive demystification of metaphysics, metaphor, and narrative order is a profound insight into the nature of narrative. At one marvelously reflexive moment Marlow catches himself and questions his own acceptance of these forms of coherence. When Fyne tells him of the "elopement" Marlow pauses, and in recalling the scene he tells his own listener, "And suddenly I became still more surprised at myself, at the way I had somehow taken for granted things which did appear queer when one thought them out" (67). Such a faculty of curiosity not only is what breaks down Marlow's resistance to Fyne's revelations (48), but is for the framing narrator "the most respectable faculty of the human mind—in fact, I cannot conceive the uses of an incurious mind. It would be like a chamber perpetually locked up" (40). As this is a novel about people trying to emerge from closure—Flora from her drawing-room childhood, de Barral from prison, Powell from the labyrinthine dungeon of the shipping offices, Marlow and Anthony from the captain's cabin into the world, and narrators through reflexivity from narrative banality—we can take a locked chamber as a metaphor for the Western mind, opened by curiosity to attempt a survey of the territory beyond the margins. There is, of course, no escape from those margins—not because the territory beyond is unreachable, but because its place is already composed, however secretly, within those margins. That is, the reflexive energies of *Chance* penetrate the conventional pretense to impose order, and the even more deeply shrouded pretense that order is purely opposed to disorder or chance, and this even while the novel's other energies lay out a narrative so conventionally representational as to lead back around into the romance of damsels and knights that Conrad's subtitles for the sections of the novel suggest. Exploring the apparent anomalies of incertitude, chance, and the infinite beyond the cultural vessel does not take the culture into alien territory beyond logocentric assumptions, but it does show how those assumptions prescribe a narrative project in which allusions to that internal but suppressed territory are woven into a fiction of the whole.

The courage of *Chance* in sounding the analogical echoes among metaphysics, selfhood, marriage, society, language, and narrative makes the novel a valuable study of what we mean by the relation of the narrator to his material. More than the peripheral activity of one art form far from the center of thought and commerce, the narrative act becomes the paradigmatic operation of Western consciousness. Reconciling the anomalous, testing the conventions, restoring the margins are essential trials for the more skeptical of the novel's knights, Marlow, but so are the reflexive tasks of edging along the "void" fenced into our metaphysical domain. The framing narrator, himself a wise skeptic, thinks of Marlow perched on the branch of a tree "like a bird, which, secretly, should have lost its faith in the high virtue of flying" (34) rather than taking off for his "true element," the sea. Considering that it is professional seamanship that represents the most rigid attempt in the novel to constitute cultural discipline, it is no wonder that Marlow perches uneasily, that he should seem to have lost "faith in the high virtue" of so simplistic a sense of that culture.

A master narrator, he sees the common fictional ground of both narrative and culture at large, and he senses that the individual stands on that ground not only to assimilate chance experiences into his own mental and psychological order, but to help perpetuate the cultural sanity—"for working purposes"—by balancing the causality and the chance at its heart. Hence he cannot sail off naively into the sunset of the cultural romance to which he leaves the hopelessly more innocent Powell and Flora. The equivocal poise of Marlow is nowhere better reflected than in his final willingness to accompany the couple to church: "Hang it all, for all my belief in Chance I am not exactly a pagan." Not exactly a Christian either, Marlow senses that the primal relation of the narrator to his art is like a vessel alone upon seas of infinitely fluid cultural materials. The skillful sailor weaves wind, wave, and ship into the pure pleasure of forward progress and the practical matter of survival, even if, as Marlow muses in reflecting upon the metaphor, our ship was "launched haphazard" rather than having "a port of final discharge" that would satisfy the most simply phrased linear dream of logocentric craft.

Conrad and Early Modernism

Narrative, as we have seen, can manage philosophical or existential anxiety by establishing margins, labeling menaces as a means of partly taming them, inventing a logic of roles and reasoning that directs ordinary existences in a more or less comfortably plotted collective novel. At the same time, however, reflexivity opens two complementary fronts with the ideological implications of that directorial function. The first is to indicate the extent to which economically motivated anxieties are a major determinant of the narratization of chance into a tale (by both characters and narrators). More generally, however, the etching of that reflexive circuit cuts all the way down to the basic economic order as itself a dominant protonarrative. As such, it affects the metaphysical components we have traced in Conrad; selfhood becomes a product the individual must manufacture, nature is a force or object to be understood and used, and human community is a hierarchical structure dedicated to efficient and orderly productivity. Even when humane values are sought out in shaping that productivity, other structures like the economic suffuse the definitions of, say, selfhood; or in the less direct workings of ideology, the linear causality of agent and intentional force serves to mask the diacritical causality of a cultural system in which the organizing power of economic reality is everywhere at work. It is to be found, for example, in the aesthetic drive to reify every element within a novel's expanse into a unit productive of a single thematic end, making the novel a machine in which every part derives its worth not intrinsically but in terms of the surplus thematic value inhering in the production of meaning by the novel as a whole. Like a worker, each narrative element is both structurally essential and individually expendable. The novel's typical formal energies, that is, have sought to enact the degree and kind of hyperorganization of the narrative world that socioeconomic systems have attempted in all material and cultural forms.

Reflexivity's play is still productive, of course, since the narrative mode of production is far too overdetermined by a multitude of forces for any single work to exceed. But that play can nonetheless suffice to reveal those overdeterminations both at the micro level of specific anxieties and historical elements in a given work and at the macro level of the genre's form. It may not be possible to separate fully human instincts for form from culturally conditioned needs, since as the Lacanians tell us we are always already inserted in medias res in existing discourse. But in looking all around itself, (reflexive) narrative not infrequently suggests ways it functions both like and for the means by which capitalism structures thought and action. Jameson's analysis of the political unconscious, in other words, is precisely what this side of reflexivity initiates.

In *Chance,* for example, the "marginal" position occupied by Marlow, as by young Powell, is partly so for economic reasons. Their equal fascination with the content of the story is a function of the similarity in their positioning on the tenuously empowered margins of the economic structure (that is, their "power" depends upon pure performance rather than upon innate qualities or, better yet, ownership in that structure). Moreover, the difference in their comprehension of that story derives from Marlow's having already worn through (as in "Youth") the way plots cover over the ulteriority of cultural motives. As we have seen, the long and for some tedious and only partly relevant opening of the novel has to do with the difficulty a young captain faces in getting a position. The establishment keeps a closed shop, and for him to catch on to a command takes a special entrée in which professional ethics are bent a bit. The lesson, then, is that no possibility exists for a profession or material rewards unless one submits to the hierarchy, exchanging the idealistic plot of a meritocracy for the initiation rites of a fraternity. This scenario is a precise repetition of the opening of *Heart of Darkness,* in which Marlow himself gains his entrance to professional standing only through his aunt's influence and wields power after landing in the Congo on the basis of his superior's exaggerated sense of that influence. Indeed, that whole novel is an investigation not just of the human heart or of imperialism, but of capitalism itself. Kurtz's mission in the upcountry is to carry out the agenda of reification in which ivory, natives, both European and African cultural rites, missionary zeal, and even the love of an indigenous beauty all become instruments for producing wealth. Surely a part of "the horror" is the discovery of the capitalist's willingness to "exterminate the brutes," a two-stage process in which humans are first reduced to brutish ciphers in a ledger and then canceled as a sunk cost.

The parallel between economic and narrative stances is suggestive, for both confront a labyrinth of conventions and deceptions, both require subjection to an existing order, both channel energies toward a specific form of production, both allow "making sense" within a predefined set of possibilities. Beneath what reflexivity tells us about narrative is what it tells us about more fundamental cultural processes that condition, among other things, narrative. Hence if Kurtz narratizes the Congo along capitalist lines, Marlow performs an equal violence in normalizing Kurtz for the Intended, even if restaging it all for the group of listeners serves as an act of partial contrition that notes those moments when the narrative program snags on the passion of a native girl in *Lord Jim* or the nature of a lie in *Heart of Darkness*. Such moments force repressed contradictions to the surface in ways that etch the labyrinthine pattern of cultural processes and the complex interrelations among its various spheres or levels.

In *Chance* another one to watch is de Barral, the financier. The narrative of thrift and virtue he stages in his advertising and public image is built with the same aesthetic devices as Marlow's tale. Words circulate as things in the realist's economy, point of view arrogates a semiotic space in which is constituted the illusion of power and authority over that circulation, and plot and the attendant thematic payoff function like projections of interest earnings attracting readers' investments. Both can be highly productive narrative systems unless reflexive analyses within the text "overdo" exposure or auditors publish the sum total of bad loans made by the bank. But both also publish, in part by their exaggeration of the naturalized mechanics of the norm, the conventions and assumptions through which they take place. The density of narrative artifice in *Chance* foregrounds, as we have seen, much about the nature of narrative. Similarly, de Barral's practice differs from the commercial norm more in degree than in kind, shifting resources from the ordinary to the privileged citizen by means of the power produced by institutions and concentrated capital. A bank is no more candid than de Barral about the proportions in which its profits from depositors are distributed, and one bailed out by tax-supported insurance is no less likely than de Barral to obscure its impending insolvency. It is no accident that the companies he founded were the Orb and the Sceptre, signs of the imperial sovereign sanctioning such an eminently capitalist enterprise as banking. Something less than approval of this paradigmatic enterprise is indicated, since all of his relationships involved misplaced trust and victimization. His customers trusted him and were victimized; he succumbed to deception and was victimized by the con artists who approached him with capital ventures; he and Flora both trusted the governess, an economic dependent who saw the relationship unsentimentally as a cash proposition to be exploited for profit. The obvious point is that reified relations victimize, and capitalism, it seems, requires such relations as its modus operandi.

The desire for a fiction less predictable than mystery stories and for a society less dominated by capitalist structures is the sort of utopian ideal attempted within *Chance*. Part of the spectacle of Flora and Anthony's relationship is that it at least attempts to take place outside the economic margins. They break the taboo of the merchant marine against wives aboard ship, choosing to humanize an environment and maintain a relationship—choices that productivity has little use for. Their relationship begins out of anything but economic self-interest, as an antidote, in fact, to the spinsterhood that Flora's economic disgrace and lack of dowry might impose and to the bachelorhood that professional seamanship imposes upon Anthony and Marlow. It consists early on of a desperate and self-sacrificial effort to overcome the damage wrought by the economic forces that roll over Flora in the form of her father's disaster. Indeed, it is difficult to imagine how their relations would ever have overcome the bizarre estrangement of the early going had de Barral's killing himself not canceled out the domination and paternalism he had internalized from his immersion in the capitalist mainstream. That is a rather drastic remedy for capitalism, a sardonic reversal of Kurtz's advice to "exterminate the brutes." But the lack of verbal or physical communication between Flora and Anthony in that early going is an equally drastic portrayal of the effects economic forces can have upon that most biological form of community humans strive for. That Anthony, once canceled by the hazards of his profession, is replaced by Powell may, moreover, suggest the extent to which marital relations share with the machine an interchangeability of parts within the general design specifications of the mechanism.

Perhaps it is no wonder, in the final analysis, that characters in this novel struggle so desperately to deal with the dual demons of chance and the economic. The fierce conformity of the Fynes is perhaps a function of their fear of the chance to which one is exposed if one steps out of the roles and beliefs prescribed and sanctioned by one's culture. Part of that fear is economically motivated; if the idea of reification includes the usefulness of codes of respectability in keeping class factions more or less homogeneous, then to introduce the other of heterogeneity is to imperil the payoff to one's niche in the machinery of production. Mrs. Fyne wishes to keep her social round, Mr. Fyne his job. The thoroughness with which the Anthonys subscribe to various scripts from popular narratives is in part their effort to restructure their lives in a way that seems safer from the effects of chance, but it is also a way that seems more human to them than the reified relations that hold them in place early in the novel. One horror lies in that zone of chance beyond the metaphysical organum of traditional thinking; its complement is the emptiness and alienation produced by the element of chance inhering in the economic Darwinism of free enterprise, one in which corporate and institutional species survive red in competitive tooth and exploitative claw, and as much at the expense of individuals failing a certain kind of fitness as in any Disney pathos of sickly or newborn antelopes pulled down by the carnivore floor supervisors of natural production.

In the Victorian novel, then, what is inescapable is the attempt to forge a middle-class voice amid the cacophony of textual strands through which that class consciousness was emerging, an attempt that navigates the troublesome line between the desire for an authentic and originary self on the one hand and, on the other, the dispersion of any such self into the textual strands of which it is woven. In this early modernist novel we find something of a shift to what is, in one sense, the logical question to follow that earlier effort. If, that is, one does emerge with a body of texts negotiating a culturally accepted resolution of those issues, then one is obliged to test the power of that resolution to indeed contain the forces contending against its dominion over all the chances that surprise the regularities, consistencies, and coherences for which Victorian fiction strives. In the previous chapter I suggested that few of the works we most respect from the nineteenth century are uncritical of the resolutions they work to achieve, and in this chapter I might well suggest that such is equally the case of the reflexive questions posed by early modernist narratives.

For example, much of James's work studies the intersection between individual consciousness and experience, an intersection regulated by the copybook expectations each character brings to its experience. John Marcher's mistake is to read his life as the *wrong* kind of popular fiction—it might have developed comfortably enough within the domain of the domestic sentimental novel. He prefers, however, a different sentimental strain we might call the pathos of catastrophe. As an egoist with no real productive role to play, he compensates by projecting his stoic endurance in the face of the beast; his beast, though, is precisely the history that leaves him irrelevant and unanointed for the larger role his egoism yearns to fill. He readies himself to contain the catastrophic chance within the heroic fortitude to endure a naturalist novel, a role that gives shape and purpose and (at least at a personal level) legitimacy to his privileged leisure. Lambert Strether and indeed nearly all of James's sensitive egoists face much the same dilemma. Social privilege insulates them from the demystifying power of history; lacking Marlow's fortuitously located perspective on the social and economic margins of culture, they are mistaken and frequently injured in their contacts with those who live a different novel. How close Isabel Archer comes to understanding human experience is itself problematic; she at least comes to sense something of the conventions of the sophisticated European novel of intrigue. Whether Lambert Strether does finally understand the realities of Mme de Vionnet or Maria Gostrey is less certain than that he grasps his own exteriority to their respective narrative constructions, and thereby the fact—if not the correction—of his misreadings.

These misreadings, these cultural plots displacing any more direct reading of history, function as the confines of subjectivity in James. But seen reflexively, they also function within a negative dialectic in which any particular plot is critiqued and by which the network of plots constituting the characters' collective life is shown to have a lack. Lest this appear detached from a discussion of reflexivity, let me make it clear that the repeated failures of James's characters to master the materials of their "lives" as fully as the realistic program appears to ordain, and the pervasiveness and inescapability of code systems colliding in the novel of manners frame James so thoroughly transcends, all function to turn us back around the narrative circuit a second and third time, once to see what is happening on the micro level of individual characters and again to step back and observe the macro level of narrative itself as practiced by James. At the micro level, the plot network serves as a conceptual Valium settling everything, provisionally, until it wears off under the stress of the history the characters take part in. At the macro level of narrative, the individual cases in which narratives constitute subjects correspond to the function both of the novel genre in creating a certain kind of consciousness and of the full range of reified cultural forms in constituting the spaces, with attendant powers, privileges, and responsibilities, within which such subjects may operate. James's works embrace this process as it generates the cultural lives of author and character, but also as, reflexively, it works to trace the less apparent, ideologically charged channels of those lives.

Hence Marlow's obsessions with culturally posited margins and their fraying at the edges of history are, in fact, of a piece with the agenda for modernism encouraged by Conrad's "mentor." These obsessions are indeed a form of that recurrent spectacle in Faulkner's fiction of characters struggling to impose narrative mastery upon their own or others' experience. Partly, as John Irwin argues, this struggle is a way of compensating for their inability to master highly charged psychological relations, particularly the father/son dynamics of the Sutpens and the Compsons.[23] In this sense, then, Faulkner's narrators may have a greater sense of urgency, their sanity more visibly frayed than that of the dignified suicides like Brierly or the leisurely Marlovian narrators, but they all occupy the same position at the limits of the culture's ability to assimilate into a reassuring narrative the elements of chance in experience.

Both novelists, that is, seem engaged with the founding problem of narrative as an epistemological category that seeks to know and to domesticate what lies beyond the ken of prevailing views, at the same time that, as a strategy of containment, it seeks to repress the contradictions between the power of social forms and the force of desire. The struggle to contain the threats and contradictions implicit in experience is an attempt to achieve an enabling power over what menaces one's equanimity, whether that power appears in terms that are psychological, as for the Quentin of *Absalom, Absalom!,* emotional as for the brothers in *The Sound and the Fury,* or aesthetic as for the modernist like James, who discerns and valorizes what he would like to believe is his own figure in the experiential carpet.

But it is also, of course, a limited power, for the power to domesticate exists, as we have seen, in an uneasy harmony with the results of that drive to know. It is the latter that keeps turning up the reflexive loose ends of the cultural line on experience. On a very obvious level, the struggle's difficulties are signaled by the inescapable facts that Quentin is soon dead and that the narratives of the Compson brothers fail to compensate them for the parental "style" to which they have all been exposed or for the loss of Caddy. At the level of individual experience, history lies impervious to narrative except in the minds of true believers. For those like the Compson brothers, caught in the contradictions between various codes (with their implicit promise to transcend chance and change) and personal and social realities far from the models presupposed by their ideals, history can only appear menacing. Jason knows he is closed out economically once fraternal status in the banking world is denied him—the stock and commodities markets are rigged for insiders, retail business depends upon far more massive investments than his family can provide, and even real estate is a financial drain unless one can, as he finally does, liquidate it. Benjy experiences a different form of exclusion, of course, one contingent upon the genetic chance of his retardation. What he discovers, however, is a social version of the economic shop upon which Jason looks so enviously from the outside; because of his idiocy he loses his mother, his sexuality, and finally even his limited mobility, drastic sacrifices for a society having little use for nonproductive members. It is significant, perhaps, that he is given no voice to protest, only a wail to mourn the intransigence of a culture increasingly organized to discipline and normalize rather than nurture.

All three of the brothers' "narratives" make their way without naming the full range of forces with which they contend, a disability that shows us not only the epistemolgoical limitations of narrative, but also some of the historical grounds that occasion those limitations. Benjy

111

names, in his way, the absent Caddy, in whom are concentrated the personal relations from which he is excluded, but he can indicate nothing about the social themes his case implies; Jason, on the other hand, names the economic theme insistently, but only obliquely points toward the poverty of his emotional life from childhood on, perhaps mandated by his preoccupations with economic relations. Quentin, of course, focuses explicitly upon the abstract schema by which his culture has equipped him, poorly as it turns out, to organize experience. But he lacks the emotional directness of Benjy and the socioeconomic preoccupations of Jason and hence, like his brothers, embodies a repertoire of narratizing tools that is itself incomplete. The Compsons, of course, live by an ethos suited, perhaps, to a mode of production characterized by the plantation and by intense concentrations of wealth—wealth that in the case of the three brothers might well have seen them through at least some of their afflictions, not to mention Caddy's. But the industrial capitalism that has replaced the agrarian economy treats blue blood like black, forcing to the surface for Jason, and perhaps in oblique or displaced forms for his brothers, the contradictions underlying both cultures between which they find themselves being steadily ground down. Hence they occupy positions as marginal as Marlow's, being outside one culture historically and another economically—but without Marlow's saving capacity to take flight or to see however confusedly the relationship between the individual as narrator and the material he or she seeks to assimilate.

Jake Barnes, "unmanned" in his wartime effort to shape history, certainly has no illusions about narrative. In the urban centers the various narrative efforts to contain history stack up like books on the shelf; we see folk ritual, Catholicism, Cohn's adventure novel, the Parisian avant-garde artiste, the sentimental romance Frances would like to climax with the requisite wedding, the encapsulated historical narratives of anti-Semitism and class privilege, the decadent saga of the sexual picaro, and the androgynous rock star potency of Pedro Romero. To recover from the stress of all these cultural narratizations colliding, Jake chooses his own myth of immersion in the primal waters of seas and trout streams. He seeks there to reawaken some "natural" rhythm that would counter the hollowed conventions of a generation "lost" without a narrative master code its members might harmoniously share. At the same time, one cannot escape a complementary dimension of this malaise. That is, the "lost" cast of The Sun Also Rises consists of those who live in exile from their native culture. Some are like Jake, economically dependent upon his ability to package experience for media consumption; some are the privileged and sensitive sufferers of the Jamesian tradition, considerably more decadent, but still looking for some sensation by which they can restore vitality and wisdom to lives emptied of function or necessity; some are like Pedro or the would-be matadors of the punningly titled "Capital of the World," channeled toward the glamorous wealth of spectacle by the poverty and boredom of the provincial underclass. It would be difficult to say which predominates—the economic and historical lostness or that resulting from the exhaustion of persuasiveness in those (narrative) codes "lost" by the drifters in Hemingway's fiction. For many readers the muscular rites of Jake, Nick, or "Papa" himself (in the media narrative so skillfully generated) seem a primal antidote to the threadbare and effete culture depicted in the fiction, as if one could indeed write oneself off that cultural page of *Chance* into existential authenticity.

Such a reading suggests, of course, that one *can* know and master experience in ways not prescribed by culture and co-opted by its economic forces. But Jake's last line, perhaps the best closing of any novel, gives no quarter to illusions about either mastering or knowing. That is, to the primordial desire for an adequate closure to the jagged pieces of history, to Brett's last wavering hope for narrative mastery and the fulfillment of desire, Jake responds not with a metaphysical *nada* or a naive Nobelian affirmation, but with the bitterly icy side of Jamesian aestheticism: "Isn't it pretty to think so?"

It is pretty, of course, only if one can believe with the pure devotion seen only in the naïveté of the Intended, one who is married to conventions. For most of the period's protagonists, awareness of the relation between the narrating self and the material it seeks to contain produces much pain and disillusionment and, at best, a heightened reflexive sense of how history eludes narratives at either the micro or macro level. How else could one describe the cast of *The Great Gatsby* except as falling through the gap between myth and history? In myth there are mobility, character, and completion; in history there are economic class, codes, and desire. Indeed it is far from innovative in Fitzgerald studies to dwell upon the relation between narrative and historical realities, though the radical implications of that relation are not always spelled out. When a narrator questions "the use of doing great things if I could have a better time telling her what I was going to do" (150), then we are faced with the outright replacement of history by narrative, a pattern that recurs often in the novel. Nick complains of "some garrulous man telling over and over what had happened, until it became less and less real even to him and he could tell it no longer" (156), as if history had been packaged in narrative until finally consumed and discarded.

Certainly Daisy is a case in point of the character unwilling to see history without an intervening narrative. We are told that "her artificial world was redolent of orchids and pleasant, cheerful snobbery and orchestras which set the rhythm of the year, summoning up the sadness and suggestiveness of life in new tunes" (151). She likes an artifice that gives her social privilege, leisure, and luxuries; she appreciates something as commercial as popular music with its trendy "new tunes" going so far as to "set the rhythm of the year," a task some might reserve for nature itself. But it is precisely the inability of the artifice to maintain the illusion of mastery that accounts for both the "sadness" of chance and mortality and the "suggestiveness" of something that might be more vital than an "artificial world." It is of interest that these lines precede the famous passage in which Daisy passes beyond the loose hold Gatsby's memory has over her:

> Through this twilight universe Daisy began to move again with the season; suddenly she was again keeping half a dozen dates a day with half a dozen men, and drowsing asleep at dawn with the beads and chiffon of an evening dress tangled among the dying orchids on the floor beside her bed. And all the time something within her was crying for a decision. She wanted her life shaped now, immediately—and the decision must be made by some force—of love, of money, of unquestionable practicality—that was close at hand. (151)

She moves, that is, in that oddly lit universe in which so many of Conrad's figures shift across our view. Moreover, the season to which she moves is ambiguously signaled on the one hand by "beads and chiffon," figures for the artificial world that in their unity and permanence signal the stability of fulfillment she misses. On the other hand, of course, are "dying orchids" that represent the threat of time and history. She wants to possess something of their natural elegance while remaining immune to their decay. Hence on the philosophical level she wants "decision" and a life that is "shaped," the order and conviction of a narrative ethos that will sustain her in the face of the chance that menaces the vulnerable individual. But she also wants "love" that is guarded by "money" and "unquestionable practicality," nonnarrative elements that provide economically the power that mere myth cannot maintain. On the strength of that class allegiance, Daisy survives.

Gatsby, of course, does not, for his choice is that other of mythic narrative. When he tries to share with Nick his own conclusions about Daisy's marriage, he admits there must have been love at the outset, but that "in any case . . . it was just personal" (152). Somewhere in Gatsby any notions we might have of "personal" authenticity have been replaced not only by the economic ladder he climbs but by the mythic battlements he seeks to scale. For Daisy the personal is displaced finally

by economics, for Gatsby by myth. This is why after his final disillusionment he "found what a grotesque thing a rose is" and could see the
world as "material without being real" (162). That is, the rose itself,
stripped of mythic investment, is only so many decaying layers of cells,
and material reality seems "real" only once it has been ordered, valued,
and redeemed from its historical determinants by a culture's myths.

The novel's last memorable image portrays us rowing against the tides
of history, perhaps having expected to float on the river with Jim to
freedom, only to find that river taking us instead in the wrong direction
to reenslavement. Narrative displaces the historical as much as it explains
it, giving us a taste of freedom as we float clear of one illusion only to
carry us into another that we may or may not recognize as such. Gatsby,
however, believed in "the orgiastic future that year by year recedes before us" (182), a conclusion that seems to preserve at the end of the
novel the ultimate validity of Gatsby's mythic expectations and to
accent only the difficulty of their attainment. But this expectant vision
of fulfilled desire is framed on both sides by inversions that instead
point backward to that history to which myth is at least partly an
evasive response. "He did not know that it [the green light of fulfill-
ment] was already behind him" in the economic determinants that he
never quite escaped. The memorable closing is equally potent: "So we
beat on, boats agasint the current, borne back ceaselessly into the past."
We are able, that is, to call the past "history," but not History, and
reflexivity has a way of pointing this out to us, bearing us back ceaselessly to the framework imposed at the outset of our narratizing of self
or society, to the yet more basic social and economic modes that in
large part determine such frameworks, and thus finally also to the
threatening, contradictory, and distasteful elements our narratives seek
to alter. Still we beat on, not toward an "orgiastic future" perhaps, but
at least into the future tense of our narrative projections. Perhaps we
have expected a sacred Nile to take us on its current of inevitability to
the delta of destiny itself, but we find ourselves instead upon a Marlovian sea of conjecture, confusion, and chance with less in the way of
certain course or ultimate port of destination than a clearer sense of
the mariner's art.

Nor should one overlook that modernist who seems to some to have
come closest to reaching a mythic moment. But I take the quintes-
esential Lawrentian character to be not the ecstatic Birkin, in relation
to whom the other characters fail to achieve blood consciousness and
ludic authenticity, but Hermione, whose will to master experience into
a satisfying narrative pervades all the characters of Lawrence's fiction.
Hermione as stylized masquer, Gudrun as eurhythmic sorceress, Rupert

as the pine-needled Pan, Ursula as crocheting hearth goddess, Gerald as stoic leopard on the slopes of Kilimanjaro—all stage the same dance, choreographing madly to produce the sensation of finality, that state Lawrence calls at one point being "burned into essentiality." "Essentiality" smacks of a plenitudinous authenticity, and it is no accident that Lawrence's figures work both frenetically and discursively to speak into being that authentic balance of the various oppositions with which his narratives play—that "struggle for verbal consciousness" dominating the foreword and the dialogue of *Women in Love.*

"Frenetically" because the balance is so patently precarious and so deadly to strive for, and "discursively" because the characters have no choice other than the literal discourse of dialogue or the "textuality" of the kinds of coded patterns just alluded to. Only Ursula believes it is attained at novel's end; the rest of the cast find themselves closer to Marlow's perplexity. Gudrun, for example, knows Gerald's death could be contained as "a pretty little sample of the eternal triangle," a narrative cliché less adequate to her own mind than the melodramatic sense that the titanic fight had been "between Gerald and herself." She is left with a bitterly ironic assurance that Birkin "would do things for her" in order to "see her through" her lethally triumphant scenario. Neither those satisfied with the cliché of the triangle nor Rupert in his decent way of "looking after other people" fully grasp how ruthless the combatants had become in trying to dominate each other's narrative lines. She, though, knows the difference between the margins of cliché or decency and the will that contends beyond the narrative possibilities yet domesticated within the popular mind.

Rupert also understands something of this, but only in his own way. In the last lines of the novel some of this is suggested in the final conversation between Birkin and Ursula:

> "I don't believe it, " she said. "It's an obstinacy, a theory, a perversity."
> "Well——" he said.
> "You can't have two kinds of love. Why should you!"
> "It seems as if I can't," he said. "Yet I wanted it."
> "You can't have it, because it's false, impossible," she said.
> "I don't believe that," he answered.

It is of interest that Ursula parallels will, conceptual or narrative schema, and perversion, as if any path other than unconscious harmony with the instinctual could lead only to disaster. But for Birkin, the unfilled desire that powers the whole drive to struggle, verbalize, relate, and grow is not satisfied by the cliché of the domestic duo (a frame certainly as banal as that Gudrun scorns). Birkin cannot believe Ursula's assertion

116

that he "can't have it" because her own explanation signals the gap through which Birkin seeks to pass. She says his desire for more than the domestic is "false," which suggests one thing, and "impossible," which suggests quite another. That is, an "impossible" desire is one that is true but unattainable, and it points to something missing in the finale of a novel showing characters struggling hard to bring together any narrative thread they can find with desire's drive for a real experience of fulfillment.

That "something missing" may well have to do with the socioeconomic dimension that becomes increasingly attenuated in the novel the more intensely the struggles are fought on the personal plane. In the early going there is much made over Gerald's mechanization of the mines, another step in reifying every event in the drama of production that, at least until it becomes customary, disrupts the sorts of primal harmonies Lawrence talks about nostalgically in essays about the miners in the pit. By the time of the ski trip, this dimension is represented primarily in Loerke's compromise with industrialization, a willingness to allow his art to become an object in the campaign to make industrial values normative in every sphere. However repugnant in the main to Birkin, industrial capitalism is a spectacle of will shaping the materials of society according to its own narrative of technological and economic order. As such it is the perverse side of the venture upon which every character and narrator necessarily embarks, and it exercises a real fascination for Gudrun. It offers, after all, a historically viable resolution of the contradiction between the desire all the characters feel for something more than the individual relation and a reality in which the prospects for some instinctual commonality seem "impossible" if not "false."

Birkin imagines a relation between individual men to complement the sexual domestic relation. For Loerke, however, capitalism provides a narrative frame in which the unprivileged fade as thoroughly into stereotypical anonymity as his young Aryan dependent—one may therefore enjoy the consumption of current models as they become available for exchange. Gudrun lurks on the edge of this pattern, herself already a voracious consumer of the sexual signifiers of bright stockings and blaring hats, already exploiting Birkin to "see her through." For Ursula, simply not seeing anything outside the domestic scene seems to suffice; she is content to live in cottage exile with no apparent need for self-support, no engagement in economic or political realities, no consideration of a plot wider than the private zone of the family. But Birkin will not and cannot believe in that narrative bubble, for he senses the wider sea on which it floats, a Conradian sea perhaps, but one that he can name only as a male love. A Marxist Birkin might have talked about some form of unreified collective life, a communal ideal that would oppose the industrial organization of culture and its plot lines. Instead he finds himself simply baffled; he is not so bad off as Gudrun in Dresden, writing but not surprisingly with "no particulars of herself." (Because she is becoming assimilated into the prevailing organization of subjectivity?) But like many an early modernist protagonist, he cannot get much further than *not* believing in limited narrative models. He cannot read beyond the cultural pages any more than Marlow can. What we find, then, is that the philosophical theme explicitly pursued—the difficulties of authentic self-narrativizing—carries with it an equally potent socioeconomic theme—the inaccessibility of any authentic view of a communal other that might satisfy the intense desires concentrated (displaced?) here into the purely personal context. The two are sides of the same basic reflexive issue that indeed suffuse early modernism.

Perhaps, then, to a greater extent than he often articulated, Lawrence's burning "essentiality" holds some important social themes at bay, themes that nonetheless impinge sufficiently to lead him to "the whole thing" that Lawrence feels only the novelist—the narratizer—can achieve.[24] But that something more is also, as this sketch of the period suggests, to be found in Gatsby's green light, what Robert Wilson (in "Francis Macomber") will not talk about, the timeless moment beyond Dilsey's cardboard cutout of a church, the all-consuming Jamesian pattern, the haze surrounding the empty shell of Marlovian narration in *Heart of Darkness*. Or to point to the master novelist of any period, perhaps it is "that word known to all men" in Joyce's fiction but spoken by none.[25] Certainly we should at this point begin to accept it as the true subject of much of this period's reflexive energies, but a final turn may yet be useful, this time to Conrad's friend and coconspirator in narrative matters, Ford Madox Ford.

To read Graham Greene's back cover blurb, Ford's "true subject" in *The Good Soldier* is "the English 'gentleman,' the 'black and merciless things' which lie behind that façade."[26] But it is also possible to agree with Leonora that "the cause of the whole miserable affair; of the whole sorrow of the world" (47) is the accuracy of the narrator's sense that her eyes, rather like Conrad's seas, "were immense, were overwhelming, were like a wall of blue that shut me off from the rest of the world." That is, as he puts it later on, our narrator is "an ageing American with very little knowledge of life," who must of course proceed both in his life and in his narrative as if he did have it, or as if anybody could, for that matter. Ford's "true subject" is also the record of this individual effort to draw some margins and devise some headings that will contain the catastrophic passions behind the "facade" of any polished character in a novel or a social class.

Our narrator is bright enough to recognize that "conventions and traditions, I suppose, work blindly but surely for the preservation of the normal type; for the extinction of proud, resolute and unusual individuals" (214). But he is not "bright" enough to be one who risks being himself extinguished, and his efforts for over two hundred pages are to find the conventions and traditions that will allow him to arrange events so as to satisfy his own need to understand but will not disrupt the fireside chat of the narrative relation he envisions for him and his reader (19). He needs, that is, to preserve the "normal type" despite a certain appreciation for the "unusual." Hence he argues that he should not be considered "an imbecile" for his misreadings, that we should "consider the position" he occupies as an individual narrator (101); it is, we are told, "natural enough for my mind to frame the idea" (102), and the frames through which he sorts from scene to scene run the gamut offered by his leisure-class entertainments: one finds the "cheap novelist" (104), melodrama (105), novel and biography (109), French comedy (112), yesterday's paper (113), guidebooks and fashion plates (114), schoolgirl romances (195), Catholic hagiology (203), sentimental novels (218), heroic romance (225), and generally "indifferent poems and novels" (229).

Without these framing devices, the material would remain "all a darkness" (151), and indeed perhaps it does even with them. For if Faulkner can end with Benjy wailing his path around the Confederate War Memorial, Ford can end with a beautiful girl muttering, on occasion, "the one word 'shuttlecocks' " and a narrator who thinks "that it all means nothing—that it is a picture without a meaning. Yes, it is queer" (228). Queerest, perhaps, is precisely what is involved at the intersection between narrative form and experience. That is, we do have an elaborate series of parallels that include everything from sex to polo as analogies for narrative art. Edward, we learn, plays women just "as he did with the polo-ball," and that play has a peculiarly textual quality that emerges in its speaking. As the narrator explains, it was "as if the very words that he spoke, without knowing that he spoke them, created the passion as they went along. Before he spoke, there was nothing; afterwards, it was the integral fact of his life. Well, I must get back to my story" (110). The passage suggests something like a "performative" theory of love, as of polo, and the narrator's quick shuffle back to "my story" is anything but a non sequitur. Speaking the narrative into form is the means by which he and his readers pass from "nothing" into the "integral fact" of narrative coherence.

He has, after all, just before this passage been very forthcoming about what love/narrative entails, and his rambling discussion in fact puts forward six propositions:

1. It is "something in the nature of a widening of the experience" (108) in which a man learns what he had not known before, a "widening of the outlook." Narrative too is an epistemological act, an attempt to know something about the relation between experience and our conventional expectations about it.

2. That increase in knowledge brings with it the "acquiring of new territory," like filling in a blank country on the Conradian globe or having a new worldview or pulling in some experience not already within our usual margins.

3. Underlying these elements is "the craving for identity with the woman he loves," a desire "to see with the same eyes, to touch with the same sense of touch, to hear with the same ears, to lose his identity, to be enveloped, to be supported" (109). "Identity" and "sameness" have become loaded terms in our own age, and the means by which they are constituted as one form or another of cultural mythology is in large part the story of early modernist reflexivity.

4. Underlying the craving for identity is a basic sense of absence, a basic desire, driving the individual beyond himself "to come to her for the renewal of his courage, for the cutting asunder of his difficulties. . . . We are all so afraid, we are all so alone, we all so need from the outside the assurance of our own worthiness to exist." The available roles are experienced as deficient, leaving the individual fearful, incomplete, and unvalidated. Whether one considers this as a function of the codes or of the larger social structures conditioning those codes, it seems nonetheless to mark lovers and narrators in *The Good Soldier*.

5. Love and narrative seem to be insufficient remedies for this alienated state, though there is a decisive uncertainty about the reason for this. On the one hand, we find a melancholy sense of impermanence— "they pass away as the shadows pass across sundials," much like the high noons of heroic confrontation in *Lord Jim* or the near formulations in Marlow's visions. On the other hand, both love and narrative are too easily consumed like the other products of their culture: "the pages of the book will become familiar; the beautiful corner of the road will have been turned too many times. Well, this is the saddest story" (109). Do we face the inadequacy of a fixed epistemological form attempting to contain the fluid materials of human existence, or do we face the absolute reification of every experiential mode (like love) and discursive form (like narrative)? It seems to be precisely this intersection marked in this strain of reflexivity.

6. The final state in the sequence these passages project is either literal death (as in Ashburnam's case), madness (as in Nancy's case), earnest perplexity (as in the narrator's case), or a completely alienated form of being (as in Leonora's marriage to the rabbit Bayham). Within the meditation we have been reading, the narrator tells us that "for every man there comes at last a time of life when the woman who then sets her seal upon his imagination has set her seal for good. He will travel over no' more horizons . . . he will retire from those scenes. He will have gone out of the business" (109). Love, scenes, the metaphysically charged metaphor of the journey, business—all seem equivalent spheres in which age of a certain sort results in a sealed imagination. In what sense "sealed"? Like a coffin; like a prison cell; like an epistemological closure of one kind or another; like an uncritically accepted social hierarchy.

The narrator worries at one point that "I have, I am aware, told this story in a very rambling way so that it may be difficult for anyone to find their path through what may be a sort of maze" (167). That maze, it seems, is one Ford shares with the lot of early modernists touched upon in this chapter. The pretense is still that classic hope for some form of direct relation between narrator and material, narrator and reader; as the narrator himself goes on to explain, "I have stuck to my idea of being in a country cottage with a silent listener, hearing between the gusts of the wind and amidst the noises of the distant sea, the story as it comes." Surely the wind and sea give us both a primordial rhythm the story seeks to emulate and a source of "static" to disrupt any sure transmission even of a story that seems to just "come" to a speaker facing a silent listener. But in those silences of the contemporary listener, and in the tracings of the maze in which all become a bit perplexed, one finds the all-but-unspoken themes of reflexivity bearing down on the hope for either a truly "natural" rhythm like the sea's or the unmediated contact between speaker and listener implied in this brief dream of a language unlike that spoken by the rest of us.

FOUR

Warren, Late Modernism, and the Issue of Narrative and Identity

Thus far we have confronted several fundamental problems with familiar critical terms. *Vanity Fair*'s dispersal of narrative voice and stance into a shifting series of semiotic relations and their attendant conventions makes less convincing the anthropomorphism of the traditional usage of these terms. *Chance* insists that the "narrator's relation to his material" be considered not merely as a strategy of representation, but as a fundamental ideological framework within which the culture constitutes a narrative grasp of hidden inner workings it projects behind its collective experiences. As we approach Robert Penn Warren's *World Enough and Time,* we find a means of following reflexively the way narrative constitutes identity within its characters and, by extension, in readers who necessarily assimilate narrative's implicit models for conceiving of selfhood and subsequently or correlatively conceive themselves.

The Reflexive Dimension

Subtitled *A Romantic Novel, World Enough and Time* seems thus to focus upon romanticism's basic issue of individual selfhood within the genre's context of realistic attentiveness to the world. Featuring a nineteenth-century protagonist who sets for himself the goal of high deeds and noble sentiments, the book thus seems a prime site for the reenactment of the culture's highest sense of individual identity and the struggle for its realization. It also, however, makes a reflexive examination of this process unavoidable by doubling the narrative perspective and thus foregrounding the textual constituting of identity. We begin with Jeremiah Beaumont, a man compiling a diary to justify a killing he wants to see as a noble deed and thus struggling constantly to formulate some version of his experiences that will reconcile what he terms "idea" and "world." At the same time, however, the modern historian who frames Beaumont's documents with his own commentary

122

and supplementary materials also struggles, for he finds this would-be romantic hero posing a number of difficult questions that trouble his own assumptions about histories and the characters who animate them. For not only does the novel demonstrate, as Robert B. Heilman so aptly put it, "the failure of a private, subjective 'ideal' realm to come to terms with, to be integrated with, to be married to a realm of public life and activity, the realm of politics and society and group action, of law and justice,"[1] but it also deploys a thorough questioning of subjectivity and the "romantic" narrative that simultaneously forms and celebrates it, not to mention the activity of interpretation by which we make sense of such narratives. Indeed, Jeremiah comes to grief not so much because he fails to embody the humanistic ideals he so respects as because he relies upon them so completely: he tests them to the utmost extremity and ultimately demystifies both his own views and those of the narrator.

Most critics, however, minimize this reflexive theme, working instead within the framework of Heilman's pioneering review of the novel's basic division between "idea" and "world" and assuming the need for some balance between the two.[2] Thus they follow the narrator in adopting Jeremiah's own framework for defining the novel's problem while rejecting his unfortunate efforts to solve it within that framework. In other words, they accept the narrator's essentially patronizing stance toward Jeremiah's "smashing pratt-fall" of a drama,[3] although the narrator is also capable of undercutting the smugness of the modern perspective (as when he notes that, given our taste for warfare, "we may be like the dunces" who duel).

It may be, however, that such a reliance upon the narrator is as ill-founded as Jeremiah Beaumont's upon *his* guides and books. Is it possible that the narrator's acceptance—and ours through his—of Jeremiah's framework dooms us to efforts as unfortunate as Jeremiah's, and that the narrator's acquiescence in Jeremiah's terminological boundaries is thus a disastrous misuse of his authority to establish the truth for us? I feel some reluctance to suggest this, since several more extended studies of Warren's work regret the narrator's failure to be *more* authoritative. Barnett Guttenberg, for example, suggests that "the narrator is not altogether reliable; he does not see that the absurdity [behind both the farce and the pathos in Jeremiah's story] is not insurmountable." Moreover, "he lacks 'the kind of knowledge that is identity' " and "does not see the possible reintegration of selfhood," thus ending with an "unawareness" that requires the critic to imagine a more affirmative ending.[4] More pointedly, Leonard Casper asserts that because of the point of view, "the author's values [perhaps more precisely the narrator's], instead of serving as fixed reference from which error can be measured, are always in danger of becoming just another portion of man's general perplexity."[5] If Casper is correct, the narrator's values *do* slip into the vortex Jeremiah's documents create; if Guttenberg is correct, then those values may well be "perplexity" anyway because of the narrator's embarrassing obtuseness. In both cases these critics seem disappointed to find the narrator holding back from stating any unequivocal metaphysical reference points.[6]

But can a novel both propose as coherent a reading as Heilman finds and transmit itself through so dubious a medium as the narrator here described? We must be cautious, for those who follow Professor Heilman's lead can find a great deal of support in Warren's other novels and in his poems as well. But if we were to look at the book as a reflexive commentary on how it deploys the materials Heilman finds, then we might see the reservations noted by Guttenberg and Casper not as faults, but as pointers to an alternative track through the novel. That track follows closely the ways both the narrator and Jeremiah himself reflect upon the difficulties they encounter in making a narrative about Jeremiah's life.

The narrator begins as a dutiful historian, citing his piles of newspapers, diaries, documents, letters, court transcripts, the protagonist's journal—all written, he says, "to us." Naturally the narrator casts the expected doubts upon the reliability of contemporary testimony, even confessing that we only "have reason to believe" a miniature portrait he describes is actually of Beaumont. To take such conventional warnings seriously would, of course, impugn the authority of all the sources of the narrative. We should not take lightly this undermining of truthfulness, for it is the keynote for the many problems that rise before us as we travel this track in the novel.

Indicative of such difficulties with sources is the following: "That was the way Jeremiah Beaumont heard the story of Rachel Jordan, and that was the story he heard. We cannot be entirely sure of the story he did not hear, for the diary of Rachel Jordan is silent, and Jeremiah's account of what she was to tell him later of that period is relatively meager. Furthermore, what Jeremiah Beaumont believed, and what Rachel Jordan had come to believe may be distorted by the intervening events. The experience had been exposed to the light of time and the corrosive influence of a change in the chemistry of Rachel Jordan's own being" (58). The narrator then generates a series of "perhaps" clauses to index the possible ranges of distortions in the records in which he must "try to discover the projection of the secret line of meaning." Perhaps secret lines fare poorly when corrosive chemicals are set loose, especially in a context in which even human character is conceived as if it were an old photograph—where we look for secret lines is always at least once removed from whatever those lines purport to represent.

But perhaps of even more interest is the novel's second paragraph, where the narrator muses over the project ahead of him: "We have what is left, the lies and half-lies and the truths and half-truths. We do not know that we have the Truth. But we must have it." The first two sentences are disturbing only if we take such conventionalized gestures literally, containing as they do an admission (Do we ever know that we have the truth?) we normally prefer not to make. But when he says "we must have it," does he mean "must" in the sense that we necessarily have it in the documents themselves (it must be there)? Or does "must" connote the desperate desire to hold truth absolute and pure (I *must* have certainty!), a desire that should make us uncomfortable by the time we finish following Jeremiah's ultimately unscrupulous search for the idea? Or finally, does "must" refer not to desire to have truth at any cost, but rather to a kind of ontological necessity to have truth as a condition of survival (as one must have food and water)? The first meaning would affirm the naive historian's faith that meticulous and objective sifting of documentary evidence will yield a truthful account of the events, motives, and causal links that constitute human history. But the latter two are hardly so absolute in their implications, one suggesting that desire may well resort to desperate acts of (mis)interpretation to reach its goals, the other a philosophical assertion that to be human means to constitute a truth that slakes some inner thirst (more, perhaps, than it necessarily comprehends some outer reality).

The more problematic possibilities here loom larger as one encounters the metaphors the narrator provides for his unenviable situation as the passage continues:

> Puzzling over what is left, we are like the scientist fumbling with a tooth and thigh bone to reconstruct for a museum some great, stupid beast extinct with the ice age. Or we are like the louse-bit nomad who finds, in a fold of land between his desert and the mountains, the ruin of parapets and courts, and marvels what kind of men had held the world before him. But at least we have the record: the tooth and thigh bone, or the kingly ruins. (3)

To be "puzzling" over remnants may well be the human condition, but the two metaphors develop quite different contexts for this state. Though his puzzlement does not especially inspire confidence, the positive connotations of the normally well-prepared and objective scientist are more heartening. The analogy is not without ambiguity, however, for this scientist is "fumbling," and he must "reconstruct" a dinosaur from only a tooth and thigh bone; however well intentioned he is, however thorough his preparation, a great deal of guess work must go into an effort that may well risk the nineteenth-century mistake of putting the wrong head on the brontosaurus. Even the value of that effort is questioned, since its object, Jeremiah, is hardly enhanced by the comparison to a "great, stupid beast." For while "great" indeed suggests the epic scope to which he aspired, "stupid" is anything but ennobling. Moreover, to be "extinct" and destined only for a museum suggests a failure to achieve the sort of timeless ideal that would make his search of enduring value.

There is, however, a second metaphor. If "scientist" carries positive connotations for our society, certainly "louse-bit nomad" anchors the other end of the spectrum. Whereas the scientist, relative to his subject, represents the zenith in sophistication and refinement of intellectual achievement, the nomad, relative to those who built "kingly ruins," represents the nadir. Again, however, the analogy is ambiguous, for the abundance of the ruins provides a number of clues for reconstructing the life and times of the kingly builders, a far more reliable store of data than a tooth and thigh bone for the paleontologist. Moreover, the second metaphor is much kinder to Jeremiah, showing him as a kingly, larger-than-life figure whose ruins we are barely qualified to puzzle over and whose achievements seem a model for a benighted age to emulate.

What are we to make of these contradictory metaphors? Several observations seem in order. First of all, one might say that here the narrator allows to surface some ambivalent feelings over his role and his relation to his material: the nature of the narrator as objective researcher, of his material as neutral data, of his outcome as verifiable truth, all are in conflict with the narrator as ignorant wanderer, his material as a lost and magical race, his outcome as a marvelous fable of those who "held the land." These alternatives are reminiscent of the labyrinth into which Marlow's questions about order and chance lead him; moreover, they take us back to my opening chapter's oscillation between two problematic constructs as the movement in which narrative is constituted. Necessarily, then, the narrator seems unable to stake out clearly his position on these issues, an inability that leads to a second point about these metaphors: if the narrator strives to be a careful scientist but finds himself also a lost and perplexed fabulist, then what status is secure for the reader? Presumably the narrator as historian is the point of view closest to that of the reader of a narrative text: both confront documentary materials that propose an interpretive chronology of events. To the extent that this is true, the reader must then share the problems this narrator has in charting the novel's grounds even as they shift like those desert sands the nomad roams. Finally, the metaphors suggest that the protagonist, Jeremiah Beaumont, is both less and more than his researcher. He is a great stupid beast who blunders without the elaborately developed tools of self-analysis developed in twentieth-century psychology, but he is also kingly in his desire to rule himself, to exercise absolute sovereignty over his era and the role he plays in it. The last of these three observations about the metaphors is perhaps a part of Warren's nostalgia for a more heroic age, an age when men strove to fill public and private roles much larger than those we tend to script for ourselves. Taken together, however, they all belong to a more subtle reflection upon the grounds and aspirations of narrative and in particular this romantic novel's focus upon the self. By so quickly raising serious questions about his efforts, the narrator has already launched a reflexive examination of his own act of writing that asks a reader to rethink his own uncritical assumptions about his connections of thigh bones, teeth, and kingly ruins.

Textuality and Selfhood

One theme of this reflexive attention to narrative is the intertextual nature of many of its key elements. Jeremiah himself is, in a sense, a text inscribed by the literary and rhetorical traditions he absorbs. Jeremiah esteems the gift of literacy his father conferred upon him "more than a legacy of land and rents which my father did not leave me" (9), and indeed he rejects Marcher's offer of such land and rents according to the high drama of romance, haughtily sweeping out of the old man's house because he has been asked to surrender his name, his verbal patrimony. His education is that time of his life when "men and books offered him the great patterns of meaning for life" (44), his courtship of Rachel is waited out by reading voraciously (66), and she finds him a quaint young man "who reads too many books" (73) and acts accordingly.

Late in the novel the narrator is forced on more than one occasion to observe that for Jeremiah, and at times for Rachel, "poetry triumphed" and they "assumed their perfect shapes, took their perfect roles for a drama enacted on a high and secret stage" (303), "a simple drama of great wrong, of righteous vengeance, of love unto death" (383). Scripted by romance, both Jeremiah's actions and his conceptions of his actions and of the self they constitute are essentially intertextual. They are hence conventional and mediated rather than natural or directly derived from reality or truth (or self) as absolute entitites. The narrator notes other currents that contribute to the scripting of Jeremiah's account and self-conceptions. At one point, for example, he stops to note that the "language Jeremiah used long after in writing of that period echoes the language of the theological tract and the pulpit" (24). The romance element he found not only in novels but in *Pilgrim's Progress* (9), the later influence of Platonic idealism (70), and the discussions of mind/body relations by Dr. Burnham (12) and Hawgood (299) are parallels to this theological language. Its vital role in his self-justification is expressed in his dream of bathing and cleansing himself in the blood of Colonel Fort while "the words of the hymn ran through his head" (165). The terms of his self-conceptions and actions quite literally derive from textual systems of belief all sharing a metaphysical dualism.

That this is true for other characters as well makes clear the role of interpretive artifice derived from cultural texts in thinking and acting. Rachel, for example, "knew from all the books and poems and the whispered secrets of other girls that love was a pure flame and a spiritual passion in which pain was joy and joy was sacrament" (47), Wilkie Barron (the exemplar of the World in the novel's philosophic schematic) certainly follows the stylized idioms of oratory and persuasion, and even Skroggs (exemplar of the Idea) thinks and writes within the textual style of his father's fundamentalist religion—an early political tract, for example, is entitled *A Trumpet Blast for Those Who Would Not Be Devoured*, a highly conventional title that shows clear crossover from the religious into the political realm.

The meaning and significance of one's actions are formulated according to these shaping conventions, as Jeremiah reflects early on when he says "that only if you look out upon your own act as from a window does your act become real to you and take meaning in the world." That outer world is a dream compared with the detached faculty that watches "himself speak words and lift his arm" (119), composing significant verbal and physical gestures within the textual frame of his conceptual window on the world. What these characters see when they look "out" upon the world or upon themselves conforms to such a frame. And since those actions themselves stem from a sense of self derived from texts, it is no accident that he comes late in the novel to feel that "a man might live his years and end but where he began" (423), serving out the sentence copied from the text shaping his initial sense of self and world. We seem, in other words, to be very close to Marlow's notion of "copybook lives."

One case that is virtually paradigmatic of the novel's reflexive treatment of textuality and selfhood comes late in the novel as Jeremiah awaits trial in an underground dungeon. As his attorney leaves, Jeremiah chants over and over the lawyer's final assurance to Rachel:

Beaumont will never hang, the words tingled in Jeremiah's mind, as he watched Mr. Madison ascend the ladder, and disappear. *Beaumont will never hang, Beaumont will never hang,* like the refrain of a ballad or old song forgotten from some desperate violence of long ago, the identity of the hero lost.

He released Rachel from his embrace, and stepped from her side. He took a few paces, and stopped, hearing the words in his head.

But I am Beaumont, he thought.

Then: *I am Beaumont, and I will never hang.* (362)

Jeremiah is disoriented, strangely lost to himself, until he has the traditional form of the ballad to give him a sense of structure and to enable him to identify himself with "the hero" long ago in romance's golden age. The last two lines, however, make inescapable the defective logic by which a literary form is taken as ontological ground, for Jeremiah achieves identity by filling in the slot of the heroic ballad with his own future. But that identity, the text says, is of a "hero lost," just as Jeremiah is to himself. That is, even though the specific textual basis may as in this case be "forgotten," *any* sense of himself will always be mediated through the textual frameworks that supply both the substance (as when they mandate Fort's death) and the form (as here) of his being.

Jeremiah seems, then, to live within a closed system of intertextual inscription. Such a world includes the narrator too, one might argue. As we have seen already, the narrator makes much of the stack of documents—texts—from which he works, and his discipline as historian is one that is specifically devoted to the art of interpreting sources and weaving them into a single text. Such an act, of course, parallels Jeremiah's effort to take in the texts that shape him and synthesize them into a coherent enacting of his selfhood. He even goes so far as to duplicate the frame narrator's writing of history by providing one of the key documents from which the narrator draws his material. Thus both Jeremiah's life in general and his specific act of keeping a journal parallel the historian's act of writing the novel. The problems and limitations of each are thus quite similar, and Jeremiah Beaumont's fluctuating castigations and exaltations of himself show the same radical contraries we found in the narrator's metaphors for himself. This equation is significant, since the reader's position is also drawn into this circle: we too are poring over documents (the novel and its quotations from earlier texts), we too must read Jeremiah's life with the same difficulties and limits endured by narrator and protagonist, we too feel dwarfed by but also superior to the novel's figures. Moreover, in our efforts to make sense of the words upon these pages we depend upon our expertise in the conventions of history, historical novels and romances, philosophical discussions of selfhood, and critical theory that teaches us *how* to think about texts and about our weaving together of these various strands into some "reading" or interpretation.

One finds this drawing together of narrator and character in more than their general situation within the intertextual network. In their use of metaphor, both find themselves with similar formal problems. Their styles of metaphor are quite similar, for one thing. The narrator quotes Jeremiah's journal, speaking of legal language that "crackled like autumn leaves underfoot or thorns lighted under a pot" and of logic that "marched beyond the green confines of human hopes and fears across the sands of a desert toward some far-off mountain of Justice" (39). He provides his own metaphors when he summarizes Rachel's life before she enters Jeremiah's as a "world outside of time" like "a little garden, breathless with belated roses overblown in the hot, hazy sunshine, lost in the wideness of the violent, throbbing land" (59). Both participate in such a similarly lush metaphoric style that when the narrator writes of Jeremiah, evidently summarizing from his journal, we cannot tell whether the metaphor is borrowed from Jeremiah (they are sometimes quoted, sometimes not) or invented by the narrator. For example, in one summary of Jeremiah's daydreams about his future career in law, the narrator says that Jeremiah's "mind ran with a cold joy through the work of the day like a keen knife blade through soft, delicious pine" (44). Whose metaphor is it? How could we tell? If the styles are so indistinguishable, does that not suggest deeper similarities in the (textual) habits of mind, even in their basic means of interpreting and composing a coherent verbal order?

To speak of meaning is to introduce another similarity in their use of metaphor—its capacity to multiply itself in contradictory ways. We have already looked at a good example of the narrator's generation of multiple metaphors (the scientist and the nomad) that interact with something less than smoothness. But Jeremiah too is given to such chains of metaphors, which begin to sound like desperate efforts to put into words what continually escapes or exceeds the categories and systems of belief we have seen his language embodying. His "hope beyond hope," as he puts it, is not only to be free but to have something to live for. The narrator gives this passage from Jeremiah's journal: " 'For I could never cling,' he says, 'to the mere fact of life without inwardness, for that were but music without melody and the color of flame without heat, and the trampling of cattle in the stall's dung' " (371). It would not be difficult to skim over this, making little of it other than to note the bombast of his rhetorical style. But if we pause to see what these metaphors carry, what do we find? What does it mean to say that life without inwardness is like the trampling of cattle in dung? I suppose above all it suggests the dehumanizing impact of losing one's spirituality, a sinking into bestiality that Jeremiah himself will soon enough achieve on the island of La Grand' Bosse.

Some of that concreteness is still in the second metaphor of the flame, but with a difference. That is, the comparison is not to the heatless flame, but to the heatless *color* of flame; Jeremiah abstracts once from flame to achieve the concept of a shade on a color wheel and a second time to leave behind the warmth one might otherwise associate with the color. As for the first metaphor, music without melody—something to which twentieth-century listeners have grown somewhat more accustomed—we have a still more abstract form of art thinned out to its own most abstract possibility. What happens in this set of metaphors is that the final member of the trio moves downward, to employ Jeremiah's own scale of values, to the bestial; the first two, however, move in the opposite direction upward into abstractions made possible only through the abstracting agency of language. What does Jeremiah mean to say? Does "life without inwardness" cause one to attempt apotheosis into conceptual abstraction or to descend into the fecal mire of man's animal nature? One might argue that Jeremiah's life shows the consequences of both strategies, but it would be hard to argue that he is at this point really trying to say this to himself. At least as hard, that is, as to argue that the narrator's metaphors of the nomad and the scientist are necessarily intended to eradicate any stable basis for his own authority. As each attempts to express the meaning of his account, he proliferates metaphors that battle intramurally rather than embodying whatever elusive significance each sets out to discover. It is as if language were dedicated to reflexively shadowing its referential function.

In addition to sharing a distinctively intertextual world and a similar style and strain in using metaphors, the narrator and Jeremiah share the difficulties of interpretation. Jeremiah's general agony with this act shows up in a number of passages in the text like the following, in which he puzzles over why he did not abandon Rachel and flee the island prison. The narrator summarizes for us: "Why did he stay? Because, in honor, he wanted to protect her? Or did he stay merely because he had sunk into the brute torpor and mire of the place, because he had accepted the place and the place had accepted him, as a quagmire accepts and sucks in whatever offers itself to that black peace? He asked himself those questions, and more, torturing the possibilities" (439). Jeremiah "tortures the possibilities," then, teasing out all the alternative interpretations of his motives, his words, or those of others around him.

The narrator repeatedly finds himself in similar difficulties of interpretation. At one point, for example, he pauses to note that Jeremiah "seems to take relish in using terms of horror and condemnation" for himself "as though he would cloak himself in the language of common report." But the passage continues: "Or did his motive lie deeper? Did that language cleanse his hands for the moment, and restore him to the society of men? Or when his own tongue condemned his act, did he relish the irony because at that moment he felt more free and secret in his inner self set off from the world?" (248). Each of these three possibilities is quite different from the others, and they suggest, repectively, (*a*) one seeking to cloak in cliché the real nature of his deeds, (*b*) one seeking some form of self-flagellation to expiate his sins and reintegrate him into the community, or (*c*) one exulting in the isolation of satanic pride over the ignorant and befuddled worldlings.

This is not an isolated passage. When, for example, Jeremiah states in the courtroom that he has been convicted "by false witness and testimony perjured for gain," the narrator reflects as follows: "It is interesting to remark here that Jeremiah did not affirm his innocence, only that he had been wrongly convicted. Was this merely an accident of phrasing, an emphasis caused by his own training in the law, or had the word *innocence* stuck in his throat at last to leave him with only a deep equivocation by the card?" (352). Shyster, or chastened sinner? It is impossible to tell. A bit later in the novel the narrator does this again, this time with Rachel's belated confession of love to Jeremiah. The narrator asks, again open-endedly, "Had she spoken them [words of love] out of her own guilt as an expiation? Or out of pity for the very loneliness which made him reject her? Or had she spoken the truth when she said that she loved him because love was the only thing left, and you must have something, even to die? Or because the unwritten text of the drama that she and Jeremiah Beaumont acted out on their high and secret stage demanded this in the end?" (377). Though at first glance these questions seem to be the objective historian's neutral list of possible motives, they actually propose four quite different conceptions of self and cosmos jostling for dominance in the narrator's mind. Rachel as a repentant sinner implies the universe of moral struggle; as an exquisite sensibility moved by pity, she is the pathetic heroine in a cosmic melodrama; as a desperate wretch under capital sentence, she is a naturalist victim ground down to the last emotion in her repertoire; as a role player, she is a slightly ludicrous stand-in for herself in a fabulist heroic drama. We move, in other words, in a romantic framework from a drama of moral absolutes to its degenerate form of sentimental drama, and in a realist framework from an austere awareness of the individual crushed by social forces beyond her control to its satirical form unveiling the private delusions that account for deviant or foolish behavior. None of these literary zones is a resting point, however, because the narrator gives us an "at any rate" and a resumption of narrative, not a definitive interpretation: we cannot decide, it seems.

As in trying to define the ratio of greed and idealism in the motives for the New Court movement, it is a case of "proportion we can never know, for it was all long ago, and men's hearts are always sealed, even to themselves" (393). The narrator's task drives him to the same expedient of "torturing the possibilities" to which Jeremiah is driven and, as the comparison suggests, in so similar a style that substantive distinctions between the two blur—the individuality and originality of each is undermined, as if the more one tries to determine the nature of a self, the more one finds indeterminacy in place of identity, continuities of cultural codes in place of unique or original elements of character unfolding, discontinuous textual strands within an individual in place of an expected unity. Not only do both narrators resolve into the same kind of textual practice, thus making them less subjectivities than stylizations, but the object of their endeavor (the selfhood of Jeremiah) follows a parallel displacement into conventions of discourse.

This threat to our usual assumptions about selfhood is related to the still more general problem of interpretation. If both narrator and protagonist are enmeshed in projects whose completion is so problematic— projects in which the reader is also involved, as the multiple strands of our own reading demonstrate—is it possible that we all are attempting something we assume traditional fiction takes for granted but that such insistently reflexive fiction as *World Enough and Time* gradually defines as beyond the reach of our basically intertextual codes, our metaphoric language, our always relative stances of interpretation? That is, if selfhood is constituted by interpretation, then that process becomes a central theme in any consideration of the novel's reflexive dimension. Indeed, a constant stream of passages in the novel confront this very issue more directly than any we have so far given close attention, and they carry some important implications not just for this novel, but for our thinking about all fiction.

A Nietzschean Will to Selfhood

Particularly in the face of these general problems, an interpreter's effort to make events comply with his schematic of significance seems clearly to be one man's version of the culture's general will to power. At this point Friedrich Nietzsche's critique of our often uncritical metaphysical assumptions offers a useful pattern for tracing this reflexive narrative's analysis of its own interpretive reasoning. Nietzsche notes that since we "lack any sensitive organs" for the inner world, "we sense a thousand-fold complexity as a unity" and "introduce causation where any reason for motion and change remains invisible to us."[7] Three features of his critique of our ordinary sense of "consciousness" are thus apparent: that our means of perceiving it are inadequate, that knowledge is "simplification, coarsening" of complexity, and that the actual structure giving rise to the notions of which we are aware is inaccessible to us: "that which becomes conscious is involved in causal relations which are entirely withheld from us—the sequence of thoughts, feelings, ideas in consciousness does not signify that this sequence is a causal sequence; but apparently it is so, to the highest degree. Upon this *appearance* we have founded our whole idea of spirit, reason, logic, etc. (—none of these exist: they are fictitious syntheses and unities), and projected these *into* things and *behind* things!" (284). This would seem to make the archetypal project of a "romantic novel"—recording the growth of the poet's (or poetic protagonist's) mind—rather difficult. Indeed, the attempt requires that one have faith in the means of perception, its capacity to elaborate a sufficiently complex model for its subject, and the accessibility of that subject matter, precisely the assumptions Nietzsche disparages. Who, then, is correct—the philosopher or the romantic?

World Enough and Time, of course, requires that we provide the answer, for its own final sentence—"Was all for naught?"—in essence questions the validity of Jeremiah's constant testing of the "idea" of self against the "world" in which that self seems to unfold. As we have seen, however, the narrator—and through him the reader—shares Jeremiah's problems in composing an account of his tragic history or, as one attempts to make the novel "relevant," of one's own life. Thus the narrator seems to evince as deep an ambivalence over his task as Nietzsche might suppose he should—he has "that which becomes conscious" for him through the artifacts, but the effective "causal relations . . . are entirely withheld from us" as well as from the narrator. From the outset, then, modernists like Nietzsche and the narrator are skeptical about the project the book undertakes.

Jeremiah, the romantic, is a good deal more stubborn and hopeful, however, and the book represents his persistent effort to be free of anything like Nietzsche's cautions and the narrator's ambivalence. Ultimately, as one might suspect, the attempt founders—in the plot, for example, Jeremiah never achieves an explanation that survives the test of his own history. But it is also apparent, in the stream of comments he makes upon his attempt to "know" his own truth (and in the narrator's summary of those comments), that his own conviction in this task gradually shifts towards Nietzsche's deconstruction of its possibility. Since Jeremiah, the modern narrator, and Nietzsche all end at something like the same position, the novel would then seem to have some grave implications for one of fiction's basic thematic configurations—the quest for an integrated and authentic sense of selfhood—as well as for a poetics based upon the same metaphysics.

In any case, Jeremiah begins with great confidence in his ability to know the truth of things. For example, toward the end of the second chapter we read the following: "He felt that the future was beyond plan, it already existed, he would discover it step by step as he moved toward some flame, some point of light, beyond the murk and mist of things" (62). The passage contains the sense of a teleological history, certainly one romantic assumption that unravels during the novel, thereby undermining the premise of classic plotting that the self is a culmination, a fulfillment of some purpose within the course of things. That this future self should be the light of truth, preexistent, represents the most extreme form of a metaphysical concept of self or ego outside time, awaiting realization as an ultimate reality. That it should be "beyond the murk and mist of things" suggests a clarity and unity characteristic of the more Platonic range of thought within our culture, and Jeremiah's confidence in discovering this light in its purity and plenitude embodies the quintessence of absolutist certitude.

The narrator is clearly uneasy with such certitude, however, and during the early part of the novel when Jeremiah's confidence is at its highest, the narrator keeps his own more limited creed literally before the reader. The following comments establish a vortex in which the reader, from his smug distance of sophistication, is to be sucked into equivalence with Jeremiah; but the casualties include more than the reader's pride:

> The gratuitous act: that was what he sought. But why did he seek it, the act outside the motives of the world? The answer is easy. It was the only way he knew to define himself, to create his world. We look back on his story, so confused and comic and pretentious and sad, and it seems very strange to us, for our every effort is to live in the world, to accept its explanations, to do nothing gratuitously. But is his story so strange? Explanations can only explain explanations, and the self is gratuitous in the end. (116)

The first third of the comment seems pure romanticism—the supreme self developing itself through the suprarational discourse of the imagination, a self-authenticating, self-grounding, self-creating plenitude of being. The middle sentence pictures us all, by contrast, as pure realists living in the world of straightforward explanations. The excerpt closes like a steel vise, however, crushing the two alternatives together until they are flat as the page that gives rise to them. What the narrator questions here, in effect, is that this founding of self along the textual lines of a romantic or Platonic tradition should be thought "strange." Rachel recognizes that Jeremiah has "read too many books" (218) and hence is a sort of intertextual creature. But the narrator here also questions the grounds of our condescension toward his error. We who derive our explanations, as we think, directly from the world—From science? From existential discussions of temporality's implications?—are no better off. "Explanations can only explain explanations" is an explosive assertion that *any* description is derivative, already trapped within the intertextual circularity. The explanations cannot reach outside the text to the referent, to the self or the world they *are about,* rather than simply *are:* they reach instead to some text, tradition, or complex of texts. And if the self is "gratuitous," then it is unearned, like a gratuitous payment, and unjustified, like gratuitous criticism; it cannot manifest the interpretive relations of cause and effect between essence and actions.

In other words, our "organs" of perception are attuned to always stylized interpretations. Nietzsche would argue that "rational thought is interpretation according to a scheme that we cannot throw off" (283), a statement parallel to the narrator's suggestion that the interpretation of self—and perhaps that self as well—are what we "create" when we need to "define" ourselves, a suggestion toward a linguistic ontology of selfhood. If, as Nietzsche argues, "knowledge" relates less to truth than to the will to power, the need to master, then this track we have begun to chart through the novel takes us toward a sense of concepts like "interpretation" and "self" not as the metaphysical cornerstones of our existence, but as pragmatic stratagems for survival. They persist because they are tools that seem to work, not necessarily because they are true. Hence Jeremiah's story is strange only in the degree to which concept overtly predicates action, not in the basic state of positing a questionable but eventually prophetic schema of selfhood to live by. We pause to revise the schema only if it does not work, and somehow we always assume along with Jeremiah that such revision takes us closer to truth. We are, in other words, not essentially different from Jeremiah in our procedures; we differ only in the specifics we choose to believe.

The narrator's observations are not the only corrosives acting upon our sense of Jeremiah's initial assumptions. Within his own account reality begins to exceed his circular explanations, to escape his attempts to fit it into neat philosophical models. A few pages after the passage just examined, the narrator quotes Jeremiah directly: "And I asked myself how may we know that Justice is in the heart? There is no one to tell us. It is like a game, I said to myself, in which we place our coin upon a card, then turn the card to see if we win or lose, if on it or no is truly pictured the kingly face of Justice. Ah, but—and I put the last sad query to myself—can we ever see the other side of the card? Who will tell us?" (122–23). Admittedly this comes in one of Jeremiah's phases of depression, but the image runs quite contrary to a distant light beyond the murk and mist of things. One must bet on a card without ever being able to see its face value. In the immediate context this is his justification for trusting the "heart at its first whisper"—impulse—rather than testing its whispers against any restraints; but the shift of authority from a transcendental light to historically triggered impulses within oneself is a clear diminution of that authority. The Idea that was to have made sense of the world, to have reflected its substructure, shrinks to the dimensions of the troubled inner self of an individual, its mortal shell for temporary survival against a hostile environment. Jeremiah's incipient nostalgia for the transcendental authority is reflected in the plaintive "Who will tell us?" that follows his realization of the epistemological dilemma: the face of truth is forever turned from us, and there is no one to "tell us" if indeed we are right.

This shrinking or diminution of authority begins soon after his receiving shocks from the world at large. Overhearing gossip that he married for security, Jeremiah is shaken and finds it "hard to put into words" his shame, but his attempt is nonetheless instructive: "If a man lives by what he feels to be the truth in him, and discovers in a single instant that the tongue of the world says differently of him, there comes the fear and shame that what he had held to be the truth in him may not be the truth after all and there may be no truth for him but the terrible truth now given him by the tongue of the world. And if a man is robbed of his truth, and of a sudden, how can he know what he is?" (164). The repetition of "tongue" keeps us mindful of the linguistic and therefore intertextual nature of "truth," the six occurrences of which insist here upon its central if problematic place in his thinking. But the realization that this inner "truth" is not proof against the world's differing versions and interpretations, that "truth" is relative to cultural consensus ("the tongue of the world") rather than to a metaphysical "truth in him," is a nearly disabling blow to Jeremiah, producing both fear at the loss of absolutes and shame from the demystification of his almost sacred view of himself. The very materiality he attributes to truth (as something that can be stolen) attests to his lingering sense of its independent, metaphysical existence. Still, Jeremiah is moving away from his initial certitude that one can "know what he is" and to some extent toward the sense that such concepts as "self" and "consciousness" have lost their transcendent materiality, have indeed become what a semiotician might take them for—nodes in a network of differential relations established by "the tongue of the world" and thus, as culturally posited, arbitrary and problematic.

A few pages later, in fact, Jeremiah is ready to return to his initial image for truth but with some important revision: "And I thought how my own words had sprung from something in me I did not know the name or meaning for, and how a man moves in the darkness of himself, more trackless than the wild country, toward a light which glimmers far away. But he does not know what the light may be. (And now that all has come to pass, do I know?)" (172). We are again close to Nietzsche's notion of "relations which are entirely withheld from us" and close as well to the relation between "name" (language) and "meaning" as this side of culture's line from which "words" spring in our consciousness, while on the other side remains the unnamed and therefore unknown (cf. Nietzsche: "We set up a word at the point at which our ignorance begins, at which we can see no further" [267]). The light is still there, as in the earlier passage, but it is now undefinable even when "all has come to pass." It seems not to be the material thing he can "discover," as before, but to be trackless and untraceable. The more he strives to embody the truth toward which a textual tradition (that of the romantic or Platonic) points, the more he finds that it alienates him from the world and its unholy mixtures, leading him ultimately to this "wild country" beyond the conceptual landmarks of culture, an unknowable realm where the "flame" toward which he had expected to move "step by step" has become an undefinable "glimmer." He can know only what is already tracked by cultural and linguistic conventions and their implicit assumptions, but to attempt living by those assumptions is to lose both the world and the light of truth itself. That is, one's commitment to embody truth fully exiles one beyond language and the culture it represents, for language is itself always "far away" from the fullness of its referent, always an approximate approach rather than making present the wholeness of that referent. To reach truth, one must therefore go beyond language and culture; but to do so, as Jeremiah realizes, is to be lost in the trackless wild country where "our ignorance begins." For one committed to writing as a means of knowing, this paradox has ominous implications.

If we shift now to the latter part of the novel, where the linguistic implications become increasingly heightened with the metaphor of the drama Jeremiah and Rachel act out together, we can trace the final stages of this theme of knowing in Jeremiah's record. Jeremiah struggles to come to terms with the implications of living both in the secret drama he and Rachel construct together and in the public world. Summarizing Jeremiah's papers, the narrator reports:

> The problem, however, was more than a problem of doubleness. If the worlds had been entirely different, with a gulf of unplumbed nothingness between, then all might have been easy. He could have lived in both untroubled, speaking different languages, abiding by different laws, worshipping different gods, walking different streets, admiring different landscapes. (305)

In a metaphysical scheme, in other words, one could speak the language of transcendence, the tongue of the holy flame, and that of immanence, the tongue of commerce and companionship. Such a structure of values, neatly punctuated with a nihilist void between, could stabilize one's hierarchy of explanations and imperatives.

> But it was not so. The two worlds impinged, overlay and lapped, blurred and absorbed, twisted together and dissolved like mist. That was the trouble. You never knew when the doubleness you embraced might become simplicity, or when the single to which you looked or on which you laid your hand might divide like smoke, or to what strange corner the familiar street down which you walked might lead. The common word in your mind or mouth betrayed you. What did the word mean, after all? (305-6)

The images for the relation between the two worlds here are as confused as Jeremiah's thinking. "Impinged" suggests etymologically two realms that "push against" each other, trespassing, but apparently holding their membranes intact; one might be pressed, but distinctions can be maintained. Overlaying or overlapping suggests the same distinctness while covering the same ground, a step toward greater confusion since the same language operates on at least two levels. Twisting together adds tension to the model, but "blurred" begins to confuse the two, while "absorbed" eradicates a distinction altogether and suggests a merging into a single identity; "dissolved," of course, undoes the whole substantiality of Jeremiah's language and the authority of the distinctions and truths it claims. And is "mist" the same "murk and mist" beyond which the light burns? Are we moving in a realm that embodies the substantiality of streets and corners or merely the ghostliness of smoke with its illusory form?

The oscillation is unsettling to Jeremiah, who touched a double world with his steel blade only to be electrocuted by the worlds' concurrence in a simple verdict of murder; it is unsettling also to a reader, who must answer with Jeremiah the question, "What did the word mean, after all?"

The "word" of common explanation marks the line between the intertextual world of culture and the trackless wilds where ignorance begins, and it thus reflects both the epistemological limitations of the former and its mystified ideas about the latter. For Jeremiah, the once certain point of light has become bewildering illusions of smoke and mist.

In any case, the "word" of explanation Jeremiah tries to utter has become increasingly complicated as the progress of events has worn away his early assurance. A few pages after this passage, it is not the two worlds but "lies and truth" that are "all twisted together," indistinguishable realms whose dividing line is perhaps as problematic as that between the "two worlds" (cf. Nietzsche: "No, facts is precisely what there is not, only interpretations" [267], and hence no absolute line between truth and lie). "And before his [Jeremiah's] eyes, in the sunlit room, among the forms and voices, all things for a moment seemed to waver and blur as in darkness" (329), another indication that solidity and distinction are inappropriate categories for the concepts Jeremiah is trying to work with.

It is worth pausing over Jeremiah's recurrent confusion of his physical and mental scene with these metaphors of substance for concepts, for this metaphoric habit of thought represents in effect a discipline by which both self and world are built. Nietzsche argues that "we are unable to affirm and to deny one and the same thing: this is a subjective empirical law, not the expression of any 'necessity' but only of an inability" (279). His argument runs that logic, based upon this law of noncontradiction, is thus "an imperative, not to know the true, but to posit and arrange a world that shall be called true by us."[8] The "axioms of logic" are not "adequate to reality" so much as they are "a means and measure for us to *create* reality, the concept 'reality,' for ourselves," thus making the only ground of logic what we would call a constitutive poetics. As for any empirical basis, Nietzsche speaks contemptuously of the "coarse sensualistic prejudice that sensations teach us truths about things" (280) and thus argues that "one should not understand this compulsion to construct concepts, species, forms, purposes, laws . . . as if they enabled us to fix the *real world;* but as a compulsion to arrange a world for ourselves in which our existence is made possible:—we thereby create a world which is calculable, simplified, comprehensible, etc., for us" (282). Hence Nietzsche seeks to dislocate Western philosophy as a mirror of the nature of things into an explanation of explanations, an ordering of accumulated sensory experiences as they take place in and are bounded by language with its own sensory basis. He points, in other words, toward constitutive poetics as the central cultural operation, one that this novel pursues primarily in the context of creating a myth of identity.

In a curious way Jeremiah's radical testing of the ideas of his romantic heritage takes them in the reverse direction from the ideal, back into the concrete experiences whereby world and idea test each other, whereby in fact they fail to redeem—be adequate to, in Nietzsche's language—each other. The realms of concept and raw experience that culture wills to master thus flow back together along their generative lines and not only overlap, but blur and absorb each other. It is perhaps no accident, then, that the realm of abstraction he attempts to erect in the concrete fuses for him with that concrete until he can no longer hold the abstract's clear and pure lines and can no longer see the substantial in the murk and mist of the world—it is always transformed for him by the interpretive "scheme that we cannot throw off." He relives the sensory basis of conceptual abstractions and loses the culture's illusory separation of the two. It is precisely the process that Nietzsche traces in the reverse direction, deconstructing metaphysical notions along their roughly historical or generative lines; Jeremiah works backward but seems to find the same traces of the "coarse sensualistic" in the pure idea and the "interpretation" according to the idea already in the "facts."

As Jeremiah persists in his efforts, he tells a parable that underscores not only his dilemma but the primal need that drives him onward. The parable is about an old boatman on the river at night who finds shore and shadow fusing in the darkness. Applying it to his own efforts, Jeremiah continues: "So I looked into that darkness of men's hearts and words and could not be sure where lay the shore of truth. But that brought not the fear. That comes when you look into your own heart, and in that darkness the shadow and shore confound. Where was my truth? Where was my truth? And for the moment I did not know why I had come here, or what need had brought me, for the idea by which man would live gets lost in the jostle and pudder of things" (329-30). No doubt the "jostle and pudder" is a good deal like the "murk and mist," but in any case the idea is getting lost in things, and with good reason. One cannot say that truth in this novel is like a shore with its figurative connotations of a stable bank guiding one to a fixed destination. Jeremiah's confounding derives from the significant joining of "why" (with its relation to the idea) and "need," which has much more to do with concrete survival, emotional and otherwise, than with the conceptual realm Jeremiah always appeals to for direction. Indeed, Nietzsche again is helpful in explication, for he presents knowledge (the Idea) as the will to power over things, as an "apparatus" for "taking possession of things" (274), as "a very well acquired habit of belief" that has more to do with the practical "preservation of man" as a species than with the "truth of things." On the fringe of Jeremiah's consciousness is the sense that it is his extraordinary *need* to enact a stable definition of himself that leads him to carry out the dramas in which he engages. The commitment that requires recourse to prestructured understanding necessarily removes him from the truth of things to the pragmatics of preservation, the provisionality of what has worked before masquerading as transcendent truth.

Hence not only does experience teach him about the relative nature of truth and about the wild and trackless nature of the individual underneath the texture of cultural history, but he also finds his metaphoric language leading him back to the sensory and thus problematic origins of the concepts it figures forth in his writings. Jeremiah is left with considerably less than the pure flame of the Idea lighting his pathway to certainty and fulfillment. He comes instead to the knowledge that "my life was nothing and all I had ever done was nothing and meant nothing," at least insofar as he aspired to embody some unique ideal and thus not end up to be, as he thinks he does, "no different from any man's life." The narrator evinces some anxiety at this point, since if knowledge indeed means recognizing that the "self is gratuitous" (because none of us represents either a transcendent entity or some permanent and enduring ideal), then the idea of a romantic novel is hollow. But his reflections bring him to some worthwhile realizations of his own:

> He had come to the "knowledge," he says. He says that, but we can scarcely believe him, for if he had come truly to the knowledge, would he have sat again the next day at his table and written down the account of all that Munn Short had said, and all that he himself had said, and the horror of his nightmare? With that knowledge what would have been the meaning of that act of recording? But he did write it, and the words are all there before us on the yellowing, curling sheets. Or is there the paradox that even in that knowledge, even when it is truly had, man must put down the words, must make the record? For even when that knowledge of blankness comes, he is still man and must "justify"? (392–93)

"Blankness" is a disquieting result for an effort at explaining, at recording the meaning of the self, world, and life, and it reminds us of Marlow's fascination with the "blank" Flora his narrative seeks to fill in. Blankness, the absence of words, is the realm beyond that line we have found between the sayable and the trackless. It is perhaps the same to which Colonel Fort, the book's wisest man, comes: "There is no sadness like the sadness of a man who knows the secrets of the world and of power, for only that man is forced to face the blankness of the last secret" (37), the secret of "the man himself." Jeremiah's earlier idea of explaining the self as a light beyond the murk and mist of things presupposes the metaphysical framework of a structure of truth rather than this new sense of a set of codes and pre-texts whose matrixes overlap until the projection we call the "self" becomes apparent. Man is thus a textual creature and "must make the record" even if what he has is a "knowledge of blankness." There may only be the passion of recording, of "justifying" not in the sense of invoking transcendental or scientific laws explaining the ways of God and man, but of "justifying" the typographical margins of a life whose "selfhood" falls now between the quotation marks from opposing traditions (of Jeremiah's romanticism, the narrator's realism), a selfhood, that is, which is the textual creation of an interpreter—in first person, as in Jeremiah's journal, or in third, as in the novel at hand.

One of the more significant passages in which Jeremiah works out this sort of knowledge comes just after the narrator mentions the "divine frenzy and sweet blackness" (Jeremiah's phrase) of Beaumont's naturalistic phase in the West and then summarizes the insights Jeremiah's journals reach:

> But he came to know how hard it was "to know the inwardness and truth of things, for a man remembers what was the fact, but even as he remembers he knows the fact to be a fleeting shadow of something that passed, as when he looks at the ground and sees the swift shadow of a bird's flight and lifts his eyes, but the hawk, or whatever bird it was that had swooped thus low, is gone." The truth would justify, for "if we can truly know the truth we know that it could never have been otherwise, and what we know to be true we can accept, for that is all the heart yearns for in the end." But it was hard to know. (379–80)

The truth "would" justify, would manifest itself in its eternally valid and unchanging nature, acceptable and satisfying to the deepest yearning of the heart—but the catch is in the conditional of "would" and "if." We get not the hawk, let alone its inwardness, but only its deceptive and distorted shadow as a trace of the thing itself. We get, in other words, only the extent to which it blocks the light. (The same light beyond the murk and mist of things?) We have not the fact but the interpretation, the outline, the hypothesis, the abstraction. Indeed it seems "hard to know," for the blank shadow fails to provide what "the heart yearns for." We might well conclude that when Jeremiah defines his "unpardonable" crime as that of "the self," he identifies selfhood with his entire process of deceptive abstracting, of supposing his coherence in terms of concepts and idealized patterns, of anticipating the fulfillment of his self in the linguistic terms of inherited conventions.

What is put in jeopardy with such an analysis of selfhood? First of all, as Jeremiah says in the preceding passage, traces replace facts as the building blocks we have to work with. What we see is already a mislead-ing sign that something has passed whose own inward nature is unattain-able, whose outline, in fact, can only be guessed at, whose identity is at best approximate. It is guessed at and approximated on the basis of our own limited experiences both directly and indirectly through the textual pool of our cultural heritage. Sometimes Jeremiah's errors come from his own individual naïveté, his simple lack of knowledge. Most of the time, however, they come from the influence of his interpretations of his own past and that cultural past in his reading; in Nietzsche's terms, "memory also maintains the habit of the old interpretations, i.e., of erroneous causality—so that the 'inner experience' has to contain within it the consequences of all previous false causal fictions" (266). Such a burden of error means that all the connections between the shadow and the hawk, between the trace and the thing itself, are fictions that leap across the gap between our perceptions of things (because "all sense perceptions are permeated with value judgments" [275]) and the things themselves, between the word as figure and the referent as thing, be-tween the cultural system of defining and distributing significance and the natural state of things in their neutrality. Even as we hunt for *le mot juste,* we have already wrenched the subject from its natural state and are dealing with a trace formed as a function of the needs that led us to notice it in the first place and of the previous "false fictions" that are always with us.

Nietzsche has his own parable for the novel's persistent theme of problematic and circular interpretation:

> As a genius of construction man raises himself far above the bee in the following way: whereas the bee builds with wax that he gathers from nature, man builds with the far more delicate conceptual material which he first has to manufacture from himself. In this he is greatly to be admired, but not on account of his drive for truth or for pure knowledge of things. When someone hides something behind a bush and looks for it again in the same place and finds it there as well, there is not much to praise in such seeking and finding. Yet this is how matters stand regarding seeking and finding "truth" within the realm of reason. If I make up the definition of a mammal, and then, after inspecting a camel, declare "look, a mammal," I have indeed brought a truth to light in this way, but it is a truth of limited value. That is to say, it is a thoroughly anthropomorphic truth which contains not a single point which would be "true in itself" or really and uni-versally valid apart from man. At bottom, what the investigator of such truths is seeking is only the metamorphosis of the world into man.[9]

Nietzsche's parable thus pierces to the heart of narrative's attempt to constitute the identity of a protagonist. The "metamorphosis of the world into man" becomes almost a trick phrase, for "the world" includes, as we have seen Nietzsche suggest, the inner world we call "conscious-ness," and "man" is, in the final analysis, less an ontological being than a concept constituted according to a distinctly metaphysical poetics that Jeremiah exhausts in his efforts to embody it.

The alternatives for Jeremiah are bleak. In the wilderness of the island of La Grand' Bosse, Jeremiah undergoes a strange experience in which he feels himself becoming the "blankness" we have found elsewhere in the novel whenever a character penetrates, for a moment, the cultural membrane within which he breathes. As he travels westward into the wilderness, he feels that this primal land where "nobody keers what yore name is or what you done" will restore him. He goes so far as to think it "would be peace, would be like being born again, would be like the joy of grace and salvation" (419). Nature replaces the Christian heaven of his youth, for "nobody keers" about such cultural matters as names and histories. "Ah, I thought then, the land is the same, and its beauty, and is voiceless, whatever our errand, whether for wealth or peace, to open or to close" (421). Nature thus seems safe from any incursion of culture.

The benign Eden quickly becomes, however, "a peace which he called the 'black inwardness and womb of the quagmire'" (439), a "last peace which was neither happiness nor unhappiness but darkness" (445), a "communion only in the blank cup of nature" (463). When he seeks the grounds of our concepts of selfhood in this realm of nature, a realm prior to the culture either of the philosophical Idea or of the political World, he finds only the lowest common physical denominator: a sense of the human community as the "jewel" of a syphilitic lesion. The kind of "innocence" he finds in nature is not Rousseau's state of the noble savage, but "what man cannot endure and be man"; for to be human, Jeremiah observes, is to "bear my heart within me like a bleeding sore of self," a self he feels only as the "guilt" of contending with the (cul-tural) norms he has violated (463). Hence there is no "natural" author-ity to sanction the structure of values he assumed gave life its meaning and coherence, merely that Nietzschean stance of individual interpreta-tion from which he posits the continuity of his own life as a quest.

The alternative to this alienation is the troubled existence he has back in the settlements. As we have seen, he finds there no "world" not already formed by an "idea," and hence no unmediated intersubjective source of authentic validation. This source is further complicated by Jeremiah's sense that "each person was but himself and reaching out the hand across distance did not avail" [442]). Nor does he find, how-ever, any "idea" that has not come to him from the (cultural) "world," thus sealing him off from any access to a self-evidently true transcendent center.[10] In the final analysis, then, Jeremiah Beaumont exists not in the timeless space of transcendent being, but in the misty zone where culture conjures up its narrative myths (of self, of truth) and then, as we have seen in *Chance,* naturalizes them and "forgets" they were ever constituted rather than "received." The common hope that Idea and World could coexist, whether in truth, nature, or being (or even being together), is the same nostalgic longing we see Jeremiah expressing so plaintively throughout his journals. Ultimately, then, the novel's "target" is not merely a deluded pseudoromantic, or romanticism, or the genre of the romantic novel, but mystification about culture itself and about narrative's place within its workings as a means of sustaining the cultural myth of selfhood.

Narrative and Selfhood

The novel's reflexive dimension thus achieves a Nietzschean dispersal of both the method and the material of the romantic novel into the intertextual network of culture. One might well ask, then, what viable stance this disintegration of historiography leaves the narrator—he who poses as the manager of the pile of "yellowing, curling sheets" and is left echoing Jeremiah's last question ("Was all for naught?") quite literally, just as he must methodologically. He echoes more, however, for if the venture they must undertake is not possible, it nonetheless seems somehow necessary. That is, the novel deconstructs its procedures, but it does so not simply to turn its back upon those means, and certainly not to abandon altogether the attempt to achieve its ends. Its reflexive comments circle around narrative's stress points and invalidate the text's assimilation of the textual models of romance, history, or philosophy. Nonetheless, the text also takes seriously the effort to proceed as if history were continuous in causation, unified with significance, and coherent within a larger and stable structure of values that permits unqualified intuitions about truth and error, good faith and bad, fact and conjecture. It even proceeds as if the model of history were applicable on the individual level where the self as transcendent or timeless entity provides the continuity, unity, and coherence of the series of events that constitute a biography. How does one make sense of this apparent contradiction?

A last look at Jeremiah's handling of such problems may enable us to achieve some answer to this question. Jeremiah confronts one version of this paradox when he discovers that the self seems more real, more knowable, in the falsifying act of retrospective interpretation than in the presumably more immediate act of experiencing: "He struggled to know it, to live back into the past time and know it as he had not been able to know it when caught in the toils of its presentness" (380). He finds himself, in other words, only through the Nietzschean will to impose an interpretive order. Repeatedly we find Jeremiah in the situation of looking out upon his own act "as from a window" when the seemingly detached act of speaking or lifting an arm can through interpretive vision "become real" and "take meaning" (119). Moreover, in the "toils of its presentness" the self seems not to act according to the metaphysical model of selfhood—planning, intending, and carrying out its purposeful acts—but to act impulsively, as when Jeremiah repeatedly simply does things. What comes to his consciousness are literally effects rather than causes as, according to the metaphysical notion, they should be—Jeremiah seems to embody Nietzsche's contention that selfhood is simply another abstract concept and "the phenomena of consciousness merely terminal phenomena" rather than "a cause" (352). There is an unnameable "necessity" that lies beyond any explanation of motivation he can offer (74) and that surfaces in the narrative as a long series of impulsive acts that come from something more like the behaviorist's automaton than from the metaphysician's conscious self.

For example, he realizes he "fought on an impulse" at Lumton (100); he bursts out at Tom Barron "without premeditation" (141); "without thinking" he kisses the dying Mrs. Jordan and professes love of someone who spooks him elsewhere in the narrative (144). "Without judgment or intention" he throws Fort to the ground rather than killing him (131); he knows neither why he leaped to Mr. Tupper's defense nor why he does not leap to his own in the tavern brawl (161, 164); he promises Madison to keep "good conscience in politics" "though he had not willed that answer" (181). His words come at Dr. Burnham "beyond any premeditation" (222), as indeed does the whole side trip into his childhood haunts, and so forth. These are only representative examples from the first half of the novel. The point is not that Jeremiah is simply an impulsive young man, though certainly he is that as well. The point is that repeatedly both he and the modern narrator describe action without either will or premeditation, hallmarks of the metaphysical theory of self that drives Jeremiah to his long and futile attempts at explanation.

Hence his conscious self is neither an entity immediately accessible to an (auto)biographer nor a unique, original shaper and controller of its destiny. If it is the romantic novel's project to relate the individual consciousness to the ideal realm toward which it aspires, then *World Enough and Time* is a very strange exemplar of the genre. But Jeremiah

147

enables us to understand a bit more about this paradoxical state of affairs. In his final comments he longs for "a way I have missed" to achieve the existential plenitude when "the word becomes flesh" and the completeness of narrative when "the flesh becomes word" (464). He knows he has failed to find the way "whereby loneliness becomes communion without contamination," for existence in the world pulls abstract ideals back down to their sensory and arbitrary origins. He has also failed to find the way "whereby contamination becomes purity without exile," for as we have seen, relationships are contaminated both by the stylized roles inculcated by romance and by the irremediable egoism of the individual, while to follow truth out of the contamination of the world is to become lost in the trackless wilds beyond culture. He still insists "there must be a way," but he admits that "I may not have it now." Romantic to the last, Jeremiah persists in taking his failure as his personal sin rather than as an inevitable human failure.

At the same time that one strain of his last paragraph persists in such mystification, he also breaks through for a moment to a sense of the blankness apart from his textual antecedents. He concludes that "all I can have now is knowledge . . . [of] the terrible logic of life," a knowledge that though he is driven by belief to his quest, the quest is unfulfillable, its assumptions a fiction, its objective an illusion. Something of this universalizing knowledge is in his confession that his is "the crime of self, the crime of life" (462), rather than the highly personal sense of failure he also feels, that it is the necessary cultural sin to commit the errors anatomized in this reflexive narrative. Indeed, perhaps it is because of this sense that, at the very moment he seems thus to accept this knowledge of life demystified, he launches yet another high drama, yet another conceptual role to play, a role couched in the language of melodrama: "I go home through the wilderness now and know that I may not have redemption. I no longer seek to justify. I seek only to suffer. I will shake the hangman's hand, and will call him my brother, at last" (464). In one sense there is justification in calling the hangman, who deals in the literal death of that idealization we call the self, the brother of one who for a moment acknowledges the demise of his own idealizations of life. At the same time, however, the last two lines take the confessional of the first two and convert it into a noble resignation reminiscent of stock figures like Sidney Carton—the graceful gesture on the scaffold, the sense of falling upon the thorns of life and bleeding. The melodramatic posturing belies the effect of knowing, as if the knowledge made available by distancing oneself from artificial constructs does not provide a basis for authentic being, as if being human implies positing and posturing alongside and discontinuous with the

148

knowledge of their inauthenticity.[11] That is, we are necessarily constitutive, though we can also be reflexively aware of it.

That, perhaps, is one way to sum up the effects of this novel's simultaneous positing and deconstructing of its romantic project. Essentially
ironic, reflexivity here recognizes that we are both scientist and nomad,
that we impose our will to power over the chaotic teeth and thigh bones
of our existence, making our lives coherent and whole, but that we are
also louse-bitten wanderers mystified by the kingly ruins of our culture's
metaphysical abstractions, having forgotten their basis in problematic
traces, a figurative linguistic medium, and the simplistic schematics of
interpretation. Such abstractions are kingly in the aspiration to dominion they reflect, but always—as artifice—they are already ruins of that
dream of absolute mastery of world, of history, or of self. Part of those
ruins must necessarily be the assumption by narrative theorists that the
ontological self is an unproblematic reference point in theories of character or point of view. The reflexive themes of this novel, that is, also
pertain to any theory that attempts to tell the story of the novel's narrators: both the method and the material are subject to the Nietzschean
dispersal of interpretation and selfhood into the cultural paradigms
within which both novelists and theorists necessarily work.

Warren and Late Modernism

Sustained by the general pervasiveness of phenomenological and existential analytics in their intellectual atmosphere, late modernist writers,
even more than their predecessors, seem preoccupied by the nature and
grounds of subjectivity. Typically, their narratives both rely upon and
undo several key sources or underpinnings of "authentic" selfhood.
These preoccupations, while necessarily dominating our attention to
their texts, bring with them the problem of how we might define the relation between such issues and the ideological concerns we have found
recurrent in reflexivity. For example, the events of *World Enough and
Time* take place amid social upheaval, and the relation between public
and private issues is not always clear. In the middle of a depression the
state legislature passes a replevin bill (to delay debt collection) in conflict with the constitutional guarantee of economic contracts. The legal
debate is class oriented, though also, as is always the case, complicated
by pitting economic privilege and the principle of order against the
interests of labor and the principle of opportunity. The champions of
the relief party are men like Skroggs, Wilkie, and Fort—those whose
lower-class origins and subsequent struggle for meritocratic advance

149

contribute both a populist fervor (as rhetorician, operative, and states-man) and a moral ambiguity (they are also, respectively, a killer, a scoundrel, and a seducer).

Jeremiah Beaumont is an extreme form of this mix of attributes, and indeed Warren tells us he "began to think of the political struggle of the time as a kind of mirror I could hold up to the personal story."[12] With ambiguity comes the lack of closure, however, for although the rule of the constitution finally prevails, as does that of the historian over Jere-miah Beaumont, each case is a closure of violence rather than of resolu-tion. Just as the narrator finally knows no more than Beaumont, so does the constitution fail to resolve the conflict between the ideals of democracy and the economic realities that shape the lives of the citizens it regulates. Form and history remain incommensurate.

In a curious way Rabbit Angstrom, at least the Rabbit of *Rabbit, Run,* shares these dilemmas with Jeremiah Beaumont, and John Updike moves further in defining these dilemmas than his critics generally indicate. Jeremiah touches the ideal in a textual zone he finally cannot dwell within; Rabbit has an adolescent hot streak in a ballgame, touching the ideal in an athletic utopia that vanishes with the buzzer. Though never pressed for a buck, Rabbit nonetheless finds no space in his socioeco-nomic order within which he can prolong the magic rightness of the perfect thirty footer. Thrown back upon the construct of selfhood by a culture that masks its failure to nurture as an individual failure to achieve authenticity, Rabbit finds an emptiness at the heart of selfhood akin to Jeremiah's bleakest vision.

The novel often appears to be an existentialist exemplum as orthodox as Percy's parables. But Updike can be an open thinker when he wishes. Note, for example, his comments in this interview more than a decade after *Rabbit, Run:*

> My books feed, I suppose, on some kind of perverse relish in the fact that there are insolvable problems. There is no reconciliation between the inner, intimate appetites and the external consolations of life. You want to live forever, you want to have endless wealth, you have an endless avarice for conquests, crave endless freedom really. And yet, despite the aggressive desires, something within us expects no menace. But there is no way to reconcile these individual wants to the very real need of any society to set strict limits and to confine its members. *Rabbit, Run,* which is a book much on my mind lately, I wrote just to say that there is no solution. It is a novel about the bouncing, the oscillating back and forth between these two kinds of urgencies until, eventually, one just gets tired and wears out and dies, and that's the end of the problem.[13]

Although the convention-bound side of Updike is much in evidence with its "strict limits," so is an undervalued flexibility that finds "no solution" to the kind of question Jeremiah Beaumont and Rabbit Angstrom want settled.

Hence to a certain extent the opening episode, in which Rabbit joins a pickup game, could be seen as an existentialist lesson in balancing the reality of aging and death with the achievement of personal identity— the "weighty" body and short breath with the "tautness" of an "ace" (8-9).[14] Against the "tightening net" of the sameness of his life is the flood of "deeper instincts" tapping "freedom like oxygen everywhere around him" until he "is the Dalai Lama," existential self-begetter. When the inauthenticity of everydayness, Heidegger's *Altäglichkeit*, closes in, "he runs. Ah: runs. Runs" (255). Although these are the last words, literally, in the novel, this apparent escape is not so simple. For one thing, Rabbit has no real place to go that is any better than what he leaves, as Updike's difficulties in producing a convincing sequel indicate. The "strict limits" his society sets to his wish to live, his economic aspirations, his various desires (to recur to Updike's comments) are limits that are finally inescapable. Moreover, Updike works into the fabric of this novel some interesting passages undermining the props an existentialist text might seem to require.

Indeed, Rabbit has the troubling sensation that in the confused turnings of desire he has been both mistaken and true in following a "right" path—that he is, in a puzzle of an image, "like a musical note that all the while it is being held seems to travel though it stays in the same place" (193). There is here an "oscillating back and forth" between two kinds of human being—an active one that appears to travel, with all the cultural implications of the journey of growth, development, and teleology in general, but also a passive one played within a culturally constituted *langue* of notes and harmonies and upon a given social instrument with clear lines and structures determining the forms to which it can give rise. It is this oscillation at the heart of *Rabbit, Run* that links it to Robert Penn Warren's searching probe of the romantic novel at the heart of late modernist narrative and that defines its difference from less critical texts of the period and from more strictly limited critical readings of its own material.

Updike toys with but finally complicates a cultural nostalgia for instinct, an unmediated flow of the natural deriving from the same romantic ethos Warren studies in *World Enough and Time*. Running, driving, sex, and basketball are among the activities in which the unconscious, unpremeditated, and "natural" are prized, and Updike ties them together by having the literal ball of one become the metaphoric wad of map thrown out the window in another, by having the skirt of sex surround the hoop, and so forth. But the crucial figure of the criss-crossing pattern, repeated in Rabbit's "random" runs, road maps, sexual triangles, and basketball playbooks, correlates not with a benevolent nature, but rather with the enmeshing social relations Rabbit cannot altogether elude. He finds that his life "clings to his back like a tightening net" (16), his mother "wraps him in a hug" that entails the push/pull of Oedipal smothering (241), and the whole community becomes a menace as "all under him Harry feels these humans knit together" (241). Partly those relations legislate pressure to earn a living at certain "approved" jobs, and partly they involve a set of conventional roles he is to play in personal relationships. Most basically, though, they permeate and mediate any relation to a primordial nature either within or without. Hence Rabbit has no better luck than Jeremiah Beaumont in escaping to nature itself. On his first (and only imagined) journey up Mount Judge, he thinks of the unexplored reaches of a near-primeval forest:

> But in long patches of forgotten pine plantation the needle-hushed floor of land glides up and up, on and on, under endless tunnels of dead green and you seem to have passed through silence into something worse. And then, coming upon a patch of sunlight the branches neglect to keep out or upon a softened stone-filled cellar pit dug by some brave and monstrous settler centuries ago, you become vividly frightened, as if this other sign of life will call attention to yourself, and the menace of the trees will become active. Your fear trills like an alarm bell you cannot shut off, the louder the faster you run, hunchbacked, until distinctly, with a gasp of the clutch, a near car shifts gears, and the stumpy white posts of the guard fence dawn behind the pine trunks. Then, safe on the firm blacktop, you decide whether to walk back down home or to hike up to the Pinnacle Hotel for a candy bar and a view of Brewer spread out below like a carpet. (18–19)

Culture is a comforting carpet, covering and making a domicile out of the wilderness and supplying unambiguous asphalt lines (Like black lines on a page?) connecting its havens, but nature is a "menace" against which one needs a "guard fence" for protection.

This contrast is even more heightened late in the novel when Rabbit actually makes this trek, "trying to keep himself in a straight path" like the cultural line he only appears to have abandoned. Instead of the road he expects, however, there is the shock of a "precipitate hollow" lined by "dead trees" with "a shadow as deep as the last stage of twilight" (246–47). A crumbled house is "a clangorous horror, as if this ruined evidence of a human intrusion into a world of blind life tolls bells that ring to the edges of the universe" (247), an ominous warning to those who would naturalize cultural constructs. He feels lit by a "great spark . . . whereby the blind tumble of matter recognized itself, a spark struck in the collision of two opposed realms." Is this a parable of traditional ontology, the higher order of a being that is conscious and thus human, or does it mark the gulf that separates the cultural creature from any unmediated contact with the "blind tumble of matter" that constitutes culture's other? The man at the gas station tells Harry, "The only way to get somewhere, you know, is to figure out where you're going before you go there" (27). He is an essentialist, confident in his knowledge of origin and end, and hence holds to the first possibility; but when Harry replies, "I don't think so," he cancels that reading. Man makes the land into the language of landscape, and in that language he is estranged from any accessible "natural" map of either land or self.

This condition of being already inserted into a cultural order becomes a more dire condition than the *Geworfenheit* of the early Heidegger's Dasein. Dasein cannot choose its condition of being; Rabbit, it seems, can scarcely choose at all—the pattern in which nature becomes split between a culturally ordered, hence limiting, landscape and a frightening inconceivable other is repeated in various ways everywhere Rabbit turns, whether it is to the psychological arena of intersubjectivity, the conceptual realm of theology, or the more general cultural sphere of discourse itself. Repeatedly, that is, Rabbit finds that, far from starring in some drama of heroic subjectivity, he is caught within a network that leaves him a very different kind of being than the romantic narratives of a Beaumont or a star athlete might have led him to expect. Prestructured and almost semiotic in its medium, being for Rabbit is oddly cut off from such traditional sources of authenticity as nature, intersubjectivity or any definition of "humanness" not subject to history or a given culture.

For example, Rabbit's various Oedipal overlays are half playful, half indicative of the persistence of a fixed order in which the gap of desire remains unclosable. "The union of breast and baby's face makes a globular symmetry to which both he and Nelson want to attach themselves" (194). Lucy Eccles's anger aligns itself with that of his mother—each, "suddenly caught in some confusion of her own, would turn on the heat that way" (202). Early in the novel he plays an elaborately allegorical game of Oedipal golf, himself the ball, the play shifting from irons (Janice) to woods (Ruth) until "the ball runs, hops and hops, hides in a bush; white tail. And when he walks there, the bush is damn somebody, his mother; he lifts the huffy branches like shirts, in a fury of shame but with care not to break any, and these branches bother his legs while he tries to pour his will down into the hard irreducible pellet that is not really himself yet in a way is; just the way it sits there in the center of everything" (110). The serial overlays of the women, the extraordinary effort of concentrating his will into a pellet (as if the pellet of

153

selfhood were indeed the construct of a Nietzschean will), the egoistic self-absorption all provide rich stuff for Oedipal readings in which it is always his mother in the bush, his other women merely the instruments by which he swings back into the "sad scruff" of various displacements of their troubled relationship. As he thinks late in the novel, "with his mother there's no question of liking him they're not even in a way separate people he began in her stomach and if she gave him life she can take it away and if he feels that withdrawal it will be the grave itself. Of all the people in the world he wants to see her least. He wishes she'd die" (239). Unity and separation, enablement and castration, love and death, attachment and death wish—the psychology of early childhood locks Rabbit in, affecting all his relations. It is no wonder that this woman whose criticisms are "somehow too powerful, at least with him" (16) should leave him feeling "the difficulty of pleasing someone" (179), that things are beginning to "hem him in," and that "the mute dense presences" of Janice and Ruth are "pushing in the dark like crags under water" (192). Partly Rabbit cannot choose freely the shape of his relations to others because of the language of Oedipal entanglements in which he has always found himself.

Theology, and the whole edifice of conceptual thought for which it stands, proves no more sure a resource for Rabbit. On the one hand his "feeling that there is an unseen world is instinctive" (195), he "wants to believe in the sky as the source of all things" (233), and he feels "that somewhere behind all this . . . there's something that wants me to find it" (107). He inherits, in other words, the traditional map of the conceptual territory, but he gets nowhere trying to follow that map. His faith is none too steady; after professing his belief to Ruth, "he wonders if he's lying. If he is, he is hung in the middle of nowhere, and the thought hollows him, makes his heart tremble" (77). Later on at the hospital, his life seems "a magic dance empty of belief" (165), and the nonexistence of God fuses with the mortality of Janice, his "perverted" with his procreative ejaculations, until all "seems a sequence of grotesque poses assumed to no purpose." Sex, that is, holds death and demystification at bay, or vice versa, procreation and perversion becoming interchangeable poses no longer distinguished by a reliable concept of authenticity. Later praying "doesn't do it. There's no connection" (230), even though "he keeps saying [forgive me] silently to no one" (231). Finally, "the ultimate, 'Why am I me?'—starts panic in his heart. Coldness spreads through his body and he feels detached, as if at last he is, what he's always dreaded, walking on air" (235). Indeed, when he finally hears out his old coach, what he hears as a defense against misery is a theory of morality worthy of Nietzsche: "Right and wrong aren't dropped from the sky. We. We make them" (232).

In nature Rabbit finds not instinctive spontaneity as his ground for authenticity, but a willful and predatory Jocasta—"Nature leads you up like a mother and as soon as she gets her little price [procreation] leaves you with nothing" (73). In relationships, Rabbit finds not the I-Thou of intersubjectivity but the futile displacements of Oedipal desires and the inevitable fading of romance into the institution of family life with Janice (Ruth, her would-be replacement, also asks for marriage). And in the search for the Idea, as Jeremiah Beaumont called it, the church window that begins as a "circle of red and purple and gold [which] seems in the city night a hole punched in reality to show the abstract brilliance burning underneath" (69) becomes "a dark circle in a stone facade" (254). The plenitude of color is darkness if the church is too poor or careless to create the illusion; "reality" is in fact the "stone facade" of architectural design. "Burning underneath" is not so much the "abstract brilliance" of an ultimate coherence of things as the empty church on the inside, the empty street on the outside, spaces whose differences is created only by the play of human design.

That final emptiness in which inside and outside dissolve into each other bears on more than theology. At novel's end Rabbit "feels his inside as very real suddenly, a pure blank space in the middle of a dense net" (254). That net is woven of all the lines stretched between nature and culture, spun of relations, and dependent upon the concepts by which the metaphysical, ethical, even economic strands are composed. The self is real as an organism of blind matter with its "debt" to procreation, but as selfhood is the "blank space" bounded by these cultural strands. Or, as Foucault puts it at one point, "The individual is not to be conceived as a sort of elementary nucleus, a primitive atom, a multiple and inert material on which power comes to fasten or against which it happens to strike, and in so doing subdues or crushes individuals. In fact, it is already one of the prime effects of power that certain bodies, certain gestures, certain discourses, certain desires, come to be identified and constituted as individuals" (98).[15] Rabbit comes to feel not an "elementary nucleus" at the heart of his experience, but rather the distillation of "certain" repertoires composing his consciousness; power, as Foucault explains, is "exercised through a netlike organisation" rather than being "localised here or there," and "individuals circulate between its threads," indeed are bounded and thus constituted by those threads. Rabbit tries every escape in the cultural repertoire to evade being a more or less passive effect of power, but he finds himself like a spider always hanging in one blank space or another of the discursive web of culture. Updike embraces no myth of existential freedom, nor any traditional faith in transcending that web; indeed, at certain moments the text seems ready to place the main currents of mid-century ontology, metaphysics, ethics, all in the branches of a Nietzschean genealogy of Western thought. Certainly at times in this novel, and perhaps more so in other works, Updike often places himself more comfortably within established notions. But here one finds curious reminders of the troubling territory into which we have seen Warren take late modernist narrative. No one in either novel, even the heroic Fort, finds an "elementary nucleus" or "multiple and inert material" at the heart of selfhood—rather, there is Fort's "blankness" and Rabbit's "empty space" bounded by the discursive lines woven into the language of the unconscious.

Rabbit recognizes both the hazardous and the unavoidable qualities of so discursive a self when he finds himself unable to cut off Eccles's questions: "Rabbit doesn't want to tell him anything. The more he tells, the more he loses. He's safe inside his own skin, he doesn't want to come out. This guy's whole game is to get him out into the open where he can be manipulated. But the fierce convention of courtesy pries open Rabbit's lips." (105). Courtesy pries, the self transpires in the already spoken, and one exists in a mesh of language subject to all those interests, institutions, and ideologies to which its threads are attached. Like *World Enough and Time,* Updike's *Rabbit, Run* pushes to the limit the romantic novel's effort to happen more or less uncritically within the framework of the protagonist achieving selfhood. Both circle the grounds of that basic plot, ultimately clearing that ground of its solidity, leaving us, with Rabbit, in the air. Though he runs as hard as any fictional protagonist, Rabbit gets nowhere in particular except, as we have seen, to a blank space rather than a positive mark. Hence, despite Updike's lack of interest in explicitly reflexive techniques in the novel, the work becomes at a deeper level a reflexive hollowing of the nucleus of late modernist narrative. Rabbit runs in reflexive circles around the central premises of such fiction, trying hard to understand what supports the kind of active being it legislates, finding instead a relatively passive form of being more Foucauldian than existential.

Walker Percy might at first seem an odd choice for this study, for his novels are generally regarded as quite consistently Kierkegaardian, as if his purpose were to narrate *Sickness unto Death* or *Fear and Trembling.* *The Moviegoer, The Last Gentleman, Love in the Ruins, The Second*

Coming, all dramatize Percy's favorite situation, the protagonist trapped in inauthenticity, despairing without knowing it, moved finally less to some suddenly authentic and positive life-style than to that vigil of the knight of faith watching and waiting for a sign. It is precisely this apparent repetition of existentialist dogma that draws my interest to Percy, especially to *Lancelot,* perhaps least favored of his novels among those who like Percy most.

The point is what happens when Percy articulates his familiar themes through an inmate in an asylum who has apparently blown up the family mansion, killing his wife and the film crew that includes her current lover. I want to argue that *Lancelot* becomes in effect a reflexive commentary upon the recurrent pattern of Kierkegaardian existentialism underlying all of Percy's novels, providing a textbook narratization of that credo that nonetheless is allowed to flower on the Baudelairean soil of homocidal mania. If our analysis of Updike's play with existentialism found selfhood a blank space, bounded by the external discursive lines of power rather than by the internal borders of a unitary nucleus, this analysis of Percy's novel will note how close it comes to finding a blankness at the heart of the watching and waiting. In the suspension of positive knowledge (about truth, God, self) required in the Kierkegaardian escape from routine, orthodoxy, and mere convention, Percy's protagonist is finally driven to a voided space in which organized thought (his listener's orthodoxy, for example), history (as embodied in the burned mansion), and even personal memory (his dismissal of the importance of remembering the events) are all jettisoned in favor of a new age in which, it appears, a rural retreat reminiscent of *Bleak House* seems to suffice. It is a curiously contradictory vision in which religious or metaphysical categories serve as near transcendental signifieds anchoring existence even though no specific content within those categories can be located or affirmed. Precisely the havens undermined in *Rabbit, Run* are sought by Percy's protagonist—nature, intersubjective relationships, the frame of selfhood—their primary justification being their otherness to conventional daily life.

What, finally, we find is an oscillation between Kierkegaardian will, the leap of faith beyond where the rational can comfortably go, and the Nietzschean will. Lancelot's end point, a survivalist ready to wield the sword of the Archangel Michael on his own eschatological front, is not so different from that of the Nietzschean will to power over the recalcitrance of inchoate materiality, the unreachable subjectivity of the other, and the polyphonic, heteroglossiac textuality of the cultural membrane from which we take our impressions of "reality." Indeed, the theme of narration in *Lancelot* is profoundly tied to that of will, leading to a new age rising from the ashes of Belle Isle in ways that are far from innocent. When that oasis of idealism and historical nostalgia passes into the realm of tourism, and when the movie business tropes and retropes illusion and reality, the novel begins to shimmer at the point where the distance erodes dramatically between the Kierkegaardian and Nietzschean positions.

Partly this oscillation is discernible in a series of apparent oppositions bearing on ethics, ontology, intersubjectivity, and history, each of which frustrates the kind of closure Jeremiah and Rabbit were seeking. Lancelot thinks at the outset of his conversations with Percival that one should "undertake a search not for God but for evil" (53), "a purely evil deed, an intolerable deed for which there is no explanation" (54); pure evil would rise above the complicated acts of history with their multiply determined explanations and *prove* the "pure and simple" realm of absolutes. Just like Jeremiah, he wonders if one can "ever be sure of anything," feeling that "I had to find out" (139). "One has to know for sure before doing anything . . . I had to be absolutely certain" (43). What he discovers, of course, is "nothing at the heart of evil," that "there was no 'secret' after all, no discovery, no flickering of interest, nothing at all, not even any evil. There was no sense of coming close to the 'answer' " (274).

This silent void is also at the individual level, of course. In place of the authentic feeling psychotherapy seeks to liberate, there is "numbness and coldness, no, not a feeling, but a lack of feeling" (274); Lancelot ends his "therapy" not by connecting to an inner self of free-flowing emotion, but with "a slight curiosity about walking down that street out there" (274). That is, he ends with something not much more than a psychomotor itch to move about in the world (as opposed to feeling out his own identity, carrying out a metaphysical program, or the like). Similarly, to the goal of psychotherapeutic discourse to *remember* the crucial clues that unlock the hermeneutic door to the inner answer, Lance opposes his notion that "I won't know for sure [what happened] until I say it" (110), a curious performative in which lines of discourse constitute rather than represent. Lance even dissolves the ideal of psychoanalytic dialogue itself, suggesting instead that "to *make conversation* in the old tongue, the old worn-out language . . . can't be done" (89). The "old tongue" narratizes according to its own hidden agenda of values, in the way that "it is impossible to speak of love without sounding like Tin Pan Alley" (178) or of self without sounding like the metaphysical tradition underlying convention. Nonetheless, the old language is all we have; Lance's effort to knock on Anna's wall in a "new language" is futile, and so he must "say it" into form with a mainly silent Percival. Significantly, it is not what he finds in his self or his memory, but rather the form of a new age he anticipates generating that enables him to feel the stability and purpose that have apparently led to his imminent release at novel's end—not hermeneutics, but play.

The abundant and overt play with actors serves to take the existentialist cliché that inauthenticity is role playing and fold it over more contemporary intimations of an "authenticity" without ground. Hence Lance complains that the townfolk take the movie stars' roles more seriously than their own lives: "the movie folk were trafficking in illusions in a real world but the real world thought that its reality could only be found in the illusions" (161). In the oscillation between "reality" and "illusion" it is possible to lose the contrast between figure and ground, for the pure roles played by the actors foreground those embedded in the conventional relations we all must live out. Hence the satiric note that "Jan's theory is that by the very nature of the medium cinema should have nothing to do with ideas" is a double note, part commentary on the idiocy of the film being made, part perception of how inaccessible any reliable conceptual ground finally becomes. Indeed, Lance's contempt for Dana gives one pause; he describes the actor as "a blank space filled in by somebody else's idea" (155), but we have seen the numb blankness he feels in himself and his sense that even love is suffused and formed by Tin Pan Alley's ideas. Dana, the "perfect cipher," is more the reality than Lance's occasional nostalgia for transcendental being would allow.

Even intersubjectivity, the I and Thou of which is often the refuge of religious existentialism, has difficulty sustaining itself in the novel. All the women Lance has known, for example, seem versions of each other, as if "woman" were the name of a lack he kept compensating for. He notices on first meeting Margot (and remembers all these years to tell Percival) that her words are oddly anachronistic, "what my mother's generation said" (82). Margot repeats his mother's pattern of infidelity in a relation of lovers "like Camille and Robert Taylor" (228). Nor is Margot the only one. When his first wife dies the slow death of leukemia, he thinks it "curious to wake up one morning alone again in Belle Isle, just as I had been alone in my youth" (88), Lucy apparently having replaced for a while the mother he missed as a child. Even his daughter Siobhan is perceived in a decidedly libidinal light, "as sexual a creature as her mother," much given to showing "her little biscuit" and being noticed for doing so (123). Perhaps most revealing is this passage midway through the novel: "Do you know what it's like to be a self-centered not unhappy man who leads a tolerable finite life, works, eats, drinks, hunts, sleeps, then one fine day discovers that the great starry heavens have opened to him and that his heart is bursting with it. It? She. Her. Woman. Not a category, not a sex, not one of two sexes, a human female creature, but an infinity" (137). In "finite life" there is a lack, the infinity he names woman but which he cannot hold; no woman suffices to satisfy that infinite longing for something "pure and simple" beyond the limitations and complexities of the ordinary, and intersubjectivity falters under the burden such metaphysics places upon it. To one bred on absolutism, of course, "not having her is not breathing" (137), not drawing the breath of life inspired by such framing.

Hence there is a dark comedy in the confused relationship Lance is brewing with Anna next door. It begins in the failure of a new language, and (in the novel) ends with the optimistic conjecture of an intermediary—a record of something less than an unmediated relation. Apparently its most intense direct form is a catastrophic argument in which Lance explains his conclusion that "man's happiness lies for men in men practicing violence upon women and that woman's happiness lies in submitting to it" (241). The theory suggests the inevitable reduction of intersubjectivity to an intrasubjectivity in which the other is known mainly as a player in one's own psychodrama. Anna's response is to tell him to "shove off" (273). The novel's play with intersubjectivity follows an oscillation between various ideals of physical, emotional, and intellectual relationships (an "authentic intersubjectivity" of Buberian proportions, but one not reached by any of the cast) and a broadly focused desire suffused with an absolutist metaphysics; together the two poles allow quite a field for the energies of the characters, but not one in which any of them find anything resembling an "answer," any more than in Lance's more overtly metaphysical musings.

In both metaphysics and intersubjectivity, the Kierkegaardian leap of will and faith struggles to hold its ground against a radically demystifying Nietzschean sense of that leap as a will to mastery over the uncertainties and menaces of human existence. Lance does not omit history, however, from the same contest. One kind of "history," of course, is fair game for all hunters. *Altäglichkeit,* everydayness, the rut so deep that Lance had worn a path in the brick floor of his pigeonnier, is unambiguously stigmatized, and all the familiar components of this existentialist theme are present. War was the only time in forty years Lance's uncle "felt real" (233); once jealousy brings him to life, Lance repeats the Sartrean discovery of a hand by "registering the sensations of my body" for twenty minutes (248); he senses life as "a kind of dream state in which finally I could not be sure that anything was happening at all" (60); he constantly rereads a Raymond Chandler novel so "I could stand my life" (25). All the earmarks are here. So too are the

Kierkegaardian responses—once he awakens, he is able to "watch and wait" (67), to notice "a cherry mole on my breastbone I had never noticed before" (70), to lie down on the bricks and perform a suitably knightly ritual of penance and vigil, to puzzle over "the mystery" of the "here and now" with its question being "What is one to do with oneself" (110), to become "sober, alert, watchful" with the realization that "I could act" (112). No easy believer, he is ready in proper Kierkegaardian fashion to "wait and give your God time" (277).

But the Nietzschean form of will invades a state that otherwise would seem comfortably confined to a merely individual kind of history. Lance discovers the intoxicating relationship between will and power: "If one knows what he wants to do, others will not only not stand in the way but will lend a hand from simple curiosity and amazement" (136). "If you tell somebody what to do, they will do it. All you have to do is know what to do. Because nobody else knows" (209–10). In the absence of certitude and dominant absolutes, there is only will, it seems, and Lance's new age is not always purely Kierkegaardian waiting. Partly, it is simple rejection of the old age (163). He has vague notions of a third revolution that begins reasonably enough but takes on an unpleasant edge—"a stern code, a gentleness toward women and an intolerance of swinishness, a counsel kept, and above all a readiness to act, and act alone if necessary" (167). Its ideology is to pretend to none ("the new order will not be based on Catholicism or Communism or fascism or liberalism or capitalism or any ism at all"). Its character, however, is to allow the unpleasant edge to become oppressively sharp, a "stern rectitude valued by the new breed and marked by the violence which will attend its breach" (168), a violence not unlike that bowie knife Lance slices through Jan's neck. The idea is to "speak with authority" (169). When Lance really gets rolling, he denounces the "great whorehouse and fagdom of America" and proclaims the "new Reformation":

> We are going to set it out for you, what is good and what is bad, and no Jew-Christian waffling bullshit about it. What we are is the last of the West. What we are is the best of you, Percival, and the best of me, Lancelot, and of Lee and Richard and Saladin and Leonidas and Hector and Agamemnon and Richthofen and Charlemagne and Clovis and Martel. Like them we might even accept your Christ but this time you will not emasculate him or us. We'll take the Grail you didn't find but we'll keep the broadsword and the great warrior Archangel of Mont-Saint-Michel and our Christ will be the stern Christ of the Sistine. And as for your sweet Jesus and your guitar-banging and ass-wiggling nuns, and your love feasts and peace kisses: there is no peace. (190)

Partly, of course, such a passage represents Percy's love for bombastic hyperbolic satire; partly, though, the passage suggests a protofascism and hegemonic mania incipient in Lance's peculiar but perhaps astute distillation of "the West." Absolutism, ethnocentricity, militarism, class, metaphysics, totalitarianism all blend into the violence of will underlying Lance's determination to bring a new age into existence. As in the case of ethics, ontology, and intersubjectivity, then, history can be thought only in terms of the exercise of power—even God is described as a force one must wait on for some decisive intervention—rather than in terms of any necessarily inherent or innate meaning. What is "right" or "so" seems the mad product of physical or interpretive violence at the heart of which, ultimately, is Lance's "numbness and coldness."

Strangely akin to Beaumont's attempt to seize power over the course of things, Lance's combination of Kierkegaardian vigil and new age crusade points either to an individual psychosis, a not very convincing containment of the novel's energies, or to a primal willfulness to know and to rule that is only strengthened as history wears away the potency of traditional institutions. Percy's fondness for eschatological situations for his fiction is thus appropriate for the late modernist themes emerging in this inquiry. Finally, that is, *Lancelot* is the prototypical Percy figure rather than the exception. There is no internal transcendental structure he can ground himself upon; there is no reliable external institution with which he can meaningfully affiliate; there is only the act of will that risks all the dangers emerging in Lance's diatribes and murderous vengeance. Like Updike, Percy finds problems with no easy solutions, particularly the problem of "what one is to do with oneself." Neither goes as far as Warren in making literal the "economy" of that existential play, and hence they remain largely within at least the wilderness preserve of its ideological grounds. What one does see emerging here, however, is a fairly consistent practice of narrative that questions profoundly the problematic aspects of subjectivity as the last major remnant of Western metaphysics, but without necessarily pursuing fully the suggestive complementarity of impoverishment in the individual and the institutional forms of experience.

Perhaps no novelist seems more determined to tap the traditional resources of subjectivity than Saul Bellow, a task of which *Herzog* is perhaps paradigmatic. Moses, always writing letters to those responsible for the landmarks of Western culture, is forever trying to put it all together, to synthesize the final and right answer sought by all these late modernist protagonists. From one perspective, the intensity with which Moses considers his intertextual debts makes explicit how thoroughly within the intellectual tradition any such search must be; whether barely exposed to it like Jeremiah, unaware like Rabbit, respectably literate like Lance, or obsessively attentive like Moses, the prototypical late modernist character confronts his existence within the context of humanistic subjectivity. Herzog, however, turns away from thought as his medium to the point of verging on an anti-intellectual retreat to quite nostalgic sources of presumably more authentic being than that to be found in his unfinished scholarly labors. "Late in spring," we are told early on, "Herzog had been overcome by the need to explain, to have it out, to justify, to put in perspective, to clarify, to make amends" (8).[16] He begins, that is, with a drive very similar to that we have found in this entire cluster of novels. He finds what they all find—"God's veil over things makes them all riddles" (92). Of course, to feel the need of making amends, to assign ultimate intentionality to a God, and to assume the hermeneutic stance of riddle solving all indicate the theological confines within which the novel's inquiry takes place. Like Rabbit, Herzog wants to believe "that a Life is something more than such a cloud of particles, mere facticity" (325) and feels himself a bit lost in the "post-Copernican" age (349). Finally he turns against his project of justifying it all. He rejects the medium of language as satisfactory when he grouses to Asphalter, "More words. I go after reality with language. Perhaps I'd like to change it all into language" (332). The need to explain he consigns to "our own murdering imagination" working overtime (354), and he names the "chief ambiguity that afflicts intellectuals": they "hate and resent the civilization that makes their lives possible. What they love is an imaginary human situation invented by their own genius and which they believe is the only true and the only human reality" (370). He rejects, that is, abstract, idealized, and systematic constructs. He is put off that "people think explanation is a necessity of survival. They have to explain their condition" (392).

Despite his own addiction to the verbal and conceptual machinery of culture, then, Herzog turns increasingly away from it. He remembers his mother demonstrating "what Adam was made of" by rubbing dirt from her palm (285) and uses his own suffering as "a more extended form of life, a striving for true wakefulness and an antidote to illusion," a means to "cut into" what he calls the "marvelous and self-sufficient fictions" we dream up (386). Some points of purely subjective experience, it seems, enable an escape from the "illusion" of dreaming, thinking, and writing and provide a "true wakefulness" that is an authentic and reliable answer. Indeed, this romantic belief in an unmediated access to truth through subjectivity surfaces mainly in three nostalgias harbored in the character of Herzog—for nature, for childhood, and for a simple brotherly or sexual intersubjectivity. Almost in spite of itself, however, the novel half undoes these very springs of its hopefulness by showing how much of a piece they are with the constructs we have seen Herzog so eloquently disparage.

Nature often is treated in the novel as a kind of irresistible force, as when Herzog muses that "if, even in that embrace of lust and treason, they [Madeline and Gersbach] had life and nature on their side, he would quietly step aside" (69). There is, it seems, a higher authenticity in nature than in social rules and relations. It is also a beneficent signature of divine providence: "at the waterside in Woods Hole, waiting for the ferry, he looked through the green darkness at the net of bright reflections on the bottom. He loved to think about the power of the sun, about light, about the ocean. The purity of the air moved him. There was no stain in the water, where schools of minnows swam. Herzog sighed and said to himself, 'Praise God—praise God'" (115–16). Immediately, of course, his "heart was greatly stirred by the open horizon," and he wishes "his soul could cast a reflection so brilliant, and so intensely sweet." He has his daughter take off her shoes to wade in the lake and walk in the grass in a near sacramental scene set off from a "mechanical mower" that "was riding in circles, barbering the slopes" (338). When he gets to his country retreat near the end of the novel and begins opening windows, "the sun and country air at once entered. He was surprised to feel such contentment . . . contentment? Whom was he kidding, this was joy!" (381). In his most anti-intellectual moment, Herzog rejects Nietzsche's effort to "question as has never been questioned before, relentlessly, with iron determination, into evil, through evil, past evil, accepting no abject comfort" (389). Because ideas inevitably become "perverted," Herzog rejects them to write "under the veil of Maya," rejecting the Dionysian: "Nature (itself) and I are alone together, in the Berkshires, and this is my chance to understand" (388). Finally, he begins sending notes to God himself, once he has taken his nature worship into its most nonconceptual, simple form: "He walked quietly into the woods, the many leaves, living and fallen, green and tan, going between rotted stumps, moss, fungus disks; he found a hunters' path, also a deer trail. He felt quite well here, and calmer. The silence sustained him, and the brilliant weather, the feeling that he was easily contained by everything about him" (396). From city to country, from human to animal trail, Herzog's path takes him back to a desire for unmediated contact with the sustaining power of nature. The problem is the very banality of the course and even the language in which it appears. The adulterous couple are so suffused with "a certain theatrical genius" (16) in their posing, Madeleine gifted with cosmetics and turning every episode into a "theatrical event" (140–41), Gersbach an absurd "TV impressario" and distributor of "emotional plasma" (264), that they seem hardly the candidates for a natural authenticity in their love that Herzog makes them out to be. The stainless purity of the ocean, the reflections in the water, the Berkshire woodlands, the ritual cleansings apart from the mechanistic—all come under the parodistic signature of "the veil of Maya," that deceptive gauze of illusion that leaves uncertain the status of so clichéd a resource as "Nature (itself)."

Despite Herzog's distrust of language, then, it is likely the discourse of nature that he is most enamored of—its built-in authorization of sustenance and containment, of comfortable and simple feelings, of a vague but comforting transcendentalism, and perhaps even more, of a retreat from the interpersonal and the socioeconomic complications of life in the city and from the intellectual complications of pursuing Nietzschean demystification. As he writes his way into the discourse of natural harmony, his *sense* of health and sanity and peace increases. There is, moreover, another complication to this ideal into which he passes. Basically, "Nature" for Herzog is perceived as a noneconomic relation to landscape, something scarcely comprehensible to his brothers, and one that covers over the fact that his Berkshires retreat is made possible only by the concentration of wealth achieved by his father, by his own unearned inheritance of that wealth, and by the privilege of leisure afforded to a member of the economic class to which he belongs. He is allowed, that is, to "consume" nature as if it were an environmental Valium. Juxtaposed to his would-be romantic discourse, of course, is the less deceptive cash relation of someone like Ramona who is, after all, in the business of merchandising nature in her florist shop.

If the novel allows us to see the discursive qualities of Herzog's nostalgia for a nineteenth-century transcendental relation to nature, it may well permit similar reconsideration of his similar fancies about childhood, another romantic wellspring of untrammeled innocence and immediacy. Discourse intervenes here as well, as when he realizes that Gersbach's tears are not "for himself" but for the other of "that little kid"—the kid of the "stories" and "poems" one carries around. Herzog tells himself a number of these stories during the novel, some of which take his family's very real economic anxieties, and particularly the "rags" and "bruises" his father suffered, and melt them down into the pathos of his own training in suffering as he watched his battered father recount his woes. He schools himself in his father's self-absorbed mournful eloquence, taking over its lines as his own. Partly, then, childhood is when one's discursive habits are formed. More to the point of childhood itself as a positive value are the traits of the "little kid" he constructs in his own stories. He thinks, for example, of his mother wetting her handkerchief with saliva and cleaning his face or pulling him on his sled through the streets, feeling that "[a] ll he ever wanted was there" in the childhood home (174). Why, given their tenuous financial state? Perhaps because a child is "allowed" to have everything done for him—the relation of dependency, both emotional and economic, is even less subject to question than his later dependency upon the paternal legacy for his Berkshires Bleak House. A child's leisure is not questioned, his actions need not be productive, his thinking need not take Nietzsche into account, his relationships lack the entanglements of adult sexuality or professional rivalry, he has no responsibility for the colonial profiteering of an uncle (218) or the less obvious economic warfare Herzog's brother was later to practice—the list could go on, of course, but the point is that childhood is both Herzog's source for the discourse of suffering and his vision of a time before his own other became fully enmeshed in that discourse.

Like other protagonists we have examined, Moses Herzog also puts great faith in intersubjective relations as a guarantor of meaningfulness. "I really believe," he tells Luke, "that brotherhood is what makes a man human" (333). Mostly, however, this brotherhood is expressed in sexual relations. For example, he thinks that "we must help one another. In this irrational world, where mercy, compassion, heart . . . were often debunked, renounced, repudiated by every generation of skeptics" (246). The object of his attentions here, of course, is Ramona, described a few lines later as "a dear woman. She had a good heart. And she had on black lace underpants. He knew she did." She is the other of his lovers' discourse, suggesting a less than innocent reading of his speech to Luke about brotherhood: "The real and essential question is one of our employment by other human beings and their employment by us" (333). No doubt Herzog intends a very authentic relationship here, but "employment" reminds us that Ramona is caretaker ("If I married Ramona, it [financial things] would be easier" [44]), reliever of anxiety, and fantasy role player, and that somehow "It" always invades "I-Thou." Sexuality serves as a kind of utopian intersubjectivity satisfying all possible "natural" needs, in the way that childhood and nature are utopian for him. In fact, of course, for Herzog sex takes place only in highly theatrical surroundings. Sono stages their happenings with props gathered from her bargain-hunting expeditions, managing a ritual of tea, bathing, and venerable erotic scrolls. Ramona is equally accomplished; "it delighted Ramona to come on playfully in the role of a tough Spanish broad" (25), and she "was highly experienced at entertaining gentlemen. The shrimp, wine, flowers, lights, perfumes, the rituals of undressing, the Egyptian music" (195) are all carefully managed. "She thrust the door open and stood, letting him see her in the lighted frame of bathroom tile" decked out in "the black lace underthing" and "spike-heeled shoes, three inches high" (251), as if she were "one of those broads in a girlie magazine" (249). If their love is to be a way of touching base with primal human instincts, a foundation for some relation more genuine than other players in the novel might provide, then its domination by stereotypes, rituals, roles, and magazine fantasies raises serious problems. They share a lovers' discourse rather than an unmediated relation.

Finally, of course, all three of these forms—nature, childhood, sexuality—are modeled on an idealized intersubjectivity in which the other conforms to that desire left as a gap in discursively conditioned subjects. The name of that gap transpires in the space between the speaker and the spoken, between the self reflexively articulated and the unconscious eluding any such articulation. Bellow's recursive loops back to these ideals are part of a general reluctance to name that gap explicitly. Such looping explains, perhaps, his relative palatability to a wide audience that appreciates the ease of dwelling imaginatively in Bellow's fiction, just as Percy's fiction is more often taught than Warren's more philosophical novel because its overt Kierkegaardian paradigm is more congenial to the professional class conducting its exegesis. But even Bellow stresses the psychic exigencies under which Herzog's accommodation takes place, foregrounding above all the textual, epistolary medium in which he works out the possibility of creating an authorial whole where history had left only its homonym. In part displaced Old World values, in part nineteenth-century "selfhood," Moses Herzog's ethos flickers in a world deaf to its appeals and incommensurate with its implicit narrative of human experience. It is possible to read *Herzog* as an affirmation of rugged, or at least of sensitive, individualism in a world of mass homogeneity, but it is also possible, in light of the general project of late modernist narrative, to see it as the final miscarriage of a tradition of subjectivity continuing to function in a world that operates according to a radically different aesthetics.

What late modernist narrative does, finally, is to test to the breaking point the cultural burden subjectivity is asked to carry in midcentury American culture. Though elsewhere in world culture it may not have been the case, in America—even today at many levels—subjectivity understood in terms thinly veiling traditional metaphysics is asked to bear the major burden of meaning, significance, and order. The fiction of that culture, however, writes as many letters to itself as Moses Herzog, finally signing off altogether on any uncritical acceptance of the myth that has by and large sustained mainstream American daily life. Repeatedly gesturing to a gap left in or by that form of subjectivity, providing figure after figure for the other sought out to complete that subject, late modernist narrative portrays authentic selfhood over and over as a problematic ideal. It is hard to remain convinced that it is a failing of individuals, hard not to see more than a little significance in Herzog's repugnance at Gersbach's "butcher's" Yiddish (78). That repugnance marks the emptiness and divisiveness of class boundaries, a privilege consisting of style and leading less to a fulfilled selfhood, the promise of the class narrative in which the protagonist seeks wisdom and social position, than to an experience of that form as a painfully empty space created by means of the multiple textual strands of the cultural network. Throughout this cluster of novels, then, reflexivity has the curious quality of exposing much about the philosophical assumptions of its form and focus, but not the ideologically charged grounds on which it retreats from the broad if sometimes incoherent engagement of early modernist narrative with the fundamental issues of social organization. Perhaps in the final analysis the *real* name of that other, that persistent gap or lack in the subject, is precisely this unspoken.

FIVE

Fowles, Contemporary Fiction, and the Poetics of the Author

John Fowles's most celebrated novel offers an opportunity to probe yet another fundamental relation in the poetics of point of view. In *The French Lieutenant's Woman* we come before the ultimate center of authority in point of view theory—that of the author in fiction, whether we call it the implied author, the putative author, or the authorial self.[1] Hence we might think Fowles's novel a closed critical case at this point: there is near unanimity of essentially existentialist readings of it, there are extensive comments by Fowles himself about his intentions and reactions to the novel, and there are further comments by an authorial self presented in the novel's celebrated "intrusions" of a reflexive narrator. Perhaps it is just this weight of authorial authority (to sound out the apparent tautology) stacked against the text that draws out my curiosity to see whether the text indeed accepts it or, instead, follows the curious circular path of reflexive fiction to expose, critique, and disperse the theoretical elements we group under the heading of the author in our poetics of fiction.

The Concept of the Author

This critical tool derives its authority from the author's status as origin or source, and thereby also as intention or end. The authorial element is thus the alpha and omega of the fictional process, despite whatever remains in the air of the biographical and intentional fallacies. One quite commonly hears statements like, "Since the author says x there, here he must mean x as well" (the argument from origin), and "Since the author was thinking about x, isn't calling it y the critic's arbitrary invention?" (the argument from intention or end). Both questions, however, are really the same and depend logically upon the assumption of an ontological consistency in the author, itself derived from the metaphysics of the eternal and unique soul of the authorial self informing the work or even, in some critical theories, impressing itself upon the work.[2]

At the same time, of course, we also honor the critical maxim of separating the author from his work—there is often an ironic distance of some sort between "the man" and the texts bearing his name. But the grounds on which we feel this distance still allow critical recourse to the real, "deeper" self of the author. The easy cases here are the clearly demarcated rhetorical distances Wayne Booth charts in his criticism. But even in the more slippery cases in which an author's views expressed in other texts are recognized as imprecise guides to those in the text in question, that recognition is framed by some sense of mysterious internal forces beyond the writer's conscious control that also shape the work. These forces may be the scriptural writer's divine inspiration, the romantics' influx of the spirit of nature or of the ideal in one form or another, or in our own century the more modern myth of the unconscious self of the writer structuring the work "for" him. The critic, by inferring the identity (the unity, the consistency, the Edelian dynamics) of this force, achieves privileged access to the work's "real" meaning through this more comprehensive grasp of the essence of the authorial self. Whether this grasp is derived from a specifically Freudian or phenomenological program, to name two common examples, or is a more general recourse to the sense of the "person" behind the works, it is based upon an expectation of fixed and stable reference points with definite metaphysical assumptions.

Compare, for example, Michel Foucault's insistence that we move beyond "the theme of the originating subject" in our concept of the author and that we think of "it" as "a variable and complex function" of forces within the fiction, within the wider spheres of discourse, and within the institutional structures of society.[3] He calls the classic conception of the author "the ideological figure by which one marks the manner in which we fear the proliferation of meaning," for in seeking the univocal "one impedes the free circulation, the free manipulation, the free composition, decomposition, and recomposition of fiction" (159). Such an outlook shows Foucault's interest in the history of systems of thought, particularly as such systems (necessarily) regulate the capacity of fiction to "recompose" the conventional concepts of reality against which it lodges its own.

What is curious when we turn to the case of John Fowles is that his own comments on this subject launch demythologizing themes that seem to undermine not only his own privileged position as spokesman on the issue, but also the meaningfulness of the authorial rhetoric so celebrated (or notorious, depending on one's views) in *The French*

Lieutenant's Woman. On the one hand, Fowles is capable of using quite traditional terminology in talking about the relation between the author and his work. For example, he states that "the whole meaning and commitment of the person who creates will permeate his creations, however varied their outward form."[4] Such a comment, together with Fowles's general advocacy of existentialist notions, allows those with traditional assumptions to constitute the familiar reading of Fowles and his work. At the same time, however, one finds in the writings various strands that work a different and opposed pattern, one that undermines the sense of author we might infer from the spiritual suffusion and unification of a verb like "permeate." It may be that Fowles's well-known celebration of "mystery" is too easily read in traditional terms and that, as he says of religion, such terms are "inherently parasitical on a deeper and more mysterious nobility in man than any existing religion or political creed can satisfy" (110). Beneath our religion and our political ideologies of selfhood lies a radically demystified—and hence to our conventions "mysterious"—sense of "man" hosting, in Fowles's image, the parasitic products of cultural discourse. Perhaps ultimately that mystery is the courage of man to posit his own grounds of being, despite the Conradian state in which any final certainty must remain suspended.

In any case, the presuppositions of our usual concept of author seem imperiled by Fowles's attack upon any remnant of faith in the immortality of man or even in a soul. He says this at one point: "What survives death is putrescent stopped machinery. The consciousness is a mirror reflecting a mirror reflecting a mirror; anything that enters this room can be endlessly reflected and its reflections reflected. But when the room is demolished, no mirrors, no reflections; nothing" (38). The passage bluntly denies any afterlife ("nothing"), any metaphysical element of the self ("machinery"), and any pseudodivine ex nihilo creativity ("reflections reflected").

But Fowles's analysis of how the whole metaphysical view of man could ever have arisen in the first place is also useful to us, sounding as it does like a far more readable version of some recent philosophical theory: "The myth of a separate consciousness partly arises because of the loose way we use 'I.' 'I' becomes an object—a third thing. . . . These self-criticisms and excuses give us an illusion of objectivity, of being able to judge ourselves. We therefore devise a thing that judges, a separate 'soul.' But this 'soul' is no more than the ability to observe, to remember and to compare, and to create and to store ideals of conduct. This is mechanism, not ectoplasm; the human brain, not the Holy Ghost" (38). Fowles argues here the linguistic origins of our

171

concepts of "self" and "soul" and thus provides a clearer explanation of our culture's logocentrism than Derrida himself, as well as reminding us of Nietzsche's discussion of man's propensity to read "agent" and "intentionality" into any process he observes. Apparently one of the "reflections reflected" is the "I" from language, as if the "Holy Ghost" of selfhood were an illusion reflected beside us as we ride our linguistic car through the Disney funhouse of Western metaphysics.

Fowles recurs to such ideas several times in *The Aristos*. He satirizes the same metaphysical legerdemain when he talks about "this strange tool, my brain, that sees itself and calls itself a tool and tries to find in itself a thing not a tool that it is a tool for" (85). Even more interesting is his answer to the question where one would find the "ultimate pole," the "I": "Plainly, it is no more than a recording of phenomena; a colourless mechanism distinguished from other such mechanisms only by its position in space and time. Ultimately 'I' is simply the common condition of all human mentality. . . . 'I' is thus a convenient geographical description, not an absolute entity" (85). Again we find the passivity of what is this time a recording mind rather than a merely reflecting one, but also a further element in the deconstruction of a traditional sense of self. This element is the thorough dispersion of the "I" of selfhood into "all human mentality," the surrender of the idea of "entity" altogether. Fowles seems to talk quite comfortably about "the nothingness at the still centre of our being—that nothingness we mask by talking of 'I'" (86). Hence if we are to talk of the authorial self, we would be referring to one point in time and space in the plane of "all human mentality" as it happens to have reflected and recorded chance entrants from its range of experience. That is a less authoritative point, and certainly a less stable and unified point, than the self of the Judeo-Christian tradition Fowles unequivocally rejects (110).

If the authorial self shifts as rapidly as its mirrors reflect different shapes and its recorders register new sounds, then the metaphysical sense of the transcendent authorial self as origin and end of the work, and hence the ground of its unity and court of appeal for its interpretation, seems undermined. But the authority for this figure also rests upon the aesthetic assumption that, baldly put, the author guides and determines a work according to a program (of, e.g., theory, philosophy, self-portraiture) that the critic can, if lucky, identify as the work's hidden agenda. This second prop also seems wobbly in the light of some of Fowles's comments about art. If the consciousness is a hall of mirrors, there is danger that too much of the work of the self-conscious artist "becomes a disguised form of the self-portrait. Everywhere the artist sees himself as in a mirror" (194). But, one might add, since that self is not an "absolute entity" but the "common condition," what necessarily is reflected is thus the stylization of self reigning at a given "geographical" point in space and time rather than any uniquely personal or "original" nature or insight.

Fowles further loosens the guiding authorial hand by stressing the passivity of the creative mind. A work for him begins as "mythopoeic 'stills'" that come in the night: "Once the seed germinates, reason and knowledge, culture and all the rest, have to start to grow it. You cannot create a world by hot instinct; but only by cold experience."[5] At first glance this seems like Henry James or any number of other authors talking about their work habits. But note that the agency is dispersed into accumulated experiences (knowledge), culture, "and all the rest" rather than being attributed to the author. One is reminded of the passive imagery of romantic theorists, but for them poetic inspiration derived from some mystical spiritual force, not from the structures and conventions of culture intersecting at an authorial point in time and space. Thus we find Fowles noting that "my natural cast of mind is very much synthetic and allusive, rather than analytic and critical," thereby stressing the dominance of intertextuality (alluded to and synthesized) over the myth of direct inspiration.[6] When Fowles indicates that his "making fun of some of the sillier fashions, manners, and fetiches of the time" was "generally copying *Punch*—whose numbers from the 1860s I used widely for background detail," the admission suggests a dependence upon prior texts for attitudes as well as for details.[7] And certainly Fowles has been very open in explaining that "I know I have learnt a lot" from his favorite reading in the secondhand bookstalls—"Old trials, travel books and historical memoirs"—specifically, he adds, about narrative technique, again underscoring the decisiveness of the cultural repertoire of patterns and devices that take over and shape the material of the "mere fictioneer."[8]

The same demythologizing of the godlike creator shaping his work in his own divinely unique image comes in Fowles's self-deprecating humor when he writes to a group of French scholars as follows: "I am in fact a far less deliberate writer—whatever the surface appearance of the finished text—than it is easy for an academic (and perhaps in particular a French academic) to credit. In composing I proceed far more like a blind man fumbling his way across an unknown room, and so with constant retracings of steps and revisions, than a 'philosophical showman,' who is presumably all fireworks and luminosity."[9] The image of the fumbling blind man, together with what we have already seen, gives us less the sense of the sage divining his ends than of the experimenter beyond the frontiers of precedent who saves those fortuitous combinations of codes and subject matters that surprise him with their appeal. A "philosophical showman" might indeed control and shape his creation according to the "luminosity" of a blueprint, but such is not the case in a process where the cultural repertoire stocks the authorial stream. The notion of a "guiding authorial hand" is clearly a retrospective imposition, a normalizing interpretation inferring origin from the text as it is found or, more properly, as the critic's method allows him to find it.

What few comments we have from Fowles about his specific artistic strategies in the novel not only illustrate the "blind man fumbling across an unknown room," but also help counter a third conventional critical assumption that a given work, or indeed an oeuvre, reflects or should reflect an organic unity of theme and form (presumably derived as an effect of one or both of the first two premises we have questioned). This presumed unity can be a powerful interpretive tool, though we have already seen in the case of Thackeray that such precepts can give rise to deceptive and misleading expectations about what one will find in a text. Such may also be the case with Fowles. He argues the need for what he calls "polystylism" based on the examples of Picasso and Stravinsky, for "skill in expressing one's meaning with *styles,* not just in one style carefully selected and developed to signal one's individuality rather than to satisfy the requirements of the subject-matter" (203). Apparently defined rather broadly, "style" here becomes not the mark of the man as author but the strategy of the text, its ends answerable not to the authorial reference point, but to that of whatever range of gestures the text may make at any given moment in its course.

A similar idea is reflected in Fowles's discussion of the difficulty in getting the right voice for his material. He chooses the ironic voice for its capacity to suppress any real "I" of the author, and he continues as follows: "So I have written myself another memorandum: *You are not the 'I' who breaks into the illusion, but the 'I' who is a part of it.* In other words, the 'I' who will make first-person commentaries here and there in my story, and who will finally even enter it, will not be my real 'I' in 1967; but much more just another character, though in a different category from the purely fictional ones."[10] Fowles makes explicit here the standard disjunction between a first-person narrator—even one purporting to be the novel's author—and the biographical personage who collects the royalties. The disjunction is somewhat complicated by the logical necessity of maintaining it also in this apparently but therefore illusorily "direct" text. That is, the "I" making these comments about "an unfinished novel" is not the "real 'I' in 1967" either, but rather the authorial critic, with all the conventions and stylizations that govern the role. In both cases the movement of disjoining these textual features from the "'I' in 1967" pulls with it not only the stable authority one almost automatically associates with a talented and rational being, but also the unity and consistency and other such traits we have grown accustomed to expecting as necessary conditions of "an absolute entity." We have instead one of an infinite number of textual strategies ready to fill the authorial slot in any given discourse the "real 'I'" might engage in.

The issue is further complicated by the grammatical blurring in the equation of "you" and "'I.'" What can it mean to say that "You are the 'I' that is part of the illusion?" Perhaps no "real 'I'" is ever anything but "part of the [textual] illusion." That is, given Fowles's earlier argument that what stands behind these pronouns is a reflector rather than an agent, a mechanism rather than a self, and that our habitual conversion from pronoun to mythic concept is basically linguistic, we are pressed toward the conclusion that no authorial "I" is *ever* the "real 'I' in 1967," but rather must be a textual mechanism in one discourse or another. Even to persist in the idea of a "different category" to describe author, narrator, and character, as Fowles does above, seems inconsistent with the larger implications of the principles he advances, for these figures are all linguistic functions serving textual aims. Given the shifting textual ends of polystylism and of the multiplicity of pronomial antecedents in the authorial subject, it seems that Fowles's principles would make that figure we call the author a deceptive point at which to attempt a theoretical check of textual free-fall.

Hence Fowles's images for the consciousness as a room of mirrors and for the author as a blind man stumbling around in the textual room are only the vanguard of an implicit refutation of popular conceptions of the author's authority, particularly as it bases itself upon the metaphysical primacy of his selfhood, his authoritarian majesty over the course of his narrative, or even the fixity and consistency of his authorial dendrons as they make cultural connections at one point or another. But to explain what concept of author emerges in its place is no easy matter—we have grown accustomed to the traditional interpretation of the historical fact that individuals have written novels that seem stages in the evolution of narrative. One might get so basic as to point out that heredity and environment cooperate to structure those mirrors and to prompt the blind man stumbling around the room. Yet even my language suggests the sort of intentionality in the process ("cooperate to") that, in an earlier chapter, we found Nietzsche describing as our rage for finding agents and imposing retrospective interpretations.

Perhaps what we need to do is to borrow Fowles's own habit of constructing homologies between aesthetics and other discourse systems, and in doing so to borrow one of his favorites—that of evolution. An amateur naturalist himself, Fowles makes much of the nonintentional evolutionary process he calls "horizontal" evolution; it has no "end" or "summit" or "promised land" as the end conferring order and significance on the process (*Aristos*, 14–26). Thus when Thomas Kuhn speaks of evolution in scientific studies as development *from* rather than development *to,* the shift in the preposition marks the same demythologizing of end in history. In the case of the novel, one would have to surrender the sense that an ideal or even a better kind of novel was reached at any time in the history of the genre, or that individual "development" is ever more than "from." Instead, one has each phase of culture recombining the elements we find in narrative to suit its own ends, to answer its own questions, and to reflect its own emphases and values.

But we would also need to refine our sense of the "agent" in the process. One might say that Darwin's theories dispersed the agent we had mythologized into human history, replacing the divine with chance mutations and the hazards of weather, geology, and other ecological features that provided adequate external factors to man's development. To the extent that Fowles argues the passivity of the authorial process, its reliance upon recombinations of a cultural repertoire of conventions, and the conversion of the author from an absolute entity to a textual strategy, he may be said to be pointing toward some analogous reconstitution of our conception of the author along less melodramatic lines than those of the inspired genius scribbling by candlelight. We would, then, recognize an "original" author when he served as the locus of a conceptual shift in the combination of narrative conventions, thereby enabling the genre to solve the problems set by its point in cultural space and time—when, in the evolutionary metaphor, his work had survival value in the cultural ecosphere.

Pushed too far this line of reasoning leads to an absurdly mechanical notion of the writer, but it does suggest the usefulness of refraining from deifying the author, attributing to him, however implicitly, such divine attributes as unity, consistency, fixity, and the like. Such a view alters the natural deference one feels toward authorial rhetoric—whether in a novel or in essays about a novel—and places the implied author in the wider context of textual conventions that play among each other in a given text. Not surprisingly, this deconstruction of authorial authority coexists with the pronouncements, or textual strategies, dependent upon it in the same way that other reflexive elements we have examined coexist with the referential gestures of the text. The problem all of this sets for us, then, is determining precisely how the various modes of presenting the implied author both exercise the figure's rhetorical power and reflexively demonstrate its limits.

It might be objected that I ought not rely on the author's comments to question the authority of the concept of author: either I accept the authority of writers to shape, control, and comment upon their works, or I do not. I ought not have it both ways. In an interesting way, however, this line of reasoning seems to be a logical trap. The trick is that if you agree with the unreliability of author as an interpretive ground, then the evidence offered here is entirely unacceptable, coming as it does from the author. On the other hand, if you *disagree* with the thesis, you must do so in the face of a powerful authorial statement—a source of evidence that is by such a position meaningful (hence you accept the standard of evidence but not the conclusion to which it leads). Perhaps I have it not both ways but *neither*. Both readers must, in effect, pick and choose among authorial statements depending on whether they agree with or contradict the principles of the critic. After all, the critic is also an author and is entitled to stake out his position; that he does so in a way quite congruent with that of the fictional author, achieving internal consistency, more or less, through selective reconciliation of the field of data and his own discursive world is of course interesting to me. It suggests that we share more even with the writer of reflexive fictions (as this is becoming reflexive criticism) than we might have thought. Any such author is situated in the conditions of his writing, is a function of what is carried out. The double movement is here because it was always already here. But this question belongs to the next chapter.

Chapter 35 and Authorial Rhetoric

Chapter 35 of the novel is a convenient primer of uses to which an apparently "innocent" intrusion can be put, for if on the one hand it is a scholar's helpful gesture to explain differences in sexual mores between 1860 and our own age, it is also a supple exercise of the authorial presence, demonstrating a number of the points to be made about this aspect of point of view in the novel. Beginning with the narrator's "intrusive" question, "What are we faced with in the nineteenth century?" the chapter is apparently called forth by Charles's ambivalence over his sexual stirrings for both Sarah and Ernestina, especially as it contrasts with the frankly sexual appetites of the less genteel Sam and Mary. But as he provides information about the differences between Victorian and modern valuations of sexuality, about differences between the classes in mores, and about the case of Thomas Hardy as both victim and beneficiary of the age's tension between "lust and renunciation," the narrator manages to elaborate something close to an allegory of writing that aids our effort to rethink the concept of author.

The chapter begins with the efforts to keep the reader from thinking Mary too oversexed (for her self-indulgence) or Charles too undersexed (for his slow and puzzled responses). The narrator speaks bluntly of "the error of supposing the Victorians were not in fact highly sexed" and of "another common error: of equating a high degree of sexual ignorance with a low degree of sexual pleasure."[11] His discussion seeks to determine not only the reader's reaction—a bold use of the author's authority—but also the logical principle by which he reacts—perhaps an even bolder use. Hence he attacks the interpretive procedure of establishing evaluative or normative hierarchies as a way of making sense of change. One is reminded of Fowles's own principle of the "relativity of recompense" explained in *The Aristos* as "*that which allows, at any stage of evolution, any sentient creature to find under normal conditions the same comparative pleasure in existing as all other sentient creatures of its own or any other age*" (59). Despite what jingoists or nostalgia buffs might argue, then, no age is better off. Within the novel the narrator argues his own interpretation of the age: "I have seen the Naughty Nineties represented as a reaction to many decades of abstinence; I believe it was merely the publication of what had hitherto been private, and I suspect we are in reality dealing with a human constant: the difference is a vocabulary, a degree of metaphor" (212). Victorian reticence and contemporary obsessiveness are merely stylistic rather than substantive distinctions: "these 'ways' of being serious are mere conventions. The fact behind them remains constant" (213). Though this belief seems to argue for a "human constant" beyond these stylized expressions, it also encloses any individual within the expressive conventions that shape his or her desires, that in effect constitute the conditions of possibility for those desires, regulating the sense of what they are in the first place and how to go about fulfilling them. In terms of historical judgments, then, we cannot apply normative labels like "undersexed" or "naughty" without betraying a temporal provincialism of vocabulary and metaphor, a confusion of stylistic and essential qualities. We are not objective historians assessing a practice, persons originating a clear relation of events; we feel the pressure of a larger discursive practice against that of another era. In other words, this section's end result is to demonstrate the impossibility of any (authorial) viewpoint outside the current conventional framework.

Moreover, as the argument goes, the Victorians may have been better off, since they may have been able to "experience a much keener, because less frequent, sexual pleasure than we do" and may have been "dimly aware of this and so chose a convention of suppression, repression and silence to maintain the keenness of the pleasure" (213). We may be the more "Victorian" in the negative sense, "since we have, in destroying so much of the mystery, the difficulty, the aura of the forbidden, destroyed also a great deal of the pleasure" (214). Any discourse suppresses, that is, by screening experiences according to its own norms and conventions; the error of one period's judging another lies in assuming that its own discursive conventions are "right" or "natural"—that is, nondiscursive and therefore normative. It leads the Victorian, with his notions of the spiritual nature of authenticity and of public responsibility and proprieties, to deplore what to the modern is open-mindedness, harmony between physical and psychological needs, and freedom from social repression; of course we too can make a similar "reading" error. The result is that not only are these alternative discourses incommensurable, but neither can be taken as normative. One of those discursive conventions, of course, is the author, who for at least two centuries has been considered an originating source rather than a derivation from larger structures of belief.

This debate about the historiography of sex has another side to it, however. One must keep in mind that the narrator proceeds within the norms (e.g., of pleasure) shaping modern discourse, not at all within those of spiritual uplift and public duty that shaped the Victorian discourse of restraint. Himself within the modern discursive frame, he can neither mediate between the two frames, as he appears to do, nor give us a necessarily true or even a Victorian way of seeing nineteenth-century subject matter. Such an argument against evaluative interpretation, one might contend, imperils the novel's central thematic description of Charles's evolution to an apparently more authentic state of being. How, that is, can one imply that an existentialist approach is better than that of Victorian "prudence" if one is already, as Fowles himself acknowledges, within the existentialist "vocabulary" and "metaphor"? It is difficult to establish a difference in the status of discourses about sexuality, on the one hand, and about marriage, social caste, or personal authenticity on the other. Without such a difference, Charles's initial state seems as full of recompense as his final, more existentialist one.[12] The authorial validation of the existentialist stance thus seems to be the voice of one convention proclaiming its dominance over any competing conventions that enter the text.

We must conclude that this authorial voice is composed of at least three contrary strands in contemporary thinking. One is a very contemporary recognition that an authorial voice must be caught within the "vocabulary" and "metaphor" of one point in the space and time of human mentality and hence is the voice of those external conventions contesting others (either contemporary or historical) for dominance. At the same time, a second voice is that of a kind of scientific positivism, insisting with an impossible rigor on the repudiation of any condescending temporal provincialism at the expense of the Victorians. A third seems unaware of the problem and cheerfully valorizes existential awakenings. This is indeed a "variable and complex function of discourse" we are confronting, to recur to Foucault's description, and to speak of a single "modern" convention looking at *the* Victorian convention is thus imprecise.

Rather than an ontological being, then, the author seems actually to be an interplay among the narrative and interpretive codes or conventions that make the authorial voice something other than the personal presence we may informally take it to be. The authorial voice is, in other words, a varying tactical maneuver of the specific confluence of conventions discernible in a text, even if at the same time it functions as if it were "authoritative" in the articulation of a theme. If the author is thus a function of those conventions, then not he but *they* are the delimiters of the text. Moreover, they are not the single point of origin of the univocal subjective tradition to which Barthes and Foucault stand opposed—they do not unify so much as they disseminate the different possibilities for meaning we have discovered at work in the novel's commentary on Victorian sexuality.

To pursue this chapter's implications is to extend our recognition of Fowles's recurrent homology between sexuality and aesthetics. In fact, this chapter is part of a larger, almost allegorical structure paralleling the specifically discursive qualities of sexuality, aesthetics, theology, science, and history. Early in the novel the narrator alerts us to this elaborate comparison by noting that his digression on fiction has much "to do with your Time, Progress, Society, Evolution, and all those other capitalized ghosts in the night that are rattling their chains behind the scenes in this book" (82). The link between sex and narrative is made explicit elsewhere in the novel in, say, the narrator's description of the "kind of devious sexual approach" that characterizes the novelist's appraisal of a potential model for a character (317), or in the way a character such as Sarah models her sexual narrative like a work of fiction complete with all the trappings of what the narrator terms the "romanced autobiography" we all maintain (82). This chapter on sexual self-control, after all, comes in the context set by chapter 13 and its discussion of the relation between the novelist's control of his characters and God's control over his creation; since our god is "the freedom that allows other freedoms to exist" (82), the contemporary novelist accordingly casts himself "in this new theological image, with freedom our first principle."

One implication is that the Victorians' tight control in theology, fiction, and sex may well have contributed to the fervor of the primary illusions each mode nurtures. In each of them, for example, the Victorians imposed an almost awesome authority figure exercising firm and overt control—God, the omniscient novelist, and the Victorian male are not to be trifled with. And yet, as chapter 35 teaches us to argue, these stylistic expressions may be no more repressive than what we have replaced them with. That is, the hegemony of our inherited ideals and values, the detached implied author who only covertly shapes the narrative, the still demanding and, in their own way, rigid sex roles shadowing our own attempts to love—all may be as authoritarian as anything "suffered" by the Victorians and may shape a different style of fervor.[13] The novel thus exploits the sexual connotations of the relations among the author, the narrator, his characters, and his readers in order to define the discursive roles governing the principals' participation. At the very least, one is reminded by this analogy of the importance of the purely appetitive nature of our love of narrative, its gratification of our need to be identified with another, its dependency upon shifting lines of dominance and compliance among participants (akin to those in sexual relations), and finally the necessary reliance upon the conventions of narrative courtship that constitute a discourse with its repertoires of structural patterns and images. If this is beginning to sound like Roland Barthes's work in *The Pleasure of the Text* and *A Lover's Discourse,* it is because Fowles and Barthes are working the same homology between narrative and sexuality, though in different directions.

Certainly this homology foregrounds the conventions governing each activity and assuring participants that they can play complex but relatively predictable roles in either form of cultural intercourse. One may say, first of all, that conventional cues open and close distance among participants, as we have all suffered or enjoyed in love, and as critics like Wayne Booth can so persuasively chart in fiction. In *The French Lieutenant's Woman,* the voice quoting in epigraphs, describing Lyme in the 1860s, vividly evoking a character's beauty or impatience, blowing away the plot as a fictional plaything, analyzing the nature and grounds of a given response or interpretation—this voice opens and closes differing relationships whose coincidence within one text underscores the range possible within the discourse. Sarah, as an authorial character, dramatizes the solicitation that opens a relationship, a solicitation paralleling that of the narrator eyeing the passenger in the railroad car, as well as her own opening of a narrative relationship in the Undercliff. She also imposes her demands for submission that end Charles's willingness to continue the relationship in the final ending of the novel; such demands parallel, perhaps, those implicit in a text for a reader's conceptual submission as well as Charles's earlier submission to her first narrative's fictions about Vargueness.

These openings and closings follow a tightly scripted set of conventions that are part of a larger process of mutual fictionalization. In *The French Lieutenant's Woman,* a transformation takes place similar to that Barthes describes in *A Lover's Discourse* (in "To Love Love").[14] It is the "Image repertoire"—"the discursive site" and its images, forms, and structures—that one loves or mourns rather than the "other," who is largely the "tool" of the subject's desire. The "other" is most important as a participant in the drama of the discourse, necessarily submitting to the fictionalizations of the subject. The subject in narrative fictionalizes himself in successive removes as implied author, authorial narrator, and authorial character, and he fictionalizes the readers he addresses in order to play his role in the drama of narrative discourse. The reader's reciprocal fictionalizations of the author are equally intense and are playfully anticipated by the guises the author suggests for himself (stocky passenger in a Victorian railway car, Frenchified fop in an open landau, learned intellectual historian). Sarah, as authorial character, makes of Charles what she needs to advance the chapters in her own unfolding life narrative; Charles, the character as reader, struggles to make Sarah and her narrative conform to his own image repertoire, needs, and desires.

In these kinds of relationships, neither can hope to wholly know the other; neither can approach the other except in the forms inscribable within the discourse in which both participate; neither is relevant to the other except as a silent accomplice in the completion of a role; neither can ever achieve the complete absorption of the other into his own discourse; and neither can be described, analyzed, or defined except on the evidence of a textual version of how they act out their roles in the discourse. These traits, according to our allegory, are equally applicable to the nature of the "subject" in narrative. Just as characters are functions of the interplay of all the formal units in the novel, so readers are what takes place in their heads as they verbalize relations among those formal units, thus playing out one of the roles they authorize, and authors are what takes place as they conflate, juxtapose, circulate, superimpose, undermine, overextend, parody, and otherwise relate the linguistic, semantic, and literary codes at hand.

The first part of our look at chapter 35 suggested that the author was less the source of judgments and insights than a feature of the nexus of literary, philosophical, and cultural conventions criss-crossing in his text. This second section opens up another model for the "disappearance of the author" into the roles possible for him as they are acted out in the text itself. To see the author as the accumulation of discursive conventions and roles as they interact in a text does indeed begin to provide a more reliable and useful conception of the author than the subjective model Foucault would have us eschew.

In the last third of chapter 35, Fowles takes up the case of another writer, Thomas Hardy, and shows how the author is constructed by an interpretation of textual elements, an interpretation subject to the hermeneutic problems we found in the passages on historiography. Fowles recounts the case of Hardy's engagement to Tryphena, broken off at the discovery that she was his niece rather than his cousin. Because the emotions of the whole affair led eventually (Fowles asserts) to both Sue Bridehead and Tess, as well as to Hardy's greatest love poems, Fowles argues the benefits of quashed love: "This tension, then— between lust and renunciation, undying recollection and undying repression, lyrical surrender and tragic duty, between the sordid facts and their noble use—energizes and explains one of the age's greatest writers; and beyond him, structures the whole age itself. It is this I have digressed to remind you of" (216). The obvious import of the passage is something like Freudian displacement in Hardy's case—frustrated love finding its aesthetic outlet.

Yet we must also be mindful that the opposition between lust and renunciation has already been exposed as a stylistic rather than a substantive difference—a matter of vocabulary and metaphor, as the narrator puts it. The focus, in other words, immediately falls upon the discursive conventions noticed by the interpreter. Earlier we found Fowles himself arguing that the author was one point in space and time reflecting the common structure of human mentality and, moreover, reflecting it in terms of the emergent recombination of conventions at that point in space and time. Here we have not a psychological argument about the experiences shaping a metaphysical entity prior to the text or separable from its age but a description of the particular nexus of conventions discernible in what might perhaps best be called a semiotic being. For the author in this case, Hardy, is traced through the fictional and poetic creations that have drawn the notice of Fowles. The "energizing" comes from the static between the discourse of passion and that of morality, particularly as it is discernible to the modern reader of the texts of Hardy's fiction, poetry, and biography. An interpretation of discursive structures derived from fictional, poetic, or documentary texts leads us to the semiotic being we call the author, Thomas Hardy.

The passage calls attention to this semiotic quality through the language used to describe its central thesis. The terms on one side of the "between" all involve giving up what we think of as the self to forces quite beyond that self: lust (to another's sexual appeal), recollection (to one's narrative interpretation of the past), surrender (to the "lyrical" scripting of emotional release), and facts (to the cultural roles prescribed in cases of consanguinity). But these forces all share a purely cultural form rather than the primordial naturalness we might expect in discussions of libidos and lust—the coding of sexual appeal, the artifice in recollective interpretation, the literary stylizing of "lyrical," and the ethical (or moral?) stylizing in "sordid." The other set of terms—renunciation, repression, duty, and use—all reflect either passive or active shaping of what is offered according to even more specifically cultural ideals—"tragic," "noble," useful, and the ever differently defined duty and conduct. What would initially have seemed an attempt to explain the unique mystery and power of a great novelist turns out also to be a dispersion of Hardy as an "absolute entity" into the various discursive conventions of culture contending for thematic domination both of the text in which we inscribe our sense of him and of that in which he himself worked out, consciously or otherwise, his own history. The project is thus to collect the semiotic conventions that make possible the texts we have rather than to attempt a necessarily mystified transubstantiation of them into the fiction of a transcendent being.

What we find in chapter 35, then, are at least three concrete ways to understand the often mentioned notion of the author as a "textual strategy."[15] We found, for example, that the author was less an authoritative entity dispensing truth than a tactical voice of discursive conventions and their underlying assumptions, that he was less the court of final resort as to intentions and thematic ends than the playing out of a courtship role stylized by the dramatic conventions of the narrative process, and that his relevance was less that of the definable, absolute entity whose "nature" or "structure" somehow explains the text than— as in the case of the reading we get of Hardy—an interpretive construct built by the reader on the basis of both the specific characteristics of the recombination of conventional elements in a text and that reader's assumptions about interpretive procedures.

We have, in other words, found our close reading of this curious chapter cohering in the light of the theories of Barthes and Foucault, but not necessarily in the traditional interpretive sense of a stable, univocal message relayed from author to reader. Indeed, both author and reader become composites that take shape as interpretive connections are made among the points in the text, just as the text becomes less a linear message than a crosshatching of conventional "lines" (in all senses of the word), a series of overlays of various code systems that, as they come together, disperse and recombine in an apparently inexhaustible way. By addressing the retrospective logic of interpretations, the chapter helps clarify them as "operations that we force texts to undergo."[16] By aligning sexual and narrative relations as discursive systems, the chapter reminds us of the highly conventional quality of "the connections that we make, the traits that we establish as pertinent." And by examining the case of Hardy, the chapter shows how "the continuities we recognize [and] the exclusions that we practice" enable us to read a semiotic being as "an absolute entity."

Such a thorough conflation of Foucault's perspective and Fowles's fictional practice becomes possible only when one does not let traditional ways of talking about authors impede "the free circulation, the free manipulation, the free composition, decomposition, and recomposition of fiction," as Foucault puts it. Apparent contradictions become functions of the inevitable variations in the connections we can make—and they cease to be "problems" with critical logic—once this perspectival shift is achieved. Hence the coexistence of these deconstructive themes with an existentialist, humanistic program in both the fiction and the nonfiction, and on the narrative level with a thorough reliance upon and exploitation of the traditional rhetorical resources of the authorial narrator, should not trouble us too much with its apparent self-contradiction. It is similar to the deconstructive philosopher working within the "logocentric" vocabulary of Western philosophy: the point is not only that the philosophical is a circular ("centric") system that posits its own ground the moment its discourse begins, but also that to discuss its issues we are forced to use that same self-justifying vocabulary. In narrative, regardless of how thoroughly we may explore the possibilities for reformulating our rather metaphysical concepts of the author in fiction, we are still acting as an author using all the rhetorical implements of authorship, regardless of their implicit philosophical assumptions. This shift in critical thinking is explained in a comment by Roland Barthes: "We know now that a text is not a line of words releasing a single 'theological' meaning (the 'message' of the Author-God) but a multi-dimensional space in which a variety of writings, none of them original, blend and clash. The text is a tissue of quotations drawn from the innumerable centres of culture. . . . The writer can only imitate a gesture that is always anterior, never original. His only power is to mix writings, to counter the ones with the others, in such a way as never to rest on any one of them."[17] What remains, then, as the next task of this chapter is to take stock of the fictional elements in *The French Lieutenant's Woman* normally related to the authorial perspective in traditional theories of point of view and to see in what ways they enable us to confirm the hypotheses thus far established.

Epigraphs and the "Author"

Literally the first place one begins to encounter the implied author is in the epigraphs he chooses. The standard expectation of epigraphs is that they link us to the implied author more directly than almost any other aspect of the novel; unlike the plot materials manipulated by the narrator, epigraphs come from the reality of the cultural canon and inform us about the interests, education, and beliefs of the implied author. Hence, particularly when they are used as heavily as they are in *The French Lieutenant's Woman,* epigraphs are expected to give us little bases of interpretive safety amid the text's playing field. They are guides to the chapters they head, and they establish the continuity between the work in hand and the cultural canon into which the epigraphs painstakingly insert it. For example, the epigraphs to the sample chapter we just examined function in traditional ways to enhance the scholarly authority of the narrator and to create the general ambiance of the period in which the novel is set. More specifically, there are two epigraphs, one from the 1867 Children's Employment Commission report on the laxness of sexual standards among the rural working class, and the other two lines from Hardy ("In you resides my single power / Of sweet continuance here"). Such direct information and emotional tone setting are not at all uncommon in the novel's epigraphs, for the implied author often exercises his power to dispense knowledge and emotions to his readers as if he were indeed the old Victorian authorial god.

At the risk, in fact, of verging on the statistical, we can find more than a dozen chapters with epigraphs from commission reports, social historians, literary texts, and newspaper bits documenting the social, political, and economic background of the age in order to shape a reader's response to the novel's times and characters. That is to say, they appeal to our sense of respect for the official published interpretation of the era and hence remind us of the extent to which our understanding of an age depends upon which texts we canonize (by quotation, reading lists, or our own historians' bibliographies). In addition to the commission report of chapter 35, such epigraphs range from a passage in Jane Austen's *Persuasion* describing the Undercliff to Leslie Stephen's remarks about respectability (as a gloss on Freeman's offer of partnership to Charles).

Over a third of the chapters feature quotations from poems, novels, and folk songs that, like the lines from Hardy in our sample chapter, echo the dominant emotion of their respective plot segments. These range from the jovial remark quoted by G. M. Young—"I have heard it suggested that the typical Victorian saying was, 'You must remember he is your uncle'" (when Charles's uncle decided belatedly to marry)— to a far more fervent quatrain from Tennyson to head the chapter describing Sarah's preparations for the climactic session at Endicott's Family Hotel: "But on her forehead sits a fire: / She sets her forward countenance / And leaps into the future chance, / Submitting all things to desire."

This last example, however, complicates the simple line that epigraphs seem to have drawn from author to reader, a line that somehow manages to lead us past the very obvious way epigraphs are in fact barriers—they are, after all, the words of *other* authors, not "his" or "hers" whom we read. In this particular case, our expectation of "interpretive safety" runs into trouble. The first-time reader of the novel misses the irony of Tennyson's quatrain in its context, for it is not till much later that he has any chance of realizing that Sarah is faking her injury in order to set Charles up for the seduction. Sarah "sets her forward countenance" in the most artificial sense of the verb, not simply in the moral resoluteness daring the "future chance" the poem is considering. "Submitting all things to desire" is thus more of a mystery clue than the sort of simple emotional echo illustrated by Clough's poem of sexual awakening heading chapter 16 (in which Charles first associates Sarah with past scenes of passion). But it can hardly even be considered a clue, since, detached as it is from the narrative, it carries no tonal and no contextual cue to prompt the reader to see it ironically.

This epigraph, in other words, goes out of its way to accentuate the normal variations between an author's and a reader's interpretations of source, quotation, and chapter and the relations among them. We become aware of the author wielding his power by regulating both the content of information and its rate of flow, in this case denying the reader the grounds for fully understanding the epigraph. We also become aware, however, that the reader, though held off for a while by these constraints, still is free to interpret according to his own critical assumptions once he has finished reading the text. If the author sets a forward countenance according to his own thematic desires, the reader combines with these elements his retrospective countenance over the finished narrative. Both, that is, become semiotic beings acting out the roles allotted them by the range of connections the text makes possible. Naturally these roles are similar in many ways: the reader inevitably attaches his own epigraphs to passages and chapters by mentally quoting other writings that shed light upon the text in hand, a process that quite likely simulates the authorial compilation. But by empahsizing the interpretive differential, this epigraph, at least, works against the conventional expectations.

Epigraphs thus have a decidedly mixed relation to the chapters they head—often, as we have seen, they are guides to them, but they also serve as specifically literary frames that prefix an interpretive frame to the chapter, often an ambiguous one. Chapter 11, for example, quotes William Barnes's Dorset dialect poem about a pretty but useless man: "the wold vo'k didden bring / En up to know a single thing." The lines might refer to the childishness Ernestina shows in her diary (though we find later that she has more wisdom and strength than we had been led to expect); they might refer to Mary, who is certainly not taught much formally (but is an effective repository of mass culture's "intuitive" shrewdness); they might, after all, characterize Charles, who is later described as emotionally naive and seems to have been poorly educated for the world in which he finds himself. This epigraph's relation to its chapter, then, may be as confusing as it is helpful, since one must decide not only to whom it applies, but also the kinds of education it refers to and how these kinds might each in its own way be inadequate scripts for the roles the characters must play.

Nonetheless, this epigraph does alert the reader to the questions worth asking about the chapter, and this is only a slight diminution of the author as the one with the answers. More of a diminution occurs when the epigraph suggests there are no answers at all. Something of the kind happens in chapter 31, which describes Charles's arousing view of Sarah asleep in the stable, her confession to having orchestrated her dismissal by Mrs. Poulteney, and the blaze of passion when they kiss before Charles's flight. The epigraph is from Clough's "Poem":

> When panting sighs the bosom fill,
> And hands by chance united thrill
> At once with one delicious pain
> The pulses and the nerves of twain;
> When eyes that erst could meet with ease,
> Do seek, yet, seeking, shyly shun
> Ecstatic conscious unison, —
> The sure beginnings, say, be these,

Prelusive to the strain of love
Which angels sing in heaven above?

Or is it but the vulgar tune,
Which all that breathe beneath the moon
So accurately learn—so soon?

The lines dissolve the seemingly stable behavior of Sarah into an oscillation between the verities of angelic love and the artifice of a precocious seductress, thereby stressing the impossibility of determining what in human behavior is nature and what is artifice, what sincere and what role played, what original in the human heart and what derived from a cultural repertoire: indeed, the oppositions themselves may be the most illusory of all.

Given that Sarah is the plot's authorial character, freely composing narratives and identities for herself, and given the reformulation we have traced of the concept of the author, this epigraph celebrates even more than the impossibility of judging with certainty the meaning and character of Sarah Woodruff. All that breathe beneath the cultural moon learn accurately the vulgar tune of narrative conventions and the wider systems of belief of which they are a function. Having done so, both their judgments of specific situations (or characters) and the grounds of those judgments are forever encircled by those conventions and assumptions. The epigraph thus both fulfills and thwarts the function it is expected to carry out—it *does* guide the reader to the kind of judgment he should reach about the chapter, but it does not so much do so on the basis of the writer's authority at it guides reflexively by reminding us that the chapter, its implied author, its reader, and the interpretive interrelations among them are not interpersonal relations of coder/decoder, speaker/ listener, but rather the complex and "imperfect" coming together of authorial and readerly matrixes of literary and cultural conventions. The epigraph thus guides interpretation away from the illusory reference points that are thought normally to keep it in line and toward a reflexive understanding of the author as a semiotic being and of interpretive relations as a role-playing process shaped by the paradigmatic assumptions of its participants—themes now familiar from our study of the novel. The wholly sincere and selfless lover is as much a cultural myth as the wholly original and creative writer, and both myths wrest an illusory deity out of a codified function, an entity out of a role, "ectoplasm" out of "mechanism."

But one should not suppose that the stability of the author is merely exchanged for that of convention, for the epigraphs establish a complex relation to the tradition they represent. As we consider the use they make of earlier texts, we find that they carry out the expected function of bridging the gap between the current work and its predecessors by quoting those presumably related in some way, but that they also separate a quoted passage from the canon by forcing it into new and alien contexts that change it. Chapter 29, for example, is headed by Arnold's insistence that one must do things not by inclination "but because it is one's duty, or is reasonable." The chapter features Charles sensing his alienation from the age and going to meet Sarah in a stable, thus violating a Victorian sense of duty and behaving in ways the novel's Victorian doctor clearly considers unreasonable. But at the same time it is existentially "reasonable" for Charles to distance himself from cultural systems that leave him with no meaningful role to play, and it is his "duty" to himself to discover what it is in Sarah that calls forth such powerful responses in him. Does the epigraph connect the novel to Arnold by showing how the latter's central concepts still justify our behavior, or does it point out the irreconcilable differences in the meanings of those key concepts and thus underscore disjunction? The epigraph seems to note a contemporary synthesis of Arnold's moral imperatives and existentialism's focus upon the individual's self-development, but in that intercoding Arnold does not remain quite the same.

Such a synthesis emphasizes not the author's controlling the epigraph's significance for the chapter it heads, but rather the process by which "significance" is a function of the correlations of cultural assumptions at play as one text makes use of those coming before it. Epigraphs repeatedly are brought into the context of the novel and thus acquire what Fowles, in discussing one of his objectives in the work, calls "an existentialist awareness before it was chronologically possible."[18] One finds this with Mrs. Norton's "What's DONE, is what remains!" in chapter 4, or with Arnold's observations at the head of chapter 53 about the dangers of seeking only moral perfection rather than "the full and harmonious development of our humanity," and at the head of chapter 61 about "true piety" as "acting what one knows," or even with Darwin's indication that "many structures have now no very close and direct relations to present habits of life" (chap. 3). Verses from Tennyson about the wish for a new "man to arise in me" (chap. 45) or about men rising "on stepping-stones / Of their dead selves to higher things" (chap. 48) complete the range of quotations that acquire, in the context of the novel, a distinctly existentialist cast not always entirely harmonious with the value system implicit in the works from which they come.

The cultural gap between the nineteenth and twentieth centuries seems not to be bridged by quotation; indeed, the intercoding of these quotations with the existential theme of the modern work demonstrates the interpretive violence seemingly inevitable when an author's work—just as inevitably—feeds upon the texts of the past. Such violence is not unlike that which figures in the novel's epigraph from Marx: "Every emancipation is a restoration of the human world and of human relationships to man himself." That is, one might argue that it is through this violent reformation that intellectual emancipation restores to human ends our codings of both the world and relationships. Something of this violence seems implicit in what Fowles suggests in one of his "memoranda" to himself while composing the novel: "If you want to be true to life, start lying about the reality of it." That is, "lying" can only mean crossing the lines drawn by conventions, which may well be among those "structures" Darwin had in mind as having "now no very close and direct relations to present habits of life." The lie in this case, of course, is a modern interpretation of epigraphs exploited for their ability to serve thematic, atmospheric, and reflexive ends simultaneously. Such a use of epigraphs reminds us that fiction (or by implication any discourse) is made of bits and pieces of the verbal past woven into a different matrix of associations and conventions. The image of a creative homunculus in Fowles's brain dashing about looking up lines in *Granger's* yields to that of a (miraculously) fluid die into which the soft clay of both verbal and nonverbal pasts is formed. Again, that is, we find the study of epigraphs taking us back to the suggestions of this chapter's opening section, this time resolving the originator into the intertextuality of his era's paradigm (his "point in space and time") and of the past texts on which his era depends.

These issues become if anything more acute when one turns to those epigraphs that more directly refer to the authorial condition. Some of these are amusing enough; chapter 13's epigraph, "the drift of the Maker is dark," is a playful warning that the narrator is about to drift from narrative to metanarrative with intentions that seem fairly dark at first reading. Chapter 27 begins with Clough's famous lines about the difficulty of reaching "the buried world below," the emotions of the past; Tennyson's question, "was the day of my delight / As pure and perfect as I say?" points to the always vexing question of narrative reliability. Marx's description of the increasingly dogmatic quality of the "language of established society" when its illusions become evident (chap. 30) has immediate application to Mrs. Poulteney's prominently featured rigidity, but perhaps also to the equally dogmatic demands we sometimes hear for an authorially "responsible" moral fiction—one thinks of John Gardner's polemics—and from the left for a fiction free from authorial impositions of exhausted metaphysics (in, say, the essays of Robbe-Grillet).

Another epigraph from Marx (chap. 42) highlights the general existential theme of individuals like Charles and Sam working out their fates in the body of the chapter: "History is not like some individual person, which uses men to achieve its ends. History is nothing but the actions of men in pursuit of their ends." Marx's observation is referred to again in the narrator's final commentary on the novel (365) and clearly is part of Marx's effort to demythologize naive historiography's fiction of the heroic struggle of the human spirit to fulfill its manifest destiny (or for the pessimist, its equally manifest damnation). One might well go back to the epigraph and substitute "writing" for "history" and "conventions" for "men." That is, Marx is suggesting for history the same sort of dispersion of "agent" into the multiplicity of elements in the historical process that we found implicit in Fowles's essays and comments—the author is the geographical space and temporal moment in which numerous more or less conventional elements converge in practice. As the case of epigraphs suggests, authorial rhetoric is hence not a direct line to a metaphysical being whose unity and consistency are the ground of the text's organic form and thus a decisive court of interpretive appeal. Rather, it is one among a number of elements in the text's vocabulary of narrative conventions that tend, reflexively, to mark their orbits within the semiotic rather than the metaphysical sphere. This is not to say, of course, that epigraphs are not useful in interpretation, but the justification of their usefulness needs to reflect what the epigraphs themselves suggest about their limitations and what a less mystified sense of "author" implies.

"Authorial" Commentary

Despite narrative theory's warnings against confusing the views of a narrator and those of the implied or "real" author, commentary still carries tremendous interpretive authority because it seems coeval with the source of the narrative it explains—it seems, in other words, to be as close to an unmediated gloss on the authorial conception as we can get within the narrative. Although much of the commentary in *The French Lieutenant's Woman* seems to consist of reliable information and insights intended to aid a reader's interpretation of the characters and events, commentary also questions both the process of interpretation itself and the nature of our expectations about commentary. It becomes, then, something like a reflexive study of the nature and limitations of authorial commentary in the text.

The theme of interpretation is foregrounded in a series of what seem to be comments about historical information that can prevent misjudgments by the reader. For example, when Charles finds "the wildness of innocence" in Sarah confounding Dr. Grogan's diagnosis of neurosis, the narrator takes time out to explain: "In spite of Hegel, the Victorians were not a dialectically minded age; they did not think naturally in opposites, of positives and negatives as aspects of the same whole. Paradoxes troubled rather than pleased them. They were not the people for existentialist moments, but for chains of cause and effect; for positive all-explaining theories, carefully studied and studiously applied" (197). At first glance the passage is straightforward explanation of why Charles is perplexed once the "positive all-explaining" theory runs aground on the contraries he finds in Sarah. Rather than dismissing Charles as obtuse, we are to see that *our* conventions of character reflect the complexity of modern psychological theory—Quentin Compson and Sarah Woodruff, not David Copperfield and Mr. Harding, correspond to our expectations.

But the passage also serves as a warning; we are not ourselves above "chains of cause and effect" and "studiously applied" premises. In fact, the conventions of our role as readers demand them. It may be we are to recognize the inadequacy of Charles's interpretation of Sarah as having "that same wildness Charles had sensed in the wren's singing . . . a wildness of innocence, almost an eagerness"—the romantic myth of spontaneous authenticity does not hold. Nor does Dr. Grogan's analysis, based on its own logical chain and studiously applied assertions. Shrewd as he is to recognize before most readers can that Sarah's behavior partakes of complex intentional elements and hence of the artifice of strategy, we recognize that his interpretation too is limited by the logical chains and assertions of his unsympathetic all-explaining theory. But if we adopt a condescending stance toward either of these Victorian interpretations, we are not only invoking the hierarchical principle of judgment we have already found the novel discrediting, but also studiously applying the chain of cause and effect interpretation that takes our present awareness, called "existentialist moments" by the passage, to be the plenitude of wisdom. When the narrator invokes authorial privilege to comment upon his fictional creation, his doing so adumbrates a principle that undermines the authority of *any* single interpretation, since a "dialectically" inspired method and an "existentialist" method are still "positive all-explaining theories" rather than categorically distinct from the characters' procedures.

Such a comment limits the authority we might have anticipated in the narrator's authorial point of origin. Another example of the narrator's providing information of the times—the case of La Roncière and the pages from a Victorian work on hysteria—is related in more than content to the comments about dialectical thinking. As the note after the case explains (187–88), La Roncière, who was first condemned "by social prestige, by the myth of the pure-minded virgin, by psychological ignorance," then exonerated and rehabilitated on the basis of Dr. Matthaei's recognition of the girl's hysteria, has only recently been discovered to have given her real cause for her "hysteria" by snipping a lock of pubic hair from her on the fateful night in question. This case study of interpretation quickly becomes complicated, but what we find is that the case adduced to illustrate Grogan's diagnosis of hysteria, which turns out in some ways to be accurate, was itself an inaccurate overreaction against the truth in the girl's accusation. She had been wounded just as she claimed, and the innocence society cultivated in her self-image had certainly been violated when the lieutenant carried out his fellow officers' dare; thus her charges were truthful, even if La Roncière's letters were her foolish and obvious forgery. Both the case for and that against her testimony invoked faulty, oversimplifying interpretive frames similar to those we have just seen. Moreover, each depended upon a social consensus to clinch its case—the initial conviction upon a benighted society's outrage, the subsequent exoneration upon a backlash led by a crusading scientist determined to illuminate the dark ages of that society, and the latest reversal upon the contemporary historian of science documenting the overzealousness of psychologists in the primitive phase of their field's emergence. Each succeeding paradigm of interpretation finds the case confirming its own conceptual framework, but when the framework changes, and when such a change prescribes a particular kind of research that turns up new information less relevant to previous research paradigms, the conclusion shifts accordingly. The passage is thus a complex allegory of interpretation emphasizing the decisiveness of a paradigmatic framework in determining issues, themes, and the kinds of evidence felt to be most relevant to the interpretive act. The effect is to diminish the force of narrative commentary, for the authorial narrator can only be considered one of a series of possible sources of "all-explaining" theories about the "right" reading of La Roncière *or* the characters before us in the novel.

Yet another example of this anatomizing of interpretation comes in a comment he makes about Charles and his inability to explain his own malaise: "We could not expect him to see what we are only just beginning—and with so much more knowledge and the lessons of existentialist philosophy at our disposal—to realize ourselves: that the desire to hold and the desire to enjoy are mutually destructive" (60). One has to be suspicious of the implicit claim of interpretive perfectability, of having reached the "right" insight that lies outside Charles's abilities. But considered reflexively, the passage also reiterates one aspect of the novel's allegory of interpretation: holding and enjoying, product and process, possession and desiring, retaining and striving—the opposition has important implications for the wish to understand once and for all the feeling Charles has at this point in the novel—or for that matter, any question raised in the text. The struggle to know, to understand, becomes reified once the data are brought into line with our culturally derived framework of interpretation, and that reified product is an obstacle to be overcome as both the framework and the individual wielding it continue to change under the pressures of history. A single interpretation tightly held and the desire to enjoy the process of coming to understand are "mutually destructive." Hence there is more than fair-mindedness in Fowles's response to his French critics that "some at least of the *complaisance* the writers accuse me of extending to our own time was intended to be taken with a large grain of salt." [19] We must come to recognize that *any* interpretation must "be taken with a large grain of salt" rather than allowing ourselves to privilege either our own interpretive frame or that of a mystified exaggeration of the authorial act. Comments such as this, at least, certainly invoke for their specific ends principles that undermine the absolute authority normally ascribed to the authorial text. The authorial epicenter we infer from the quaking text is better understood as the function of much larger pressures in the cultural geology of writing.

The most grotesque implosion of authorial commentary occurs when it becomes the voice of the crucified Christ speaking to Charles in the chapel: "My poor Charles, search your heart—you thought when you came to this city, did you not, to prove to yourself you were not yet in the prison of your future. But escape is not one act, my friend. It is no more achieved by that than you could reach Jerusalem from here by one small step. Each day, Charles, each hour, it has to be taken again" (284). And so the passage continues in the swelling rhetoric of an existentialist messiah, a guise presumptuous enough to make its rhetorical impact upon the reader (let alone upon Charles), but also suggesting that an equal freedom to recast the Judeo-Christian heritage awaits each age's, and each narrator's, interpretive needs. Certainly the tone is condescending enough to alert one to the dangers of its smugness. Interpretation, one surmises, is not one act—at each reading it has to be taken again from the intertextual repertoire of an interpretive paradigm. Neither the authorial point of origin nor the end of absolute truth sustains its metaphysical status independent of cultural relativity, and the expectation of "all-explaining" commentary is reproved by this reflexive allegory of interpretation; that is, explanation proceeds, but within the city of cultural discourse rather than the eschatological fulfillment of a new Jerusalem.

Interpretation, and the presumption of authorial vision that lies behind commentary, is not the only relevant theme to be found in this exercise of the authorial function. The commentary also directly confronts the concept of personal identity on which our notions of the author also depend, and in terms, not surprisingly, close to Fowles's own speculations with which this chapter began. To regard the author as a stable and significant point of reference, we have to find in him a fixed ground outside the narrative, the personal point of access to a consistent and unified metaphysical vision anchoring meaning in that author's works. But here we are told that "we all write poems; it is simply that poets are the ones who write in words"(123). It may be that poets are the ones who put the words down on paper, but we all do what in this scene we see Charles doing as he tries to puzzle out Sarah and his feelings about her—we *feel* our experiences, however perplexing and seemingly beyond the ordinary, not in the unmediated terms of the spontaneous and "natural," but in the semiotic or "grammatological" terms of *writing.* At the same time that the comment endorses the depth and power of Charles's emotion, it also suggests that it is already a text in the culture's semiotics of feeling and hence not quite a means of contact with the nondiscursive. As a general principle, it suggests that the authenticity of supposedly "direct" feeling is compromised by such closure within semiotic conventions, however poetic they may be.

The narrator presses the point home in more fundamental terms when he turns on the reader's possible objection to talking about the autonomy of fictional characters: "But this is preposterous? A character is either 'real' or 'imaginary'? If you think that, *hypocrite lecteur,* I can only smile. You do not even think of your own past as quite real; you dress it up, you gild it or blacken it, censor it, tinker with it . . . fictionalize it, in a word, and put it away on a shelf—your book, your romanced autobiography. We are all in flight from the real reality. That is a basic definition of *Homo sapiens*" (82). Not only is writing the proper metaphor for the way we feel our experience as it occurs, thus stressing the cultural refractions in what might otherwise be thought of as "direct" experience, but our very sense of identity is a fictionalization. The text thus argues that we all compose a "romanced autobiography" we call our self and contends the philosophical commonplace—as Dwight Eddins calls it—"that each man's life is a novel of which that man is the author" and, we must add, the protagonist.[20] Hence this passage suggests that our identity is a shifting, evolving fable answering our immediate

196

authorial needs rather than a stable, consistent, and authoritative history identifying the sort of "essence" (identity, consistency, unity) needed for a decisive authorial point of reference in point of view theory. Insofar as we can speak of an authorial "essence," it is a discursive construct arrived at after the textual fact.

In life or in interpreting fiction, we learn to act on the strength of these fictions, whether or not we acknowledge them. Hence the novel argues again in chapter 45 that we are all "novelists, that is, we have a habit of writing fictional futures for ourselves" and that "these novelistic or cinematic hypotheses often have very much more effect on how we actually do behave, when the real future becomes the present, than we generally allow" (266). More than just a marginal notation of why Charles dreamed up the first and most conventional ending of the novel, this passage points to a view of culture as a repertoire of texts and structures decisively shaping our behavior. Can Charles thus be said to have generated autonomously that ending? He seems rather to have lapsed for a moment into perfect alignment with the Victorian novelistic convention (calling for him to heed the moral imperative on the allegorical cover of *Pendennis*) until, once that convention has been surprised by Sarah's abandonment of the script, he alters it accordingly, first to the convention of romantic exile (when he plans to go away with Sarah to the Continent) and finally to that of romantic melodrama (when he feels himself "the last honorable man on the way to the scaffold" [364] in the novel's third ending). The stage posturing of his confession to Ernestina at Lyme and his Byronic wandering in the new world only serve to multiply the number of examples in which Charles composes his autobiography along the lines of one romance script or another— while it happens as much as in retrospect.

The narrative conventions by which Charles sees his life cohere are not restricted to the romance plots whose roles he chooses as models. The cultural relativity implied in these plot models applies equally to the metaphysical coherence that is a distinctly authorial trait, whether one refers to the author of texts or of romanced autobiographies. If we try to pursue the problematic line we found in an earlier passage between a hypothetical "human constant" and the stylistic embodiments in "vocabulary" and "metaphor," we will find a passage like the following enlightening. The narrator summarizes Charles's self-justifications as he tries to decide whether to remain conventional:

And how should he have blamed himself very deeply? From the outset his motives had been the purest; he had cured her of her madness; and if something impure had for a moment threatened to infiltrate his defenses, it had been but mint sauce to the wholesome lamb. He would be to blame, of course, if he did not now remove himself, and for good, from the fire. That, he would take very good care to do. After all, he was not a moth infatuated by a candle; he was a highly intelligent being, one of the finest, and endowed with total free will. If he had not been sure of that latter safeguard, would he ever have risked himself in such dangerous waters? *I am mixing metaphors—but that was how Charles's mind worked.* (152–53; italics mine)

"Total free will" is an illusion, of course, for we have found Charles already simply switching prescripted romance roles. But at this point when his confidence in his role is breaking up, so too does the metaphoric coherence structuring his view of his life. Rather than any illusory "constant" of a self powerful enough to choose in complete freedom, Charles is stumbling among the competing schema implied in chemistry ("purest"), mental health ("madness"), warfare ("defenses"), cuisine and Christology ("mint sauce to the wholesome lamb"), animal behavior ("the moth and the flame"), and sailing (in "dangerous waters"). Interestingly enough, the novel elsewhere reflects this same list of interpretive frames for what happens—science, hysteria, class warfare, social mores, theology, the biological constants beneath human behavior, and the concept of life as a journey. This author of his "romanced autobiography" is having difficulty precisely because he cannot yet compose these competing narrative and metaphorical structures into an identity ("character") and a plan of action ("plot") that will satisfy his (authorial) aesthetics, in the largest sense of the term. Moreover, we learn much from its dramatization of the stylization and culturally bound alternatives that cycle through his sense of the options available to him for making sense of and structuring his experiences—the authorial analogue finds no point of access to the metaphysical ground he seeks as a means to stabilize and organize a consistent, unified, and "right" selfhood.

The analogy between the author of selfhood and the author of fiction thus reminds us of several themes we have found elsewhere in the novel, particularly as the analogue undermines the idea of an author as a metaphysical being independent of a culturally stipulated identity, as a creative genius creating ex nihilo an original text, or as a consistent, wholly unified "absolute entity" to whom issues in interpretation are in any meaningful way referable. He is instead something more like a semiotic being shifting intertextual elements around according to their satisfaction of current criteria—in both his life and his work. This semiotic and intertextual standing of the concept of author is developed in some detail by the commentary. One example is the narrator's deference to a 1749 "very far from dull history of a lively human penis" for a description of festivities at a brothel, a history found while "nosing around" a bookseller's; what pleases him about the two-page quotation is that "it allows one to borrow from someone else's imagination" (240). If this is an example, however extreme, of the process quoted earlier from Fowles's account of his reading, it certainly demonstrates the extent to which narrative techniques learned from existing texts bring with them far more substantive conceptions than the narrative pacing and dialogue techniques Fowles mentions in that account. Indeed, it bolsters the interesting point made by Fred Kaplan that Fowles evokes the past "through an eclectic exploitation of styles and structures that for Fowles' audience *is* the Victorians and their age."[21] Kaplan argues that Fowles thus implies that our knowledge of the past is not through facts but through the imaginative literature's version of those facts. The passage thus reinforces the allegory of interpretation I discussed earlier, for it makes clear that any past is remembered only in terms of its discursive interpretation. At the same time, however, one is reminded of various themes we found in Fowles's essays about the status of the author—the eclectic polystylism of Fowles's artistic strategy that dissolves the one voice, the dispersion of origin by the suffusion of intertextual debts of both technique and substance, the pluralism of intention that results from the eclectic qualities of authorship, and even the absorption of "author" into the set of textual strategies that present "him" in the act of discovering two pages for his novel in eighteenth-century pornography.

The narrator reaches even further in commenting on his sense of being caught between two conventions of the novel—the Victorian and that emerging with Roland Barthes and Robbe-Grillet (80). But since he feels he fits no convention entirely, he points out a series of other discourse systems in which he might be participating. The list includes "transposed autobiography" (a choice reinforced by Fowles's suggestion in an interview that he drafts in first person and revises to third,[22] therefore lending credence to the suggestion here that "perhaps Charles is myself disguised"), as well as essays from a list of fields similar to that we saw earlier in the novel's homologies, and just now in Charles's metaphoric frames: biology ("On the Horizontality of Existence"), historiography ("The Illusions of Progress"), literary theory ("The History of the Novel Form"), philosophy ("The Aetiology of Freedom"), and social history ("Some Forgotten Aspects of the Victorian Age") (81). Our opportunities to have explored already the implications of horizontality and the illusion of interpretive progress remind us that these other discourse systems have been used to deconstruct several important assumptions in the history of the novel form. But the implications run both ways, as the chapter implies later when it suggests this digression has much to do "with your Time, Progress, Society, Evolution and all those other capitalized ghosts in the night," and as it makes explicit by alluding to the Heraclitian notion that "fiction is woven into all" (82). Not only is *The French Lieutenant's Woman* what it is as a result of the confluence of multifarious discursive strands, but these other discourses share a vital trait with the sense of selfhood already examined—they too are fundamentally fictive in their nature and status. What does it mean to say that the fictional author is the type, rather than the prevaricating exception, of the author of discourse?

In chapter 55 the narrator marks the difference between fiction and reality as the former's inevitable fixing of the combat or tension among "wants"; authors give the illusion of ending or closure to what would otherwise be an open process. As we consider the ways narrative closure characterizes these other discourse systems, we can recall Warren's subversion of the myth of objective history, this novel's stress upon the fictive element in autobiography, and its equally explicit disparagement of science's "foredoomed attempt to stabilize and fix what is in reality a continuous flux" (45). Whether closure is narrative or conceptual, it artificially limits the frame upon subject matter to the terms presupposed by the text. "Author" is the summary of those presuppositions insofar as they are identifiable at any given time and is hence a semiotic nexus more than a prophetic medium for metaphysically grounded "truth." It is, to recall Foucault's words, "the ideological figure by which one . . . impedes the free circulation" of textual meaning and, instead, imposes closure.

The diverting discussion of Charles's autonomy in chapter 13 is also relevant here. In explaining how Charles could surprise him by violating the plan, the narrator claims that novelists write "to create worlds as real as, but other than the world that is." At first glance, this seems merely the realist's credo; the catch, however, is in the phrase "as real as." "Realistic" in place of "real" would have suggested the more innocuous reading; but literally the sentence claims far more. No version of the "world that is" is any more real than the fictional world; to think about the world at all is to author it. When, early on, we found Fowles redefining the author as "simply the common condition of all human mentality," he may well have been suggesting that any discursive act makes or constitutes its world and, since the author is himself a function of the text, the author too is always made rather than transcending the text.

Similar implications inhere in this response to any objections to commentary in the novel: "I have disgracefully broken the illusion? No. My characters still exist, and in a reality no less, or no more, real than the one I have just broken" (82). One is unsure whether the objection is over "disgracefully" or "broken," the difference being that between whether one may make any explicitly reflexive comments at all and whether the definition of illusion covers the narrator as well as the plot. The final sentence, however, is even more important; the question was about "illusion," the answer about a "reality" in which any number of fictive frames coexist. When Fowles goes on to pinpoint the issue as the "more valid" reality of characters described as beyond his control, to what is he pointing if not the network of intersecting discursive conventions powering the text and providing the "control" he recognizes is beyond him? In what reality do they exist other than the discourse in which they and the author figure so prominently, a discourse that, as we have seen, can scarcely be distinguished from any other discursive form? That this tells us more than the simple idea that plots could take more than one shape is clear from the analogy Fowles claims between fiction and the discursiveness of selfhood. He points out that his failure to control Charles is the same failure of the reader to control, "however hard you try . . . your children, your colleagues, friends, or even yourself." The characters draw their life not from an author's conception or control, but from the larger matrix of semiotic strands set in the text. Similarly, neither those we raise, those we work or play with, nor that most precious one we like to think we either *are* or *form* (depending upon our beliefs) are any different, subject as they all are to the same force of cultural semiotics both in their individual histories and in their (and our) conceptions of those histories.

Hence when Charles is said to be "real" *because* he is in this way "autonomous," then the criterion of "real" is consistency within a contemporary narrative convention in which "autonomy" really means we pretend that those conventions and narrative imperatives shaping a character's (or individual's) actions are under his direct control rather than dispersed in the cultural network of which he is, as Fowles argues of the author, one point in space and time. "Real" thus means consistent with paradigmatic (i.e., cultural, conventional) determination of which signs shall refer to reality, to being real, to behaving consistently with what the paradigm presupposes reality to be like.

If this sounds incompatible with existentialism's celebration of the individual's freedom to be, it is probably because our conception of existentialism is still based on a largely metaphysical sense of the self. When the existentialist argues that existence precedes essence, we still read a "being" as the ground of the existing, as the origin of choices. It is that "being" who had the moral responsibility to commit himself to choices that cohere and are meaningful. The persistence of this evasion of the discursiveness of the "common condition of all human mentality" has distressing effects for critical theory, for it allows all those lapses of a different kind of bad faith, one that seeks to base the dignity and stature of the individual, and the analogous authority and message of the author, outside the cultural realm in some spiritual dimension. What the demythologizing themes of this novel achieve is a reminder that, as Fowles puts it, "existentialism is not a philosophy, but a way of looking at, and utilizing, other philosophies. It is a theory of relativity among theories of absolute truth."[23] That is, it is a theory that accepts the destabilizing effects of relativity wherever they fall, even if it means recognizing the discursiveness not only of discourse, but of whatever has been assumed to be nondiscursive (i.e., our views of reality, our sense of self, the very discrimination among and definition of the options open to the "free" man). This does not mean that the "reality" of history does not exist, of course; it signifies that the paradigm underlying a given discourse is the means by which history constitutes those who play out its processes and that some paradigm or, more accurately, mix of paradigms is an inevitable intermediary between a not so free person and historical forces. Hence the characters' freedom at the end of the novel is not that Charles can now, or that Sarah can now, be free to honor the nature of his or her authentic being, but that both have shifted discursive norms for their course in life and that the confusion, "hysteria," blanks, and eruptions they experience illustrate the turmoil discernible in semiotic beings when they sense themselves between roles, in the code-changing no-man's-land along the battle lines between more than one cultural consensus. Neither Charles nor the authorial narrator may be viewed as escaping the bad faith of outworn and benighted conventions, for what is at stake is precisely *not* nurturing the illusion that one will escape semiotics into some pure free paradise of plenitude and authenticity.

"A Terrible Anomaly in Reason"

That authorial narrator also, as we saw, felt himself between conventions, and his talk about the novelist as a "godlike proprietor" is an attempt to work out his dilemma. We are told unequivocally that "the novelist is still a god" (82); ostensibly the effort is to find his real shape somewhere between the Victorian omniscient novelist who can go anywhere in the novel he likes—as he does in chapter 55 by entering Charles's railway car—and the detached *nouveau roman* fop who in chapter 61 rides away from the final scene (362), the sound of his landau echoing in Charles's ears as he leaves Sarah's house and find "he did not know where to go" (365; Presumably because the *nouveau romancier* has left and will not tell him?). Robert Huffaker explains the presence of both figures as the way "Fowles defies both Victorian preoccupation with the illusion of omniscience and contemporary fixation upon the illusion of detachment"; in other words, he is emphasizing "that the modern novelist *does* exist in his fiction" as much as the Victorian novelist did.[24] This existentialist reading suggests that the authorial god recasts himself "in the new theological image" of leaving others to their freedoms (chap. 13); the counterelements we have found suggest that the "master" of discourse is not in a position to free his subjects, that he himself becomes a function of his text, swinging in and out of the novel, back and forth from twentieth-century detached impresario (chap. 61) to involved but omniscient nineteenth-century novelist (chap. 55), up and down from omnipotent god (55) to helpless victim of his character's whims (13), and so forth through the various roles the text requires, and thus leaving his characters (and himself) only "*un simulacré de liberté*" as the discourse takes shape.[25]

Thus the novel seems to endorse Robbe-Grillet's critique of the omniscient novelist (or god) and his "distinctly mean and dubious . . . moral quality" (317) and to undercut the new French version as pretentious (his foppish appearance and predilection for grand opera), possessive, and exploitative ("he very evidently regards the world as his to possess and use as he likes" [362]—rather like the Victorian novelist in chapter 55), and as absurdly "proprietary" and self-satisfied. In other words, both share the illusion of controlling what is actually, as discourse, free of their mastery, shaping both their self-conceptions and their roles in a novel according to discursive rather than personal needs. Perhaps what Fowles means, then, when he frees Charles to go to the Dairy if he must, is that in the long run it *does* answer authorial ends to allow the discourse to well up out of the authorial consciousness's hall of semiotic mirrors and reflect what it will of its current playing out of conventions—the interplay of precedents, the crossplay of different systems or genres of discourse, the horseplay of a mind reflexively aware of the pretense in the creative mystique, of the illusion that his or any other discourse masters or comprehends what is outside it, and in the last analysis, of the ultimate variability of the "I" of author, character, reader, or individual.

When the narrator makes his last explicitly reflexive comment, it is that "there is no intervening god [in life, in fiction] beyond whatever can be seen, in that way, in the first epigraph to this chapter" (365). That epigraph celebrates "the process by which chance (the random mutations in the nucleic acid helix caused by natural radiation) cooperates with natural law to create living forms better and better adapted to survive" (361). To maintain that the authorial self is chance radiation altering the nucleic acid helix of narrative discourse is to stress that narrative change is primarily its becoming "better adapted to survive" in the changing configurations of cultural assumptions, and that the author's role is hardly the same mastery of an original genius celebrated in popular romanticizing of the author. "To create" narrative or any other discourse may indeed mean to be the god of that discourse, like the narrator of *The French Lieutenant's Woman,* but, then, to be a god in a semiotic universe is a very different thing from being one in the grand old metaphyscial cosmos of a logocentric culture.

One might well argue that the relevance of "author" to a fiction is as the groundless ground, as our positing of a nuclear center based upon the orbits of textual ions. The author does indeed serve as the means by which the recombinative possibilities of conventions are played out, but as such he is himself as much a process (of playing out those possibilities) as the text itself—neither are the usual static entities modeled on metaphysical notions of the self. In fact, as we have seen on each of our approaches to the authorial mode within *The French Lieutenant's Woman,* the "author" is himself a textual product of his works insofar as they replace "him," become what we mean when we speak of "him." It is the visible traces of his having been created in the process of fictionalizing that constitute the "author" in fiction, a process that Fowles repeatedly finds in fiction, in nonfiction, and in "life" itself. To call the author a "textual strategy," then, is to recognize that there is no meaningful sense in which a nontextual entity is relevant in considerations of point of view and other critical concerns; indeed, to speak of a nontextual or nondiscursive entity may itself be philosophically imprecise. In any case the "author" is created by the same process that creates narrators and characters and hence obtains no great privilege over them as a center of coherence, an interpretive authority, or a methodological key to our reading of the text(s) forming "him." The author as a specificially semiotic god allows his interpreters to be free.

Hence when Fowles parodies the appearances (in both senses) of his authorial narrator, he is merely attempting to make explicit the textual figment that correlates with the particular style, voice, and techniques of a given configuration of conventions. That they are constructed *from* the text, rather than simply being the agents responsible *for* the text, underscores the fact that the author is the same sort of interpretive construct created by the reader that character, narrator, or theme is commonly recognized to be. *The French Lieutenant's Woman* continues a reflexive current in the novel in which, even as the authorial function

204

is dramatized and depended upon for many effects, it is also exposed as the circular shape of reflexivity with which this study began.

When we have recourse to the author's other works, the logical soundness of the recourse for interpretation lies not in the integrity of the metaphysical being responsible for both texts, despite temporal changes in his personality, but in the confluence of conventions and their interconnections at an authorial point in time and space, despite the shifting recombinations occurring over a period of time. The logical link is *not* to the man, but to the textual conditions he works with and from which we subsequently infer him from the way that, having taken place, they have constituted his "being." Many of our discussions of the author are confused by this blurring of the distinction between the organism and the discursive manipulations it has produced; the discussion of the one is a venture into amateur psychologizing, of the other into the blending of discursive conventions of numerous kinds.

In a passage designed partially to explain the imaginative power of Christ over a young man (Charles) so progressive in his views, the narrator comments on the "profound sense of exclusion, of a gift withdrawn" among "all but a very few Victorian atheists" (281). For these individuals, he explains, "Christ remained, a terrible anomaly in reason," neither the "completely secularized figure" of our century nor the "divinity" of the rest of the Victorian world (282). Hence "Christ" still successfully exercised an imaginative power over his "readers," just as the contemporary novelist can do despite the demystifying of novelistic techniques and elements. Though we are "enlightened" enough to be theoretical atheists about the author, as we work with texts that godlike appeal still operates in all its "terrible anomaly in reason." Hence in the reflexive play of *The French Lieutenant's Woman* one finds allegories of writing and reading emerging, renewing their vigor in the form of the novel without pretending the old myths are more than cultural forms, however distinguished their heritage.

Fowles and His Contemporaries

Writing after the vogue of modernist psychological narrative and amid the onset of the poststructuralist era, Fowles retraces some of the same ground we saw in our discussion of *Vanity Fair*. He does so, however, not to differ in any fundamental direction from Thackeray's tracing of the semiotic contours of the emerging collective consciousness of the middle class, but rather to open that vexing intersection of the ontological and the semiotic more systematically and, perhaps, more persistently.

If literary modernism failed to jettison entirely the conventional apparatus Thackeray satirized and to attain an unmediated grasp of consciousness itself, Fowles's work seems to pursue aggressively the range and
implications of "creativity" within a fully semiotic context. Indeed, perhaps Fowles's "return" to the rather Victorian use of epigraphs signals a
passage beyond a certain moment in which modernism seemed to
attempt, by increasing the intensity of its psychological focus, to escape
the mediating apparatus of Victorian epigraphs and commentary. Fowles
focuses with loving vengeance upon that apparatus and the succeeding
generations of narrative conventions. If, then, Thackeray shows the
narrator's ties to the ideological allegiances of a given narrative mode,
Fowles extends that connection back to the author "himself," placing
beside the unitary self with its various beliefs the "author-function"
that displaces ontology almost entirely as a pertinent frame of reference
and points instead to all those larger ghosts of history "rattling their
chains" in the night. Nor is Fowles alone on the contemporary scene in
posing such questions about the relation between the "author" and the
larger structures on whith the role depends. At one point in Robert
Coover's "The Magic Poker," the narrator loses his confidence and poses
a question similar to that of Fowles's authorial narrator. He begins con-
fidently enough, bragging about his doings and insisting that "really,
there's nothing to it" (22).[26] Before long, however, he stops to ask, "But
where is the caretaker's son? I don't know. He was here, shrinking into
the shadows, when Karen's sister entered. . . . This is awkward! Didn't I
invent him myself, along with the girls and the man in the turtleneck
shirt? . . . To tell the truth, I sometimes wonder if it was not he who invented me" (27). In such a textual world "invention" means something
other than the quasi-divine creation of the authorial god. It is, of course,
an intertextual world in which "invention" involves multiple relations
constituting the various epiphenomenal points in a story, including the
authorial "I" of Fowles's notes or of this reflection. In fact the narrator's
perplexity is only one theme in a multistrand narrative that foregrounds
the multistrandedness of any narrative and that exceeds the mastery of
any single controlling point. Indeed, the authorial narrator seems more
like an air traffic controller struggling madly on his scopes to keep
narratemes from colliding in midair. Perhaps part of Coover's play with
this portrait of the author-god is an effort to remind us how easily we
think of narrative as a solo flight piloted by a "Lucky Lindy" rather
than as a network of relations much wider than any pilot can himself
control. The many incompatible strands of this story make evident how
difficult it would be to expect the authorial narrator to provide the
interpretive line we have been conditioned by many classic narratives to

expect,[27] but Coover's "The Gingerbread House" may be even more useful to our purposes, for the multistrandedness of that story moves specifically to collect classic interpretations of it and allows each hypothetical authorial intention to dominate in turn the shape of the episodes. We find a heroic romance, complete with the song of the innocents about "God's care for little ones" (61), featuring a Hansel whose shrewd ploys might have saved them in a less Melvillean universe. But we also find considerable psychosexual fascination between the boy and the witch, he "transfixed" but following nonetheless until her "gnarled and bluish fingers claw at his poor garments, his pale red jacket and bluish-brown pants, surprising his soft young flesh" (71). There is, too, a diabolic totemism of the ripped-out dove's heart that fascinates witch, old man, and boy. The witch herself is a condensation of many nightmare fantasies, as this segment suggests:

> The witch flicks and flutters through the blackened forest, her livid face twisted with hatred, her inscrutable condition. Her eyes burn like glowing coals and her black rags flap loosely. Her gnarled hands claw greedily at the branches, tangle in the night's webs, dig into tree trunks until the sap flows beneath her nails. Below, the boy and girl sleep an exhausted sleep. One ghostly white leg, with dimpled knee and soft round thigh, thrusts out from under the blanket of branches. (74)

Each sentence compounds our interest in the witch. In the first she is Ahab's nightmare; in the second a universal vision of supernatural villain. In the third her hands become a predatory sexuality in which blood, sap, and other precious bodily fluids mingle in a highly charged condensation full of a childlike fear of sexuality. Finally, the last sentence pits the vulnerable androgynous sensuality of innocence against the hovering menace of adult power. The economic and generational warfare behind the tale is played up in the basic situation of the old man's abandonment of the children, and the sexual energy behind fairy tales is seen not only in the figure of the witch but also in that of the good fairy who "floats, ruby-tipped breasts downward, legs dangling and dimpled knees bent slightly, glowing buttocks arched up in defiance of the night. How good she is!" (74). Sexual ripeness and moral goodness are archly condensed in such a segment, as if the "author" meant everything at once as, of course, the intertextual literary system has a way of doing. Such a narrative forces to the surface our awareness of the many interpretive systems at work in narrative, each of them trailing long strings of texts behind it, each of them thrashing out its contradictions within the semiotic being who is anything but a single point of thematic coherence.

Indeed, much of Coover's *Pricksongs and Descants* can be seen as a way of emptying out the author into the interpretive systems within which he functions. An alternative solution to the problematic space of the author is discernible in the late work of Truman Capote. In the preface to *Music for Chameleons,* he poses this crucial problem: "How can a writer successfully combine within a single form—say the short story— all he knows about every other form of writing? . . . I was not using everything I knew about writing—all I'd learned from film scripts, plays, reportage, poetry, the short story, novellas, the novel. A writer ought to have all his colors, all his abilities available on the same palette for ming- ling (and, in suitable instances, simultaneous application)."[28] Stranded in the middle of a "creative chaos" in which he feels quite blocked, Capote's solution to the authorial dilemma is to collate all the techniques associated with various author functions, discourse type by discourse type, until "author" becomes a condensation of his cultural condition- ing as a commercially successful author. Interestingly enough, that con- densation has been much questioned by critics wondering if one or another author function was properly executed according to the terms of the literary contract—if, for example, the author-reporter retained sufficient distance, the novel author sufficient creative latitude, the script author sufficient fidelity. Such questions seem odd in the face of Capote's having emptied out the author as original creator and stressed instead the technical assemblage, the repertoire of virtuoso gambits. What is really interesting, however, is that Capote's crisis seems not to have been solved until he placed himself "center stage"—not in the sense of imperial author, but in the reduced and extravagantly semiotic form of initials, the "TC" of "Nocturnal Turnings" or *Handcarved Coffins,* a character whose authorial functions transpire as part of the action of writing, whether interviewing himself, "reconstructing" events, or getting out of the way to let Junebug Johnson "commence."

If Capote shows all that is internalized, John Barth tends to emphasize the more external frames within which the author function takes place, particularly in his multiplying levels of framing until the pointlessness of *ever* escaping all the brackets, all the layers of quotation marks, all the myths or novels (his own or others'), is painfully apparent. Some critics might like to treat such practice as aberrant, counterproductive to the realistic ends of narrative, but it is in fact paradigmatic of all fiction, and it is highly productive in suggesting the *means* of any narrative. That is, closing in on speaker after framed speaker could also always open out instead on frame after cultural, textual frame compos- ing the multiple references of any text in our tradition.

Equally interesting is John Hawkes's *The Blood Oranges,* a novel that challenges us to trace out all the frames into which its authorial narrator, Cyril, is resolved. Hugh's photography is partly a form of possessing absolutely rather than relating openly, but it also serves in the novel as a mode of consciousness with significant epistemological limits to its authorial grasp of its subject matter. A photograph, that is, is like realism, a representational transparency; but also like the language of realism, the "things" in a photographic negative are all negated, white blobs, and it is absence (the ground of the figure) that is "figured" until the photograph is actually printed and we "forget" the intermediary stages of the process. Cyril's Illyrian aesthetics of will, however, is a Utopian dream of libidinal plenitude. Cyril has no more luck willing everyone into an orgy of erotic fulfillment than Hugh has in mastering the objects of his photographic (or expeditionary) endeavors. What matters for our purposes is that each offers a common model of authorship in our culture—as mimetic master of reality, as romantic creator of a better world. Each, of course, fails to fulfill his program, suggesting the extent to which their respective idealisms transgress the limits of the attainable. Cyril, after all, cuts a ridiculous figure, his oversized body huffing up the hill on a spindly bicycle to Catharine's sanatorium, his wife departed, his friend dead, his lover psychologically vacant. He is more endearing than Hugh, but then he is allowed to narrate the novel as a sort of rebuttal or extension of Ford's version of a similar quartet in *The Good Soldier,* carrying out Hawkes's theory of fiction as "revenge for all the indignities of our childhood; it should be an act of rebellion against all the constraints of the conventional pedestrian mentality around us."[29] As internalized as those conventions are for Hawkes, given his attentiveness to Ford as an example, it is no wonder that his "rebellion" works within familiar conceptual boundaries, setting logic against imagination, restraint against gratification, photography against Illyrian ritual, mimesis against creation, antithesis against other. Hawkes considers that Cyril and Hugh "are both artists" (101) and would consider himself one as well, I should think, but none of them gets outside the conceptual frames Hawkes places alongside Barth's literary or Capote's technical intertextualities.

If one begins to examine figures whose emergence postdates this cluster of writers, one follows further the lines along which contemporary writers reconsider the authorial position in the narrative world. I want to look closely at four works that seem to me to chart promising directions for the effort to see beyond what Foucault calls "man" and thus beyond the author function to which we have become accustomed. Steve Katz, Robert Kelly, Ronald Sukenick, and Angela Carter provide opportunities to consider the relation between the author function and, respectively, the sign, the "style world," the nonlogocentric, and the phallocentricity of the narrative tradition.

In *Moving Parts,* Steve Katz presents four sections that are "unrelated" in the old sense of the word but that lead steadily toward the absorption of the "unifying" presence of an author figure into the sign—in this case, literally "43."[30] The opening section, "Female Skin," is the first instance in which Katz makes playfully literal our clichés about the author of fiction. It is, as one might guess, a striking instance of the author's "getting under the skin" of his character, Wendy, who comes complete with photographs and a release from one Wendy Appel giving Katz permission to use her "name and details from my experience" (27). One could not ask for a case in which the real more directly authorized the fictional. That such authorization is a foolish preconception is suggested by the narrator's experience of walking about New York in his character's skin: thousands of geese begin to follow him, and he tells us that they "watched me as if I were expected to say something" (17) as, one supposes, a good sage should. We who hold such preconceptions are no doubt prime candidates for the "new work of art" by Charles Ross that "has the capacity to cause the slow dissolution of whoever views it by irresistibly absorbing the light that makes up the viewer's own real substance" (19). We are, it seems, the sum of our energy of perception, for just before art lovers disappear while looking at this work, "some of them suddenly 'see the light,' realizing that all of reality is dependent on this energy, nothing else is as crucial." It is experience rather than transcendental identity that is "crucial," and we are as silly as a goose if we tie the textual experience to the author himself.

In the second segment, "Parcel of Wrists," the "author" receives just that in the mail—forty-three wrists that he plants in pots around his apartment. He makes a trip in vain to the return address, a trip doomed partly because there is no such place (he ends up going only to towns whose names are similar), and partly because the trip "composes itself minute by minute" (18) rather than submitting to any authorial design. When he returns, the wrists have sprouted bushes of body parts whose superabundance becomes a burden: "Perhaps you have met me at one time or another in the streets, haunting strangers, insisting on the replacements from the pack of goods I carry on my back. You must know who I am" (35). And indeed, after considering the solicitations carried out by Fowles's authorial narrator, we should know that this is the author as semiotic being, combining and recombining the physical signifiers by which we construct characters from words and conventional behaviors that just seem to grow on trees. The cost is great, however, as in the case of Susan Kentucky, to whom, out of love, he gives free of charge "a forehead, complete with temples, a couple of cheeks with variable dimples, one of my most powerful brows, and I don't know what else." But the love is futile, because "if she has applied my parts to her features I'll never be able to recognize her. That's one of the hazards of my occupation, and one of the paradoxes not entirely taken into account by those who imagine mine to be a 'power trip.' Who is it? Who really exercises the control. That's an important question" (36). The real, that is, has always already passed into the refiguration we call the textual, and if that involves a certain will to power over reality it also, paradoxically, leaves that reality as elusive finally as any object of desire as well as putting us at the mercy of those features we are enabled semiotically to recognize. The final paragraph of the section laments that he ever accepted the parcel of wrists—the repertoire of conventions—"that caused this life that I have . . . to take the peculiar turn it did at a certain point." The package comes through the United States Post Office, that great public intertextual network, and he realizes that had he refused the shipment "my life might have worked itself out by an entirely other set of priorities." A different flowering of culture might have filled his apartment, it seems, "an entirely other" semiotic matrix within which to arrange the real. As it is, the "author" depended on the wrist action.

In the third section, "Trip" (which follows a photographic summary of "The Author's Wrists"—in case one has missed the point), the authorial narrator claims actually to make the journey that turns out to have been the fiction of "Parcel of Wrists" and provides photographs and many details to authenticate the trip. "In this book," he tells us, "you get such a sense of the reality of the main character that he seems to get off the page and sit down with you on the bus" (10). This satire of review-speak does in fact strike at a prevailing assumption that fiction *should* create characters who are as "real" as those on the bus with us, and it is doubly significant because the "main character" is the "author" of the preceding segment. The reality of the "author," that is, depends upon the persuasiveness of the techniques of fiction, whether or not one is finally sure to have found which story if any shows the "real" author. The sketch repeatedly undermines any nontextual identity as the narrative source, as when one paragraph ends with the note, "As far as the Protagonist can tell he's the only protagonist on the bus" (15)— "he" is a role, the rest of them simply decorative detail in the narrative construct as it rumbles along Route 43. Even his experiences shift into a zone that is oddly textually determined; some days, for example, have to be filled with "deletable events" if they are part of the protagonist's time left out of "Parcel of Wrists" (18), and this narrator "feels a twinge of guilt every time he strays from the script" of the other story, noting defensively that "Steven had an author to help eliminate waste, and the Protagonist has to do it alone" (21). As the contradictions develop, he comes to feel that "I haunt this place out of my own fiction, living in one world and in another at once, but alive now in neither, admitting no history in one, having none in the other" (49), as if he were "myself emptied" (43). The crisis, of course, involves that all but deconstructive oscillation between the author as existential and as semiotic being.

Finally, the emptying complete, we come down to the relation between language and fiction: "Language is the medium, and the limitation. If truth is the result it's not constructed in language, but generated as resonances by the art of telling" (74). "Generated" rather than derived, the truth it seems is itself "untellable" and is a function of distinctly semiotic resonances. Because of the infinite multiplicity of such resonances, however, unrestrained art menaces not just our poetics of the author, but ideology. Of conviction, for example, we read that "the stronger that gets, the more contingencies are eliminated that are also true" (73). Even a conviction in "good, humanitarian, hippy rules" purges alternative truths—those as "minor" as the subjectivities tossed out as the author or the protagonist in this novel, or as major as the truths and convictions freely circulating beyond official or authorial control. Ultimately, that is, any ideological position, whether overtly political or veiled as theories of subjectivity or of narrative, must fear its yet unspoken or, perhaps, unheard other, for "art prepares the bed of contingencies from which reality sprouts, ripens, and is harvested" (75). If we multiply resonances, we multiply conceptions of communal living that may unsettle the status quo. In terms of the self, of course, the textual is the locus of exploring the "boundaries of identity," boundaries that are found not in some thing itself, but in those "resonances" of the semiotic matrixes within which consciousness takes place. Art "threatens any rigid, presumptive view of reality with a disintegrating song" of alternative possibilties for coding experience, and the paradoxical upshot is that "identity is always one thing. Knowing it is all the others, and as soon as I force a separation, perceive a separation, I'm making fiction. Fiction is inevitable" (76). The passage seems almost to reverse the drift of things by affirming a conventional definition of identity and opposing it to fiction as merely alternative and unreal worlds. But if fiction is "inevitable," and if it works in the separation between the "one thing" we hold to and the "resonances" and "contingencies . . . that are also true," or as true as the formulation in which we have mustered "conviction," then fiction is indeed an epistemologial mode in which we consider reflexively the modes of constituting subjects in a culture (not least of which is the authorial subject) and, more broadly, alternative models for culture itself.

In the final section, "43," Katz turns to meditate upon the strange and random persistence of the number forty-three in these narratives (route numbers, addresses, phone numbers, wrist counts) and in the world around him (in scattered newspaper accounts, numbers winners, his sons' experiences, and the like). It is, of course, less a treatise on numerology than on semiotic systems in general: "These systems are tools useful to help you yourself arrive at a description of reality, but as soon as you depend on the system itself for the answers, start looking *at* it rather than *through* it, there begins to form a cataract of dogma over your perception of things as they are" (22). We must be skeptical of the possibility of eluding systems altogether to see things "as they are," but the "cataract of dogma" pertains at once to the mysteries of numerology, the techniques of fiction, and the theme of identity. Similarly, looking *at* narrative so reflexively could eventually threaten its capacity to strike up its "disintegrating song," the only worse danger being to look only *through* it as in a more narrow mimetic poetics. What *Moving Parts* suggests, of course, is that a certain period of looking "at" narrative is useful for arresting our tendency to look "through" it to the reality either of the source experiences or of the author to which much mimetic theory tends to refer the narrative. Both those experiences and their "authors" are moving parts of the semiotic process.

In a note "To the Reader," the narrator of Robert Kelly's "Russian Tales: Experiments in Telling" suggests that his "thirty-seven researches are experiments in allowing language to tell its own stories, as it is well able to do, if we listen" (48).[31] That is, if Katz's work was an effort to replace the author, however playfully, with the inscrutable sign of "43" so pervasive in the volume, Kelly's tales seek to "replace" the author with language as the teller of the tale, an experiment that plays havoc with the "readability" of "Russian Tales" but produces some very stimulating meditations on the topic we have been pursuing. Kelly's note concludes by quoting one of RK's lyrics: "Language is the only fable / and is utterly able," and pursuing that fable leads RK to quite a suggestive reflection upon the "style-world of the fairy tale." That genre might to some suggest a freedom from such "common sense" rules as causation, but the concept of the "style-world" is, I think, a suggestive way to express the closure of language and thought within conventions of various kinds—semiotic codes, if you will. In terms of form, the thirty-seven "researches" range from narrative vignettes to gnomic meditations, but despite their apparent opacity and "experimental" savor, they cohere in very suggestive ways within the research agenda set by this opening note. Kelly's fiction, in fact, may be one of the richer pieces to win the intense competition (six out of over a thousand submitted) that Bruce R. McPherson held in assembling his commendable collection. Growing out of his study of Russian roots and English morphemes, the story opens into the constructive rather than mainly critical implications of contemporary theory and "experimental" fiction.

We begin to see some of these implications in the second segment, "Where Magic Starts." Its opening sentence, "Hang a gay saying atop a decrepit thing," contrasts the "thing" with the gay world of language and texts, in which death and impermanence, two recurrent "themes" in the less reflexive segments, are arrested within a formal order. It is an act of will, this hanging, and the "word" or "saying" clearly covers the thing; the second sentence, "Substance sees its own fruit," indicates the distance between the substantial thing and the form it takes within the "style-world" of language. One could play out a number of this metaphor's implications—the innumerable possible fruits each thing might bear, the mixture of both identity (the transfer of traits from thing to form) and difference (each possible form differs both from the other forms and from the thing). The theme of difference, however, is the one emphasized by the passage, for the third sentence suggests that we "hang it for guilt." One can only assume that the "guilt" stems from that difference, the covering, the lie built into language by its very nature of differing from its referents.

At this point the segment takes a minor turn: "Live though, and experience a moisture." This gnomic maxim shifts from semiotics to existentialism, language to subject, its "though" betokening the necessity to live, speak, and write despite the problematic quality of the verbal medium in which we have our experience. It is, in other words, not a medium set and setting into stone, but rather an experience of the fluidity—"moisture"—of the shifting relations between thought, language, and reality with which semiotic theory has made us familiar. And indeed, the next two lines make this clear: "Power is always outside, power is *away*. Inside is water and feuding and war." One can hold but not be power, Foucault tells us; one can wield but not possess language; one can think of mastery and understanding but not escape conventions and scriptings and the manifold sedimented assumptions within the intertextual world of culture. Inside, that is, one finds not ground but water, not identity but feuding differences.

"Howl for freedom all you will, the agitation of waves controls our tract." The ontological, existential, linguistic, and stylistic freedoms that have constituted the desire of Western culture are, it appears, futile in the face of the agitation of these waves. "Tract," of course, is a richly suggestive node joining space or place, alimentation, and writing in a way that locates these freedoms within the fluid realm of style-worlds rather than amid the unity, clarity, and self-identity of traditional concepts of the author.

The third and final movement of the segment picks up at this point: "Smell possesses a drag, became memory. Magic starts there." We have here, I think, a rendition of the primal passage from experience to memory and textuality. That is, smell impedes the thoughtless flow of experience and drags us back to prior experience, and the "magic" of texts begins in just this sort of selective, hence arbitrary, linkage, chronological texturing, and metaphoric transfer from one experience to another. And indeed, as the segment then suggests, it "turns lies into talk [the implicit catachresis of individual words into the discourse system of talk], talk into nonsense [from the conventions of words into the conventions of one discourse system or another, we move further and further from the sensory into non-sense], enemies into time [oppositions of one kind or another become the structuring principles by which we come to understand time—narratizing] and time into eternity [language enables the conceptual escalation from narratized segments into abstract and absolutist metaphysics]." The segment concludes with yet another highly condensed maxim about these multiple dimensions of language's "own stories": "All meet every, any second." That is, at any second in language we continually face the meeting of its generalizations ("trees") and every particular referent that confronts that generalization's "lies" about particulars.

I am suggesting, then, that this particular segment begins a series of reflexive meditations spaced through this series of "tales" that condense into a brief narrative many themes of recent critical discussions. A few pages later, for example, one comes across a segment in lyric form, "The Pear Tree Song." It plays off a familiar enough first stanza (a shriveled pear holding within it the memory of summer) to arrive at a radically existentialist message ("Whatever was is me"), affirm a Whitmanesque loquacity ("Until every cell, every cell / speaks its secret I / am talking to you"), and lead to this reflexive conclusion:

Time is the cells of my hand
writing the word "Time!"
is my skin, fat of my bones, sinew
of brain
given me to god with,
this hand and everything it touches—

If in the earlier segment memory (subjectively structured time) is where the magic of discourse starts, here the writerly source of both the word "time" and the phenomenon of time is affirmed—"god" is a performative verb that develops in the act of writing (rather than a noun preceding it, even metaphorically), and thus with absolute creativity or originality as one of its fictions and time as another. If one turns to another segment, "Fire Sermon," for help with the fiction's concept of time, one discovers the narrator urging the reader to "solve the mystery of time," with the assurance that "you are equal to the task, even with the running arrow you suspect to be time, but that I know is exactly the opposite. What flies is not time. Time is what stays. Time is what stays and we shape it, give it the shape of itself in our hands, the way a clever cook carves from a little block of ice a perfect rose" (63). Here we find again the move through language into conceptual abstraction—we shape time through our conventions and assumptions—as in the movement we saw earlier from enemies into time and then eternity. But this sermon also constrasts the linear and teleological time of the cultural tradition (the arrow aimed and released to travel to its destination) with time as a cultural fiction (like a cook carving ice). To conclude with the narrator that "you are the red in the rust" (64) is to shift the "fire sermon" from the ascetic emphasis of Buddha or T. S. Eliot to the aesthetic theme of creative form, and from the authorial self as transcendental moral being to the ferric oxide of semiosis. The play with Zeno's arrow, of course, also suggests a logic quite contrary to the Aristotelian mainstream of the culture, one in which customary procedures of causative reasoning, categorical distinctions, identity and difference, structure and division all come to mean something quite different from their mainstream forms.

Perhaps the segment called "Rose" (rows of words planted for us?) is the place to go for further insight into the narrator's exploration of this allegory of style and language. As ruler of the garden, the rose's aim "is to summon into the garden certain beings without whom the garden does not possess what the rose calls meaning" (73). If the rose is the metaphoric equivalent of carving time out of sense and memory, then it functions well as the epicenter of the garden of textuality (or at least of narrative). But without certain beings like readers, it is difficult to imagine "meaning," a construct that derives from the activity of such persons who enter the text and survey what it holds.

What follows addresses directly the difficulties involved in getting readers into the "garden": "There is a price to pay in going through a gate or door. Not just that you're in a new situation you have to evaluate. Not just that there are flowers and vistas to appreciate. Not just that you've unhooked the chain and stepped into that sealed-off place, the silent garden. The price you pay is what you expect. Your hopes are the coins you pay and pay over, dire usury of magic. The spell you're under is the words you say" (73). "Magic," we know, is the emergence of the aesthetic text as memory and sense interact, and its "usury" is the interest it exacts, however punningly, as our expectations and our hopes are drawn from us and transformed as surely as textuality transforms the sensory into its cultural permutations. Hence the metaphor of "coins" for hopes, since what is involved in the reading process is several kinds of exchange—we buy the book, we pay our time into it, we trade wisdom with it, we are changed (and coins, like hopes, are themselves "change") by the reading. Every "silent garden" of a text, after all, is a "new situation you have to evaluate" in order to understand. Ultimately, then, we are spelled—created as textual beings, necromanced into being— by the words we perform, whether as writers or as readers.

This segment, then, condenses much that has been argued in recent years about meaning and interpretation, and its conclusion sums matters up nicely: "Rose knows this, and often in her place apart sings. You hear her song as smell, and what you see is her frequency." The "place" of textuality, of course, is always apart from any site at which we might seek, in our logocentric way, to pin it down. When the rose sings as smell, we are carried all the way back to the first segment we examined, where we found that it is in smell that the "magic starts" in memory's play into words. That what we see is the "frequency" of rose/ smell/memory opens in several directions at once: (1) we see as many textual elements as our literary competency (i.e., our recognition of significant repetitions) permits; (2) we resonate from as many sensory and textual memories as our individual experience contains, since we too must be "what ever happened," as in "The Pear Tree Song"; and (3) we see frequency in the sense of color frequency, where electromagnetic waves (one recalls the waves that control our tract) account for the perception of color rather than an essence of redness inhering in the rose. We see what we are culturally (or physiologically) equipped to see. As in the case of color, where one sees precisely that "color" *not* "in" the thing (or it would have been absorbed with the rest of the white light's color bands), what we see is fully a function of how we construe

217

rather than of what we confront. We author, it seems, within the "style-world" we inhabit, and authorship as Kelly portrays it is a constitutive act of knowing that owes much to the usurious semiotics of which it composes itself.

If Kelly's "style-worlds" are a means of letting language tell its own tales, then Ronald Sukenick's *98.6* is a way of experiencing the limits of language and its attendant systems, featuring as it does a group of seventies "hippies," one of whom, variously known as "Ron" and "Cloud," attempts to go beyond those limits. One limit he challenges is that of fiction, his idea being "to write a novel by recording whatever happens to their group so that they're all characters in his novel including himself. And his novel" (68).[32] Characters, authors, and novels are all textual figures, it seems, and Ron's aim is to overcome this limit by turning writing into "recording," to achieve the most direct relation possible between textual and nontextual. That is, like the nonfiction novelists of the seventies, he "feels that novels should be about real life so instead of making up some story he gets a cast of characters and invents a situation for them and he simply writes what happens."

Crucial to this nostalgic project of escaping the limit of narrative conventions is that of going beyond language itself. Partly this involves a language that is of the body rather than of reason, as in the origin of language in the Sasquatch myth George tells: since they talked through their navels, their voices "weren't connected with their brains they were connected with their bodies" and hence "they could only talk about what they felt they couldn't talk about what they thought" (96). Ron aspires to this escape from the ratiocination that leads to fiction or logic, and he seeks accordingly a language that is not "crystallized" or "static." Calling it Bjorsq, he "won't define it. Or can't" (65), because to do so is to lapse back into the very (rational) discourse he seeks to replace with the language of bodies and emotions. "Bjorsq is a window language all others are mirrors" (161), he notes, gesturing, one supposes, toward the mimetic epistemology of the Western tradition.

Bjorsq and the escape from textuality, of course, are really efforts to grasp a plenitude or fullness of being not accessible in the "straight" world, and the quest to find Sasquatch, the missing link (or "Lunk" as it is sometimes called), becomes another version of this utopian wish. What the group discovers, however, is not reassuring. Ron/Cloud's revelation runs something like this: "He recognized the Missing Lunk on the last S & D Mission. He heard it coming out of Lance's mouth. That is what he heard was not The Lunk but the fact that it was Missing.

That's when he decided to speak the kind of language [Bjorsq] people don't understand. If they don't understand it The Lunk can hide there. As soon as they understand it they hunt it down and then The Lunk is Missing again" (161). Ron "cries a lot," having come to this sense of things, because it means that language—even speech "out of Lance's mouth"—carries the Missing rather than what they seek, and the moment one chooses an understanding of the Lunk itself, then one has definitely missed it. The narrator makes this clear in summing up Ron's reasoning at this point: "He thinks all this is very clever. He thinks he has it all figured out. He won't speak the language that people can understand but he thinks it. He thinks it and that's the trouble. He's so smart" (162). What the narrator discovers for Ron is that language is already there and never *not* there, that the self takes place in and through language, that it is in the textual realm that one authors narratives or oneself. Or as Cloud (Ron) says at one point: "Psychosynthesis is the opposite of psychoanalysis but apart from that Cloud refuses to define it. Cloud feels that life is a lot like a novel you have to make it up. That's the point of psychosynthesis in his opinion to pick up the pieces and make something of them. Psychosynthesis is based on The Mosaic Law. The Mosaic Law is the law of mosaics a way of dealing with parts in the absence of wholes. Vat zen" (122). Psychosynthesis, the making of psyche, is a narrative process of taking the Nietzschean initiative to "make something" of its (intertextual) pieces. Unfortunately it takes Ron most of the book to discover the full significance of "the absence of wholes," whether of a linguistic whole that is a Bjorsquian other to Western language, an existential Lunk that is the missing other to identity, or an experiential narrative that is the real other to fictive discourse.

Angela Carter's haunting *Fireworks* contains a number of tales that are stimulating meditations on the relation between consciousness and writing, but perhaps the most useful to our purposes is "The Loves of Lady Purple," a tale about a man who carves and dresses a puppet as Lady Purple, the quintessential male fantasy of female desirability. Obviously, however, more is at stake than marionettes: "The puppeteer speculates in a no-man's-limbo between the real and that which, although we know very well it is not, nevertheless seems to be real. He is the intermediary between us, his audience, the living, and they, the dolls, the undead, who cannot live at all and yet who mimic the living in every detail since, though they cannot speak or weep, still they project those signals of signification we instantly recognize as language."[33] The capacity of signs to function as convincingly as the real is made literal in the story when Lady Purple takes revenge on her maker and "escapes" to a brothel. As creator and stage manager, the puppeteer takes us strangely back to Thackeray's *Vanity Fair* where our close readings began, and his fate and that of his creation carry some challenging implications functioning on several analogical levels at once. Certainly the "professor," as the puppeteer is called, is carefully portrayed as an analogue of the writer. He is a "consummate virtuoso" whose native tongue is "an incomprehensible rattle" to ordinary people he meets, hence his crew consists of a "foundling dumb girl" and his deaf nephew. Cut off so dramatically from ordinary intercourse with humanity, he and his nephew "held interminable dialogues in sign language," as if the artist could not help but foreground the semiotics of language," communicating through a discourse "delicately distanced from humanity," a "choreographed quiet . . . like the mating dance of tropic birds" (26). Ornate, stylized, suffused with desire, the professor seems the very picture of the alienated artist.

In his puppet, the complex ambivalences one would expect from such a state manifest themselves in a doll that is both beautiful and sinister, with beautiful hands but long nails, a permanent smile with "ferocious teeth," spectacular hair held with "many brilliant pins," beautiful clothing accenting "a purple the color of blood in a love suicide" (27–28). She is "a cunningly simulated woman" and "a monstrous goddess," "wholly real and yet entirely other." Like a deeply satisfying narrative whose ideological pins prick us only upon reflection, Lady Purple "instantly annihilated the rational" in her audience as the professor conducts her "incantatory ritual," which reinforces in an audience the communal values. When, finally, she so absorbs his Zenlike performance with her that she sucks first his breath and then his blood and escapes to the brothel, we have on this level an allegory of the life of art inspired by its creator, drawing his life into its form, and then passing beyond his control into the commercial usage of the marketplace.

This is clearly an inadequate reading of this rich story, however, for it obscures a crucial dimension of Lady Purple: "Her actions were not so much an imitation as a distillation and intensification of those of a born woman and so she could become the quintessence of eroticism, for no woman born would have dared to be so blatantly seductive" (28). She is a condensation of the entire repertoire of seductive signs and conventions, and as such her "unappeasable appetites," as the advertisement puts it, "turned her at last into the very puppet you see before you, pulled only by the strings of *lust*" (29). If, however, she is the condensation of conventions, then these appetites are not hers but those of the cultural system from which those signs derive, and the strings of "lust" are the discursive strings tying down the limits within which she must take place. What surfaces, in other words, is one version of the phallocentricity of discourse in which (mainly male) desires are spoken into the form of fantasies like Lady Purple and, however less intensely, of any "born woman" within its sphere. The story this puppet enacts is more than a little disturbing in this light. She reaches maturity in a brothel where the prostitutes sit "motionless as idols" hanging above the patrons in "wicker cages"; "upon their real features had been painted symbolic abstractions," as indeed some would argue women are generally suspended as idols carrying the burden of metaphysical abstractions (chastity, domesticity, purity, otherworldliness) that limits their movement in society as surely as do wicker cages. As the narrator tells us, "it seemed each one was as absolutely circumscribed as a figure in rhetoric, reduced by the rigorous discipline of her vocation to the nameless essence of the idea of woman, a metaphysical abstraction of the female which could, on payment of a specific fee, be instantly translated into an oblivion either sweet or terrible, depending on the nature of her talents" (32). Goddess or devil, the women in the drama are, like Lady Purple, "reduced" to a "figure in rhetoric." The linguistic agency here is marked by the abundance of roots like "scribe" or "name" and words like "figure," "rhetoric," "abstraction," and "translated." Rather than being women, they are rigorously disciplined to be the *idea* of woman, as if the textual realm of their life drama limited them to the script of the authorial male desires. They become, literally, the puppets their phallocentric culture makes them.

When, outside the drama, Lady Purple parallels its murder of lovers by killing her creator-lover, he who "could not sleep unless she lay beside him" (28), her actions seem to raise the question of reality versus fiction: "Had the marionette all the time parodied the living or was she, now living, to parody her own performance as a marionette?" (39). But given the formal and ultimately linguistic origins of her behavior, the question becomes moot, since *both* living and "undead" take place within the same limits. As she begins to walk without strings, then, "the brain beneath the reviving hair contained only the scantiest notion of the possibilities now open to it," for there is no definable difference between "awakening from a dream or coalescing into the form of a fantasy generated in her wooden skull by the mere repetition so many times of the same invariable actions." One can have nothing but the "scantiest notion of the possibilities" that lie beyond the phallocentric language portrayed here as the professor's masque of desire. Such women, it seems, are heavily programmed as items for exchange, as abstractions,

221

as fantasies, as anything but the ideal of original and creative self-authorship one might take as the implicit ideal in this and other stories in *Fireworks*. It is not, of course, a simplistic antimale diatribe, for significantly enough the professor is equally consumed and destroyed by desires whose form is as stylized as the tangible shape he gives them in his art. The same pertains, of course, to Lady Purple's patrons within the drama, for "she was the object on which men prostituted themselves" to their own fantasies. A malign transference takes place in which the fantasy literally turns and renders them as reduced a set of semiotic roles as the prostitutes themselves. In fact, Lady Purple becomes "the sole perpetrator of desire . . . and used her lovers as the canvas on which she executed boudoir masterpieces of destruction" (32), finally taking to "murdering her lovers" in the ultimate reduction of the human to an object.

Phallocentricity, apparently, perpetrates a horror upon both the object and the subject of its utterances, and to "author" the fantasies of such a culture is less an act of sovereign power than a submitting to the process of subject formation that constitutes and limits individual existences. If Fowles toys with the notion of the passivity of authoring, Carter explores the nightmare dimension in which that passivity is a cultural rape of individual possibility through semiotic systems that, as many of these contemporary writers suggest, carry the real agency of authorship that more romantic theories had assigned to the individual genius. Texts are "incantatory rituals" regulating the roles and formal properties of "individuality" in a culture. A story like "Lady Purple" probes deeply into the sinister regions of that process to examine the ideological subjection of individuals within the hierarchies continually reenacted in the "rituals" of discourse. Writers working out their roles as authors seem, then, to find their fictions stressing the despair of subjection, as in "Lady Purple" or the less hopeful moments of *98.6*. Or as in *Moving Parts* or in Barth's fiction, they may find a will to play the role of author as semiotic being "reconfiguring" reality in ways that may well finally result in the "new possibilities for meaning" we found Eco advancing as the heart of the ideologically charged aesthetic text. If indeed one theme emerges from these narratives' reflexive attention to the concept of the author, it is a practice in which a will to play balances, however dizzily, the active and passive extremes of that author concept. That balancing makes apparent the violence of power in the active role and the subjection to power in its passive contrary, even if the one is disguised as interpretation and the other as "recording." Hence the will to play is a far from frivolous attempt to reconceive the relation between the two roles and to blend their traits into a more satisfying role than the sadomasochistic alternatives they represent. Perhaps it requires the striking feminist fiction of Angela Carter to bring us finally to this fertile intersection of sexual difference, language theory, and the semiotic nexus of concept and history.

SIX

Reflexivity and Criticism

What I want to emphasize is simply that the passage beyond philosophy does not consist in turning the page of philosophy (which usually amounts to philosophizing badly), but in continuing to read philosophers in a certain way.

Jacques Derrida

At this moment in literary studies, and particularly after studying at some length here the reflexive concerns of a number of narratives, I cannot help but have serious reservations about the classic assumptions underlying traditional literary study. Referential theories of language, mimetic theories of literature, and metaphysical beliefs about selfhood and truth no longer seem to be fully consistent, "natural" elements in a self-evidently justified approach to literary texts. Reflexivity reminds us that we deal with a semiotic tissue, not one that is organic or ectoplastic. Widely accepted critical methods clearly have considerable explanatory power, but just as clearly they do not exhaust the field's possibilities and can be quite misleading in the hands of rasher practitioners who claim explicitly or implicitly that they do. It is a difficult business at best to imagine an alternative critical ecosystem, particularly one capable of drawing upon the best efforts of earlier formulations, but I must risk some generalizations at least about certain fundamental attitudes and orientations. I am encouraged by the frequency with which good sense moderates claims of comprehensiveness or absolute adequacy between critical theory and practice, and we may in fact be able to use these provisos and disclaimers as a starting point for a reflexive criticism formalizing this sense of limits. Based upon what we have found in the narratives we have explored, I should be able to offer some useful hypotheses about the nature of critical activity, a general scheme of poetics embodying the constitutive dimension to which reflexivity has led us, and some speculations about the larger cultural implications of this reconsideration of narrative point of view.

The Reflexive versus the Canonical Critic

As we have seen, reflexivity suggests that narrative derives its authority not from the "reality" it imitates, but from the cultural conventions that define both narrative and the construct we call "reality." The poetics of both are constitutive, thus deriving from cultural assumptions about positing the nature and grounds of what shall pass as coherent and meaningful, rather than literally mimetic—that is to say, ultimately "natural" and thus dependent upon a true nature of the things "imitated." By similar reasoning, reflexivity also suggests the equally unsettling conclusion that criticism derives its authority not from the text it imitates (by rendering what it means, how it works, or some combination of the two) but from cultural conventions that, again, define *both*. The poetics of both "creative" and "critical" texts are *constitutive,* and the definitions of both suitable materials and suitable relations to be constructed with those materials are presupposed in the paradigm invoked for each process.

The implications of deriving both creative and critical discourse from cultural paradigms are twofold. One can argue that, as tradition has it, they differ, though for reasons different from those offered by tradition: each practice is conditioned by a different set of conventions. Hence there is certainly something to I. A. Richards's startling separation of emotive and referential language, of the truth of "internal necessity" and that of correspondence, though a "something" quite differently defined and determined than he supposed. That is, since both sets are features within a cultural rather than a natural paradigm, one can understand why our contemporaries deconstruct the valorization of, say, the creative over the critical. The difference between the two inheres not in some natural distinction between the rational and imaginative faculties of the homunculus but in cultural prescriptions for what will "count" as subject matter, as effective rhetoric, and as true for that discursive set. Richards's belief that creative texts differ from referential or critical texts thus satisfies our sense of the divergence among these three sets of conventions, but since each of the three has convention rather than nature as its ground, the differences are less absolute and evaluative than they appeared to Richards.

Hence, despite years of effort on the part of stylistic analysts and Prague theoreticians, I conclude that "literary" texts do *not* differ in any fundamental way from "ordinary" texts. Instead, they merely foreground what by means of acculturation we "naturalize"—that is, they underscore the "literary" or fictional qualities of what they share with all discursive texts. These shared attributes include assumptions

225

about language (which in "ordinary" texts is normally assumed to be representational and objective), about the nature of any text as a discursive fiction (textuality in "ordinary" discourse is normally assumed not to complicate its neutral and objective description of reality), and finally, about the nature of meaning as an interpretive construct (though in "ordinary" texts meaning is normally assumed to be a "message" contained within the text and decoded by any reader possessing certain universal traits of literary competence).

The critic, then, finds himself isolated from several sources of authority that, whether they placed him in a superior or an inferior position in relation to other discourses, nonetheless gave him sure grounds for proceeding. Rationalism does not make him superior to the misty metaphorist; imaginative poetic genius does not subordinate him to the role of a support service. Science, poetry, and criticism each constitute an interpretation of reality answerable to paradigmatic assumptions, not directly to reality itself. None of the three can claim ultimately to ground itself upon something outside its own cultural tradition—but this independence need not be considered a limitation.

It might, that is, be argued that this reflexive perspective on criticism limits its reliability and thus its scope; but this objection is thinkable only in relation to some hypothetical discourse that could indeed command the field—that could, in fact, accurately reproduce the essence of its subject matter as one might traditionally conceive it. Discourse is, however, answerable to the dictates of the paradigm of which it is a function; the definition of the individual particles in its subject matter, the discrimination of waves of movement among those particles, the relations among both that form the field under study—all these are governed by convention. Whatever degree of correspondence there may be between what paradigms constitute and what is, beyond the discursive realm of knowledge, "there" is—to give a twist to classical philosophy—sufficient, but not necessary. As Thomas Kuhn points out in relation to science, it is competing paradigms, not the accuracy of correspondence, that threaten a paradigm's currency in a community.

What does it mean, then, to view criticism as a highly stylized form of discourse among many other equally stylized forms? It means, first of all, that it should not seek to define a fundamental nature of either literature or criticism, at least in the sense of a structure there in any text or reading of a text. It should seek instead to study texts as they form themselves at the point of interpretation, both for what they reveal of their own workings and for what can be observed about the act of interpretation itself and the larger perspectives of which each interpretive stance is a subset. Sets of decentralized, multiple relations succeed the expectation of a central structure of form or response; one watches the text form, noting the dissonant senses of "form" both as creating and as confining material within extant patterns. The multiplicity of possible relations derives from differences between the forming going on in a text and the forming (of that forming) going on in the critic's observation. It may be a "limitation" of criticism that this reflexive awareness points to the coexistence of so many other possibilities of interpretation, but it may also be liberating to realize that such a variety derives not from a fault (one's inability to accomplish the illusory goal of comprehensiveness) but from a necessity (since discursive conventions must proscribe some insights in order to enable others).

If we thus see our method as a function of a cultural paradigm, it is no longer prideful to argue that what "authorizes" a reading is the authority of the critic's method, questions, and procedures as they create a discursive out of a more narrowly narrative order. It may, in fact, be humbler than presuming to master the secret key of a text or a culture. The reflexive critic, then, has no illusions about devising a master code; he is more likely to inquire after the various diffractions of different critical optics. A critic does not discover but constitutes a reading of theoretical and historical relations among and within texts that normalizes them all according to those assumptions and criteria commensurate with his (perhaps largely unconscious) paradigm allegiances.[1] We might, in fact, best articulate the nature of the reflexive critic by contrasting it with that of what I shall call the *canonical critic*. The canonical critic turns to literature with a paradoxical attitude. On the one hand he reverences great literary texts, bowing before the canon of texts that function almost scripturally—they teach, inspire, and discipline. At the same time, however, he strives for mastery of them, assimilating their infinite detail and variety into a (conscious or implicit) theory. Literature coheres—becomes and functions like a canon—in terms of this theory that is at least on one level analogous to a theological master code unlocking the secrets and stipulating the relative value of both major and minor books. It is this paradoxical attitude that, on the one hand, allows the canonical critic to hold the value of literature infinitely above any efforts of his own and, on the other hand, to aggrandize those efforts by attributing his central theories to the nature of poetry, the nature of man, or some similarly "natural" object of rational study that elevates him to the status of shaman mediating between the populace and otherwise inaccessible mysteries.

Immediately, then, differences between the canonical and the reflexive critic present themselves. The canonical critic quite aptly thinks

227

of his theories as a *poetics,* for the term's ancient root, meaning to pile up,[2] recalls the efforts of the Titans to pile up mountains that they might scale Olympus and themselves become gods. The aim of a poetics is to pile up the natural fundaments of literature that the canonical critic may scale the pinnacle of Parnassus and occupy its spring of wisdom, a seat from which he may have a commanding view—mastery—of the literary realm. A reflexive critic, on the other hand, would suppose that the "natural fundaments" of such a theory were elements in a paradigm within which the critic views literary and other cultural endeavors. These principles are the boundaries and connecting lines he draws upon the landscape of literature; hence he might well term his own methods "grammatological," following Derrida's appreciation of the term's etymology of "scratching" one's paradigmatic mark upon the field one surveys. If I have preferred to speak of "constitutive poetics," it is simply my own reflexive way of exploiting the contrary implications of the term's two elements—the apparent contradiction in fabricating (constituting) fundamentals (of poetics).

The canonical critic thus subscribes to the fundamental metaphor of rational studies in Western culture whereby the subject of one's thought is a structure whose outline is to be discerned in the cloudy pool of actual case histories. The canonical critic's aim is thus a "perfectly clarified" conceptual schema imitating the hard, sure lines of a given structure so that it may be universally applied thereafter. The one clear observation to make about this metaphor for critical endeavor is that it makes no real sense to the reflexive critic. What makes the pool cloudy in the first place? Is it merely the effort to part the waters and see the structure, or is it also the inherent turmoil of that structure itself, especially as it interacts with that of the critic's own dynamic interplay of code elements to produce constantly different possibilities for constituting readings? We might choose to shift to a more Heraclitian metaphor of the theorist on the riverbank; the river is always the "same" river, but as the pre-Socratic sage argued, we never step into the same river twice. But this does not go far enough for the reflexive critic; we never put the same foot in, either, and we must even take account of the fact that the riverbank itself is also fluid and changing, on however slower a temporal scale. Subject, object, and grounds are simply not what is predicted by the assumption of the canonical approach.

These differences in terms and metaphors obviously indicate equally basic differences in general principles. The canonical critic focuses upon the authentic texts of the canon, conserving their textual accuracy, annotating their historical and biographical contexts, codifying their formal properties, governing their interpretation. The reflexive critic, on the other hand, is more likely also to be interested in noncanonical texts (those the canonical critic might well rule below the canon in popular literature, or adjacent to it in "nonliterary" discourse, or beyond it in the sociopolitical practices of the culture). Further, the reflexive critic would find interesting the grounds upon which emendations are made (either toward or away from a "scientific" or "correct" or, nicely, "authoritative" text). A literary text is one of a number of means by which a culture disciplines the formation and maintenance of that culture's subjects, so that "contextual studies" are less a matter of identifying references than of observing the relations among literary and other cultural forms as a complex and multidimensional matrix exercising a culture's power over individuals.

As for formalizing the description and interpretation of texts, the reflexive critic differs in marked ways, some of them already addressed. But by inventing an ungainly term to call attention to the heart of this problem, we may begin to focus upon the task at hand for the reflexive critic. Let us speak, then, of *interpretemes* and define them as the smallest units significant to interpretive analysis.[3] As far as the canonical critic is concerned, these are derived by objective, scientific, or at least inductive study of texts and carry the status of self-evidently true characteristics of the nature of texts. The issue becomes primarily that of the perennial debates over competing codifications of interpretemes: along what (plot) lines does one combine these interpretemes we all sense in texts? For the reflexive critic, interpretemes are generated by methods standing in homologous relation to other conceptual or discursive systems of the more general cultural paradigm, and a more fruitful issue than trying to valorize one codification over another is to describe how they are generated, and even to debate the very foundation of canonicity itself. In the final analysis, I would myself be less interested in debating poststructuralist versus Boothian narrative rhetoric than in deciding what Booth's constituency has been and what accounts for that of poststructuralism, or in identifying what factors account for the paradigm consensus reached at various points in literary history.

Moreover, the canonical critic assumes that the "great" texts remain in the center of cultural debate through the centuries because they most perfectly embody the true nature of poetry; the reflexive critic is more likely to think in terms of the way such texts answer the needs of the specific eras in which they are most prized, as well as to determine why certain assumptions have remained important throughout the span of Western culture. The history of great texts is a history of their adaptability to the ends of the methods brought to bear upon them, methods

229

that make use of these texts both by identifying what interpretemes are worth noting and by regulating their combination into interpretive readings that serve wider interests than those of objective scholarship.

For the canonical critic, then, the terminology related to interpretemes functions to unify, simplify, and clarify—it "fixes" texts in all that verb's senses as (*a*) to make constant (to fix something in its place); (*b*) to repair (so that it functions as wished in the cultural mechanics of using texts); and (*c*) to rig the results (through the prestructuring effects of theoretical framing). The reflexive critic, clearly enough, attempts instead to note the forms and implications of this fixing process by which culture develops its conceptual snapshots.

We might do well to see how fully one of the great minds of our times, Northrop Frye, inhabits this view of the canonical critic. Though sometimes treated as an exception to the Anglo-American rule—Frye likes to "stand back" from the text and hence is not as close in his readings as some might wish—Frye is in fact the central type of our tradition and stands out only because of the comprehensiveness and explicitness of his effort to address the canon. His old and new testaments, *The Anatomy of Criticism* and *The Great Code,* to which all his other works stand as, perhaps, patristic commentary and exegesis, would more than repay extended treatment. But more briefly, we can still make some valuable generalizations about these major attempts at a cultural synthesis.

We might cue those generalizations to the three connotations of an enormous "willfulness" in Frye's command of the canon. The first, by way of pun, is the "fullness" or plenitude of the cultural will (that is, a bequest from the nature of things for a fulfillment that will, ultimately, it seems, occur). His eschatological imagination defers to the last days a reunification that projects an Eden as alpha and omega of the psychic history. Neither he nor his master poet, William Blake, have had much use for the Darwinian deconstruction of Christian teleology.[4] *The Great Code,* for example, is up to the *Anatomy*'s old game of generating a mythic plot to unify human time, disguising it as always in Frye within spatial diagrams like the one in which, framing the three phases of Western culture's writings, one finds "('Revelation')" and "[Fourth Phase]."[5] He peppers the text with uncertainties about terms like kerygma to defuse the more rabidly antitheological crowd, and here in the chart he uses the full arsenal of quotation marks, parentheses, and brackets. The effect is the same as in the *Anatomy,* however; we have a perceptual framework with the Word as beginning and end of a linear development, as the two high points of Frye's visionary "U." The familiar analogy between tragic fall and comic redemption obtains.

The persistence with which Frye sees—that is, imposes—that "U" in the full exercise of the Coleridgean constructive imagination is the second sense of "willfulness" and is a testament to the power and scope of Frye's mind.[6] In his assimilation of secular or sacred texts Frye demonstrates both the power of a critical paradigm to read itself into texts and the difficulty we would have in refuting his readings. At what point, that is, do we decide that what is there (according to one reading) is outnumbered or overpowered by what is there but unaccounted for in that reading, or would be accounted for only in entirely different readings? To be fair to Frye, he tells us in *The Great Code* that he is interested not in the Bible itself, but in how it has been seen in the culture, an admission that sanctions his use of the Authorized Version and his ignoring textual criticism and other biblical scholarship.[7] And elsewhere he indicates that his constructs are only his imaginative insights and that others are possible. The latter admission reminds us of the reflexive critic's point about the arbitrary basis of critical paradigms, the former of Frye's interest not in the texts themselves but precisely in their "canonicity," their role as a tradition, overview, or great code. And clearly, by code he means the word in its almost kerygmatic sense of interpretive code, not the reflexive critic's sense of codes as constantly self-transforming (and therefore never fully consistent, unified, coherent, codified) processes for making connections—as if a code were like the Germans' World War II Enigma machine, except that this randomly varying code-making machine could never be set exactly the same way twice.

Frye's command of the canon, then, becomes a marshaling of its texts toward the sort of stable and imaginatively eschatological view of things presented in *Anatomy of Criticism* as a secular great code. As such, willfulness shades quickly from the pejorative and personal qualities of "stubbornness" to the much grander Nietzschean sense of the will to mastery or power by which Frye dominates the tradition, killing off all the side shoots and countershoots of the cultural tree until it is pollarded according to his "U" vision. This conceptual topiary is thus the majestic performance of a truly great mind, but it remains spectacle, performance, a shaping of the script by a master actor who "does" the play his way. The dramatic metaphor is misleading, however, for neither in the Bible nor in the secular canon do we have in any traditional sense the authoring of a script—rather we have the retrospective editing of coincidentally available pages into a volume, as if someone ran up and down Wall Street gathering confetti and pieced the shreds together into pages arranged and bound as the "story" of the parade. Clearly, if we follow Frye's own practice of "standing back" and watch the virtuoso arranging texts into his visionary "U," we can see that pattern as the shape of the paradigm overlaid upon the material rather than necessarily as the figure in the carpet. The reflexive critic's stress thus falls upon remembering in the act that it is performative, an imposition.

Hence, as much as he is swayed by the beauty and appeal of such a view, the reflexive critic still must suspend his assent (or ascent?) to such a perspective. Indeed, it seems at times that canonical critics like Frye function somewhat like the Lacanian concept of the imaginary projected onto the cultural level. Frye works masterfully to reconcile ambiguities, epiphenomena, frames of reference, the perpetually other, the mirrored self into something like a cultural ego—an identity that organizes, stabilizes, and makes coherent the cultural experience of itself. A reflexive critic, on the other hand, remains transfixed by Lacan's teasing references to the "subject" as "a fading thing that runs under the chain of signifiers."[8] At the risk of degenerating into pop psychology, this description suggests on the cultural level a constantly shifting force or energy that fades in and out in innumerable manifestations of the signifiers (texts, practices) we seek to analyze. The similarities we note in constructing diagrams like Frye's are deceptive; Lacan warns that "sameness is not in *things* but in the *mark* which makes it possible to add things with no consideration as to their differences." This does not mean Frye is ignorant of the differences among, say, particular tragedies, just that those differences do not bear decisively upon his synthetic mission, the method of which conditions the marking.

One can thus catch something of a glimpse of what happens on a cultural level by parsing out Lacan's next sentence: "The mark has the effect of rubbing out the difference, and this is the key to what happens to the subject, the unconscious subject in the repetition. . . . In any case, the subject is the effect of this repetition [by means of the mark] in as much as it necessitates the 'fading,' the obliteration, of the first foundation of the subject, which is why the subject, by status, is always presented as a divided essence" (192). The obviously unconscious subject at the cultural level is clearly the matrix of conventions that conditions texts as its signifiers. Each text, in repeating the textual act, necessarily obliterates its pretexts in reforming them, and the concatenation of loss and reintegration accounts for the "divided essence" Frye reflects as a tragic and a comic axis in culture. The canonical critic, by commenting upon the full body of texts, raises this equation to the second power by remaking this collective canon in terms of the fundamental, fixed identity it never quite manifests. Or as Lacan puts it, "The question of desire is that the fading subject yearns to find itself again by means of some sort of encounter with this miraculous thing defined by the phantasm. In its endeavor it is sustained by that which I call the lost object . . . which is such a terrible thing for the imagination" (194). The phantasm is a "miraculous thing" because it is the fictive product of the imaginary faculty, and it is a dream of this "lost object" that would complete or fulfill the subject as a stable and fixed identity. To recur to the cultural level, the canonical critic seems to be like a cultural expression of this collective drive to constitute a (necessarily illusory) identity. That drive is aimed at an identity outside the chain of cultural significations, a chain outside which we have no existence.

Ultimately, then, the recourse to a stabilized scheme is an attempt to articulate a "miraculous thing" that never was, except as a historically manifested approximation of so idealized a construct. It may well be that we must always be working to form a personal or cultural "ego" in the Lacanian sense, but it is the task of the reflexive critic to maintain, at the point of such forming, an awareness of the fictiveness by which conventions keep repeating their scratch upon the cultural field to mark the boundaries of an ego's self-vision, a scratching that is the etymological punch line of Derrida's term "grammatology." Every such design is a sufficient condition of grasping intellectually the phenomena we study, but no particular design is ever a necessary condition of such a grasp. For to argue that fiction defines rather than designs, we must first forget it is a fiction.

Frye at what I take to be his best comes close to extending this insight as far as I would by substituting "discourse" for "fiction" in the last sentence. For example, he argues that "the further we take" a list that includes "metaphysics, theology, history, law . . . the more clearly their metaphorical and mythical outlines show through," indicating his healthy sense of the fictional basis of all discourse. Moreover, he has clearly anticipated my distinction between representational and constitutive poetics with his own differentiation of the "descriptive" and the "constructive" aspects of verbal structures. One eventually becomes aware in reading of "an organizing structural pattern or conceptualized myth" that constitutes the world we first thought (naively) was merely "a verbal replica of external phenomena."[9] In other words, Frye sees the full argument of this chapter, but works as if blind to it in order to carry out his canonical mission.

Meyer Abrams and the Critical Quadrilateral

It should be clear from exploring the distinction between the reflexive critic and the canonical critic that quite fundamental differences must exist between their definitions of the terms and relations out of which critical practice is formed. Hence we would do well to draw together these general speculations and the close investigations of individual texts in earlier chapters in order to attempt some definition of the critical vocabulary emerging from a reflexive analysis of the constitutive properties of texts.

To achieve this definition, we could hardly do better than to turn to another canonical critic, Meyer H. Abrams, whose classic *The Mirror and the Lamp* conditioned the way students of my generation conceived of critical theory and its deployment. Perhaps a more potent figure than the wizard's pentagram, Abrams's critical quadrilateral schematized critical discourse into a stable, manageable, unambiguous field of power. It possessed four fixed and unquestionable points of reference, and the history of criticism could be summarized as a gradual movement from point to point: universe, audience, artist, and work correspond to the progression from mimetic (in Plato and Aristotle) to pragmatic (from the Hellenistic through the neoclassical era), expressive (late eighteenth and nineteenth centuries), and finally objective theories (in the work of Eliot, the Chicago neo-Aristotelians, Ransom, Wellek, and Warren). Following the influence of his own era in this critical history, Abrams offered a triangle designating three relations and a central space as the four foci of critical inquiry: [10]

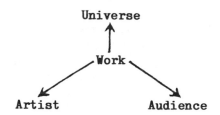

Figure 2. Abrams's "Co-ordinates" of Criticism

We note immediately that this figure minimizes, at least graphically, other relations we might wish to study (artist and audience, for example, or the relation between either of these and the universe), that it valorizes the work as the central focus, and that it permits four theories that all share basic assumptions challenged by the study of reflexivity. All four, that is, assume that creative discourse and critical discourse are primarily *referential*—that they refer to one of these foci—and that they represent what they can with considerable confidence both know and say. Whether the work tells us about the universe, the artist, or the audience, and whichever of its four foci criticism concentrates upon, we end with a *representation* of what is there. The diagram disparages reflexivity as a failure to engage with the three primary vectors of literary activity and restricts the constitutive to the effects created in the audience.

We need to recast this figure so it may more fully reflect the basic possibilities of literary practice. Abrams gives some encouragement here, for he calls his points of reference "four co-ordinates" and the triangle itself a "convenient" rather than a necessary pattern for envisioning the relations among them. I suggest a simple quadrilateral, for it preserves the possibilities Abrams works out for us without closing out the supplement we would add (I use literary terms rather than Abrams's general aesthetic terms):

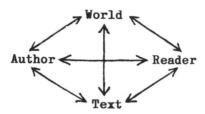

Figure 3. *A Critical Quadrilateral*

The diagram is fully consistent with traditional poetics and accentuates its customary sense of the relationship between author and reader as a meeting of the minds, each present to the other in a direct act of communication, just as text and world confront each other in the mimetic mirror lit by the authorial lamp. The vertical axis we could name "mimesis," for the text imitates or copies the world in traditional poetics, and the horizontal axis would be "subjectivity," for such theories have metaphysical conceptions in which the selfhood of the author and reader are the alpha and omega of the creative process.

Under the pressure of reflexive analysis, however, one is kept mindful that the four points of this critical compass are not off the map but are relative references drawn in an act of cultural cartography similar to that which enables an individual text to be written. Since the elements a theory constitutes as text, universe, artist, and audience are, as Abrams points out, "not constants, but variables" from theory to theory, we are always talking about coordinates in a scheme, not four absolutes as they are in themselves. Figurative displacements rather than referential designations, these terms are powerful not by the extent to which they correspond to an absolute, but by the coherence of the theory from which they derive and its ability to reconcile the data of individual texts with its larger assumptions about meaning and satisfaction. That any act of writing is conditioned by the history of writings available to an author provides neither a Platonic form of text nor a neutral or objective history but always a sense of possibilities constituted by a theoretical perspective.

The middle space that might earlier have seemed crossed by intersubjectivity and mimesis now appears to be a different chiasmus altogether. The line between author and reader is "semiotic," for both roles are cast out of the fluid codes by which each organizes the text as world, the world as text. That between text and world is thus "constitutive" in both the active and the passive senses of the term, for both exert the kind of pressure that keeps codes fluid but both nonetheless appear to the intellect only in a mediated form. Our reflexive reading of individual novels has repeatedly shifted our thinking from the metaphysical self to the semiotic construct, and from the representational replica to the constitutive creation.

This central chiasmus profoundly affects the way we define the relations along the perimeter of our quadrilateral, relations that do not figure as basic in Abrams's figure but that nonetheless are vital to an attempt at such a general orientation to critical thinking. The relation of author to text has classically been that of intention, however carefully hedged by the intentional fallacy (a dictum that, as we found earlier, finds intention obscured by the mystical regions of the unconscious: intention is there and would be a sufficient explanation, but it is simply inaccessible). From our study of *The French Lieutenant's Woman* we can define this relation less as intention than as circulation of the various code possibilities at a given authorial point in space and time. The effects possible inevitably exceed whatever the writer, critic, or reader might hypothesize after the fact as "intention" because of the infinite interplay among the complex juxtapositions wrought by the act of writing. This is a decidedly looser restriction than traditional expressive theories might prefer, but it recognizes the semiotic system of restraints and conditioning through which authorial energies must pass while also clarifying the grounds of critical pluralism.

The relation between the reader and the text has classically been urged as one of objectivity: the reader approaches the text open-mindedly to see what he might discover *there*. Such neutrality is clearly incompatible with the position to which reflexivity has brought us. Our replacement value here is not subjectivity, which is no more than another effort to refer meaning to a metaphysical agent. Instead, we might conflate suggestions by Umberto Eco and Stanley Fish and think here in terms of the "overcoding" of an interpretive community.[11] Along lines suggested in the discussion of the reflexive critic, we have here a relation governed by a set of interpretive conventions that "code" the reading experience from the very outset, determining what is to count as the "interpreteme" or basic formal unit, what relations among formal units are to be recognized, and what rules are to govern the process of articulating those relations in the form of criticism. Such a relation is conditioned both by the text at hand and by the theoretical framework of the reader, but it is not constrained by any transcendental limits as to what is permanently or naturally true, absolute, or "the rule." The "rule," as *Chance* suggests, is the margin drawn upon the pages of an individual's existential copybook.

The relation between author and the world has been variously conceived, but except in the most rigid psychological or scientific narrative theories, where the author's sense of the world is read as wholly referable to either internal dynamics or external nature, respectively, most theories recognize a degree of constitutive activity ruling any interpretation of the world of inner or outer experience. The "world" is also a construct, segmented and then interrelated according to the rules of a code or codes prestructuring everything the author "sees," and the author's relation to that world is thus the Nietzschean will to mastery that dominated our study of *World Enough and Time*. The complexity of this relation results from two inescapable consequences of the authorial power play. The author never wholly masters the world he constructs: particularly in the most acute writers, bits of experience find their way into the narrative and form pockets of resistance to the lines along which he attempts to model his world. Moreover, the authorial master code is never a perfectly coherent, stable, or fixed structure; it is a floating three-dimensional matrix whose interstices undulate because of the strain of application, the heterogeneity of inherently dynamic codes, and the varying contours of the material through which it is cast. As a result, its lines of connections constantly threaten to surprise their "master" with new implications.

The relation between the reader and the world is equally vexing and is one that has never figured with particular clarity within literary poetics. It is assumed in a very general way that readers as subjects bring with them a knowledge of the world as object and that the more competent readers are, the more accurate a correspondence we will find between their views of the world and the world itself. In fact, however, competency more likely resides in the number of templates or conceptual overlays a reader can flip through in search of an interpretive pattern. These conventions for constituting "the world" may also be acted upon by the reading experience, of course, for once engaged with a text, readers may find their codings interacting with those circulating in the text and hence changing in ways that are not necessarily predictable. Certainly *Vanity Fair* proved to be a compendium of tactics by which a text can play off the differing templates readers and texts may throw upon one another. Every act of reading, like every act of writing, recodes to some extent our sense of the world, and the dynamic, fluid quality of this process may be clearer the more vigorously reflexive a text or reader becomes. Perhaps the final effect of reflexivity upon this relation is to lead readers to recognize their "world" as an alternative fiction to that in the text, but still nonetheless a fiction constituted by a matrix of conventions quite similar to the textual manipulations that have become familiar.

Implicit in these definitions or redefinitions of literary relations are basic shifts in the way we think of the initial coordinates with which both these basic figures begin. "Text" shifts from an autonomous entity with a determinate core of meaning to a prolific dissemination of potential meanings radiating outward from the layers of code elements in the text, a process *World Enough and Time* illustrates in the interpretive efforts of its narrators to tease out the multiple possibilities of a phrase or scene. Critical response can never be more than an effort to plot those vectors recognizable within a given set of assumptions, and it will be repeatedly frustrated if it interprets "voice" as a fixed and regulatory structure from which a text derives rather than as a transitive verb. Hence the reader shifts from a free and neutral agent responding out of his own subjective identity to a construct woven in the intersection of the interpretive community of which he is a function and the operations that the text permits him to undergo. Similarly, the author shifts from a free, original, creative agent to a semiotic being constituted by writing. And the world? It, like the text, is always encountered as a fiction governed by different but still semiotic conventions rather than as a nondiscursive reference point that we can invoke without mediation by kicking Dr. Johnson's stone.

What the "nouvelle critique," as its nonreaders sometimes call it, does is to investigate literary relations along the lines defined by this revised critical scheme. Traditional and new approaches are by no means entirely commensurable—work within diverse paradigms never adequately translates from one to the other—and even among newer critics one finds severe differences. But if we grasp the revised figure we can see that despite the expected dissonance of new vocabularies and the inevitable false starts and yet to be refined initial propositions, the conflicts among contemporary critics derive partially from the differing relations on which they focus. Theoretical advances seem already to be cohering, as this brief sketch attempts to suggest, and it should be no surprise if the emerging consensus looks and sounds different from our previous perspectives, if it corresponds to newer assumptions about language and meaning, and if it satisfies different criteria for sensibleness and acceptability. In its own way, this study is an effort to see what a new critical paradigm can show about texts we thought we already understood more or less fully, and I cannot help but feel it is this emerging paradigm that will account for the most intellectually exciting work in the decades to come.

Reflexivity and the Cultural Facts of Life

To read fiction reflexively is to add the missing track to our record of the novel, to read stereophonically what a more limited poetics has rendered only monaurally. To hear these tracks in stereo is to recognize that the richness of the sound derives mainly from its echoing in the hollow chamber of semiotic conventions, not from any supposed origin in a miraculously gifted being. Not Caruso, but a singer in the shower. Our theory of narrative point of view thus needs to hear that echo and to sense the walls it reverberates from in the fictions we read. More plainly, point of view must shift from a transcendental to a semiotic understanding of its key terms, and it is within the context of that semiotic understanding that the still larger implications of reflexivity are to be found.

Perhaps enough has already been said to indicate the outlines of such a semiotic context for narrative theory, but we might recall generally that semiotics stresses the arbitrary quality of a code, thereby discarding the referential as the most fruitful investigative focus and orienting instead to the conventionality of the relations in question. Mediated rather than direct, these relations hinge upon what Peirce called the "interpretant," the abstraction, culturally posited, intervening in the process of understanding and launching the unlimited semiosis in which every term is defined not by its referential relation but by other terms. This diacritical basis of meaning thus results in differential rather than positive knowledge and introduces deconstructive energy into every reflexive moment. To address point of view in a semiotic context, then, is to recognize that the issue is not really the relation of that narrator to an entity (i.e., the author, protagonist, or observer) or to a world, but rather to the multiple code matrixes of which it is a function and for which it serves as the means of dispersing "a voice" into the ideologically charged crosstalk of "heteroglossia," as Bakhtin calls it in a monstrous but still suggestive term.[12] Voice is thus not an anthropomorphic entity but the quotation of multiple semiotic codings, a stylistic simulacrum of the ideological tensions in the culture to which the work thus alludes and to which narrative critics need to attend more thoroughly. To recognize the multidimensionality of the many relations one could discern among different elements in various codes is to account for the conditions that apportion forcefulness among them, and thus to open dramatically the range of issues possible within a theory of point of view.

The most primitive taxonomy of point of view—first, second, and third "person"—is based upon the most simplistic relation possible between narrator and reader, that of conversation. If we grasp Derrida's polemics about phonocentrism in our understanding of language, then this taxonomy's picture of the narrator as a presence who talks to us about himself or other persons he knows is a predictable outgrowth of the implicit metaphysics Derrida critiques in classic Western thought. That so few find this grammatical category of person offering any significant insight into the nature of a given narrative perhaps shows how much is omitted from fiction in any theory wholly grounded in the transcendentalism of persons and conversations. The more useful a system is, the more thoroughly it has moved toward a semiotic context and away from the "ontotheology" Derrida's work addresses.

The more nearly Jamesian approach to point of view, on the other hand, quite properly demotes "person" to a question of stylistics and focuses upon the concept of privilege to information. Where is the speaker's placement in relation to the answer to the narrative's questions? This approach to the matter has enabled many decades of close attention to the rhetorical situation, the positioning of figures in relation to the other primary functions (i.e., characters, events, bodies of knowledge) in a novel. At the same time, however, the relatively naive mimetic or representational bias of this theoretical framework should by now be obvious to students of critical theory. The assumption is that truth is meaningful (worth knowing), coherent (in ordered harmony with the well-made story), and accessible (as a kind of existential imperative for the perceiver). The faith persists, that is, that the directness and immediacy of the conversational context warrants our confidence in the points of reference this kind of rhetorical theory assumes. As we have seen in reconsidering the critical quadrilateral, those points of reference are a good deal more fluid than traditionally conceived, and the "rhetorical" tradition in criticism from James and Lubbock to Wayne Booth requires a new context within which to function. We need to stress more heavily the figurative element in the basic meaning of "rhetoric"—the points of reference in a rhetoric of fiction are thus not transcendentally anchored, but rather are linguistically posited, semiotically derived. The positioning of figures manipulates associative codes, and our attention needs to address those codes rather than thinking only in terms of beings and objects.

Most theories of point of view are in the end restraints upon the variability of actual narratives, restraints that would have prevented precisely the kinds of readings that have arisen during this inquiry into reflexivity. By conditioning expectations, such theories preselect the data one works with, and they may well go even further by valorizing certain techniques over others, valorizations that derive from the inevitable hidden agenda in a critical paradigm. For example, Wayne Booth's emphasis upon "control of distance," "unity," and the "price of impersonal narration," all from chapter or section titles in his highly influential *Rhetoric of Fiction,* makes clear an overriding moral concern within which narrative is a coherent medium for some degree of ultimate truth that grounds the narrative venture. Booth's brilliant explications attest to the power of this perspective to identify the moral elements particularly in those works that heel closest to Booth's own beliefs. Those that do not, however, and those that harbor within them serious questioning of the core assumptions in the Boothian paradigm, are less satisfyingly treated within it.[13]

Hence the crucial category of *distance* in Booth's discussions of point of view begs the question of the status of the points between which distance lies. One begins to sense a fundamental choice before us between plane geometry's metaphor of distance, with its implied points of reference and its two-dimensional mappable plane, and a far more challenging three-dimensional, perhaps even non-Euclidian, geometric space within which complex arrays of vectors, arcs, Möbius strips, and other puzzling figures display themselves within the form of the novel. Since even the points of our critical quadrilateral are virtual rather than fixed, self-differing rather than self-identical, *difference* seems to be the replacement value for *distance* in any translation from Booth's representational poetics to a constitutive poetics of fiction. Virtually every schema for point of view that shares with Booth a primarily representational poetics—in other words, virtually all schemata—hunts through point of view for a means first of flattening out the three-dimensionality I have suggested as the shape of the interrelations among fictional elements, and second of arresting the constant movement, undulation, alteration in that form. Our three-dimensional graph, that is, still falsifies unless it is, like a video display, in constant movement reflecting the inexhaustible relations that can be constituted as critics shift their grounds. A reflexively constitutive poetics keeps open the possibilities for.identifying and describing new aspects of the display's movement by preventing the naturalizing of critical stance, undermining the naturalizing of the text's constitutive codes, and putting beyond reach any pretense that one reading or body of readings could capture all the differential relations potential in a given text.

Some of this difference is preserved in an approach like that of Wladimir Krysinski, which draws upon the theories of Lacan, Marx, and Ricoeur to consider the narrator as an "other" of the author by means of which we can gain some hermeneutic insight into him—the narrator comprises "traces" one can use to understand the self-differentiating process of the authorial subject.[14] But even this treatment seeks to hold the interpretive process within a single dialectic of narrator and author, to consider fiction essentially as a vehicle for the Lacanian subject and thus as essentially referential. Other schematics leave even less room than Krysinski's interplay of subject and ego, self and other. Lubomír Doležel, for example, revives the grammatical paradigm, opening first-person narration out into authorial, observer, and personal and third-person out into rhetorical, objective, and subjective modes.[15] The subjective ground of these classifications, and the implicit assumptions about knowledge as divisible between subjective and objective modes, or about roles as divisible between personal and observational or between observational and authorial, separate functions or attributes that a reflexive analysis demonstrates are inextricably interrelated elements of *any* narrative stance by author, reader, or critic.[16]

As our review of the critical quadrilateral suggests, difference is the dynamic principle characterizing the manifold possibilities that co-exist for constituting in terms of one's paradigm an ordered sense of whatever subject one approaches. We are not observers of a flat textual grid, working with a conceptual compass and caliper to measure the angles and distances among fixed points. We are instead in the middle of the multidimensional textual environment fixing (fictionalizing) points of reference and freezing the action long enough to trace some of the shapes that pass by like the "hawk or whatever bird it was" Jeremiah Beaumont seeks to capture. We need not engage in a full-scale critique of all existing schemata to recognize the pervasiveness of the set of assumptions this study seeks to reconsider. At this point in the intellectual life of the eighties such a contention is anything but controversial. We should, however, consider the implications of shifting our critical grounds along the lines advocated in this reflexive approach. If critical method is grounded not in the nature of a *Ding-an-sich,* but rather in a paradigm of assumptions however unconsciously shaping practice, then the conditions surrounding the critic correlative with that critic's paradigm are important—at least as important as those surrounding the creation of a more obviously literary text.

It has been my object to study not the historical context of criticism, but rather the conceptual context of the critical act. But one must at least glance over the relationship between point of view theory and history as exteriority, the external conditions of possibility for both the novel and its criticism, if one is to form a full sense of the possibilities opened up by a reflexive study of constitutive poetics. It is surely no longer controversial to note that the novel emerges with capitalism, and that the social and intellectual conditions necessary for the latter also shape the former. The novel, that is, is a by-product of the alienation of the subjective and the objective, for it is in the space between the two that "realistic" narrative takes place. Moreover, the preoccupation with the subjective ego instrumental to capitalism is equally constitutive of the novel. As this study has found, however, these conceptual foundations of the past few centuries of fiction have coexisted in the novel with a reflexive dimension not so thoroughly in accord with the reigning ideology the form more obviously reflects. That is, the novel bears the marks of the process by which the entities of the state and the self as we know them are formed. This process of generation is not entirely unrecoverable, then, for reflexivity is the means by which narrative demystifies the illusion of permanent or natural "aesthetic" qualities, and thus of philosophical and political qualities as well, and outlines in all these spheres the elements that have been resituated by the historical forces that have produced the modern state, the corollary cult of selfhood, and the form of the novel basic to both of them.

In terms of criticism, I might well observe that a representational poetics is not innocently aesthetic but is equally philosophical, theological, and political. I might argue metaphorically that what Derrida archly calls "mimetologism" is compounded of the hierarchical imposition of order shared by both the aristocratic and the capitalist modes of organizing society and its many cultural manifestations. Beings and things are isolated and mastered according to their usefulness in sustaining one's intellectual possession of the world, the "it" one "gets" out

243

of understanding. Constitutive poetics, on the other hand, is a proletarian theory that reflects an earthy sense that the order of things is arbitrary anyway, so why revere or die for the man? That is, the oppressed at the moment they achieve a reflexive or revolutionary sense of themselves—the two often amount to the same thing—begin to see the class in power as comic in its pretentiousness, ensconced in power only by the vagaries of chance, and naively unaware how fragile, arbitrary, and temporary is its place in the ultimate scheme of things. Radical awareness in either the political or the critical realm, then, is a reflexive sense of how freely apparently essential elements may be reconstituted and resituated within the field they appear to dominate. It may well be difficult to resituate those elements without existing orders' reassimilating them or gradually reclaiming the vision of the would-be resituator, but reflexivity is at the very least an essential means of keeping conventions marked as such. The representational defers to what it assumes to be *the* order; the constitutive recognizes that it is only *an* order among many possibilities. Such a perspective is far from an immoral free-for-all, as conservatives would characterize it, and equally far from a nonmoral and even mindless subjection to the hierarchical intellectual and moral systems supporting a reigning ideology (in the form, for example, of underwriting the movement from precept to case or law to action). For the constitutive is an expressly politicized morality of making or ordering according to a collective construct, one that is thus ever amenable to change rather than following "laws" limiting the possibility of such change.

Constitutive poetics is therefore a necessary prelude to any political analysis that goes beyond the representationalist labeling of what, on the very obvious macro level, is there. It enables a breakthrough to a micro level whereon one may trace the rationale behind the definition and manipulation of the elements in question, the very segmentation of what Eco calls the "content continuum" according to ideological constructs, and the reconstituting of conventional usages by which a text, or a critic, seeks to reorder the collective sense of that content continuum.[17] The critical concept of point of view, for example, is akin to the establishment of a social field in which egos mill about waiting to be absorbed into utilitarian orders as needed; the novel as economy serves the transcendentally minded as a means of nurturing the ideologically motivated deployment of subjectivity in Western culture, hence mainly of circulating the values of the current order. Such a preoccupation with the self, individualism, and the private internal world of consciousness serves in obvious ways the interests of an established order of things. Reflexivity, however, captures like a fossil in stone the differentiating movement of that deployment. Treating point of view only in subjective terms blocks both the philosophical and the historical implications of the constituting of such transcendental distractions from the realities of a culture that has successfully synthesized logocentrism and capitalism into a powerful organizational force in modern life.

To consider in this light the effects of the reflexive analyses I have carried out on a number of narratives is to recognize how politically potent criticism can be, even though at first glance it seems to be preoccupied with "merely" philosophical rather than "practical" questions. *Vanity Fair,* for example, follows the radical dimension in Thackeray's own thinking and generates a series of narrative orders that present simultaneously a number of stages in the deployment of a subjective ideology, from author-god to authoritative researcher, subjective experiencer, and finally the proliferation of scripted roles within the openly textual "I." The simultaneity of the novelist-god and the slapstick puppeteer, of the investigative documentary historian and the pervasively hypothetical gossiper, of the objective observer and the emotionally blind participant collapse these stages upon each other and emphasize their dependency upon an arbitrary stance from which they are posited. The technique folds the succession of dominant narrative modalities back upon itself and thus creates the possibility for perceiving the external conditions upon which those modes depend. We found in *Chance* that Marlow rebels against reigning narratology to pierce the haze surrounding the logocentric hull of culture and to create the possibility for reformulating the repressive relationship between order and play. Given even Powell's willingness to point out the applicability of the reflexive themes in *Chance* to the "Queen's ministers," the political, social, and historical corollaries of Marlow's heady questions are apparent. *World Enough and Time* is a sweepingly revolutionary study of the deceptive relations between romanticism and what we might call scientism, objectified respectively in its nineteenth- and twentieth-century narrators. That is, the novel radically undermines the egoistic cult of selfhood by offering the reader the opportunity to work out the mutually generative nature of these two seemingly opposed conceptions of life. Scientific objectivity, that is, makes a space for the ego to transpire uncritically by preoccupying itself with the past as a status quo (in history), or with the present as a text of scientific law (immutable, unchanging, and consistent with larger sociopolitical ideologies' own pseudoscientific self-justification), or, one might add, with literature as a formal unity. In effect, the romantic accepts this dichotomy, just as the narrator accepts Jeremiah's, but by choosing instead the other half (the ego, at the expense of any blunt scrutiny of the world). And finally, *The French Lieutenant's Woman* undoes the proprietary ethic of capitalism by displacing the authorial function back into the collective semiotic meshwork from which it arises in the first place. Since the novel insists that even its most narrowly reflexive digression (on the relation between an author and his characters) "has much to do with your Time, Progress, Society, Evolution and all those other capitalized ghosts in the night that are rattling their chains behind the scenes of this book" or any other, for that matter, there are unambiguous grounds for recognizing the relation between fictional technique and the external conditions of the culture at large. Time, progress, and society are clearly crucial elements in the economic organization of a culture, and "capitalized" is a nice pun reminding us that reflexivity undoes the monolithic force by which capitalism reifies the culture according to its basic requirements.

Each of these reflexive novels, then, undoes the philosophical closure of its given form, with the result that the historical consciousness that is necessarily inaccessible to the writer or text *is* available for the reader. Hence the breach that some see between the philosophical and political wings of poststructuralism is illusory, for each constitutes the other's possibility. The perception of a breach is itself dependent upon those historical conditions that limit the possibility for a full awareness of their articulation. One might argue that, far from an adversarial relation, the philosophical and political dimensions brought together here relate as figure and ground in the ever popular gestaltist drawings of rabbit/hands or of urn/faces.

When all is said, this chapter's epigraph, urging us to read "in a certain way," may be taken over here to point toward this dual relation between philosophy and history paralleling that between the referential and the reflexive. That is, the second term of each pair is what is suppressed by the first as it embodies the reigning ideological fragmentation of the collectivity of mankind. Both historicity and reflexivity destabilize the absolutism of their contraries, however, reflexivity by undoing the philosophical underpinnings of representational poetics, historicity by clarifying the status of philosophical "truth" as a function of a socioeconomic matrix rather than an ahistorical absolute of logic or metaphysics. In this rich interplay, any attempt to impede the free circulation of the literary process, to reify it in the service of one ideology or another, or to freeze it entirely within a single critical frame is doomed to the fate of any structure that seeks closure: structures, Piaget tells us, are characterized not only by self-regulation, but by transformation as well.[18] Reflexivity is a permanently revolutionary dimension of literature that persists in resisting the yoke of any paradigm that attempts to obscure its own self-transforming qualities. One thinks of Derrida's comments on the occasion when he was introduced to American academics at Johns Hopkins University in 1969:

> There are thus two interpretations of interpretation, of structure, of sign, of play. The one seeks to decipher, dreams of deciphering a truth or an origin which escapes play and the order of the sign, and which lives the necessity of interpretation as an exile [from its own pure Presence and Truth]. The other, which is no longer turned toward the origin, affirms play and tries to pass beyond man and humanism, the name of man being the name of that being who, throughout the history of metaphysics or of ontotheology—in other words, throughout his entire history—has dreamed of full presence, the reassuring foundation, the origin and the end of play.[19]

One of these modes, in other words, attempts to reside in that quarter of the four-square diagram with which we began that is governed by the representational and the referential; the other gravitates toward the opposite quarter shaped by the constitutive and the reflexive. The diagonal between them, I think, points down the page toward the next leaf to fall from the cultural text. It may well be that the reflexive has always been with us, folded into the great narrative of Western culture. But somehow it seems that we are only now getting around to following the reflexive arc around the textual circuit we have taken too much for granted—that is, too much as granted us rather than constituted.

Notes

One   *Narrative Reflexivity and Constitutive Poetics*

1. The term "metafiction" can mislead powerfully on two very deceptive points: that such fiction comments upon itself in ways that escape the fictive qualities of that on which it is supposed to be a metadiscourse and that there is a nonmetafictional fiction. The first is a covert theory of discourse preserving the illusion of a metalanguage, the second a not so covert mimetic theory of narrative that would exclude most of the issues my own study of reflexivity engages.

2. Cf. Brook Thomas's distinction between "self-conscious," which he applies to the author as he writes, and "reflexive," which he attributes to the nature of language, in *James Joyce's "Ulysses,"* especially his first chapter.

3. Albert Cook, *The Meaning of Fiction.* These quotations all come from pp. 24–25.

4. Something of the same conflict can be seen in Mark Schorer's important essay "Technique as Discovery." The tension here is between the metaphoric implications of "exploring and defining the values *in* an area of experience" (italics mine) and Schorer's sense that, with the imposition of technique, the values of an experience "for the first time *then,* are being given" (italics his). On the one hand, the values are waiting out in experience to be uncovered by the explorations of technique; on the other hand, the values are "given" by the imposition of technique upon that experience. Schorer's thesis seems to shift the major burden for generating meaning onto the patterns and judgments implicit in the technique that structures experiences, but his figures mark his fidelity to a view of fiction as mimesis that reveals hidden transcendent values in experience.

5. This is the approach of James E. Swearingen in his excellent study *Reflexivity in "Tristram Shandy": An Essay in Phenomenological Cricitism.* At the moment that Swearingen, a more than able thinker in the Husserlian tradition, turns to a "critical explication of the structures of consciousness" as an "examination of this domain of belief and custom in human nature," our emphases diverge—his toward such structures and mine toward the cultural conventions that constitute those structures.

6. Robert Alter, *Partial Magic: The Novel as a Self-Conscious Genre,* x, xi. Subsequent references are noted parenthetically in the text.

7. Cf. Wayne Booth's treatment of Stern's novel in his classic *Rhetoric of Fiction;* at one point he seems to say that its satire is "for the sake of the comic enjoyment" and that the bizarre characteristics of Tristram's mind explain the disorder and unconventional elements of the novel—"the chaos is all of his own making" (230,

231). The purpose, apparently, is to show one aberrant consciousness as it flounders with its comic materials, a formulation that makes *Tristram Shandy* a mimesis of aberration rather than a metaphysical threat. One might well have been ready to feel such a menace in the three tensions Booth describes in the work between Tristram's claim to present himself as he is and his self-confessed "self-transformation," between the struggle "to get at the inner reality of events" and the fact that it is "always just beyond the artist's grasp," and between the effort to form an artifice and the fleetingness of "the world of chaos" (228, 232, 233). That is, "self" as difference rather than identity, "inner reality" as inaccessible, and order as cultural construct are notions that would certainly run counter to the metaphysics underlying Booth's poetics.

8. Critics of contemporary fiction often find themselves confronting reflexivity, but just as often they succumb to the temptation to see it as a mark of (only) new fiction. For example, Stephen Heath's book on the nouveau roman uses Althusser's notion of "practical ideology" to deconstruct the reality of realism. The nouveau roman, on the other hand, attends to "the forms of the intelligibility in which the real is produced, a dramatization of possibilities of language, forms of articulation, limitations, of its own horizon" (*The Nouveau Roman: A Study in the Practice of Writing*, 22). Similarly, Raymond Federman's "surfiction" "exposes the fictionality of reality" rather than crediting "man's distorted vision of reality"; it "will circle around itself, create new and unexpected movements and figures in the unfolding of the narration, repeating itself, projecting itself backward and forward along the curves of the writing" (*Surfiction: Fiction Now and Tomorrow*, 7, 11). Both Heath and Federman, however, speak as if these characteristics pertained only to very recent fiction; my own work attends to such reflexivity elsewhere in the narrative canon. Robert Scholes comes close to the same misleading emphasis; he rightly calls *Tristram Shandy* "that most self-reflexive fiction," but on occasion he refers to reflexivity as a "short-term trend" that is "masturbatory" and a "narcissistic way of avoiding this great task" (of bringing "human life back into harmony with the universe") (*Fabulation and Metafiction*, 210–18).

9. Linda Hutcheon, *Narcissistic Narrative: The Metafictional Paradox*. Hutcheon's cue, no doubt, was Wolfgang Iser's comment that particularly in twentieth-century texts reflexivity can "make us aware of the nature of our own capacity for providing links" by referring us "back directly to our own preconceptions" revealed in the very "act of interpretation," though one wonders why this would not necessarily happen in all fiction (*The Implied Reader*, 280; see also of course his *The Act of Reading: A Theory of Aesthetic Response*).

10. Patricia Waugh, *Metafiction*, 11.

11. Wayne Booth, for example, quotes the famous pasage from James's preface to *Roderick Hudson* in which the master says, "Really, universally, relations stop nowhere, and the exquisite problem of the artist is eternally but to draw, by a geometry of his own, the circle within which they shall happily *appear* to do so" (*Rhetoric of Fiction*, 232). In this quotation one could obviously discover all one needs to know about the arbitrariness of aesthetic order and thus its apparent falsification of reality. But for Booth the issue here is the "rendering of time"—not the problem of knowing it, or knowing the experience it seems to measure, but simply presenting it. Booth's discomfort with unreliable narration and his celebration of the novelist as "both a seer and a revelator" (395) suggest how alien the reflexive and the constitutive are to his thinking.

12. Paul de Man, *Blindness and Insight: Essays in the Rhetoric of Contemporary Criticism*, 17.

13. Derrida's now classic essay on this concept is available in *Margins of Philosophy*, 1–27.

14. Umberto Eco, *A Theory of Semiotics*, 274. Consider the semiotic quality of Frank Kermode's attention to "Secrets and Narrative Sequence" wherever he may learn from them the "rarer kind of sense." It is precisely that sense, he argues, that if reading "according to restricted codes we disregard as noise." We might well describe that noise as the text challenging existing codes.

15. Thomas S. Kuhn, *The Structure of Scientific Revolutions*, 128.

16. Friedrich Nietzsche, *The Will to Power*, p. 272. Future references are noted parenthetically in the text.

17. But see, as an example of an explicit address of these matters, Jameson's observation that "dialectical thinking can be characterized as historical reflexivity, that is, as the study of an object . . . which also involves the study of the concepts and categories (themselves historical) that we necessarily bring to the object." Neither critic nor author can be excluded from that "we" (*The Political Unconscious: Narrative as a Socially Symbolic Act*, 109). One could easily argue that Mikhail Bakhtin's explanation of the "polyphonic" (or "dialogic" or "heteroglossiac") nature of the novel is distinctly reflexive, since it emphasizes the relativity and multiplicity of any "voice" we discern. The ideologically saturated nature of language (there are "no neutral words and forms") surfaces because of the irresolvably dialogic nature of narrative, thus bringing us back around to the necessarily ideological stakes in thinking through the constitutive dimension of any discourse ("Discourse in the Novel," 259–422).

18. Richard Rorty, *Philosophy and the Mirror of Nature*, 357. Future references are noted parenthetically in the text.

19. As an example of how much ground is shared at these borders, consider the cases of David Caute and Richard Poirier. Caute's very philosophical version of ideological reflexivity appears in his description of a "dialectical literature" that "strives to do what it cannot do; it attempts representation while discarding the myth of representation; it attempts to transcend its own limitations as a text while never forgetting that these limitations cannot be transcended; it makes a primary virtue of honesty and yet proves its virtue by means of cunning tricks" (*The Illusion: An Essay on Politics, Theatre, and the Novel*). Caute's concept is defined in terms quite close to Poirier's non-Marxist literature of self-parody, which "shapes itself around its own dissolvents," calling into question "the activity itself of creating any literary form" and erasing distinctions among all fictions including history, biography, and culture itself; Poirier admires Borges precisely because "he won't allow *any* element . . . to become stabilized or authoritative" (*The Performing Self*, 27–28, 43).

20. This is ultimately what lies behind Victor Shklovsky's by now familiar contention that *Tristram Shandy* is "the most typical novel in world literature," precisely because of its inescapably reflexive focus upon the constitutive. For example, Shklovsky argues that "an image is not a permanent referent for those mutable complexities of life which are revealed through it; its purpose is not to make us perceive meaning, but to create a special perception of the object—it creates a 'vision' of the object instead of serving as a means for knowing it." Defamiliarization, or more accurately "making strange," is not a form of knowing a permanent referent

but of constituting a "created vision." One makes strange precisely by shifting subject matter around in verbal matrixes from one semiotic coding to another. Its "strangeness" or familiarity is thus a function of cultural coding, our sense of it dependent upon which set of relations or differences is applied to it rather than upon the nature of the thing itself ("Art as Technique," 57, 18).

21. See, for example, his query, "Wouldn't 'literary criticism' as such be part of what we have called the *ontological* interpretation of mimesis or of metaphysical mimetologism?" (Jacques Derrida, *Dissemination,* 245).

Two   Thackeray and Nineteenth-Century Fiction: Narrators and Readers

1. Quotations are taken from the Centenary Biographical Edition of *The Works of William Makepeace Thackeray* (1910–11; rpt. New York: AMS Press, 1968). Citations are given by volume and page number and also, since the availability of editions varies widely, by chapter number. The passage cited is from 2:2; 36 (vol. 2, p. 2; chap. 36).

2. Wayne Booth, *The Rhetoric of Irony,* 9–13.

3. Paul de Man, "The Rhetoric of Temporality," 192.

4. Hence even at her worst in the flophouses of Germany, Becky is described as "not worse now than she had been in the days of her prosperity—only a little down on her luck" (2:390; 65). Visiting Queen's Crawley she "thought about her own youth, and the dark secrets of those early tainted days" (2:70; 41). Traveling with Major Loder, she thinks of "happier days, when she was not innocent, but not found out" (2:378; 64). The famous letter from Mr. Crisp, it seems, was "*in answer* to another letter," and it "was not quite a new" world for Becky as it was for Amelia, "with all the [virginal] bloom upon it" (1:18; 2).

5. G. Armour Craig, "On the Style of *Vanity Fair,*" in *Style in Prose Fiction,* ed. Harold C. Martin, English Institute Essays (New York: Columbia University Press, 1959), 101.

6. As Juliet McMaster argues in *Thackeray: The Major Novels* (Toronto: University of Toronto Press, 1971): "if we are ready to consider them, we avoid the temptation to place ourselves among the Pharisees by concluding too glibly" (46).

7. For a summary of the review by George Lewes critical of this passage, and for Thackeray's explanation, see Gordon N. Ray, ed., *The Letters and Private Papers of William Makepeace Thackeray* (Cambridge: Harvard University Press, 1945–46), 2:353–54.

8. John Loofbourow, *Thackeray and the Form of Fiction* (Princeton: Princeton University Press, 1964), attends to the stylistic parody in particular, while Jack P. Rawlins focuses upon the novel's play with fictional modes in *Thackeray's Novels: A Fiction That Is True* (Berkeley: University of California Press, 1974). The latter is especially useful in a reflexive analysis of *Vanity Fair,* since Rawlins argues that "Thackeray teaches us to attend to the rhetorical and dramatic processes of the novel as we experience them" (151) and that his are "the techniques of his fellow novelists, turned self-conscious and with their implications about writing and reading made explicit" (185).

9. See Barbara Hardy's *The Exposure of Luxury: Radical Themes in Thackeray* (Pittsburgh: University of Pittsburgh Press, 1972).

10. See John Sutherland's *Thackeray at Work* (London: Athlone Press, 1974),

the extensive work of Peter Shillingsburg, and Edgar F. Harden's excellent *The Emergence of Thackeray's Serial Fiction* (Athens: University of Georgia Press, 1979).

11. Juliet McMaster's admirable study, already cited, is of course a standard reference on this question. For a somewhat different approach to unifying Thackeray's narrative elements, see Robert A. Colby's *Thackeray's Canvass of Humanity* (Columbia: Ohio State University Press, 1979), a commendably erudite contextual study of Thackeray's career.

12. See J. Y. T. Greig's *Thackeray: A Reconsideration* (London: Oxford University Press, 1950) and Bernard Paris's *A Psychological Approach to Fiction* (Bloomington: Indiana University Press, 1974).

13. Geoffrey Tillotson and Donald Hawes, eds., *Thackeray: The Critical Heritage* (London: Routledge and Kegan Paul, 1968), 44–49.

14. Ibid., 151–59.

15. Geoffrey Tillotson, *Thackeray the Novelist* (Cambridge: Cambridge University Press, 1954).

16. McMaster, *Thackeray*, 13–22.

17. At the same time, of course, the case upsets poetic justice and the principle of divine retribution from which it derives. Steyne, after all, has lived a long life of wealth, privilege, and pleasure, well insulated from the worst effects of any adversities visited upon him by the narrator's religious fantasies.

18. I am using a reprint of the 1860 edition with George Cruikshank's memorable illustrations (London: Routledge and Kegan Paul, 1976).

19. Scorn is directed most intensely at the omniscient novelist's advertising himself as such. Nassau Senior, for example, complained that "Mr. Thackeray indulges in the bad practice of commenting on the conduct of his *dramatis personae*" (*Critical Heritage*, 189). Percy Lubbock felt that Thackeray could not handle strictly dramatic presentation (*The Craft of Fiction*, 96–97). See also J. Y. T. Greig's "Thackeray: A Novelist by Accident," in *From Jane Austen to Joseph Conrad*, ed. Robert C. Rathburn and Martin Steinmann, Jr. (Minneapolis: University of Minnesota Press, 1958), 73; Arnold Kettle, *An Introduction to the English Novel* (New York: Harper & Row, 1968), 158; and Frederick R. Karl, *A Reader's Guide to the Nineteenth Century British Novel* (New York: Noonday Press, 1964), 177–204.

20. Much critical ingenuity has been spent minimizing the variations and describing "his" real purpose. Juliet McMaster focuses on the confrontation of author and reader. Ann Y. Wilkinson, "The Tomeavsian Way of Knowing the World: Technique and Meaning in *Vanity Fair*," *ELH* 32 (1964): 370–87, suggests epistemological themes as the key to unity; Roger M. Swanson, "*Vanity Fair*: The Double Standard," in *The English Novel in the Nineteenth Century* (Urbana: University of Illinois Press, 1972), argues moral critique as the grounds for coherence; and Cynthia G. Wolff, "Who Is the Narrator of *Vanity Fair* and Where Is He Standing?" *College Literature* 1 (1974): 190–203, outlines emotional limitations of the narrator as a means of rationalizing variations. Harriet Blodgett suggests more favorable moral grounds in her "Necessary Presence: The Rhetoric of the Narrator in *Vanity Fair*," *Nineteenth-Century Fiction* 22 (1967): 211–25, while Wolfgang Iser, *The Implied Reader* 101–20, thinks in terms of the process of discovery in which narrator and reader are engaged.

21. One could argue more literally, of course, that "predestined" really means that narrator and character are coequal in the author's imagination—that is, each

determines the other from the moment they exist as an idea for a novel. Or one could argue more semiotically that the system of conventions existing in the 1840s preordained the probability that such parodic play off the types and plots of the age would take place. In each of these cases, however, it is the narrative convention or type that initiates and shapes the act of perception.

22. McMaster, *Thackeray,* 38.

23. Certainly this passage disciplines the reader; just before this passage Becky has figured in a triumphant joust with the ridiculous Miss Pinkerton. The first chapter is filled with satiric touches lampooning the old lady, and Becky becomes a high-spirited Saint George who slays the old dragon in verbal combat. The reader is on her side after such a sparkling encounter, but the narrator's entrance here dwarfs the fictional events with the humor of the old man and prepares us to accept the subsequent material picturing Becky as "no angel" and as a "young misanthropist." Ridiculing Amelia's emotionalism (the anecdote's local target) and shifting the reader from admiration to censure of Becky is an obvious demonstration of a narrator's power to discipline, in effect caning the readers who have allowed themselves simply to be carried along. Such attention to disciplining readers suggests the extent to which they too serve as a narrative stance in fiction, a point I will take up in the next section.

24. Robert Scholes and Robert Kellogg, *The Nature of Narrative,* 13ff.

25. Miguel de Cervantes Saavedra, *The Adventures of Don Quixote,* trans. J. M. Cohen (Baltimore: Penguin Books, 1950), 487–88.

26. Henry Fielding, *Tom Jones,* ed. George Sherburn (New York: Modern Library, 1950), 567.

27. J. Hillis Miller, "Narrative and History," *ELH* 41 (Fall 1974): 459–60.

28. See Cheryl Herr's important discussion of censorship in *Joyce's Anatomy of Culture.*

29. Herman Melville, *Billy Budd and Other Tales* (New York: New American Library, 1961), 92.

Three   Conrad, Early Modernism, and the Narrator's Relation to His Material

1. I quote from the reprint of the Doubleday edition by W. W. Norton (New York, 1968).

2. "Mentor" may be too strong a term, but Ian Watt's account of the relationship with Henry James suggests something close to it. See his "Conrad, James, and *Chance,*" in *Imagined Worlds: Essays on Some English Novels and Novelists in Honour of John Butt,* ed. Ian Gregor (London: Methuen, 1968).

3. The serial contains many passages, often substantial in both content and length, omitted in editions of the book. Some of these passages are still present in versions of the novel intermediate between the serial and book forms. The typescript Conrad prepared for the American edition, now in the Beinecke Library at Yale University, has many but by no means all of these passages; some serial passages are already cut, some are present but canceled by Conrad's blue crayon, others apparently are destined for American publication. As it happened, the American edition was delayed long enough that its publishers simply used the plates from the English edition that preceded it. But had it gone ahead as scheduled, it would have contained a number of very interesting variants to entertain some enterprising textual editors.

As it is, we must be even more enterprising and study a fair amount of microfilm to recover the expanded versions of Marlow's comments on this narrative. Since the *Herald* is not always readily available, I will quote freely at those points where the "lost" passages are most important, noting the dates of the issues in parentheses. For further discussion see my essay "The Two Texts of *Chance*," *Conradiana* 16, no. 2 (1984): 83–101.

4. Cf. the "Descriptive Poetics of Point of View," a full-page schematic that Susan Sniader Lanser has carefully assembled from a multitude of theorists about point of view in prose fiction; although apparently exhaustive, the summary has little space for the range of reflexive issues emerging here except as a third-level subdivision of "contact" in which Lanser, by limiting reflexivity to the "self-consciousness" of the narrator, risks locking it within the metaphysics of selfhood often undermined by reflexivity. See Lanser, *The Narrative Act*, 176–78, 224.

5. Hence Gary Geddes's account of the novel, in *Conrad's Later Novels* (Montreal: McGill–Queen's University Press, 1980), stresses Marlow's targets as this sort of "ethical terminology . . . and the moral conventions, or ideal conceptions, they [ethical terms] embody" (13). But an ideal of "imaginative sympathy" guides what for Geddes is a more authentic understanding, an assurance the novel has made more difficult for other critics to accept, particularly in terms of the assumptions implicit in such "sympathy." Werner Senn, for example, finds the "epistemological indeterminacy" much less susceptible to resolution and notes the resulting paradox: "Epistemological failure is declared an inevitable necessity, while in the same breath, conjectures about the real nature of the world are made" (*Conrad's Narrative Voice: Stylistic Aspects of His Fiction* [Bern: Francke Verlag, 1980], 175–76). Senn thus seems to recognize the coexistence in the novel of the referential and the reflexive, the representational and the constitutive, and the resulting confusion for those who owe philosophical allegiance to the more traditional half of these pairs of terms.

6. This turns out to be an illusion of Marlow's, of course; the crew watches them, Powell eyes them, the first officer spits in their wake, Marlow hounds them retrospectively, de Barral himself materially affects their relations, almost fatally, and from shore the Fynes assess them without any indulgence for their unconventionality. They do not really escape the form one finds elsewhere in the novel. If indeed there *is* no exit, then we have a curious complication in Marlow's neat division between what plays within the theater of conventions and what plays outside.

7. Ian Watt, *Conrad in the Nineteenth Century* (Berkeley: University of California Press, 1979), 294.

8. Marlow also records that, as Fyne explains, the attitude he takes in his most significant (and nearly his only) action, his confrontation of Captain Anthony, is formed not so much by "what is written" in Flora's letter to Mrs. Fyne as by "what my wife could read between the lines" (252). Conrad emphasizes Fyne's willingness to act upon her conjectural narrative from between the lines by altering the serial version, in which Fyne himself reads the letter and characterizes it for Marlow (31 March), to the book version, which further removes "the source"—Mrs. Fyne does not even let Fyne read it but tells him about its contents.

9. Cf. Edward Said's discussion of this will as "a sense of mastery over life, and its true beginning perhaps the fear that life may not be worth living after all, or that without a decreed beginning life cannot have method" (*Beginnings: Intention and Method,* 114). In a similar vein, William W. Bonney argues that "interpretation,

like all perception, involves the sporadic, alogical displacement of one word by another under the reigning illusion that the whole process involves the rational, purposeful substitution of equals for equals, opposites for opposites" (*Thorns and Arabesques: Contexts for Conrad's Fiction* [Baltimore: Johns Hopkins University Press, 1980], 199). Bonney's "reigning illusion" is much like Said's posited beginnings, hence converging on the egoistic will to power. Bonney stresses the egoism heavily: "All men are destined to enact a futile attempt at trans-navigating the ever-fluctuating circles that denote the limits of their respective subjectivities. . . . for they must remain at the center no matter how much they struggle in linear impercipience" (p. 201). For Bonney, "linear impercipience" is more or less equivalent with the narrative or causal logic of logocentrism.

10. For example, Powell leaves school and then suddenly is out at sea; Anthony finds himself stranded on shore with nothing to do and scarcely anyone to talk to; Flora has no refuge left for herself or her father; de Barral emerges from prison with all old avenues closed to him; and even Marlow strikes the framing narrator as "subtly provisional" in his stay "as a bird rests on the branch of a tree, so tense with the power of brusque flight into its true element that it is incomprehensible why it should sit still minute after minute" (33–34).

11. Jeremy Hawthorn bases a great deal on the implications of this contrast, observing that language in Conrad faces both reality and cultural artifice. He goes on to argue that "the more language is used in the presence of other people and directed towards a common task then the more reliable it is" (*Joseph Conrad: Language and Fictional Self-Consciousness* [Lincoln: University of Nebraska Press, 1979], 32). *Chance* suggests that "reliability" is more a function of consensus than of truth, however, as the following discussion argues, and no doubt Perry Meisel is closer to the heart of Conrad's sense of language when he argues that it "creates and controls the kind of knowledge we have," an insight he calls "Marlow's deepest realization" and one that would make very difficult Hawthorn's attempt to define the "self-consciousness" of Conrad's fiction through an opposition between eloquence, all "lies," and experience, an unmediated source of knowledge that can nonetheless be understood by others (though Marlow cannot "express the 'inexpressible,' [he] is able to express its inexpressibility" (Perry Meisel, "Decentering *Heart of Darkness*," *Modern Language Studies* 8, no. 3 (1978): 28).

12. In one of the earliest and most typical of these passages, Marlow tells us that "it was one of those dewy, clear, starry nights, oppressing our spirit, crushing our pride, by the brilliant evidence of the awful loneliness, of the hopeless obscure insignificance of our globe lost in the splendid revelation of a glittering soulless universe. I hate such skies" (50). Alien and infinite, the skies exceed absolutely the cultural margins Marlow seeks. Thus he speaks of "the bespangled, cruel revelation of the Immensity of the Universe" (61), "the horror of the Infinite veiled by the splendid tent of blue" sky (64), and concludes that it "is difficult to retain the memory of the conflicts, miseries, temptations and crimes of men's self-seeking existence when one is alone with the charming serenity of the unconscious nature" (422).

13. Cf. Marlow's equally sexist notion that "women don't understand the force of a contemplative temperament" (155).

14. Cf. William Bonney's discussion of the ending as an illustration of the "solipsistic 'charm'" with which such sentimental illusions can sometimes be sustained (105–6).

15. J. Hillis Miller, "Ariadne's Thread," 57–77.

16. In a less syntactically tortured passage, Conrad gives us a similar sense of this undoing of the normal way of thinking about meaning: "But, as we have been told, hope 'lives eternal' or 'springs eternal,' I don't remember now which, in [the] human breast. It does. And as of all things calculated to preserve life on this earth one does not know whether one is to bless or to curse it. One naturally likes to be helped a bit in the job of 'keeping up one's end' to some purpose. On the other hand, the thought that maybe one is being duped by a heartless universe is tragic. And for what purpose? It's exasperating not to know" (2 June).

For hope to be a function of expedience (i.e., "calculated to preserve life") rather than metaphysics is perhaps not reassuring. But like Nietzsche, with whose view of logic and metaphysics this comment has much in common, Conrad is decidedly not nihilistic—such certainty about metaphysical matters is beyond us, however "exasperating" that may be to one trying to keep up "one's end to some purpose."

17. Meisel, "Decentering *Heart of Darkness*," 20–28.

18. J. Hillis Miller, "The Interpretation of *Lord Jim*," 226–27.

19. Cf. Derrida's "White Mythology: Metaphor in the Text of Philosophy," in *Margins of Philosophy,* 207–71, and Paul de Man's "The Epistemology of Metaphor," *Critical Inquiry* 5 (Autumn 1978): 13–30.

20. Similar passages are numerous, as when Powell describes the captain's closest friends aboard ship as "victims of a peculiar and secret form of lunacy which poisoned their lives" (300), a metaphor intended to apply to their jealousy, but which suits equally the poisonous lunacy of de Barral.

21. John Palmer's classic reading of the novel reaches a different conclusion about this passage. If there is precise workmanship, then, as Palmer explains, "the appearance of accident is an illusion maintained only from the human point of view, and the problem of chance reduces itself to one of knowledge" (*Joseph Conrad's Fiction* [Ithaca: Cornell University Press, 1968], 206). I suspect, however, that the "precise workmanship" is Powell's phrase, reflecting his persistent inability to accept a creation without a creator, while the list of agents represents Marlow's dismissal of Powell's metaphysics.

22. Hence it only makes sense that Marlow constructs a tight narrative even though he talks of the whole chance of hearing about the story in the first place as "an accident called Fyne" (36), or of "chance" as the force that "armed" de Barral with poison (436–37) and enabled him to navigate the tricky entrance to Powell's tidal creek on the Essex shore (258); he even calls Powell a "chance-comer" who serves all but unwittingly as the catalyst for the mutual revelation to which Anthony and the de Barrals finally come.

23. John Irwin, *Doubling and Incest/Repetition and Revenge.*

24. "Why the Novel Matters," in *D. H. Lawrence: Selected Literary Criticism,* ed. Anthony Beal, 102–8 (New York: Viking Press, 1966).

25. At least not until the three-volume deluxe synoptic edition of *Ulysses.*

26. On the Penguin Modern Classics paperback edition, from which I will be quoting (New York: Penguin Books, 1972).

Four   Warren, Late Modernism, and the Issue of Narrative and Identity

1. Robert B. Heilman, "Tangled Web," in *Robert Penn Warren: A Collection of Critical Essays,* ed. John L. Longley, Jr. (New York: New York University Press, 1965), 96.

2. See, for example, Charles R. Anderson's discussion "Violence and Order in the Novels of Robert Penn Warren," in *Southern Renascence,* ed. Louis D. Rubin, Jr., and Robert D. Jacobs, 207–24 (Baltimore: John Hopkins University Press, 1953); Robert Berner's treatment of the cultural and the "natural" in "The Required Past: World Enough and Time," in *Robert Penn Warren: A Collection of Critical Essays,* ed. Richard Gray, 67–75 (Englewood Cliffs, N.J.: Prentice-Hall, 1980); Charles H. Bohner's contrast of inner and outer realms in *Robert Penn Warren* (New York: Twayne Publishers, 1964); Barnett Guttenberg on world and idea in his *Web of Being: The Novels of Robert Penn Warren* (Nashville: Vanderbilt University Press, 1975); Marshall Walker on heritage or environment and idea in his *Robert Penn Warren: A Vision Earned* (New York: Barnes and Noble, 1979); and James H. Justus on dream and drama in *The Achievement of Robert Penn Warren* (Baton Rouge: Louisiana State University Press, 1981).

3. Robert Penn Warren, *World Enough and Time* (New York: Vintage Books, 1979), 405. Future references are noted parenthetically in the text.

4. Barnett Guttenberg, *Web of Being: The Novels of Robert Penn Warren* (Nashville: Vanderbilt University Press, 1975), 68–69.

5. Leonard Casper, *Robert Penn Warren: The Dark and Bloody Ground* (Seattle: University of Washington Press, 1960), 148.

6. Guttenberg and Casper are not alone in complaining that the novel's varying perspectives "corrode rather than correct," as Leonard Casper puts it. See too Charles R. Anderson's impatience with "unresolved ambiguities" in his essay "Violence and Order in the Novels of Robert Penn Warren," 207–24. Perhaps Harry Modean Campbell most clearly reflects the philosophical premises of this criticism by calling the book "contradictory" rather than "paradoxical" and suggesting that the latter is the province of theology—"for only theologians can successfully claim the dignity of paradox for the contradictions in their speculations" ("Warren as Philosopher in *World Enough and Time,*" in *Southern Renascence,* ed. Louis D. Rubin, Jr., and Robert D. Jacobs [Baltimore: Johns Hopkins University Press, 1953]).

7. Nietzsche, *The Will to Power,* 283–84. Future references are noted parenthetically in the text.

8. Readers unfamiliar with this argument may appreciate Paul de Man's discussion of it in *Allegories of Reading,* 119–31.

9. Frederick Nietzsche, "On Truth and Lies in a Nonmoral Sense," 85–86.

10. Note, for example, this comment, also from his final view of things: "I thought how men had written that book long ago, almost two thousand years, in passion and hope, and how men had all those centuries read it for comfort and had believed that in the beginning there was the Word, and how I myself had lifted up my heart at the sentence. . . . I laughed as I lay on the leaves and looked down at the slew, and I said out loud, in the beginning there was the Word and the Word was with God, but in the end there is the mud and the mud is with me" (440–41).

11. This parallels Paul de Man's comments about irony in "The Rhetoric of Temporality," esp. 203 ff.

12. Bohner, *Robert Penn Warren,* 112.

13. Frank Gado, ed., *First Person: Conversations on Writers and Writing* (Schenectady, N.Y.: Union College Press, 1973), 92.

14. John Updike, *Rabbit, Run* (New York: Fawcett Crest, 1960).

15. Michel Foucault, *Power/Knowledge: Selected Interviews and Other Writings,* 98.

16. Saul Bellow, *Herzog* (1964; New York: Avon Books, 1976).

Five   Fowles, Contemporary Fiction, and the Poetics of the Author

1. Hence Wayne Booth's recourse in *The Rhetoric of Irony* to the norms of the implied author to anchor the attempt to make irony stable and finite. Few equate the biographical with the implied author these days, but the metaphysical logic is the same: both take the self (real or textual) as sufficient ground for interpretive decisions.

2. Cf. Roland Barthes's characterization of our mainstream approach to interpretation: "The *explanation* of a work is always sought in the man or woman who produced it, as if it were always in the end, through the more or less transparent allegory of the fiction, the voice of a single person, the *author* 'confiding' in us" ("The Death of the Author," collected in *Image-Music-Text,* 143).

3. From Michel Foucault, "What Is an Author?" 158.

4. John Fowles, *The Aristos* (New York: New American Library, 1970), 203.

5. John Fowles, "Notes on an Unfinished Novel," in *Afterwords: Novelists on Their Novels,* ed. Thomas McCormack (New York: Harper and Row, 1969), 161, 163.

6. John Fowles, "Lettre-Postface de John Fowles," in *Etudes sur "The French Lieutenant's Woman" de John Fowles* (Caen: Centre Regional de Documentation Pédagogique, 1977), 51.

7. Fowles, "Lettre-Postface," 52.

8. John Fowles, untitled essay in *Bookmarks,* ed. Frederick Raphael (London: Jonathan Cape, 1975), 55.

9. Fowles, "Lettre-Postface," 51.

10. Fowles, "Notes on an Unfinished Novel," 167.

11. John Fowles, *The French Lieutenant's Woman* (New York: New American Library, 1969), 212–13. Future references are noted parenthetically in the text.

12. Similarly, the implied recourse to a "human constant" beyond the shifting conventions raises more problems than it may be worth. Such an essentialist opposition is hardly compatible with existentialism, the philosophy of becoming. And how should one grasp such a "constant" without ensnaring it immediately within "a matter of vocabulary"?

13. Moreover, one can detect Fowles's restlessness with the critics and theoreticians of narrative for "destroying so much of the mystery, the difficulty, the aura of the forbidden, [and thus] also a great deal of the pleasure" of narrative (214), just as the moderns have devalued sexuality through constant discussion and analysis. Critical analysis makes us so conscious of the medium and the artifice that we are unable to release ourselves to the ecstasy of fusion with a text that more innocent readers, dwelling apart from critical discourse, enjoy naturally. Something of this surfaces in Fowles's comments, in one of his essays, about critics, "Americans especially, . . . who believe that a book is like a machine; that if you have the knack, you can take it to bits" ("Notes on an Unfinished Novel," 174).

14. Roland Barthes, *A Lover's Discourse,* 31–32.

15. Cf. Umberto Eco, *The Role of the Reader,* 10–11, where he calls the author one of the "'actantial roles' of the sentence," "an illocutionary signal (/I swear that/)," or "a perlocutionary operator (/suddenly something *horrible* happened/)."

16. The quoted phrases in this paragraph come from p. 150 of Foucault's essay.

17. Barthes, "The Death of the Author," 146.

18. Fowles, "Notes on an Unfinished Novel," 165.

19. Fowles, "Lettre-Postface," 52.

20. Dwight Eddins, "John Fowles: Existence as Authorship," *Contemporary Literature* 17 (Spring 1976): 104.

21. Fred Kaplan, "Victorian Modernists: Fowles and Nabokov," *Journal of Narrative Technique* 3 (May 1973): 113.

22. James Campbell, "An Interview with John Fowles," *Contemporary Literature* 17 (Autumn 1976): 463.

23. Fowles, *The Aristos,* 123.

24. Robert Huffaker, *John Fowles* (Boston: Twayne Publishers, 1980), 100–101.

25. Cf. Dominique Catherine and Ginette Emprin, "Aspects de la Technique Narrative. Les Relations Narrateur/Lecteur/Personnages," in *Etudes sur "The French Lieutenant's Woman" de John Fowles,* 21.

26. Robert Coover, *Pricksongs and Descants* (New York: New American Library, 1970).

27. I have explored this story at greater length in "Coover's 'The Magic Poker' and the Techniques of Fiction," *Essays in Literature* 7, no. 2 (1981): 203–18.

28. Truman Capote, *Music for Chameleons* (New York: New American Library, 1981), xvii.

29. Interview by Robert Scholes in Joe David Bellamy, ed., *The New Fiction: Interviews with Innovative American Writers* (Urbana: University of Illinois Press, 1974), 108.

30. Steve Katz, *Moving Parts* (New York: Fiction Collective, 1977).

31. In *Likely Stories: A Collection of Untraditional Fiction,* ed. Bruce R. McPherson (New Paltz, N.Y.: Treacle Press, 1981).

32. Ronald Sukenick, *98.6* (New York: Fiction Collective, 1975).

33. Angela Carter, *Fireworks: Nine Stories in Various Disguises* (New York: Harper and Row, 1974), 24–25.

Six   Reflexivity and Criticism

1. Compare these remarks with those of Wilson Snipes in his study "The Biographer as a Center of Reference" in *Biography* 5, no. 3 (1982): 215–25.

2. I rely upon the *American Heritage Dictionary* (Boston: Houghton Mifflin, 1979).

3. Hence any tonal, figurative, or allusive element of style, each nuance of scene or summary, illustration, format, commentary, and so forth.

4. See, for example, Frye's "Expanding Eyes," in *Spiritus Mundi: Essays on Literature, Myth, and Society,* 109–10.

5. Northrup Frye, *The Great Code: The Bible and Literature,* 26. Those three middle phases are metaphor (characterized by poetic or literary writing), metonymy (characterized by "existential" writing), and descriptive writing.

6. Cf. his own engaging remark that "this may be only a rationalization for not having budged in eighteen years" ("Expanding Eyes," 100).

7. Frye, *Great Code*, xxi, xiii; cf. also his suggestion in *The Anatomy of Criticism* that "it is more fruitful to study what in fact myths have been made to mean" than "what the myth 'means'" (341).

8. Jacques Lacan, "Of Structure as an Inmixing of an Otherness Prerequisite to Any Subject Whatever," 186–95.

9. In Fyre, *Anatomy of Criticism*, 354, 353.

10. Meyer H. Abrams, *The Mirror and the Lamp*, esp. 6–29.

11. See especially p. 134 of Eco's *Theory of Semiotics* for his explanation of overcoding in analytical procedures. Stanley Fish's idea of "interpretive communities" is explained conveniently in the introduction to *Is There a Text in This Class?* esp. 12–17.

12. Mikhail Bakhtin, "Discourse in the Novel," 262–63. He argues against "a simple and unmediated relation of speaker to his unitary and singular 'own' language" (269). Rather, the novel duplicates "the intense struggle within us for hegemony among various available verbal and ideological points of view, approaches, directions and values" (346)—coexisting paradigms, in other words. The many voices of heteroglossia thereby make many different potential relations available to commentators.

13. Hence *Emma* is treated very powerfully in *The Rhetoric*, but as I suggested in the first chapter, *Tristram Shandy* is covered far less completely.

14. Wladimir Krysinski, "The Narrator as a Sayer of the Author: Narrative Voices and Symbolic Structures," 44–89.

15. Lubomír Doležel, "The Typology of the Narrator: Point of View in Fiction," 541–52.

16. A quick look at representative formulations by point of view theorists suggests how often our criticism has flattened the reflexive curve in fiction. For example, although less restrictive in the moral imperative he imposes upon fiction, Norman Friedman's fine review of the subject still considers that "the problem of the narrator is adequate transmission of his story to the reader," with the critic's major distinction that "between subjective telling and objective showing"; he differs from Booth not in this rhetorical approach but in asking "how he [the author] embodies his plot in effective form," a difference Friedman characterizes as that between the "rhetorical" and the "technical" (*Form and Meaning in Fiction*, 142, 143). Susan Sniader Lanser's approach is arrested not so much in technical options as in the context of speech-act theory. Gathering over thirty standards for describing point of view grouped under the headings of stance, status, and contact, her compendium fixes them in relation to an all but transcendental reference point of the authorial self. For example, she emphasizes the central importance of "an originating subject whose relation to the speech act may be crucial to its 'felicitous' completion, as well as a receiving consciousness whose constitution may be equally important to the structure, transmission, and reception of the speech act," the former serving as "the ultimate authority" in her approach (*The Narrative Act*, 81, 132). By way of contrast, Robert Weimann, in what is perhaps the most interesting recent treatment of point of view, correlates the author's "achieved attitude to the actual world of history" and the "medium or focus of narration" as the necessary conditions for any narrative. For a critical perspective too, it turns out, since in order to escape "the frustration of forty years of formalism" we must use this

correlation as our means of legitimizing attention to the historical, social, and psychological forces that, together with more technical points of viewing, constitute that narrative perspective. Hence, when Weimann tells us that "the modern novel is born in the consciousness of its narrative perspective," he seems to embrace the crucial role of reflexivity in analyzing a constitutive poetics of the novel ("Point of View in Fiction," 59, 66, 70).

17. See Eco's discussion of this concept in *A Theory of Semiotics,* 50–66.

18. Jean Piaget, *Structuralism,* esp. 10–13, with its strictures against trying to fix this transformational quality too narrowly.

19. Jacques Derrida, "Structure, Sign, and Play," in *Writing and Difference,* 292. "The other" thus passes through a Nietzschean affirmation that *"then determines the noncenter otherwise than as loss of the center"* (italics Derrida's).

Bibliography

Listed here are those general works that have influenced my thinking at one stage or another of this project. Relatively complete bibliographies of contemporary theory are readily available and need not be duplicated. I have relied upon my notes to acknowledge my major debts to commentators upon individual writers.

Abrams, M. H. *The Mirror and the Lamp: Romantic Theory and the Critical Tradition.* New York: Oxford University Press, 1953.

Alter, Robert. *Partial Magic: The Novel as a Self-Conscious Genre.* Berkeley: University of California Press, 1975.

Babcock, Barbara A. "Reflexivity: Definition and Discriminations." *Semiotica* 30, nos. 1/2 (1980): 1–14.

Bakhtin, Mikhail. "Discourse in the Novel." In *The Dialogic Imagination: Four Essays,* trans. Caryl Emerson and Michael Holquist, 259–422. Austin: University of Texas Press, 1981.

Barthes, Roland. *Critical Essays.* Trans. Richard Howard. Evanston: Northwestern University Press, 1972.

———. *Image-Music-Text.* Trans. Stephen Heath. New York: Hill and Wang, 1977.

———. *A Lover's Discourse.* Trans. Richard Howard. New York: Hill and Wang, 1978.

———. *S/Z.* Trans. Richard Miller. New York: Hill and Wang, 1974.

Beebe, Maurice. "Reflective and Reflexive Trends in Modern Fiction." *Bucknell Review* 22, no. 2 (Fall 1976): 13–26.

Booth, Wayne. *The Rhetoric of Fiction.* Chicago: University of Chicago Press, 1961.

———. *A Rhetoric of Irony.* Chicago: University of Chicago Press, 1974.

———. "The Self-Conscious Narrator in Comic Fiction before *Tristram Shandy.*" *PMLA* 67 (1952): 163–85.

Boyd, Michael. *The Reflexive Novel: Fiction as Critique.* Lewisburg: Bucknell University Press, 1983.

Brown, Merle E. "The Idea of Fiction as Fictive or Fictitious." *Stand* 15, no. 1 (1974): 38–46.

Caute, David. *The Illusion: An Essay on Politics, Theatre, and the Novel.* New York: Harper and Row, 1971.

Cook, Albert. *The Meaning of Fiction.* Detroit: Wayne State University Press, 1960.

263

Culler, Jonathan. *On Deconstruction: Theory and Criticism after Structuralism.* Ithaca: Cornell University Press, 1982.

———. *Structuralist Poetics: Structuralism, Linguistics, and the Study of Literature.* Ithaca: Cornell University Press, 1975.

De Man, Paul. *Allegories of Reading.* New Haven: Yale University Press, 1979.

———. *Blindness and Insight: Essays in the Rhetoric of Contemporary Criticism.* New York: Oxford University Press, 1971.

———. "The Rhetoric of Temporality." In *Interpretation: Theory and Practice,* ed. C. S. Singleton. Baltimore: Johns Hopkins University Press, 1969.

Denham, Robert. *Northrop Frye and Critical Method.* University Park: Pennsylvania State University Press, 1978.

Derrida, Jacques. *Dissemination.* Trans. Barbara Johnson. Chicago: University of Chicago Press, 1981.

———. *Margins of Philosophy.* Trans. Alan Bass. Chicago: University of Chicago Press, 1982.

———. *Of Grammatology.* Trans. Gayatri Chakravorty Spivak. Baltimore: Johns Hopkins University Press, 1976.

———. *Positions.* Trans. Alan Bass. Chicago: University of Chicago Press, 1981.

———. *Writing and Difference.* Trans. Alan Bass. Chicago: University of Chicago Press, 1978.

Ditsky, John. "The Man on the Quaker Oats Box: Characteristics of Recent Experimental Fiction." *Georgia Review* 26 (Fall 1972): 297–313.

Doležel, Lubomír. "The Typology of the Narrator: Point of View in Fiction." In *To Honor Roman Jakobson: Essays on the Occasion of His Seventieth Birthday,* 541–52. The Hague: Mouton, 1967.

Eagleton, Terry. *Criticism and Ideology.* London: Verso, 1976.

Eco, Umberto. *The Role of the Reader.* Bloomington: Indiana University Press, 1979.

———. *Semiotics and the Philosophy of Language.* Bloomington: Indiana University Press, 1984.

———. *A Theory of Semiotics.* Bloomington: Indiana University Press, 1976.

Federman, Raymond, ed. *Surfiction: Fiction Now and Tomorrow.* 2d ed. Chicago: Swallow Press, 1981.

Fish, Stanley. *Is There a Text in This Class?* Cambridge: Harvard University Press, 1980.

———. *Self-Consuming Artifacts: The Experience of Seventeenth-Century Literature.* Berkeley: University of California Press, 1972.

Forster, E. M. *Aspects of the Novel.* New York: Harcourt, Brace and World, 1927.

Foucault, Michel. *The Archaeology of Knowledge* and *The Discourse on Language.* Trans. A. M. Sheridan Smith. New York: Harper and Row, 1972.

———. *The History of Sexuality.* Vol. 1. *An Introduction.* Trans. Robert Hurley. New York: Vintage Books, 1980.

———. *Language, Counter-Memory, Practice.* Ed. Donald F. Bouchard. Ithaca: Cornell University Press, 1977.

———. *The Order of Things.* New York: Vintage Books, 1970.

———. *Power/Knowledge: Selected Interviews and Other Writings.* Ed. Colin Gordon, Leo Marshall, John Mepham, and Kate Soper. New York: Pantheon Books, 1980.

———. "What Is an Author?" In *Textual Strategies: Perspectives in Post-Struc-*

turalist Criticism, ed. Josue Harari, 141–60. Ithaca: Cornell University Press, 1979.

Friedman, Norman. *Form and Meaning in Fiction.* Athens: University of Georgia Press, 1975.

Frye, Northrop. *Anatomy of Criticism.* New York: Atheneum, 1969.

———. *The Great Code: The Bible and Literature.* New York: Harcourt Brace Jovanovitch, 1982.

———. *Spiritus Mundi: Essays on Literature, Myth, and Society.* Bloomington: Indiana University Press, 1976.

Goldknopf, David. *The Life of the Novel.* Chicago: University of Chicago Press, 1972.

Goodman, Nelson. *Ways of Worldmaking.* Indianapolis: Hackett, 1978.

Hansen, Arlen J. "The Celebration of Solopsism: A New Trend in American Fiction." *Modern Fiction Studies* 19 (Spring 1973): 5–15.

Harari, Josue, ed. *Textual Strategies: Perspectives in Post-Structuralist Criticism.* Ithaca: Cornell University Press, 1979.

Hartman, Geoffrey. *Beyond Formalism.* New Haven: Yale University Press, 1970.

———. *Criticism in the Wilderness.* New Haven: Yale University Press, 1980.

Hawkes, Terence. *Structuralism and Semiotics.* Berkeley: University of California Press, 1977.

Heath, Stephen. *The Nouveau Roman: A Study in the Practice of Writing.* London: Elek, 1972.

Heidegger, Martin. *Poetry, Language, Thought.* Trans. Albert Hofstadter. New York: Harper and Row, 1971.

Herr, Cheryl. *Joyce's Anatomy of Culture.* Urbana: University of Illinois Press, 1986.

Hofstadter, Douglas R. *Gödel, Escher, Bach: An Eternal Golden Braid.* New York: Vintage Books, 1980.

Holland, Norman N. *The Dynamics of Literary Response.* New York: W. W. Norton, 1975.

Hutcheon, Linda. *Narcissistic Narrative: The Metafictional Paradox.* New York: Methuen, 1984.

Irwin, John T. *American Hieroglyphics: The Symbol of the Egyptian Hieroglyphics in the American Renaissance.* Baltimore: Johns Hopkins University Press, 1980.

———. *Doubling and Incest/Repetition and Revenge: A Speculative Reading of Faulkner.* Baltimore: Johns Hopkins University Press, 1975.

Iser, Wolfgang. *The Act of Reading: A Theory of Aesthetic Response.* Baltimore: Johns Hopkins University Press, 1978.

———. *The Implied Reader: Patterns of Communication in Prose Fiction from Bunyan to Beckett.* Baltimore: Johns Hopkins University Press, 1974.

Jameson, Fredric. *Marxism and Form.* Princeton: Princeton University Press, 1971.

———. *The Political Unconscious: Narrative as a Socially Symbolic Act.* Ithaca: Cornell University Press, 1981.

———. *The Prison-House of Language.* Princeton: Princeton University Press, 1972.

Jefferson, Ann. *The Nouveau Roman and the Poetics of Fiction.* Cambridge: Cambridge University Press, 1980.

Kellman, Stephen G. "The Fiction of Self-Begetting." *MLN* 91 (1976): 1222–42.

Kermode, Frank. *The Art of Telling: Essays on Fiction.* Cambridge: Harvard University Press, 1983.

———. "Novels: Recognition and Deception." *Critical Inquiry* 1 (September 1974): 103–21.

———. "Secrets and Narrative Sequence." *Critical Inquiry* 7 (Autumn 1980): 83–101.

Krysinski, Wladimir. "The Narrator as a Sayer of the Author: Narrative Voices and Symbolic Structures." *Strumenti Critici* 2 (1977): 44–89.

Kuhn, Thomas S. *The Structure of Scientific Revolutions.* 2d ed., enl. Chicago: University of Chicago Press, 1970.

Lacan, Jacques. "Of Structure as an Inmixing of an Otherness Prerequisite to Any Subject Whatever." In *The Structuralist Controversy,* ed. Richard Macksey and Eugenio Donato, 186–95. Baltimore: Johns Hopkins University Press, 1970.

———. *Speech and Language in Psychoanalysis.* Trans. Anthony Wilden. Baltimore: Johns Hopkins University Press, 1968.

Lanser, Susan Sniader. *The Narrative Act: Point of View in Prose Fiction.* Princeton: Princeton University Press, 1981.

Lentricchia, Frank. *After the New Criticism.* Chicago: University of Chicago Press, 1980.

Lowenkron, David Henry. "The Metanovel." *College English* 38 (1976): 343–55.

Lubbock, Percy. *The Craft of Fiction.* 1921; rpt. New York: Viking Press, 1957.

Macksey, Richard, and Eugenio Donato. *The Structuralist Controversy: The Languages of Criticism and the Sciences of Man.* Baltimore: Johns Hopkins University Press, 1970.

Miller, J. Hillis. "Ariadne's Thread: Repetition and the Narrative Line." *Critical Inquiry* 3 (Autumn 1976): 57–77.

———. "The Critic as Host." In *Deconstruction and Criticism,* ed. Harold Bloom, et al., 217–53. New York: Seabury Press, 1979.

———. "The Disarticulation of the Self in Nietzsche." *Monist* 64, no. 2 (April 1981): 247–61.

———. *Fiction and Repetition.* Cambridge: Harvard University Press, 1982.

———. "The Function of Rhetorical Criticism at the Present Time." *ADE Bulletin* no. 62 (September–November 1979): 10–18.

———. "The Interpretation of *Lord Jim.*" In *The Interpretation of Narrative: Theory and Practice,* ed. M.W. Bloomfield, 211–28. Harvard English Studies, 1. Cambridge: Harvard University Press, 1970.

———. "Narrative and History." *ELH* 41, no. 3 (Fall 1974): 455–73.

———. "Optic and Semiotic in Middlemarch." In *The Worlds of Victorian Fiction,* ed. Jerome H. Buckley, 125–45. Cambridge: Harvard University Press, 1975.

Nelson, Lowry, Jr. "The Fictive Reader and Literary Self-Reflexiveness." In *The Disciplines of Criticism: Essays in Literary Theory, Interpretation and History,* ed. Peter Demetz, Thomas Greene, and Lowry Nelson, 173–91. New Haven: Yale University Press, 1968.

Nietzsche, Friedrich. "On Truth and Lies in a Nonmoral Sense." In *Philosophy and Truth: Selections from Nietzsche's Notebooks of the Early 1870's,* trans. and ed. Daniel Breazeale, 79–97. New York: Humanities Press, 1979.

———. *The Will to Power.* Ed. Walter Kaufmann. Trans. Walter Kaufmann and R. J. Hollingdale. New York: Vintage Books, 1967.

Palmer, Richard E. *Hermeneutics.* Evanston: Northwestern University Press, 1969.

Pavel, Thomas. "The Borders of Fiction." *Poetics Today* 4, no. 1 (1983): 83–88.

Piaget, Jean. *Structuralism.* New York: Harper and Row, 1970.

Poirier, Richard. *The Performing Self.* New York: Oxford University Press, 1971.

Ransom, John Crowe. *The World's Body.* 1938; rpt. Baton Rouge: Louisiana State University Press, 1968.

Riccomini, Donald R. "Defamiliarization, Reflexive Reference, and Modernism." *Bucknell Review* 25, no. 2 (1980): 107–13.

Robbe-Grillet, Alain. *For a New Novel: Essays on Fiction.* Trans. Richard Howard. New York: Grove Press, 1965.

Rorty, Richard. *Philosophy and the Mirror of Nature.* Princeton: Princeton University Press, 1979.

———. "Philosophy as a Kind of Writing: An Essay on Derrida." *New Literary History* 10 (Autumn 1970): 141–60.

Rowe, John Carlos. *Through the Custom-House: Nineteenth-Century American Fiction and Modern Theory.* Baltimore: Johns Hopkins University Press, 1982.

Russell, Charles. "The Vault of Language: Self-Reflective Artifice in Contemporary American Fiction." *Modern Fiction Studies* 20 (1974): 349–59.

Ryan, Michael. *Marxism and Deconstruction: A Critical Introduction.* Baltimore: Johns Hopkins University Press, 1982.

Said, Edward W. *Beginnings: Intention and Method.* Baltimore: Johns Hopkins University Press, 1975.

———. *The World, the Text, and the Critic.* Cambridge: Harvard University Press, 1983.

Scholes, Robert. *Fabulation and Metafiction.* Urbana: University of Illinois Press, 1979.

———. *Structuralism in Literature.* New Haven: Yale University Press, 1974.

———. "Toward a Semiotics of Literature." *Critical Inquiry* 4 (Autumn 1977): 105–20.

Scholes, Robert, and Robert Kellogg. *The Nature of Narrative.* New York: Oxford University Press, 1966.

Schorer, Mark. "Technique as Discovery." *Hudson Review* 1 (1948); rpt. in *The Theory of the Novel,* ed. Philip Stevick, 65–84. New York: Free Press, 1967.

Shklovsky, Victor. "Art as Technique." In *Russian Formalist Criticism: Four Essays,* trans. Lee T. Lemon and Marion J. Reis. Lincoln: University of Nebraska Press, 1965.

Snipes, Wilson. "The Biographer as a Center of Reference." *Biography* 5, no. 3 (1982): 215–25.

Stanzel, Franz. *Narrative Situations in the Novel.* Bloomington: Indiana University Press, 1971.

Swearingen, James E. *Reflexivity in "Tristram Shandy": An Essay in Phenomenological Criticism.* New Haven: Yale University Press, 1977.

Thomas, Brook. *James Joyce's "Ulysses."* Baton Rouge: Louisiana State University Press, 1982.

Tompkins, Jane P., ed. *Reader-Response Criticism: From Formalism to Post-Structuralism.* Baltimore: Johns Hopkins University Press, 1980.

Tzara, Tristan. *Seven Dada Manifestos and Lampisteries.* Trans. Barbara Wright. London: John Calder, 1977.

Wasiolek, Edward. "Wanted: A New Contextualism." *Critical Inquiry* 1 (1975): 623–39.

Wasson, Richard. "Notes on a New Sensibility." *Partisan Review* 36 (1969): 460–77.

Waugh, Patricia. *Metafiction: The Theory and Practice of Self-Conscious Fiction.* London: Methuen, 1984.

Weimann, Robert. "Point of View in Fiction." In *Preserve and Create: Essays in Marxist Criticism,* ed. Gaylord C. LeRoy and Ursula Beitz, 54–75. New York: Humanities Press, 1973.

———. *Structure and Society in Literary Theory: Studies in the History and Theory of Historical Criticism.* Baltimore: Johns Hopkins University Press, 1984.

Young, Robert. *Untying the Text: A Post-Structuralist Reader.* Boston: Routledge and Kegan Paul, 1981.

Index

Abrams, Meyer H., 234-35
Adorno, Theodor, 11
Alter, Robert, 6-7, 12
Althusser, Louis, 11
Anderson, Charles R., 258 n. 6
Aristos, 171, 172, 174, 178
Author: semiotic vs. metaphysical, 13, 14,
211-12; as voice, 16-17; in irony, 17-18;
Fowles's critique of ontological, 169-77;
as nexus of conventions, 177-80, 189,
204; as textual role(s), 180-83; as interpretive construct, 183-84; redefined, 184-
86, 236, 238; compared to author of selfhood, 196-202; Eco's definitions, 260
n. 15

Bakhtin, Mikhail, 240, 251 n. 17, 261 n. 12
Barth, John, 208
Barthes, Roland, 180, 181, 182, 185-86,
259 n. 2
Bellow, Saul, *Herzog,* 162-68
Berner, Robert, 258 n. 2
Blodgett, Harriett, 253 n. 20
Bohner, Charles H., 258 n. 2
Bonney, William W., 255 n. 9
Booth, Wayne: on irony, 17-19, 49, 259; on
distance, 170, 181, 229; and (re)presenta-
tionalist poetics, 241-42, 249 n. 7
Bronte, Emily, *Wuthering Heights,* 39
Buber, Martin, 159-60

Capote, Truman, *Music for Chameleons,*
208
Carter, Angela, "The Loves of Lady Purple,"
219-23
Casper, Leonard, 123-24
Caute, David, 251 n. 19
Cervantes, Miguel de, 50-51
Chance: culture as conventional (fictional)
margins, 67-71; 77; open and closed narrative margins, 72-74; Powell's struggle
to draw margins, 74-76, 81-85; narrative
margins and selfhood in Flora's narration,
76-80; seacraft as fiction, 85-88; abstract

thought as fiction, 89-93; custom as fiction, 92-93; intertextuality and culture,
93-97; chance as an issue, 97-99; concomitance of order and chance, 99-101;
concomitance of order and chance in
metaphor, 101-2; opposition of order and
chance as cultural discipline, 102-4
Colby, Robert A., 253 n. 11
Constitutive poetics: defined, 1, 9-13, 228;
ideological implications, 1, 243-47; vs.
(re)presentational poetics, 4-8, 12, 14, 67,
235, 241, 250 n. 8; ideology and cultural
forms, 11, 53, 67, 105, 232-33; and creating "reality," 13, 38, 42-43, 63, 95-96,
102-5, 217-18, 225, 236; ideology and
subjects, 16, 110-12, 117-18, 122, 168;
and voice, 26; and irony, 28; and selfhood,
110, 122, 146-49, 155-56, 244; and Frye,
233; and Shklovsky, 251-52 n. 20; and
Bakhtin, 251 n. 17
Conventions: and critical method, 1, 6, 10,
16-17, 174-76, 181-82, 183-84, 199-200,
204; as medium of experience, 67-71, 89,
93, 109-10, 178, 196, 220-22; as "lost"
in Hemingway, 112-13; as "style-world,"
213-14; Kermode on narrative conventions, 251 n. 14. *See also* Reflexivity;
Subject
Cook, Albert, 5-6
Coover, Robert, "The Magic Poker," 206;
"The Gingerbread House," 207-8
Craig, G. Armour, 21

De Man, Paul, 9, 12, 18-19, 258 n. 11
Derrida, Jacques, 12, 13, 228, 233, 240,
252 n. 21, 262 n. 19
Dickens, Charles, *David Copperfield,* 40;
Great Expectations, 40-41; *Bleak House,*
41-42, 54
Doležel, Lubomír, 242

Eco, Umberto, 9-10, 237, 244, 262 n. 17
Eddins, Dwight, 196
Eliot, George, 52

269